AGAINST TWO EVILS

Against Two Evils

Memoirs of a Diplomat–Soldier during the Third Reich

Johnnie von Herwarth
with S. Frederick Starr

COLLINS
St James's Place, London
1981

William Collins Sons & Co Ltd
London · Glasgow · Sydney · Auckland
Toronto · Johannesburg

British Library Cataloguing in Publication Data

Herwarth, Johnnie Von
 Against two evils
 1. Herwarth, Johnnie Von
 2. Ambassadors – Germany – Biography
 3. Anti-Nazi movement
 I. Title   II. Starr, S. Frederick
 B7.2′092′4   DD259.7H/

First published 1981
© Hans von Herwarth 1981
Introduction © William Collins 1981

ISBN 0 00 216279 2

Photoset in Ehrhardt
Printed in the United
States of America

Contents

FOREWORD

Immediately after the end of World War II, well-intentioned friends on both sides of the Atlantic suggested that I write an account of my nine years of diplomatic service in the USSR and of my role in the German Resistance. I replied that my days in Moscow were already far in the past and that the German Resistance had been a failure. Many books had even then been written about the Resistance, and anyway I did not feel the time was ripe for me to speak. During the early post-war years many people who had done little more than sympathize passively with the Resistance were, for obvious reasons, presenting themselves as active participants. Under such circumstances I did not want to tell my story, lest it give rise to suspicions that I had done so merely to ingratiate myself with the new government in Germany. In my decision not to write my memoirs I was guided by the old German military maxim that 'General Staff officers remain anonymous.' More important, I would have felt extremely uneasy writing about people who died for their cause when I, through merest accident, had survived.

During the 1950s and 1960s, my concerns were entirely different from those that had preoccupied me heretofore. By then I had nothing to do with Soviet affairs. My first post-war assignment was with the Bavarian State Chancellery. It plunged me into tasks of reconstruction in Bavaria. Then, until 1955, I served in Bonn, under President Theodore Heuss and Chancellor Konrad Adenauer, helping to build the political structure of the Federal Republic of Germany and its Foreign Service. From 1955 to 1961 I was Ambassador in London and later head of the Presidential Office in Bonn until 1965. Following a period as Ambassador to Italy until 1969, Foreign Minister Willy Brandt appointed me Chairman of the Committee for the Reform of the Foreign Service. All this occupied my time to such an extent as to make it impossible for me even to review in my mind the war years and the period before. I had no time to read the voluminous literature appearing every year about that period, nor was I much tempted to do so, since I considered the pre-1945 era to be a closed chapter in my life.

This continued down to my retirement from the diplomatic service in 1969. The appearance of Charles Bohlen's autobiography in 1973 with its chapter devoted to our mutual contacts in the late 1930s, prompted my old friend Klaus Mehnert to invite me to write about my own experiences for the journal *Osteuropa*. At about the same time I was approached by several publishers, who suggested that I also write reminiscences of post-war reconstruction. But now laziness came into the picture. Though officially I was in retirement I considered myself to be still too active to engage in what could only be a retrospective effort. From 1969 I served as chairman of the Supervisory Council of UNILEVER Germany, and in 1971 I was elected President of the Goethe Institute. I therefore declined all the invitations and encouragement of my friends to write my memoirs.

In the summer of 1974, I attended a seminar in America, at the Aspen Institute for Humanistic Studies in Colorado. At the last luncheon I found myself sitting next to a young professor from Princeton University, Frederick Starr. A historian who had himself lived in the USSR, he was keenly interested when I mentioned casually that I had once served there. The conversation naturally turned to the Moscow diplomatic community in the 1930s, and he asked me if I had known the legendary 'Johnnie', with whom he had become acquainted through 'Chip' Bohlen's book. I answered that I knew him very well, as I was that Johnnie.

As we parted, Fred Starr said he would like to continue our conversation in more leisurely circumstances, and so we met again in Princeton in January 1975. At that time, we agreed to continue in Aspen during the summer of 1975, when there would be time for me to answer all his questions and to tell him everything that I had witnessed. This in turn led to further meetings in 1977 and 1979, by which time Starr had become Secretary of the Kennan Institute for Advanced Russian Studies in Washington.

I was by no means sure that everything I had lived through was important from a historical point of view. I viewed my experiences in Russia and during the war as of priceless value to me personally but of broader note only for their human interest. As Fred Starr helped revive my memory of those years through long days spent over a tape recorder, I came gradually to agree that my reminiscences should be written down so that they might one day be used by scholars in their research. The following reminiscences were originally not intended as a book; rather, I thought of them as a record that might be duplicated in twenty or thirty copies and sent to friends, a few libraries, and research centres. If a broader group of readers should now find them of interest I would be glad, but neither Fred Starr nor I have taken this to be our primary objective.

INTRODUCTION

In the strange, ghetto-like existence that foreign diplomats led in Moscow in the years before World War II, personal friendships counted for more than political antagonisms. Amongst the more junior members of the diplomatic corps this was particularly true. The younger British and Americans and their German and Italian counterparts spent much of their spare time together and enduring friendships sprang up between them despite the ever increasing likelihood of war between their countries. One of my closest friends was Johnnie Herwarth, my opposite number at the German Embassy. Johnnie, whom I knew to be strongly anti-Nazi, and I regularly discussed the latest developments in world affairs and I received from him many valuable insights into Hitler's aims and intentions. Meanwhile the outlook became more and more menacing and the British government's policy of appeasement less and less convincing.

At a party at the Belgian Legation in the autumn of 1938 I found Johnnie deeply depressed by the news of Mr Chamberlain's recent visit to Munich. 'After this,' he said, 'the Führer will think he can get away with anything. He'll be wrong, because he doesn't understand your mentality. He doesn't realize that, whatever line your government may take, there's a limit beyond which you, as a nation, will not be prepared to let him go. This last fatal surrender of yours will embolden him to overstep that limit; it will weaken the hand of such restraining elements as still remain in Germany and it will make war inevitable – war which in the long run will bring about the destruction of Germany.'

'Yes,' I said. 'I'm afraid that before long you and I may be shooting at each other.'

'Well, anyhow,' he replied, 'if we take you prisoner, I'll do my best to see that you get an occasional drink and I hope you'll do the same for me.' And, passing to more cheerful topics, we once more turned our attention to the excellent champagne provided by our Belgian hosts.

The War we'd been talking about broke out less than twelve months later and followed its variegated course until the autumn of 1944. By then, as Johnnie had foreseen, disaster was threatening Germany and Hitler was hurriedly but belatedly pulling his forces out of the Balkans. In Yugoslavia, where I had spent the past year with Tito's Partisans, we were doing everything we could to harass the retreating enemy, who had so long harassed us in the mountains and forests. Sometimes, as I looked at the bodies of dead Germans, lying where they had fallen in the woods or by the roadside, I wondered what had happened to Johnnie and hoped that he was not lying somewhere with a bullet in him.

I cannot recall exactly when or where it was that the Partisans I was with brought me that particular batch of captured documents, but I can remember the scene perfectly: the peasant's cottage, the dim lamplight, the weary Partisans in their battle-worn tunics, slung about with a strange assortment of captured weapons. All of a sudden as we were going through a pile of signals, operation orders and ordinary wartime papers, which the Partisans had captured in some recent engagement, one of my companions gave an exclamation. 'Here's something for you, Comrade General,' he said. 'It's about what they are going to do with you when they catch you.' And he handed me a typewritten sheet.

It was an order which seemed to have originated from some military authority outside the usual chain of command and which said what action was to be taken in the event of my being captured alive. I was, it appeared, to be sent immediately on capture to the headquarters of the nearest German formation and thence to Army Headquarters, where further instructions would be issued regarding my disposal. Meanwhile, the order added, I was to be well treated. 'They'll have to catch you first,' said my companion. 'Yes,' I replied. 'They've left it a bit late.' But, as I went to sleep that night, I couldn't help wondering what lay behind that particular set of instructions and just what the Germans had in store for me if they ever caught me. It was not until some years later that I learnt the answer to those questions.

Soon after the end of the war I was delighted to hear from our mutual friend, Charlie Thayer, then serving with the United States forces in Austria, that Johnnie was still alive. Like myself, he had, it seemed, had his share of adventures, having served on various fronts as a regimental officer and on the staff.

After the war he resumed his diplomatic career and became in due course the first German Ambassador to London. One night at the Embassy we were talking things over and he reminded me of our conversation in Moscow of nearly twenty years before. 'Well,' he said, pouring me out some of that particular brand of malt whisky to which I had introduced him in Moscow, 'I had that drink waiting for you, but you never came to get it.'

'What drink?' I asked.

'Don't you remember? We said that if either of us were put in the bag, the other would see that he got enough to drink. I had a staff job in Yugoslavia when you were there and I managed to get instructions issued to all the German formations that, if you were taken prisoner, you were to be brought to me. After that, my friends and I would have done our best to see that you didn't come to any harm.'

It was then that I realized who had drafted the order we captured. But, even so, I was glad that I had to wait until after the war for that drink.

As an old friend of Johnnie's I had of course long been familiar with the general outlines of his early career. I knew of the precarious situation in which he found himself from 1933 onwards. I knew something of his wartime adventures and experiences in Russia and elsewhere and of his active involvement in the Stauffenberg plot. I knew, too, of the massive contribution he had made to goodwill between our two countries as Ambassador here in the nineteen fifties.

But it was only as I read the successive chapters of the remarkable book that he had at last been persuaded to write that I realized what a truly fantastic life he has had and the extent to which over the years he was directly involved in events of the very greatest importance both nationally and internationally.

His book fills in the background to all this and brings to life the personalities involved. Of quite exceptional interest are the chapters concerning the Soviet Union, both before and during the war. Many diplomats write well, but to the elegance and lucidity of good diplomatic reporting Johnnie Herwarth adds compulsive readability, a quality in which even the best diplomatic despatches are sometimes lacking. Suspense is maintained throughout as in a thriller. Again and again survival seems an unlikely outcome. *Against Two Evils* also reflects its author's engaging personality and unfailing sense of humour, which have won him so many friends all over the world.

There is at present a strong revival of interest in the events of the thirties and forties. For the fresh light it throws on those troubled decades, this book will rate as an important historical source. It will also be enjoyed by the general reader for the fascinating story it tells and the skill and good humour with which that story is told.

Fitzroy Maclean

ACKNOWLEDGEMENTS

I would like to thank Dr Christine Mentzschel Kraus who capably translated numerous documents and Theresa H. Stopowski who typed the entire memoir several times over. In thanking these two persons for their great assistance, Fred Starr and I also wish to acknowledge the help of Kevin Henzel of Georgetown University and Patricia Sheridan of Alexandria, Virginia.

On the German side my thanks go to Dr Klaus J. Bade in cooperation with Professor Dr Walther Peter Fuchs, Professor Dr Klaus Hildebrand, Dr Joachim Hoffmann, Professor Dr Karl-Heinz Ruffmann and Professor Dr Michael Stürmer for assistance, advice and the helpful discussions we had on the manuscript.

My special gratitude goes to my wife without whose remarkable memory I could not have written this book. Thanks also to my daughter Alexandra Marchl who helped me to correct the manuscript.

I

YOUTH

I was born on 14 July, 1904 in Berlin, where my father, Hans Richard Herwarth von Bittenfeld, was attending the General Staff College. In 1909 my father was promoted to the rank of captain and became squadron leader in the Third Uhlan Guards Regiment in Potsdam. There I entered elementary school.

My mother, Ilse von Tiedemann, came from a West Prussian family and had been raised partly in Berlin and partly on the estate of my grandfather, in the then Prussian province of Posen. The estate was a very large one but it was not my grandfather's sole concern, in that he also had been engaged in trade with the United States and South America through his wife's family firm, Hardt and Co., in Berlin.

My grandfather Tiedemann was actively involved in politics. Although he never stood for public office, he did serve for a while as president of the *Deutsche Ostmarkenverein*. The purpose of this organization was to promote the settlement of Germans in those Eastern provinces where the population was predominantly Polish. Naturally, such a programme was violently opposed by all Poles who held any nationalist convictions. The methods of this organization were mild indeed, especially in comparison with those of a later era. Its mode of operation was to buy up Polish estates at reasonable prices and then to divide them and resell them to German farmers. The rural economy was such that Polish landlords were glad to sell their estates on such terms. Only in rare instances were Polish properties actually expropriated. The *Deutsche Ostmarkenverein* left its mark on my grandfather, Heinrich von Tiedemann; on account of his connection with it, he was both well-known and well-hated.

My grandfather's estate was named *Seeheim*, its former Polish name having been Jeziorki. There my grandfather lived a patriarchal existence that differed scarcely at all from that of an estate owner in Poland proper, or even of a Russian estate owner a century earlier. I still remember riding through the fields with him and watching with awe as farm labourers came up to kiss his hand. He was, as the Russians say, the *barin*. Those servants assigned to the household were considered part of the family and were kept on through long years of retirement as well as during their productive years. In the same patriarchal spirit, my grandfather built houses and whatever other facilities were needed by the labourers on the estate.

For a child, life at *Seeheim* offered infinite possibilities, all of them intriguing. The cattle were reckoned in figures seemingly drawn from the Old Testament. The stables were on a similar scale. The widest range of crafts was practised on the estate by an army of blacksmiths, carpenters, distillers, and the like. Close by the sprawling manor house was a large, well-stocked artificial lake with an island in it. The park around the house and lake covered about fifty acres, beyond which the fields stretched in every direction. Hothouses yielded fruits in all seasons, in spite of the harsh climate. *Seeheim* was, in short, a world in itself.

While still a young child I was given an air-gun, from which I eventually graduated to a small Schubert rifle, and finally to a shotgun. Grandfather had foresters, of course, but when they and my uncles were mobilized during World War I, I was permitted to hunt some of the game for the table. The fact that I was still too young to have a permit made no difference to the local police officer, who would greet me with a friendly bow in spite of my carrying an illegal shotgun.

My playmates included both local Polish and German children. Our common language was German, and I never realized that any tension existed between the two peoples. Among the Poles I particularly liked was the coachman Witkowski, who used to pick me up at the nearby railway station of Opalinitza. His son had just returned from service in the German Army and was a friend of mine as well, though five or six years older than me. Witkowski would always arrive with a basket of sandwiches and peaches, cherries, or whatever fruit was in season. The two-hour trip to *Seeheim* by horse-drawn coach enabled us to talk at length, and we became good friends.

My grandfather Tiedemann had an immense influence on my early life. For many years I was his only grandchild and he therefore lavished on me all his enormous love for children. In return, I idolized him. As I grew older he let me listen to many after-dinner political discussions. All my mother's brothers participated in these, the two eldest being respectively a career officer and an officer-turned-diplomat-turned-farmer, the third a diplomat, and the youngest with the family firm of Hardt and Company. Thanks to the variety of their experience, my uncles and grandfather expressed a wide range of opinions on most issues.

One of the perennial subjects of debate was the effort of Kaiser Wilhelm II and Admiral von Tirpitz to build up the German fleet. My uncle Helmut von Tiedemann, who had served in our Embassy in London, opposed this furiously as a needless irritant to the British and of questionable military value anyway. My two uncles, who had served in the army, felt warmer towards the project, although even they would have preferred to see the enormous funds it required go to the army instead. In all these discussions one could already feel the apprehension that France and Britain had formed an entente. With the alliance between France and Russia that had existed since the 1890s, this entente meant that Germany would be isolated in the face of all the other major European powers.

Again and again in our dinner-table discussions the name of Bismarck was thrown into the debate, usually somebody contrasting present policies unfavourably with his. Former Chancellor von Bülow also came off relatively well, especially when compared with Tirpitz, the Kaiser, and the weak Bethmann-Hollweg. After the outbreak of World War I, my uncles found themselves in rare agreement that this would never have occurred under the chancellorship of Bismarck and probably not even under that of von Bülow.

The world of *Seeheim* contrasted sharply with that of my father's family in the south. I did not know my paternal grandfather, but my paternal grandmother presided over my early youth. She was cosmopolitan, having lived in both England and France. 'Tante Jula' as she was called, was by birth a von Haber, an influential banking family from Karlsruhe closely linked with the local aristocracy. The von Habers were Christian converts from Judaism, a fact that was to be of great significance to my later career. My grandmother owned a pleasant farm overlooking the Rhine Valley near Oberkirch in Baden, not far from Strasbourg. I passed parts of many summers there amidst the rolling hills and vineyards.

In Baden, there was no question of my hunting. I was not even permitted to shoot a squirrel. There were no peasants wishing to kiss my father's hand. In general, people were far more democratic there, probably echoing the stronger impact of the French Revolution and Revolution of 1848 in the South of Germany. It is revealing that, while Prussia was fighting Napoleon, Baden sided with him. And in 1849 when the troops of the Grand Duke of Baden had been unable to quash the popular uprising, they had to call in Prussian forces under Crown Prince Wilhelm, the future Kaiser Wilhelm I.

It was at my grandmother's estate in Oberkirch that I acquired the nickname 'Johnnie'. The name originated from the visit of an English friend of my grandmother, who referred to me as 'Master John' or 'Master Johnnie'. My mother's younger brother immediately picked this up and spread it to my friends, much to the chagrin of my father, who would have preferred the more Germanic and stiffer 'Hans-Heinrich'.

I was fond of that farm in Baden, of the local children with whom I went to school, and of the ponies, rabbits, and other animals that I took care of. Different as it was from *Seeheim*, the farm at Oberkirch shared my affection with the estate far to the east. Together, they left me with a love divided between those two contrasting worlds.

My grandparents, and particularly my maternal grandfather, exerted a stronger influence on my childhood than did my parents. It was customary in those days for parents to be rather more distant from their children than they are today, and the fact that my own parents were, as the English say, 'horsey', added further to that distance. Though my mother and I loved each other deeply, her many social obligations meant that I was looked after by a nurse. Only when World War I broke out did we really become close to each other. My father and many relatives had been mobilized, and my mother and I were left to live through the anxieties of war together. She devoted much time to my upbringing and took me often to galleries to see examples of modern art. Much later, in 1971, when I was living in Munich and my wife had to look after her house in Franconia, my mother further made up for her earlier remoteness. She would rise at seven, see that I had a warm bath and prepare a good breakfast for me. She pampered me to such an extent that my friends took to criticizing me for making my aged mother work so hard. I assured them that I was quite innocent, and that in fact this well-intentioned activity gave a meaning to her life. Not that her life had lacked purpose: from the moment Hitler came to power, she considered him a personal offence and hated him accordingly. In fact, I never knew a woman hate Hitler as deeply and as unwaveringly as my mother.

I should say a word about my family's background. Since my paternal great-grandfather had been a general in command of a Prussian army corps and two of his brothers were general and field marshal respectively, I have frequently been complimented on coming from such a fine Prussian family. But we are in fact neither Prussian in origin nor military by tradition. As far back as they appear in historical records, i.e., to 1180, the Herwarths were a patrician family of Augsburg, its members engaged in banking and trade throughout Western and Southern Europe. Towards the end of the sixteenth century nearly all the great Augsburg families went bankrupt. They had made large loans to the Emperor and various princes and found themselves unable to recover their money when it was needed. The Herwarths were among those houses that suffered. After the Reformation, the family fanned out through Württemberg and Bavaria and again acquired considerable estates. None of these estates was entailed, however, and hence tended to be divided among younger sons and daughters. Most of the family remained Catholic during the Reformation, but one member who converted to Protestantism emigrated to France, became a banker to Louis XIV and acquired the chateau of St Cloud. He prospered down to the revocation of the Edict of Nantes in 1685. As a consequence of that measure, he lost all his property. His family emigrated to England, where his son became a Member of Parliament and was sent as an envoy to Switzerland. He was buried in Westminster. Eventually all lines of the family died out but my own, which stayed at Bittenfeld in Württemberg. In 1747 the last member of the Protestant Bittenfeld line was a captain in the 'Alt-Württemberg Regiment'. For financial reasons the Duke of Württemberg placed this regiment under the command of the King of Prussia, Frederick the Great. My ancestor was killed in action while commanding this regiment at the battle of Kolin against the Austrians in 1757. His eldest son was also involved in the battle, and learned of his father's death from Frederick the Great. 'Your father is dead,' the king told him, 'I shall be your father from now on.' Henceforth, the family served the Prussian monarchy.

My father retired from the cavalry in 1912. It was common practice under the last kaisers for an officer to follow a military career until he attained the rank of captain and then to resign in order to look after his estate. From spring to autumn we stayed in Oberkirch and Seeheim. During the winter, we were in Berlin where my parents had taken a flat.

The outbreak of war in August 1914, found us in Oberkirch. Without knowing much about the Austrians or Hungarians, I was shocked at the murder of Archduke Franz Ferdinand and immediately sided with the Austrians. Back in 1912, when the Balkan war had broken out, I had sympathized with the Turks against the Italians and the Balkan nations for the simple reason that several young Turkish officers had served in my father's regiment before they were mobilized and had often visited our house. My political opinions at this phase were of a personal, rather than ideological, nature! Had I regularly received postcards from officers on the other side, my youthful sympathies might have been there instead. After their defeat, the Turkish officers disappeared completely from my life for many decades. Forty years later, I accompanied Chancellor Adenauer on an official visit to Greece and Turkey. No sooner did we arrive in Istanbul than these long-lost friends came to see me in my hotel, much to my delight.

The rest of my family took a more hard-headed view of things. My father and uncles were not at all convinced of the value of the Triple Alliance between Austria-Hungary, Germany, and Italy. In particular they doubted Italy's willingness to fight on our side. My father shared this view, although he had served three years as a diplomat in Italy under Bülow, spoke fluent Italian, and was a great admirer of that country. He was convinced that it was against Italy's national interest to make any sacrifices on behalf of Austria-Hungary and Germany. The only conceivable way of engaging the Italians' interest in the Triple Alliance, he felt, would be through major territorial concessions by Austria. This was clearly impossible. Much later, I came to appreciate the wisdom of the Bismarckian maxim that my father cited in this case: that one should not expect a country to honour agreements which are against its national interest.

Even after the assassination in Sarajevo, my father refused to believe that war was imminent. His orders were to report to Berlin, but he held out for some while, keeping contact by telephone with his cousin, a General Staff officer in Stuttgart. His personal conviction that war would not occur was passed on to the entire town of Oberkirch. The inhabitants spread the word through the region that as long as Herr von Herwarth continued to come down to the town in his horse-drawn buggy, there would be no war.

Mobilization brought an end to such illusions. We travelled at once to Berlin. Passing through Heidelberg, Darmstadt, Frankfurt, and numerous smaller towns, I was deeply impressed by the patriotic fervour that was everywhere manifest. Never again was I to see such an outpouring of national emotion. Unlike that which occurred under the Nazis, it had all the earmarks of genuine spontaneity. What a contrast there was between this mood in the summer of 1914 and that of Berlin in 1938. I remember well how, on the eve of the Sudeten crisis, Hitler marched a fully armed division through Berlin while the crowd looked on in sullen silence.

We passed through Berlin to Potsdam, where my father reported for service with the army group headed by Duke Albrecht of Württemberg. As we crossed the Potsdamer Platz in Berlin, we met a large crowd drawn there by some patriotic manifestation. When the crowd recognized my father's uniform they hoisted him to their shoulders and spontaneously bore him away. I got completely lost and it took my father some time to find me again.

As war ground on and life in Berlin grew increasingly difficult, the family spent more time in the countryside. My grandfather, being a law-abiding citizen, observed to the letter the regulation that nobody in Berlin, not even owners of large estates who had access to their own food supplies, was permitted more than basic rations. These rations were very small indeed, far smaller than they were to be during most of World War II. For this reason my mother saw to it that we spent much time in the countryside, where we could at least get fruit and vegetables.

When my father or one of my uncles came home on leave they used to bring a note of anxiety to our family discussions. There was no agreement as to what Germany should do. On the one hand, my father and uncles recognized fully the desperate situation of the country, particularly after America's entry into the war. On the other, they were reluctant simply to part with all the territories Germany had gained. In this context, one tends to forget that on certain parts of the Eastern front, German troops advanced further in World War I than they were to do under Hitler.

My family was royalist to the core and closely linked with the monarchy over many generations. Nonetheless, I often heard criticism of the Kaiser's handling of the war from my grandfather and particularly from my uncle Helmuth von Tiedemann, the diplomat. What they both objected to was the Kaiser's seeming inability to take decisive action in either the military or political spheres once war had begun; in contrast to his behaviour in peacetime. Members of my mother's family were among those many people who believed that, at the very least, he should have joined a front-line regiment and done his duty to the bitter end; nor could they understand the Kaiser when he abandoned his country and retired to Holland.

*   *   *

The family was in Berlin at the outbreak of the Socialist revolution in 1918. I clearly remember the trucks festooned with red flags racing through the city, filled with soldiers who had torn all insignia from their uniforms. This came as a profound shock to me, for it contradicted

23

everything in which I had been taught to believe. The fall of the monarchy destroyed an entire social order of which my family had been a part. For all the differences of opinion within my family, however, there was general agreement that it was the absence of responsible leadership that had brought down the monarchy, rather than the actions of disaffected soldiers and workers.

Throughout my school days I had only one desire, that the war would go on until I was old enough to join the army. Resenting that I had been too young to participate in the great drama, I ran away from home at the age of nearly sixteen and became a soldier. After a short period, my commanding officer decided that this was no place for me and sent me back to school. Thus ended my first army career.

This brief escapade of 1920 had two consequences. First, when I finally returned to school I did so with a renewed interest in studying, with the result that my record during the last year and a half in my new school in Potsdam was far better than it had been earlier. Second, even though I was in the army for only a short time, I was now considered a veteran. This had no importance for me until the 1930s, but then it was to save my career.

Upon completing my studies, I had no clear conception of what to do next. The army was ruled out, since the 100,000-man limit imposed at Versailles made that career less than promising. In the end I decided to work in a factory. My father had entered business briefly after the war and considered it a promising avenue for a young man. Partly with his encouragement but mostly on my own initiative, I went to work at the locomotive factory of Orenstein and Koppel near Potsdam. I was to spend six months there, commuting to evening courses so as not to lose my place at the university. During this time I rose from the assembly line to a position on the crew that tested the locomotives. It was great fun.

My experience at the locomotive factory exposed me to industry and to the discipline of the ten-hour day. It also acquainted me directly with the German worker and the trade-union movement. In spite of my early fears, the factory workers accepted me and I them. I also had a chance to study the differences between Social Democrats, Independent Socialists, and Communists.

My life could not have been busier. In addition to working a full day and taking evening courses at the university, I was studying English and running middle-distance events in local athletic meetings. At the end of this period, I was no longer able to contemplate immersing myself fully in university affairs and the life of a student fraternity. Meanwhile, the

24

soaring inflation of the Weimar days had affected my family deeply. The property in Baden had already been sold in 1916, as it was insufficiently profitable to maintain as an agricultural enterprise. Then in 1923 the estate in Posen was sold, in order to avoid confiscation. At this time, also, my father's business venture failed, leaving us only our house in Potsdam. Times had changed. We had enough money to live comfortably, but I was certainly no longer a millionaire's son.

One evening a guest at our house, one of the directors of the *Deutsche Erdöl A.G.* for which my father had worked, spoke warmly of the dawning era of trade and banking. When I expressed interest, Herr Groeber invited me to join *Deutsche Erdöl* at Berlin-Schoeneberg under a special training programme that he would devise for me. I accepted at once, and worked with the firm from the autumn of 1922 until 1924. In the process I gained a certain acquaintance with business and, equally important, had a chance to brush up my English.

I then spent another few months in the army. With the numbers so severely restricted, service in the army had become extremely demanding. The rigour of our daytime routine was intensified by the fact that we spent so many of our evenings dancing and enjoying the flowering night life of Weimar Berlin. Returning very late to our barracks, we would catch a few hours' sleep before the military day began, only to start the cycle again.

During this period, I was once invited to a smart ball in Berlin and, while there, made up my mind to dance with one of the most beautiful and celebrated ladies of the capital. Taking my heart in my hands, I set out on the dance floor with her. It was a disaster. Not only was my conversation pitifully maladroit, but I managed to tread on her feet as well. I skulked away in a state of well-earned humiliation. Next morning I received a summons to regimental headquarters. Apparently, an officer of my regiment had also attended the ball and witnessed my escapade. I was curtly informed that it was not my duty to dance with the most elegant ladies of Berlin but rather to devote my time to the wallflowers. To give me time to meditate on my future amorous strategies, I was confined to barracks for the next four Sundays and obliged to mount guard.

I spent the winter term of 1925 at the University of Munich. Observing my activities during those months, my parents rightly sensed that there were far too many distractions for me there and insisted that I try at least one term at Breslau in Silesia, which I did. Breslau was famous for its beautiful old buildings, but in most other respects it lacked the attractions of Munich. Fortunately, my uncle Richard von Tiedemann had a large estate nearby at Sagan, which I visited often. Another uncle, Walter Vogel von Falkenstein, was also living nearby. His home contained, among other treasures, a billiard table. He was as knowledgeable about Napoleon as he was adept at billiards, and leaning over the green felt table I learned much about the Russian campaign that I was to recall vividly during the 1930s and the war.

In spite of everything, I studied hard in Breslau and, with the help of a competent coach, was finally able to pass the first stage of the state examinations in Munich in February 1926. With this tiresome hurdle behind me, I set out for London where I spent a few weeks polishing my English and attempting to make my way amidst the chaos of the General Strike. Returning to Germany, I still had not decided what I wanted to do and was most receptive to any advice that came my way. Along with my studies, I had pursued an interest in the history of art that had been developed in me by my mother and by two of my uncles. Richard von Tiedemann had served from 1909–11 at the German legation in Japan, where he had amassed a fine collection of Japanese art that was installed at his estate near Sagan. My other uncle, Helmut von Tiedemann, was a career diplomat who had an expert taste in art, without being a real collector. These uncles both pointed out to me that, whatever frustrations it might entail, a diplomatic career at least offered the possibility of visiting the major museums, historic cities and archeological sites abroad.

Sensing that my reaction was at least neutral, my uncle Helmut gave me an introduction to the Ministry of Foreign Affairs, where I was received by the Director of Personnel and his deputy. They treated me kindly but made it clear that the service was no place for anyone who did not burn with a 'holy flame' for diplomatic work. I assumed that this was a well-worn speech and was not greatly disturbed by the absence of such a divine blaze within me. They were especially pleased by my practical experience at *Deutsche Erdöl A.G.* and at Orenstein and Koppel, all of which I had acquired almost by accident. Most of their questions I was able to answer on the basis of my readings in Ranke, Treitschke, Sybel, Lamprecht; all of which I had perused in my grandfather's library. In addition to citing the works of many historians and memoirs that I had read, I also rounded out my interview with learned references to a number of authors whose works I knew at second hand.

At the end of the interview, the Director of Personnel suggested a couple of positions that I could occupy for a year or two in order to gain experience, which he considered necessary in light of my youth. Neither of these interested me, so I returned empty-handed to Munich. Some months later I received a bland communication inviting me to appear for my examination at the Foreign Ministry. I managed to ignore this for some time, thinking that it was no more than a formal letter. At length, my uncle Helmut let me know by telegram that my silence was inexcusable. I therefore submitted my name for the examination and quickly forgot about a diplomatic career once more.

When the time came to appear for the entry examination I had to travel overnight by train from Munich to Berlin. Since I was not particularly keen to enter the diplomatic service, it did not bother me that I got no sleep on the train and instead spent the night chatting with an engineer on the Walchensee hydro-electric power station near Munich. By sunrise I was quite an authority on the subject. During the oral examination I was asked to present my views on the future of hydro-electric power in Bavaria. Not wanting to overwhelm the examiners with my expertise, let alone reveal its source, I began slowly, only gradually bringing forth my more recondite knowledge of the subject. The examiners were stunned by my brilliance.

Next came the English examination. Here, the examiner asked me if there was any work on England that had particularly impressed me. Without hesitation I cited Seeley's *The Expansion of England* and spoke eloquently about it for several minutes. Until I saw the examiner beaming I had no idea that he too was a great admirer of Seeley. Again, I passed with flying colours, with the result that I found myself in the German Foreign Service.

I entered the Foreign Service in April 1927, not quite knowing what it was or why I was there. I was assigned first to the European section. Assuming that this dealt with the most burning issues of the day, I convinced myself that my career was off to a meteoric start. I had wanted to be assigned to the French Desk, and was disappointed to be put on the desk dealing with the occupied territories in the Rhineland. To my surprise, I nonetheless found myself deep in some of the most important issues in our foreign policy. I worked with a group of diplomats and policy-makers who were trying to put the perennial problem of Germany's relationship with France on a new basis. The task completely captured my imagination.

The head of this division was Heinrich von Friedberg, the grandson of a former Prussian Minister of Justice who was an ennobled Jew. Prior to 1918, Friedberg had served in the Prussian Ministry of the Interior and had drafted the Prussian constitutional reform that might have saved the monarchy. His precise and orderly mind was a great example to me. Frequently he would call me in when he had a lengthy memorandum to dictate, so that he could turn to me on matters of detail if necessary. Many times I watched him dictate twenty or thirty pages without notes and without pausing. Rarely was it necessary to make more than the most minor corrections to his drafts.

In addition to distinguishing himself in his work on behalf of the Rhineland and the Saar, Friedberg was a brilliant pedagogue. He would frequently gather a small group of us together late in the afternoon and issue a hypothetical order such as the following:

You are secretary to the German Minister in Argentina. It is the German national holiday and your minister has agreed to give a speech before the local German colony, which is split between a majority of old Black–White–Red monarchists and a few Black–Red–Gold liberals. The minister has suddenly become ill and you have been asked to write and deliver the speech in his place. You have one hour to prepare.

My own performance was less than brilliant. The greatest value of the exercise was in comparing our own efforts with the speech which Friedberg himself then delivered for our benefit.

An all-important part of my experience in the Foreign Office was my association with an excellent group of young Foreign Service officers. We were united in our admiration for Stresemann, Foreign Minister of the Weimar Republic. In his early life Stresemann had been a convinced monarchist and nationalist. In wartime he advocated the annexation of foreign territories occupied by Germany. After the war he turned into a good republican and, with the French Foreign Minister Aristide Briand, became the architect of Franco–German understanding. For many of us younger diplomats, whose ideals went to pieces in 1918 and who were searching for new ones, he was the inspiring leader who helped us to overcome the past. He opened up new horizons for us and gave us new aims.

Stresemann impressed us by his profound knowledge of Napoleon and Goethe. He liked to quote them in discussion in order to strengthen his arguments. His knowledge of these two great men served him as a rock on which he could always take refuge. One evening after a Christmas party he strongly advised us to follow his example to choose one subject and to study it thoroughly. His wife, who had two sons of our age, was extremely hospitable to the younger group and would frequently include us in the receptions and dances that she would give. My gifted and lively colleagues, the friendly manner in which the Stresemanns treated us, and our active social life in the capital made this an unforgettable period. The Nazis were later to condemn the late Weimar years as an era of chaos and decadence. For me they were a golden age, as happy as my childhood had been.

While I was still an attaché in Berlin, I frequented the Guards Cavalry Club, an elegantly equipped and comfortable establishment that offered good food and gave a pleasant annual ball. The president of the club invited Goering to come one evening, simply in order to find out what sort of person he was. He arrived for the evening properly attired in white tie and tails and spoke calmly. We knew that he was a former flying ace, and perhaps because of this felt that he would not mind being asked bluntly how he expected his party would ever get to power. He confidently assured his audience that within a few years even the Centre Parties would be supporting the National Socialists, thus permitting the Nazis to come to power legally.

I passed my final examination in December 1929. To celebrate, I went to Gargellen in Austria, where the parents of my friend Eddie Brücklmeier had two ski lodges. Brücklmeier was later to be executed after the plot of July 1944. Just as I was strapping on my skis for the first day on the slopes, a postman arrived with a telegram addressed to me. Suspecting that it might be my orders, I told him to leave it with the porter. Later, when I opened the cable, I discovered that I had already missed the date to report, so I decided that it would do no harm if I added a few more days. The skiing and party-going connected with the Carnival at Munich was all the more pleasant, knowing that I was enjoying it on stolen time.

After a post-haste trip back to Berlin, I reported with an innocent face to the Secretary of Legation, Trutter, who was in charge of the group of which I was part. To my horror he told me that I had been originally designated for Paris, but since I had been so slow in responding I was to be sent instead to a consulate somewhere in the Soviet Union. I tried to take the news smiling and bravely remarked that I had always wanted to go to Russia. Trutter, evidently doubting my words, gave me to understand that if I could catch the eleven o'clock train that evening for Paris, I would have one last chance. I was to be appointed secretary to State Secretary von Simson, who was in charge of negotiating the return of the Saar to Germany.

I flew from his office, bade my parents farewell, and used the little money I had left from my holiday to buy the cheapest *papier mâché* suitcases. Next morning I was in Paris, face to face with the concierge at the elegant George V Hotel, where von Simson was staying. Looking at my luggage, the concierge welcomed me at once as 'His Excellency's new footman'. When I told him that I happened to be the new attaché he roared with laughter and sent me up at once.

Von Simson was of Jewish origin, the grandson of the first president of the Reichstag and of the Supreme Court. I was not sure what to expect of this well-known figure. At our first meeting he invited me to dine with him that evening. He advised me to wear my dinner jacket and, incongruously as I thought, told me that he intended to have a cold dinner. I arrived prepared for the worst. After several years of cold dinners as a student, I certainly had not expected this in Paris. No sooner did we sit down than my fears vanished. Von Simson ordered cold lobster, oysters, and Pilsner beer. Relieved, I asked his permission to order champagne with which to celebrate. He granted it, but I drank alone. We then went to the theatre, but he left after the second act, leaving me to report to him later on the outcome. This turned out to be typical of von Simson.

As my old chief Friedberg explained to me, my main task was to keep Simson from giving way to his overwhelming wish to leave France and return to his family in Germany. This was the more difficult because Simson rarely bothered to attend meetings of the subcommittees of the commission, thus providing long stretches of time that had to be filled in an interesting and distracting manner. We covered Paris, I keeping careful accounts of expenditure all the while. In short, I was like Simson's watch-dog.

Herr von Simson was a perfect *cicerone*, having a vast knowledge of history and the history of art. I believe he had read every British memoir that had appeared during the last century, and he was a great connoisseur of paintings and antiques. He had left the diplomatic service as Permanent Under Secretary for Economic Affairs in the Ministry for Foreign Affairs and had taken a high position with I. G. Farben, the largest chemical concern in Germany. With his blue eyes, white hair and great charm, he was beloved by everybody. Within a few days I too had fallen under his charm.

I kept abreast of the negotiations through daily meetings with Friedberg, who attended all the sessions. Anything of significance I had to pass to Simson. In the end, our mission failed, probably because it was premature, but I had gained a first-hand exposure to diplomatic work and found it to my taste. My upbringing and training had proved adequate for all that had been put before me and, leaving Paris, I could look forward to the future with great enthusiasm.

2

LOOKING EAST, 1930–1931

After this delightful if fruitless interlude in Paris, I returned in the autumn of 1930 to Berlin, where I learned that I was to be posted to the German Legation in Argentina. I did not oppose this idea outright, since my mother's younger brother had moved there. At the same time, I wanted to explore other possibilities. My parents were living in Potsdam at the time, and every morning I commuted from their home to Berlin by train. I used to travel with Martin Schliep, who served in the Personnel Department of our Foreign Service and who had spent a long time in the Soviet Union. He was a great storyteller and had a gift for fascinating younger people with his experiences.

Schliep told me the history of the New Economic Policy (NEP) introduced by Lenin after the war, when it was found that the purer Communism of the first post-revolutionary years was shattering the economy. He also had much to say about the abandonment of that policy and the adoption of the first Five-Year Plan, which was now in full swing.

Schliep nourished an interest in Russia which, for various reasons, I had felt since my childhood. A branch of my family had emigrated to Russia in 1807. In 1894 my father had attended the coronation of Tsar Nicholas II. His vivid description of all that he had seen and heard in Russia caught my imagination. I had inherited from my forebear, Bodo von Herwarth, a gold watch, which Nicolas I had given him in recognition of his services as his page during a visit to Berlin. My childhood memories and Schliep's stories together induced me to ask for a transfer to Moscow.

There were other reasons for my decision. To say the least, things were not going well in Germany. The stock market had collapsed in 1929, and the ensuing worldwide economic crisis hit Germany harder than any other country. In 1932 we had about six million unemployed, the Communist Party was powerful, while the influence of the Nazis was growing steadily. Young people were asking themselves, 'Can we continue on the old road? Would it not be better to work out some different system for our society?' I personally dismissed the Nazi solution. I was against it right from the beginning. In part, I had personal reasons for this, since my maternal grandmother was of Jewish extraction. Though her family was closely linked with many of the leading families in Europe, her Jewish origins put her beyond the pale and caused me to be designated non-Aryan as well.

Therefore I could not accept National Socialism, but felt that I should inform myself about Communism. With this in mind, I went to the Personnel Department and told them I would like to go to the Soviet Union. They told me that I could not be transferred before the beginning of the following year, 1931, and that I had best use the intervening time in learning Russian and acquiring the necessary training for my work in Russia.

I should say something about my preparation. As part of my final diplomatic examination I had written a thesis on 'The Liquidation of the Russo-Japanese War by the Treaty of Portsmouth, 1905', a project which gave me an introduction to Russia's Far-Eastern policy. In the introduction I described the century-old Russian dream of an ice-free port on the open ocean and stressed that the Russians never tried to expand in more than one direction at a time. Along the way, I had also attended the preparatory lectures offered to the young attachés by Professor Otto Hoetzsch, an expert on Eastern policy. Thanks to these lectures and to my own research, my curiosity had already been fed with some concrete knowledge.

Thereafter, I read everything on Russia that I could get hold of. I followed Soviet affairs through the English, French, and German press. I studied closely all the articles on Russia by Paul Scheffer of the *Berliner Tageblatt*. Scheffer had lived and worked in Moscow for many years, and was married to a lady of the Russian aristocracy. He was considered an oracle on all things Soviet. There were some excellent books available as well, even on the most recent period. Klaus Mehnert, for example, had just published his study on *Jugend in der Sowjetunion*. Mehnert had lived and travelled in the Soviet Union, spoke Russian as well as he spoke German, and was full of curiosity. We became close friends.

A particularly valuable part of my training was in Russian history. Through it, I was to discover that certain traits of Soviet policy were not so much Communist in origin as purely Russian. I also took language lessons from a former tsarist officer, Colonel Noskoff, a kindly man with a great sense of humour. In trying to teach me Russian he also endeavoured

33

to introduce me to Russian literature. He was full of wonderful anecdotes about life in pre-revolutionary Russia and, although he was no friend of the Bolsheviks, he made no effort to indoctrinate me with his political views.

Even with all this help, it was extremely difficult to gain any clear picture of Soviet affairs in 1930–31. It was all very well to be told that communistic societies had existed in ancient times; comparisons with such societies only showed more clearly the many ways in which the Soviet Union was an absolutely new phenomenon. Even if one read accurate descriptions of it, it was difficult to know just what the words meant. I studied their efforts to equalize remuneration but could not get a real picture of what that meant in practice. Similarly, I studied the peculiar Russian organization of communal property in the *obshchina* without getting any clear notion of what they were.

In February 1931, a contemporary of mine, Gustav Struve, who was attached to the Foreign Minister, Stresemann, made a trip to the USSR. So delighted was he with what he saw that he decided to request a transfer to Moscow. Immediately I went to my own boss and reminded him in no uncertain terms that I was still most anxious to get to Moscow, not only because I had studied the USSR so diligently but because I had invested in a warm fur coat. In the face of this strong countermove, Struve finally gave up his idea of a transfer to Moscow. But one further impediment arose.

Before leaving for the Soviet Union, I took a long leave in order to visit my friend Albrecht von Kessel, who was posted to the German Embassy at the Vatican. Arriving in Rome in April 1931, I met by pure coincidence the counsellor of our Moscow Embassy, Fritz von Twardowski, and his wife. I called on them at the Hotel Eden and was received most politely. Twardowski was encouraging but assured me that I would have to serve first in a consulate, probably Kiev, before coming to Moscow. I asked myself why the hell I had made such an effort to cool Gustav Struve's desire to go to Russia if I was now to be assigned to Kiev or some place even less glamorous. In fact, I was designated for Kharkov or Kiev, but just at that moment three secretaries of the Moscow Embassy were transferred elsewhere, one to Leningrad, a second to Kharkov, and a third to Abyssinia, the last having run into difficulties and been declared *persona non grata* by the Soviet government. In May 1931, I finally received my orders for Moscow.

My family was convinced that my transfer to Moscow was in punishment for some nefarious deed that I had kept from them. My father's theory was that I had done badly in Paris. They were all sure that I was being sent into exile. Many of my friends knew little about the Soviet Union other than press reports of mass executions, and were terrified at my going there. Nonetheless, I was to spend more time in Moscow than I did at any other post in my subsequent career. Being a so-called 'non-Aryan', I was denied transfer to any more desirable embassy, with the result that I ended up serving eight years in the Soviet capital.

I left for Moscow by train from the Friedrichstrasse in the centre of Berlin. On its way out of Berlin the train stopped at the Schlesischer Bahnhof. Although this station was only a few kilometres to the east of the city's centre, one could already sense that a different world lay beyond. The smells were more Eastern; the milling crowds were dressed in a more Eastern way. General Ernst Köstring, our military attaché in Moscow, once quipped that 'Asia starts at the Schlesischer Bahnhof in Berlin'. He was right. From here unrolls the vast plain that stretches from Berlin to Vladivostok, interrupted only by the Urals.

Crossing Poland, the countryside grew more sparsely populated and the train slowed its pace. We glided through stretches of deep woods and broad fields and finally arrived at the Soviet frontier. There was some barbed wire about, but otherwise the only indication that it was a frontier was the large wooden structure welcoming you to the Soviet Union and proclaiming various propaganda slogans.

At the first stop within the Soviet Union I wanted to try out my Russian. I marched up to the food counter and asked for caviar, using the German *Kaviar*, on the assumption that it was derived from Russian. I failed my first test. Realizing that the woman did not understand me, I pointed my finger at the caviar. She exclaimed 'Ah, *ikra.*' This was my first practical lesson in the Soviet Union, and it was not without interest. At the frontier station, a window on the West, one could obtain caviar with ease. I was soon to learn that it was far more difficult to procure it in Moscow. Such window dressing became familiar to me later.

At once I discovered that my diplomatic passport assured me great courtesy and preferential treatment everywhere. I noticed, though, that ordinary people were treated quite severely. A year later, when I crossed the Latvian border in the company of two prominent German Communists, Ernst Thälmann and Wilhelm Pieck, I had no difficulties whatsoever, thanks to my diplomatic passport, but they were given quite a time, in spite of being loyal Party members and officials in the Comintern. Later, both Thälmann and Pieck were arrested and deported to concentration camps. Thälmann died there but Pieck survived to become President of the German Democratic Republic.

I arrived in Moscow at the beginning of the Russian spring. As in Italy, springtime in Russia bursts suddenly upon you, the passage from first shoots of green to full-blooming summertime occurring in a matter of days. It is fantastic to experience the Russian spring and to watch nature surge suddenly back to life after so harsh a winter.

Immediately upon my arrival I was taken to one of the houses leased by the German government as a kind of ghetto for embassy personnel. My rooms were in an old house in *Kalachnyi Pereulok*, where I boarded with two other secretaries, Kurt Brunhoff and Hans Kastner. The flat was minute, and I fully expected to have to accept Brunhoff's offer to put me up on the piano. It turned out to be a well-run household. Thanks to my colleagues' diligence we had an excellent Hungarian cook and also Grigorii, an illiterate peasant from the countryside, who was as handsome as a prince, and would not explode when we returned home at 3.00 a.m. yelling for bread and cheese. Grigorii's only conspicuous shortcoming was that he was an atrocious cook, as I learned when I was alone with him. His culinary skills were limited to rubbery fried eggs and caviar on ice, the latter of which I indulged in three times a day out of necessity. This soon killed my taste for caviar. When the new military attaché, General Ernst Köstring, asked me if I could obtain some caviar for him, I did so only on the condition that he reciprocate with some good German sausages.

Once settled in my quarters, I reported at once to the ambassador, Herbert von Dirksen, an old friend of my father's. The two had served in the same cavalry company, Dirksen as a reserve officer and my father as his squadron leader. Like my father, Dirksen was immensely proud of the tradition of this regiment, the Third Uhlan Guards. Stationed in Potsdam, the regiment was renowned for the fact that every officer in it was an outstanding horseman. They rode in races and horse-shows throughout Germany. Von Dirksen's regimental pride and affection for my father were genuine, and he therefore gave me a cordial welcome, in spite of the fact that he was an extremely shy person and expressed his sentiments only with the greatest reticence.

I will later speak in detail both of Dirksen and of my jobs under his ambassadorship. For the moment it is enough to say that his decision to assign me first to the consular section proved beneficial in several respects; it kept me in close touch with events outside the diplomatic world and ensured that I had ample time to explore Moscow and the USSR at what proved to be a most extraordinary period in their history.

My first impression of Moscow was of uninterrupted greyness; except for the green of the trees and shrubs, the only colours were grey and greyer. Men wore old suits, and women old dresses, usually grey. One sensed a mood of gloomy seriousness everywhere, and, indeed, there was good reason to be serious, since there were shortages of everything. Urban life was hard indeed and one felt it at once.

Visiting Muscovites, I was appalled to discover that whole families were herded together in single rooms. Many families had to share a common bath, W.C., and kitchen. Privacy vanished; the only people who had any were those foreign engineers and experts who were assigned small flats of two or three rooms. Such experts benefited from other perquisites as well, such as higher food rations and access to special shops. They were truly a privileged group.

However poor the conditions of life for those who were more or less established in the capital, the fate of the new migrants from rural regions was truly pitiable. In 1931–32 one had the impression that Moscow was being swamped by a mighty wave of peasants driven from the country-side in search of work and food. This human tide was the result of collectivization and the resultant famine, which claimed so many millions of lives. Among these migrants were many children who had lost their parents or had deserted their families and come to the city in search of food. They were known as the *besprizorniki*, and were a pitiable group of young boys and girls, but as resilient as they were colourful.

Only the toughest among them could survive. Individually and in bands, they roamed the country in railway cars. At goods yards and other stops, they would build bonfires and sit around them in large groups, warming their hands before setting out in search of food. Many *besprizorniki* in Moscow would pass the night in one of the numerous large barrels that had been used to carry asphalt and which were everywhere in evidence in those years. In the late evening, one might even encounter such children sleeping in Red Square.

I was often warned to be careful with *besprizorniki*, since they might rob or even murder us. Russians especially would caution me not to open the windows of the train when it was standing in the station, lest a *besprizornik* reach in from the platform and steal whatever was within his grasp. In spite of such warnings, I developed a great respect for these homeless urchins, so full of life and with a remarkable capacity for endurance.

37

I suspect the Soviet government appreciated these qualities when it initiated its programme to pick them up from the streets and re-educate them. I once visited one of Makarenko's famous schools near Moscow where *besprizorniki* were brought back into society, and was much impressed by the quality of the youngsters I met there. One could not help but be depressed, though, by the fact that many of them had lost an arm or a leg through tumbling from moving trains. Thanks to Makarenko's re-education camps, the *besprizorniki* gradually disappeared as a feature of urban life in Russia. This did not happen at once, though, and as late as 1935, when I visited the Caucasus, the trains were still filled with young children travelling alone. As long as they remained, the *besprizorniki* gave a sad hue to public places, a sadness that was only partially lifted by the subsequent success of many of them – such as the famous tenor Leshchenko.

In addition to the homeless children, one met many women with their children begging together for bread. These mournful groups – the living remains of what once were families – were a common sight throughout the USSR, and were particularly numerous around the larger railway stations. The stations themselves were emblems of Russia's suffering. Visiting a Soviet station at any point in the thirties, one would encounter hundreds of wretched people lying around and waiting, sometimes as long as a fortnight, just to board a train. In such circumstances, the only way to obtain a seat was to be on good terms with the authorities. This was easy enough for those holding high government positions but extremely difficult for the hundreds of thousands of impoverished peasants driven off the land by the government's policies. For this reason, many adult Russians joined the *besprizorniki* perched on the roofs of boxcars, huddled in freight cars, or even hiding between the cars on the couplings.

This created a serious problem for those foreign diplomats whose duties required that they get out and see the country. Travel by train was all but impossible if one had to board in a provincial city that lacked a German consulate. Without the special treatment accorded to Party members or Soviet officials, we were in the same position as the peasant migrants. At such times we quickly learned that the only way to reduce the interminable wait was to turn for help to the GPU, the Secret Police. The officer in charge would issue the tickets and simply evict anyone already in the seats, ordering them to wait for the next train so that the distinguished foreigner could get his seat. This was a thoroughly unpleasant procedure, but there was no alternative if one wished to travel by train. I suspect that Party members and government officials were at least as quick as we to accept the system.

Another feature of Russian train travel in the 1930s was the legions of insects of every type, particularly bedbugs. DDT had not yet been invented. In its absence, one particularly ingenious member of our Embassy had a tailor make him a pair of pyjamas which completely covered his feet and hands, leaving only his head out. This absurd but eminently practical outfit was the invention of our naval attaché, Commander Norbert von Baumbach.

It was evident that rural life was crippled at the time of my arrival in Russia in 1931. The peasantry had been condemned to a miserable existence by Stalin's policy of financing industrialization with money extracted from the agricultural sector. Nikolai Bukharin and a few other 'deviationists' had opposed such a policy as a diversion from true Communism, but Stalin could not have cared less. He simply liquidated the peasantry, and his critics as well.

After an initial exposure, I tended to avoid extended travels in the agricultural regions. It was too heartbreaking to see the endless hordes of people starving to death. When we did travel in the countryside we had to take care not to picnic too close to a village. On one occasion we failed to follow this precept, and when we threw away some orange peel a group of peasants approached us and asked if they could pick it up. Necessity is the mother of invention. A decade later I, too, would have saved the peel for marmalade.

Otto Schiller, the agricultural attaché of our Embassy, told me several times about visits to villages in the company of local Soviet administrators, who would forbid any public discussion of the prevailing famine. If people asked the officials for bread, they would not answer. If queried about the scope of the famine, they would reply: 'You must fulfil the plan and do what the Party has ordered and everything will then be all right.' Such officials simply refused to acknowledge that the famine existed.

In 1933, Herriot, the President of the French Council of Ministers, paid a visit to the Soviet Union. When he asked to see a collective farm he was taken to a large one near Kiev. He met the peasants and spoke with them through an interpreter. Returning to France, he reported to the European press that the Ukrainian peasantry was well fed and contented with the new system, and that food was in plentiful supply everywhere. What he did not realize was that he had visited a 'Potemkin village', as in the time of Catherine II. Shops on the streets through which he passed had been carefully provisioned beforehand, and special trucks inscribed

'Bread' had been imported for the occasion. White uniforms from the hospitals were issued to the doormen en route, and neatly uniformed crews were made available to sweep the streets. Herriot was greatly impressed by all this, to the deep chagrin of the staff at the French Embassy. So embarrassed were my French friends that during the Herriot visit they avoided all contact with their colleagues in the diplomatic corps.

As the mass starvation in the countryside deepened, I kept asking myself what would happen in the army. After all, the Red Army was made up of the sons and brothers of the peasants who were dying in the countryside. My instinct was that the famine would eventually create disorder and rebellion in the army but this proved to be incorrect for several reasons. First, soldiers from rural districts were flatly forbidden to take home leave. This effectively prevented direct contact with the rural situation. Second, all letters to and from the army were closely monitored. Finally, exhortatory letters were dictated to groups of soldiers. The soldiers were asked to write them out in their own hand for forwarding to their families. As a result, those of us who had been charged with finding out whether revolutionary upheavals could be expected in the army turned in a negative report. So far as we knew, there were no manifestations of unrest in that quarter. This experience had a great influence on the thinking of many of us in the Embassy on the eve of the war. It confirmed our judgment of the Red Army as an extremely well-disciplined and effective organization.

What were we in the Embassy to do about the famine? The younger members of the staff agonized over this question endlessly. Some suggested that the German government should suspend all deliveries of industrial equipment to the Soviet Union as long as its government continued to doom millions of people to death by starvation. For my part, I considered it immoral for us to be shipping goods to the Soviet Union at all. This was decidedly not the position of the Weimar government. Its response was to pretend to be preoccupied with the problem of unemployment in Germany. Since it was assumed that the shipping of goods to the Soviet Union would substantially alleviate unemployment at home, the German government felt itself freed of all further re-sponsibility. Accordingly, German exports continued unabated, as did exports to the USSR from other non-Communist states.

As this traffic continued, the younger members of the Embassy grew increasingly incensed. Von Dirksen sympathized with our feelings, but he and the counsellor, Gustav Hilger, had both succumbed to the selfish argument that justified trade with the Soviet Union on the grounds that it alleviated unemployment in Germany. Beyond this, they argued that even if the deliveries of industrial equipment were to stop, it would not prevent the Soviet Union from continuing to terrorize the rural population. I had to admit that in this they were correct. The best we in the Embassy were able to do was collect money for the *Brüder in Not*, a German organization dedicated to providing relief for those many German peasants in the Volga Basin and elsewhere who had been stricken by famine.

Upon my arrival, the Soviet Union was deep in the first Five-Year Plan. One of the primary duties of the Embassy was to analyse its impact and consequences. I was not inclined to take the exalted claims of the Soviet government too seriously, on account of the poor co-ordination between the various parts of the 'planned' economy. A good example was the truck industry. The workers in an important factory which produced engines for Soviet trucks managed through great zeal to over-fulfil their plan by fifty per cent. Unfortunately, however, the factory which produced the chassis failed to meet its plan by a considerable margin. The result was that a large part of the engine factory's output could not be used, since there were too few vehicles to put them in. On such evidence, we reached the conclusion that in many respects the basic system of the plan was counterproductive.

The impact of the Stakhanov movement reinforced our bad impression of the incentive system on which the Five-Year Plan was based. Stakhanov himself was a champion coal miner, and his herculean achievements were daily trumpeted in the Soviet press. But numerous reports that we received indicated that Stakhanov's fellow miners knew full well the special conditions in which he worked when he set his records, and therefore resented all the more the pressure that his artificial achievements put on them. Their resentment had a negative effect on productivity.

After studying numerous such examples, I concluded that it would be appropriate to call Stalin's project a Five-Year 'Non-Plan'. The construction of factories often lagged so far behind the delivery of imported machinery for them that a large part of the equipment ended up rusting unused on railway sidings. This waste of good equipment infuriated the German exporters who had provided it. Being good Germans, they were anxious to see that their machinery was doing its duty, and were angered to discover that much of it was standing idle as if in some open-air industrial museum.

For all our frustration with the Russians, members of the German

Embassy could not help but sympathize with the Soviet effort to industrialize as rapidly as possible. The difficulties they encountered aroused a compassion that grew in part from our own national experience. After all, Germany had built its industrial order later than Britain, and had undergone many of the same difficulties as the Russians were now experiencing. We knew full well, also, that until the late nineteenth century the quality of German industrial goods was scarcely higher than that of Russian production in the thirties. Because of this, we were disposed to accept that Soviet production would improve at some point in the future. Because Germany's economy had experienced its own *Kinderkrankheiten* in the past, we understood the character of Russia's teething pains in the present.

My colleagues and I argued against those in Germany who considered that the Five-Year Plans would be an utter failure and that the USSR would collapse forthwith. Not one person in the Embassy shared this apocalyptic view. For all the clumsiness of their planning and the resistance of much of the labour force, the Soviets' effort to industrialize seemed bound to succeed. The only time at which our certainty wavered was during the famine when, as I mentioned, we wondered about the position of the army. Otherwise, analysts at the German Embassy in Moscow always accepted the Soviet system as a fact.

To an observer, the Soviet economy seemed to be overwhelmingly concentrated on heavy industry and armaments, at the expense of all consumer interests. Nonetheless, there were notable areas in which the First Five-Year Plan appealed directly to the public. For instance, the emphasis upon electrification was essential to the development of heavy industry, but it also placed a glowing light bulb in every peasant's hut – thus transforming the long winter nights. Could there have been a more vivid symbol of progress? Similarly, the construction of the Moscow underground was often criticized in the West as a superfluous luxury, but it had an immense effect on the population, which had hitherto admired such splendour only in the palaces of the former monarchs. After all, numbers of lives had been lost during the construction of St Petersburg under Peter the Great, yet the Russian man in the street came eventually to revere that awesome city. Time and time again I observed how peasants could stare in fascination at the glamour of the new underground stations, which rivalled the great salons of the Kremlin, and emerge into the daylight shaking their heads and exclaiming that 'in truth our government is doing fabulous things'.

These compensating factors help account for the positive attitude of many people even during the most grim years of collectivization and forced industrialization. One could not help but admire the pervasive enthusiasm for modernity as such. Many workers whom I met were genuinely proud of their factory, and this pride extended even to machinery and instruments that had been imported from Germany. Russians realized that their country had not produced this equipment but were nonetheless eager to show it off on account of its modernity.

The expansion of opportunities for education was perhaps the most important factor making for public optimism in the 1930s. Driving around the Russian countryside, I never failed to marvel at the presence of a new school in practically every village. Along with industrialization, electrification and the building up of the Red Army, education was surely the highest priority of the Soviet government in the thirties. Indeed the three priorities were intimately connected, since the expansion of literacy was one of the principal educational tasks of the army, just as it was a precondition for industrialization.

Acknowledging all this, the fact remains that the lot of the Soviet consumer was miserable both in terms of the shortage of goods and of their inferior quality. Only the most privileged people could get anything. In 1932 there were no coffee shops in all Moscow, and only a few public restaurants. Clothing, medicine and other necessities were in equally short supply.

One might think that such conditions would have given rise to frustration that would explode in waves of crime. Although the Soviet government did not make available any reliable statistics, my impression was that crime was no more widespread in Moscow in the 1930s than in other countries, and perhaps even less. The principal forms of crime were connected with survival – the stealing of potatoes and the like. In such areas the law of the jungle prevailed. But there were few capital offences. Russians themselves claimed that one of the reasons there was so little crime was that convicted criminals could count on being harshly punished, not by imprisonment but by deportation. Thousands of Muscovites were sent to labour camps, even for petty 'hooliganism'.

Were the Russian people happy at the time of my arrival? Here one must distinguish between those who were idealists and those who were not. The former were entirely satisfied. They were preoccupied with the future, entranced by a vision of the world that was soon to open before them. On the other hand, the population at large was living in miserable conditions. Whatever revolutionary enthusiasm may once have moved them was fast petering out. During the First Five-Year Plan, however, the idealists were still much in evidence.

Who were the idealists? By 1931, many former estates (those that had not been burned during the Civil War) had been converted to recreation centres, or *doma otdykha*. On our visits to such institutions, young people would invariably invite us to discuss events in Germany. Our hosts for the most part were the most devout of Communists – only such people could avail themselves of the *doma otdykha*. Generally, my impression of them was precisely the same as Klaus Mehnert's had been: that they were utterly sincere, enthusiastic, and even unselfish in their Communism, and willing to undergo great hardship in its name. They were also impressively well informed on events abroad.

In the early 1930s, Soviet ideology was as yet untouched by xenophobia. This openness to the outside world extended even to simple peasants. On trips into the countryside, I was frequently approached by rural folk who, learning that I was German, were eager to engage me in conversation. Introducing themselves, they would explain that they had been prisoners-of-war in Germany during World War I. More often than not they would enquire after a particular German whom they had known, and would be disappointed when I was unable to provide news of their friends. Parenthetically, this suggests that prisoners-of-war had been reasonably well treated in 1914–18, in glaring contrast to the next war.

From the day of my arrival in Moscow, I tried diligently to explore all aspects of Russian culture, past and present. Naturally, I devoted a great deal of time to weekend expeditions to historic sites. Travel was difficult since the roads were so bad. The hotels matched the roads, so my friends and I would normally camp outdoors. In this fashion we visited Vladimir, the Trinity, Saint Sergius Monastery, Novgorod, and many other historic spots. These sites made a deep impression on me, for one could experience in them the genius of the Russian people. Stated differently, one could see in them what the Russian people had been capable of doing when they worked under the command of God. Even in the 1930s, I could not help but be impressed, as so many other foreigners have been in the past, by the profundity and directness of the faith of the population at large.

During my first year in Moscow, I haunted the museums. In those days, they were still trying to present the paintings not as objects of art but as documents of social history. Pictures were chosen for exhibition on this basis, and were labelled so as to underline their social message. The curators at the Tretiakov Gallery in Moscow and at the Russian Museum in Leningrad did a first-class job of finding artistic illustrations of Russia's past as it was then conceived. One could contemplate depictions of drunken priests eating with the common servants, as if demonstrating their lack of education and culture. Nor were all such pictures merely caricatures. Germans who had lived in Russia before the Revolution assured me that more than a few of them represented reality fairly accurately.

On Saturdays several of us would often leave Moscow after finishing work at one o'clock and head by train for Leningrad. Once in the former capital, we would spend our time sightseeing and visiting friends and end our weekend at the ballet or opera on Sunday evening. Immediately after the performance we would race to the train in order to be back at work in Moscow the following morning.

More than other art forms, the Russian stage impressed me with its high quality. I soon began taking foreign visitors to the theatre, even those who spoke no Russian. Before going they would complain that it would be unintelligible; I would reply that they would be free to leave at the first intermission. They always stayed to the end because the acting was so exquisite. The absence of a star system made it the more interesting, for one would frequently find minor roles filled by brilliant actors. The quality was further assured by the directors' readiness to rehearse a play for as long as a year before presenting it to the public. In the best productions one could take a photograph of the stage at any point and see that it was always in balance. Every movement was co-ordinated, to the extent that if one actor moved to the right, a second would move to the left to re-establish the visual harmony.

During my early years in Moscow, Viacheslav Meierhold had not yet been suppressed, and in fact still enjoyed great popularity. I remember well the audiences at his productions. There were always people there who were keenly interested in theatre, of course, but there was also a percentage who had received free tickets through their factories. The former, obviously intellectuals, always seemed to contrast sharply with the latter, whose conservative tastes left them puzzled at Meierhold's avant-gardism. In the long run, the government was to side with the latter against the former, and against Meierhold especially.

When I arrived, there were still many revolutionary works to be seen in the theatres. Typical among them was the ballet *The Red Poppy*, a lively production extolling the Revolution. This was soon removed from the stage, however, since it failed to arouse any enthusiasm among the 'democratic' public, which preferred the classical ballets of Tchaikovsky and the dramas of Chekhov. One exception was Mikhail Bulgakov's play, *Dni Turbinikh*. In this play, which was based on a story that had been published in the mid-twenties, one could relive the Revolution. Audiences did so with gusto, in part because the work was well acted, I believe by the company of the Stanislavsky Theatre.

Dni Turbinikh had a particular significance for one member of our embassy, General Köstring, the military attaché. At one point in the play, Hetman Skoropadski of the Ukraine had to be evacuated so that he would not fall into the hands of the advancing Red Army. To conceal his identity, he was dressed in a German uniform and carried out on a stretcher under the supervision of a German major. As the Ukrainian leader departed in this fashion, the German major on stage remarked, '*Chistaia nemetskaia rabota*' (Clean German workmanship), all in a very strong German accent. Now, Köstring had been attached to Skoropadski at the time depicted in the play, and he had been the major in question. When he saw the performance, he objected strongly to the fact that the actor had spoken with a German accent while he (Köstring) spoke Russian with utter fluency. He took his complaint to the director of the theatre. Notwithstanding Köstring's indignation, however, the part was not altered.

Watching *Dni Turbinikh*, Russian audiences could relive their revolution, though not necessarily from the perspective that the government would have preferred. In one famous scene, a young officer on leave in Kiev sits down at the piano and plays the tsarist national anthem. I remember well the audience expressing its approval of this, and even applauding. Similar scenes occurred at the performances of the Rimsky-Korsakov opera *Pskovtianka* (*The Maiden of Pskov*). In one scene, Ivan the Terrible enters the captured town of Pskov. The stage was set with a backdrop of onion-domed churches, and the ringing of bells filled the theatre. At this point, the tsarist anthem was played and the audience would applaud enthusiastically. This occurred in Moscow in the winter of 1932–33.

Later such sentiments were to be welcomed by the Soviet government. We watched with fascination after 1933 as all the Russian national heroes returned: Suvorov and Kutuzov, who defeated Napoleon; Peter the Great; Ivan the Terrible. Viewing the flow of films and books dealing with Russia's glorious past, I could not help but feel that in this instance the government had accurately grasped what the people wanted. Even the cosmopolitan composers, Shostakovich and Prokofiev, understood and participated actively in this movement.

The rise of Soviet nationalism was also reflected in literature. When I arrived in 1931, the general tendency was to describe the Whites as the former ruling class, an evil band oppressing the man in the street. They were invariably depicted as effete, sunk in decadence, and lacking all manly virtues. As the propaganda effort to build a new 'Soviet nationalism' got under way in earnest in the early 1930s, this earlier depiction of the Whites created problems. After all, there was scant honour for the Red Army in having defeated such a gang of wastrels. Party leaders understood that an army could only prove its bravery in action against a tough and valiant enemy. This led to a willingness to portray the Whites more dispassionately. A turning point in this development was probably the film *Chapaev*, which was released on the anniversary of the Revolution in November 1934. However much this seems today yet another caricature of the Whites, it struck Soviet audiences and us foreign observers as representing a long step towards a more impartial view of the past.

Theatre, film, and music were extremely lively when I arrived in Moscow, but it was a number of years before the Soviet government began to place great emphasis upon sports. There were a few good athletes, to be sure, but we in the diplomatic community felt ourselves unusual in our interest in every conceivable form of athletic activity. This did not change until the late thirties, at which time athletics was woven into the fabric of the emerging Soviet nationalism.

One of our frequent entertainments in the early years was the circus, which in Moscow was uniformly excellent. We attended the circus not only to see the customary acts but also because we knew it was one of the few places where humour thrived openly. One instance that became famous in our community was the appearance of two clowns on the stage of the Moscow Circus, one of them carrying a portrait of Lenin and the other of Stalin. Arriving in the middle of the ring, one of them would look out wide-eyed at the audience and ask: 'What shall we do with them? Hang them or put them up against the wall?' There were roars of laughter. This indicated that, for all the confusion of the day, the regime was by now so sure of itself that it could accept humour as a legitimate safety valve for criticism. Much the same thing occured at the beginning of National Socialism in Germany, where many outrageous jokes were spread about the Nazis, some of them probably started by Goering himself. In both countries such ironical self-criticism was soon to end.

These, then, were my first impressions of Russia. In my observations of the Soviet economy and of the people of the USSR, and in my efforts

47

to follow Russian cultural developments, I tried as best I could to comprehend the situation as it existed, without bias or blinkers. Frequently I had occasion to stress to my colleagues in the Commissariat of Foreign Affairs that I was trying to analyse the Soviet system objectively, without excluding the possibility of it being the best one. At the same time, I had to acknowledge that, even if I were to reach such a conclusion for *others*, I would not do so for myself, since I understood that people like myself, members of the aristocracy, were generally either exterminated, sent to concentration camps, or deported. Whatever its merits, I knew that the system could never be tolerable for me personally, and that I must therefore be prepared to resist it in any way possible.

3

CONTACT WITH THE RUSSIANS

Contact with Russians was fraught with more difficulties and even dangers than any of us would have liked. I knew from the outset, for example, that the Russian woman who gave language lessons to many diplomats was interrogated from time to time by the secret police. By 1933 we were aware that nearly everyone who had contact with us at the Embassy was being interrogated, and we were careful not to ask too many questions of them. In spite of this, even Russians connected with our Embassy frequently made critical remarks about the state of affairs in their country, statements that surprised us by their bluntness. It was the same as in Nazi Germany, where bold people would openly criticize the regime in spite of the risk of their being arrested and sent to a concentration camp. Those suffering oppression in either country could often not hold their tongues and would give vent to bitter complaints. When the husband of my Russian-language teacher did this, he was arrested and never came back. She was arrested as well, but was eventually freed, and is today living again in Moscow, still giving language lessons.

In a similar vein, the GPU from time to time checked up on the two young Volga German girls who kept house for Herbert Dittmann and me. Had the GPU looked into their case more thoroughly, it might have been intrigued by the fact that, from as early as 1933, these girls had adorned their room with portraits of both Stalin and Hitler, thus anticipating by more than half a decade the pact that was eventually signed in 1939!

Secret police checks, arrests and deportations successfully curbed contacts between foreign diplomats and Soviet citizens. Given the watchfulness that was imposed on both sides by the Soviet government's rising paranoia, it is not surprising that between 1931 and 1933 the Soviet citizens most easily accessible to members of the German Embassy were the Russian wives of German experts living in Moscow. Whenever they held parties in their flats, we would have an opportunity to meet not only them but also their Russian families and friends. This congenial contact was cut short in 1933, when most of the experts left. Those who stayed in Russia after that date were afraid to invite their countrymen to meet their wives' relatives for fear of endangering the Soviet citizens involved. Indeed, most of those Soviet citizens in touch with foreigners after 1933 were either told to break off the relationship or were arrested. Such measures were not directly exclusively against the German Embassy but against all diplomatic missions in Moscow.

While our isolation from the general public became more marked, other points of contact remained. Indeed, for all the impediments that were imposed, a surprising degree of closeness continued to exist between members of our Embassy and various members of the Moscow elite, particularly certain intellectuals, officials, and senior officers. It goes without saying that this occurred only because the Soviet government chose to permit it, yet in the case of the intellectual leaders, such contact was fostered by the genuine interest of several of our younger diplomats in Soviet cultural life.

At the beginning of my stay, cultural matters were handled by Gerhard Stelzer, a secretary at our Embassy. Stelzer was an expert on all aspects of Russian art. He lived in a single enormous room in our building on Kalachnyi Pereulok and every few weeks held a reception, to which would come many people from the worlds of literature, theatre, ballet, opera, and painting. The guest list for these soirées was well known to the government, since a militiaman was at all times posted outside our building. Soviet artists were permitted to attend Stelzer's receptions, I believe, as a kind of payment for their loyalty, and also because the Kremlin knew that Stelzer and his guests faithfully observed the unwritten rule to steer clear of political discussions. Stelzer was a perfect host, serving food and drink like an experienced butler, conversing with everyone but never asking questions. On their side, the Soviet artists loved to come to Stelzer's because they knew they could talk there with freedom.

The language spoken at Stelzer's was Russian. Though many of the guests spoke German, the younger members of the diplomatic staff all spoke Russian fluently and had even passed the interpreter's examination. Igor Grabar, the great expert on Russian icons and paintings, came regularly to Stelzer's and was one of the few guests who liked to exercise his fluent German. Our conversations with Grabar always dealt with art history, since we wanted to take full advantage of this fine old man's rich knowledge. The one theme that Grabar constantly stressed was that Russia had not experienced the Renaissance. He spoke warmly of the continuity in Russian painting from pre-Petrine times to the present. His interests were limitless, though he clearly had a strong preference for the Baroque and Classical art and architecture of the eighteenth century. Grabar visited us often, at least in the early years, and we all profited immensely from his instruction.

The world of music was also well represented at Stelzer's, though I was to meet Sergei Prokofiev more often at the American Embassy, where he was a frequent visitor in the late 1930s. Thanks to his brief American sojourn, Prokofiev had a number of American friends, but came to these gatherings as much to breathe a bit of international air as to see specific persons. He gave the impression of an absolutely balanced man, one who was sure of himself and not at all hesitant about meeting foreigners.

Anatolii Lunacharsky, the Commissar of Public Education, also attended Stelzer's sessions, and would visit our Ambassador as well. He was particularly interesting when recounting his efforts to preserve ancient monuments and restore church icons with methods that had only recently been developed. All in all, Lunacharsky appeared to be a well-informed man, not particularly convinced in his Communism, but genuinely committed to doing as much as possible for the arts. His fall from grace in the Kremlin occurred in 1933–34, coinciding with the new idea that art must be comprehensible to the masses. Incidentally, the proletarian art movement that championed this idea resorted to precisely the same slogan as was used by the Nazis in Germany: 'Art must be close to the people' (*Die Kunst muss volksnah sein*). Besides ending Lunacharsky's career, this slogan effectively put an end to abstract painting and to world-famous experiments in other fields. Avant-garde works were removed from the museums and innovative plays purged from the repertoires of leading theatres. The directors, Meierhold and Tairov, were typical of the group swept out by this change in thinking. Like the others, Meierhold was well educated and thoroughly Western in outlook, exactly the qualities that were then most dangerous.

Until the time of the purges, the actors, artists, and musicians for the most part continued to live in the same apartments as they had occupied before the Revolution. Antique furniture still adorned these islands of sophistication, and their walls were hung with the portraits of many people who had emigrated, even members of the former royal family and aristocracy.

When Stalin set out on the path to State Socialism or State Capitalism, he put an end to all this, liquidating not only some of these artists but also the mass of political figures who had taken an active part in the Revolution. He was particularly hard on the non-Russians, with Jews such as Meierhold, Mandelstam, Zinoviev, Kamenev, Trotsky, and Bukharin feeling his wrath with particular intensity. The only exception to this anti-minority policy were the peoples of the Caucasus, which was not surprising since Stalin himself was Georgian. Scores of non-Russian administrators were liquidated. This Soviet policy of *rusifikatsiia*, or Russification, corresponded to the policy of Aryanization in Germany.

By the mid-thirties, Soviet statesmen were nearly beyond the reach of the diplomatic community, but during most of my stay senior officials of the USSR paid the normal round of calls and were sufficiently in evidence for us to gain direct impressions of them. There were two or three among them whom we all genuinely liked. 'Sergo' Ordzhonikidze, who was responsible for economic affairs, and Abel Enukidze, the Secretary General of the Party – both Georgians – were humane and decent and one could talk openly with them. Our Ambassador maintained contact with them both, and since I sat in on these meetings, I was able to observe their qualities at first hand. They were thoroughly agreeable, and did not make one feel that their personalities had been much affected by their being Communists.

Our relations with the Ministry of Foreign Affairs were correct but limited, with few opportunities to enter into private conversation with officials. An exception was Nikolai Krestinsky, the Deputy Foreign Minister, who had served for a long time as Ambassador in Berlin. He and his wife were frequent visitors at the Embassy, where they were received with cordiality. Neither he nor his wife gave the slightest impression of being serious Communists. Amiable and bland, he was the complete civil servant, who could as well have filled the same role in a dozen other countries at the time, and without being very influential. Yet it was this same Krestinsky who gained fame in 1938 by standing up to Stalin in the Purge Trials.

We had at least one indication of Krestinsky's independence and sense of compassion. When my friend Kurt Brunhoff was transferred to Stockholm early in 1933, his long-time Russian girlfriend received an order of deportation to Siberia. By an error on the part of the secret police, this reached her just a few days before Brunhoff was due to leave Moscow. Deeply shocked and worried, Brunhoff went to Krestinsky and asked him to intervene with the police authorities in order to allow her to leave the Soviet Union with him. Krestinsky acted immediately. A few days later I accompanied them both to the train for Germany.

Once or twice a year we went on excursions to the countryside with our friends from among Soviet officialdom. These gatherings, which we initiated, excluded all political discussion, and perhaps because of this were the more satisfying from a purely human point of view. Given the broader circumstances of our official relations, it is touching to recall the manner in which both German and Russian diplomats at these picnics tried to treat one another simply as friends.

Between 1930 and 1932 we would not hesitate to invite officials from the Commissariat of Foreign Affairs to our homes, but this soon ended, as did our joint picnics in the countryside. By 1933–34, it was impossible to maintain with our Soviet colleagues the kind of relations considered normal in other capitals.

One of the few highly-placed Russians who ignored all restrictions until the end was Ivy Litvinov, the English-born wife of the later Foreign Minister. Mrs Litvinov enjoyed a unique position in Moscow. She frequently visited the wives of diplomats, and generally moved quite freely among the foreign community. Mrs Strang, the wife of the British counsellor, and Mrs Rabinavicius, the wife of the Lithuanian counsellor, were her close friends, and she was treated almost as a member of both families. I doubt whether these contacts had any discernible political meaning, but they played their part in the life of diplomatic Moscow.

During 1931 and 1932, most Soviet officials and other prominent persons with whom I had contact dressed in uniforms which bore no signs of distinction, with simple jackets and boots. Andrei Bubnov, for instance, the Minister of Culture for the Russian Republic and a frequent visitor at our gatherings, always appeared this way, as did his wife, who was a tall and elegant woman reminding one of Delacroix's females except for the proletarian cap on her head. There were some, like the Chief of Protocol, Florinsky, or Georgii Chicherin, appointed by Lenin Commissar of Foreign Affairs, who were themselves aristocrats, even former members of the tsarist foreign service, and who probably dressed in this way intentionally in order to demonstrate that they were one hundred per cent conformist. Florinsky retained only one obvious legacy from his former way of life: he was a fanatical bridge player and came to play regularly with all the ambassadors. With respect to dress, however, one sometimes had the feeling with him and others that they were a bit too studied in their proletarian affectations. Florinsky never wavered either in his dedication to bridge or in his comradely sartorial taste. But between one day and the next he simply disappeared, never to be heard of again. His successor, Nikolai Barkhov, did not come from the old tsarist foreign service, dressed the same way as we did and generally was much more human than Florinsky, who had always been very reticent, as if afraid of giving away his past. Then one day Barkhov, too, disappeared.

And what of Stalin himself? During the entire period 1931–39 only the most limited and indirect contacts took place between Stalin and the various foreign missions. One might see him from time to time as he made an appearance at the Bolshoi Theatre, and, naturally, he was always present at the parades on May Day and on 7 November. Otherwise, he was as a rule invisible to the foreign community. The only non-Communist German Stalin had met before August 1939 was Emil Ludwig, a renowned and controversial writer on current events who had asked for an interview and, to our great astonishment, was granted one on 13 December, 1931.

My own impressions from observing Stalin at a distance on several occasions were dominated by the feline manner in which he moved. It was easy to think of him as a kind of lynx or tiger. This trait characterized him far more accurately in my mind than the widespread reports of his drinking and roistering at private gatherings inside the Kremlin. Not that he lacked such expansiveness. I had a chance to confirm for myself the Georgian manner in which he treated his guests when I observed him in 1932 at a reception in honour of the Turkish Prime Minister, Ismet Inönü. At this buffet-dinner, the most luxurious food was served on golden plates with golden cutlery bearing the initials of Tsar Alexander I. As the Italian Secretary, Micki Lanza, sat down to the table with his golden plate, he remarked quietly, 'Honi soi qui mal y pense!' Stalin struck me then as exuberant, not without charm, and with a pronounced capacity for enjoying himself. What a contrast he seemed to make with Hitler, who had so little zest for pleasure! As a distant observer, I was also left with the strong impression that Stalin, again in contrast to Hitler, had a sense of humour. Stated simply, Stalin was quite appealing in his way, while Hitler was thoroughly unattractive.

It was clear to me and to every Western diplomat in Moscow that by about 1934 Stalin alone was fully in charge, and all important decisions in Moscow depended upon his personal will. No Soviet official doubted this, either; nor did the Russians make the mistake of permitting Stalin's charm to blind them to the man's power and cruelty. During the meeting in August 1939, between Ribbentrop and Stalin at the end of which the non-aggression treaty was signed, Boris Shapozhnikov, the chief of the General Staff, was leaving the room when Stalin ordered him to stay. So stunned was Shapozhnikov by the command that the pencil in his hand dropped to the floor.

Travelling outside Moscow, we would from time to time encounter Soviet officials who felt themselves less bound to fall in line and would say things that one would never hear in the capital. The most striking experience for me in this respect occurred in the summer of 1935, during a trip to the Caucasus, this time with our newly appointed Ambassador, Count von der Schulenburg, his daughter and my wife. When we arrived in Tblisi, the local Georgian government gave a banquet in our honour. It was a typical Georgian feast, with an enormous amount of food and liquor. Our hosts observed the time-honoured Caucasian custom of selecting a president of the table, the so-called *tamada*, whose job it was to lead the toasts and deliver the necessary speeches. The *tamada* for the evening was the Premier of Georgia, Budu Mdivani, a descendant of the princely Mdivani family, whom Count Schulenburg had known since before World War I, when he had served as German consul at Tblisi.

Mdivani opened the celebration with a toast to Stalin and Hitler, and followed with toasts to everybody present, as well as to their fathers, grandfathers, and great-grandfathers. It was a splendid opportunity for everyone to get drunk, the more since it was expected that every glass would be drained *do dna* (to the bottom). All in all, it was a most cordial affair, in spite of the bad relations that existed between Germany and the USSR by the summer of 1935. Our local Consul General, Carl Dienstmann, was the first to suffer from this cordiality, being an inexperienced drinker. Mdivani put him out of commission in quick order. As the evening progressed, a loud crash was suddenly heard. I plunged under the table, thinking it was an explosion. My wife called me up again and I saw that no bomb had exploded but that Mdivani had hurled an unopened bottle of champagne through the large looking-glass.

As the party ended, I was sitting together on one chair with Georgi Astakhov, the representative of the Commissariat of Foreign Affairs to the Georgian government. I myself have only a vague memory of the conversation, nor did I recall much more the next morning, but my wife told me that it was in the following vein. Apparently, I had assured Astakhov that Hitler was a complete catastrophe for Germany, and Astakhov in turn complained bitterly and at length about Stalin. What passed between us was undoubtedly grounds for charging either of us with treason. Fortunately, no one in the room was sufficiently sober to

55

hear or understand anything, with the exception of my wife and the young Countess Schulenburg. Both Astakhov and I were to fare better than one might have expected that evening, he later serving as Stalin's chargé d'affaires in Berlin, where he played an important part in bringing about the Soviet-German rapprochement. Poor Mdivani was not so fortunate: having already been denounced for Trotskyite activity in 1929, he was later attacked as a British agent and destroyed in Stalin's purges.

When he left the party, poor Schulenburg found himself unable to enter his car, since he thought it was an open sedan and kept banging his head on the frame of the top. When we finally arrived home, we found our friend Dienstmann sitting on the pavement outside his consulate, quite unable to enter on his own. When the three of us finally managed to get one another indoors, we had a lengthy conversation with an enormous stuffed bear which held in its paws a silver tray for visiting cards.

Early next morning my wife, Pussi, woke me and reported in a terrified voice that Count Schulenburg was dead. I raced to his bedside and found the Ambassador with some blood on his forehead but snoring loudly. When he finally woke up, he lightly dismissed the blood and its causes, saying that he had probably collided with Mt David, the mountain overlooking Tblisi.

Nothing like this ever occurred in Moscow. The sole exception was a party given by von Dirksen for the Russian generals in 1932. It was a splendid evening. Yegorov was there, as were Budenny, Tukhachevsky, Voroshilov, Uborevich, and many others of similar rank. The food was superb and the drinks equally good, with the result that raucous fraternization sprang up. As far as I recall I ended the evening sitting on the knees of Yegorov.

Such hearty comradeship between Germans and Russians was unusual even in those early years, but it was more likely to occur among the representatives of the two armies than among any other groups. Indeed, German-Russian military co-operation was far more extensive than is generally realized today. In the late 1920s it reached something of a peak, with three military projects going forward simultaneously on Soviet soil. One took place at a camp near Kazan, where new models of tanks were undergoing extensive tests. A second camp, near Lipetsk, was devoted to the testing of new models of aircraft. Also at Lipetsk, we managed to train a number of officers for the German air force, since Germany had been forbidden by the Treaty of Versailles to carry out such training on its own soil. When Hitler took power there were some three hundred German pilots who had received excellent training, all in the Soviet Union thanks to the work done at Lipetsk. Our third base was in the south of Russia, and there both the Soviet and German armies were busy conducting tests of the latest chemical weapons. All three bases were closed in 1932.

Until the end of German-Soviet military co-operation in 1932, we had regular contact with the leading officers of the Red Army and formed clear impressions of them, both individually and as a group. All the Germans who had contacts with Yegorov had a high opinion of him as a capable staff officer. We had similarly high regard for Kork, I. Uborevich, and Mikhail Tukhachevsky. The personal favourite of many of us was Semyon Budenny, notwithstanding the fact that we knew full well that he was no strategic genius. Budenny exuded an open informality that was most attractive. His contacts with General Köstring were particularly close, and in the course of their frequent meetings, I never saw anything that led me to question my initial judgment of him. Budenny was a typical master-sergeant, a person who had come up through the ranks, and, as a result, could exercise genuine leadership in the front line. He looked like a real Cossack *Wachtmeister* and he also had a keen sense of humour. When Köstring returned to Moscow for his second tour of duty, he encountered his old friend Budenny, who immediately embraced him and expressed his delight that Köstring had not been *kastriert*, i.e., castrated.

Mikhail Tukhachevsky was perhaps the most brilliant of the Red Army generals, but he was at the same time the hardest to approach or to understand. He struck one immediately as being ambitious but complicated as well, with a lot going on behind his forehead. I first met him in 1931, and saw him frequently throughout the next year. Then he dropped from view and I heard little of him until 1938, when we got word that Stalin had ordered his execution.

We all puzzled over Stalin's motives. Some observers in the West thought that Tukhachevsky might have been too partial to the Germans. Later it was claimed that he had got in touch with Werner von Blomberg, the German Minister of War, and that several other generals had also taken part in these illegal contacts. It is true that Tukhachevsky had visited Blomberg in Berlin on his way back from Paris in 1936, on the eve of the purges, but nothing resulted from their conversation. From where, then, did the rumour of Tukhachevsky's pro-German sympathies come? In Moscow we believed it was Churchill who had reported the rumour to

Beneš. Beneš in turn passed it to Stalin, who found in it a welcome justification for liquidating Tukhachevsky.

In contrast to Tukhachevsky's rumoured links with Germany, our Moscow Embassy considered him rather cooler towards Germany than many of the other Russian generals. Indeed, we were worried over his being excessively pro-French. When he made a trip to Paris in 1936 our military attaché expressed concern on this score, and was by no means calmed by the brief visit that Tukhachevsky paid to Blomberg on his return trip.

Shortly after Tukhachevsky's return, the round-up of the generals began. It seemed to us significant that they were not subjected to any public trial as a group. We explained this by the fact that these men were far too strong to confess even under torture and that Stalin knew it would be foolish to work on people who would not play his game. Perhaps, too, Stalin feared their education and their intellect.

It was difficult to understand why Stalin felt he had to eliminate such generals. We were convinced that they were not conspiring against him. Perhaps in the back of his mind the Georgian felt that they could not possibly agree with his policies and that they would sooner or later come to him and say: 'Comrade Stalin, you have done a lot to liquidate Communism through your purges. The only thing that you have yet to do is to purge yourself, which we are here to help you do.' When war broke out we captured a number of Red Army officers who had only recently been released from concentration camps, and they, too, viewed the purge of the officer corps in this light.

Several years after Tukhachevsky's death an incident occurred which brought him back to my mind in a most unexpected manner. I had joined the German army in 1939, and at the end of the Polish campaign found myself stationed at a country house north of Warsaw. We had received strict orders against fraternization, but we paid them little heed. At every opportunity we consorted with those Poles who could speak German. One evening the captain of our First Cavalry Squadron invited me to an evening of chamber music at the nearby estate where he was staying. Several of the local Poles were excellent musicians, and our squadron had in its number an accomplished pianist.

After the concert, the hostess turned to me and said: 'I understand that you have been in the Soviet Union. Did you happen to know Mikhail Tukhachevsky?' I replied: 'Yes, naturally I knew him. He was a great general, poor man.' On hearing this, my hostess said: 'You may be interested to know that during the First World War he was a young lieutenant, just as you are now. His regiment – I believe it was the Semonovsky – was stationed near our estate here. He and I became friends and eventually we were engaged to be married. He was then taken prisoner and sent to Germany, whence he wrote letters to me regularly. I will show you one of his letters, since you may find it interesting.'

At this, she left the room and returned with a letter of Tukhachevsky's. She asked me not to read the first paragraph and the conclusion, since they were of a personal nature, but drew my attention to the middle passage in which Tukhachevsky set forth his hopes and aspirations. Tukhachevsky assured his fiancée that he would have a noble career and that one day he would become a 'Red Bonaparte' – this was his expression. This convinced me that Tukhachevsky was a man of huge ambition and, perhaps, that Stalin had good reason to fear him. But at the moment the generals were arrested, neither I nor any of my colleagues in the German Embassy thought there existed any real reason for Stalin's severity.

4

THE FOREIGN COMMUNITY
IN MOSCOW

In the early 1930s, the diplomatic community in Moscow was extremely small. By no means all governments had recognized the Soviet Union, nor did any of the 'Third World' states yet exist. There were only twenty-six embassies and legations in the Soviet Union when I arrived.

Nothing did more to shape the character of the Moscow diplomatic community than the absence of the usual distractions. Moscow gave us little choice but to get to know one another. In the long run this proved of practical benefit to many of us, since we ended up with friends among diplomats from every major nation. Many of the foreigners with whom I formed close friendships in Moscow were later to play important parts in my life.

The diplomatic group in Moscow formed a community in the fullest sense of the word. There were no barriers among us. To give but one example, it need hardly be said that the German and Polish governments had serious differences during the 1930s, but at no point did these ever affect the personal relations among members of the two Embassies. I remember well the day that the Polish Counsellor, Henryk Sokolnicki, told me that they had found microphones in their Embassy. We shared their concern as if it had happened to us. I remember, too, the events surrounding the attempt on the life of my Ambassador, von Dirksen, in 1933, which resulted in the wounding of our Counsellor, Fritz von Twardowski. At the subsequent trial of the would-be assassin the Russians attempted to argue that he had some connections with the Polish Embassy. We were able to discuss all this openly with the Poles, the more so since we both knew that the charge was untrue.

So close were the relations among members of many of the embassies that it was tempting to look on them as all part of a single staff. One day the Swedish Minister, Baron Gyllenstierna, came to see our Ambassador, Count Schulenburg, to complain that the visit of his Foreign Minister was imminent and he had no one on his staff competent to handle the protocol work. Schulenburg listened sympathetically and assured him that I could be lent for the occasion. I was therefore seconded to the Swedish Legation. As a result, of course, our Embassy was well informed on the talks between the Swedish Minister and the Soviets. There was nothing unusual about this; both the help and the information could as easily have flown in the opposite direction. In this sense, one might say that we were anticipating the spirit of the later European community.

A typical occurrence in the Soviet Union, but one which would have been unusual anywhere else, was for younger members of foreign embassies to be invited by ambassadors to discuss their impressions of Russia and the political situation generally. Many times I was invited to Lord Chilston's, the British Ambassador, where, in addition to discussing political matters we would usually talk of the arts, Lady Chilston being knowledgeable in that area.

When I was transferred to Moscow in 1931, the rate of exchange was 2.16 marks per ruble. It was still possible to get some of our rubles from special German accounts, since we not only had three military stations in the Soviet Union, but also a German agricultural concession on the Kuban in the North Caucasus. This concession earned rubles, which were then passed to us at a special rate of exchange. The Embassy thus served as a kind of clearing bank of which we all took advantage.

We would buy rubles for our private expenses abroad, whether in Berlin, Warsaw, Helsinki, Teheran, or even China. The cheapest rubles in the early 1930s came from Manchuria. It was not easy to get these so-called 'black rubles', but members of the diplomatic community always seemed to manage, often with each other's help. I don't believe that I ever changed a pfennig at the State Bank. The Soviet government turned a blind eye to the entire operation, possibly because it was itself shipping rubles abroad.

The cheaper currency made travelling far easier than it would otherwise have been. In the early thirties you could still buy tickets for foreign travel in Moscow, and pay in rubles. Thanks to this system, one could use deflated rubles to buy a first-class ticket to Venice and thence to Rome, Naples, Sicily, Greece, Istanbul, and back to Moscow, all for less than a normal second-class trip to Berlin. It was a tremendous bargain and one of which the diplomats took full advantage.

Since it was virtually impossible to obtain most necessities in Moscow, the foreign missions ordered what they needed from abroad. Food came in weekly from Poland, Finland, and Germany. Wine and liquor were ordered from France, Italy, Germany and other wine-producing countries. A collective order for household articles such as soap, nails, toilet paper and shoelaces was sent out once a year by the Embassy. Those who neglected to get in their order or who forgot to order certain items would turn for help to friends and colleagues in the other missions. This need to help each other in the elementary needs of daily life was another factor binding together the foreign community in Moscow.

Among the diplomats were a number of keen collectors of art and antiquities. These people haunted the 'Torgsin' shops, where they could buy rare objects for hard currency, and the commission shops when they could make such purchases in rubles. So diverse were the possibilities for collecting that a high degree of specialization developed. There were those who collected only china and others who focused their attention on old silver; still others, such as the Swedish chargé d'affaires Assarson, or my friend Michel 'Micki' Lanza of the Italian Embassy, put together remarkable collections of icons. I do not even speak of the ambassadors, who were in most cases quite fanatical in their collecting. The wife of the French Ambassador, Charles Alphand, and of the Italian Ambassador, Bernardo Attolico, assembled admirable collections of Russian antiquities. A particularly cultivated diplomat-collector was another French Ambassador, Comte de Jean. Not being especially interested in politics, the latter spent his days visiting the various shops, where one could see him pondering over the selection of pieces for his collection.

A number of foreign diplomats devoted their free time to collecting antiquarian books. The shops for second-hand books in Moscow during the 1930s were filled with priceless volumes dating back even to the sixteenth and seventeenth centuries. Besides the Russian editions that were readily available, one could find the rarest French and German volumes from all periods. I came across early editions of the Russian memoirs of Herberstein and of Olearius, both of whom I found to have had impressions of Moscow that were not greatly different from my own, in spite of the fact that their reports dated back over three centuries. Most of these volumes, and the antiques in general, were being sold by members of the old upper- and middle-class who had been impoverished by Stalin's 'Great Leap Forward'.

The only collecting that was disapproved of by the diplomatic community was that of the American Ambassador, Joseph Davies. During the height of the Moscow purges Davies and his wife devoted themselves to collecting not individual objects but whole museums.

They paid for their 'finds' in Moscow with rubles purchased on the black market. During his brief ambassadorship, Davies' purchases of black market rubles to pay for antiques were so large and so sudden as to drive up the black market price for rubles all over Europe. Indeed, Davies' purchases were on a scale equal to that of the whole diplomatic corps combined. Since the members of the foreign missions in Moscow were forced to buy their own rubles on the black market at an artificially high rate, we all suffered from Davies' hobby. Needless to say, this added to the unpopularity of Davies, who was already disliked for his view that Stalin's trials were justified.

There were among the ambassadors and ministers in Moscow a number of outstanding quality. I shall speak later of our three German ambassadors, all of them most accomplished men. Among the others was the Lithuanian Minister, Jurgis Baltrusaitis, one of the most respected men in the Moscow diplomatic corps in the 1930s. Baltrusaitis was himself a distinguished poet and writer, having played an active role in Russia's cultural life some years before. By contrast, the Italian Ambassador, Attolico, was far less knowledgeable about Russia but could depend upon his own astute diplomatic sense for guidance. Both Baltrusaitis and Attolico did much to enliven the intellectual and social scene in Moscow.

The American Ambassador from 1933 to 1936 was W. C. Bullitt, very impressive in his way and speaking many languages. He arrived in the Soviet Union in much the same mood as I had, with unbridled enthusiasm and an open mind. He was fortunate at the beginning to establish good contacts with the Russians, but as these were gradually cut off by the government, he became more disillusioned. Whether optimistic or pessimistic, he was held in high regard by the younger diplomats. I should add the no one is more critical of ambassadors than their younger colleagues.

I must stress once again that the diplomatic community in Moscow was a real family, and our devotion to it was as great as our loyalty to our respective countries. We were united, I suppose, by our dislike of the Soviet Union as it existed under Stalin. We knew full well that we would eventually be torn apart by Hitler's activities but up to the last moment we felt ourselves to be as one in our opposition to the Soviet policies.

It would be wrong to think of this 'community' solely in terms of its diplomatic members. As much a part of our group were the leading journalists, several of whom were German. One of the most outstanding

63

was Wilhelm Baum, who was the representative of our official German news agency, DNB. Later on, Baum was transferred to Berlin, where he commited suicide. We did not know precisely why, but I suppose at the time that he was so disturbed by events in Nazi Germany that he simply could not bear to live. A Baltic German by origin, Baum was a sensitive and highly civilized man, and, in my opinion, the most balanced of all the foreign journalists in Moscow. After Baum, the most competent of the German journalists in Moscow was Hermann Poerzgen of the *Frankfurter Zeitung*, who was a late comer to our group. During the war he entered the diplomatic service and, having been captured, spent some ten years in Soviet prisons. In the late 1950s, he returned once more to Russia, where he remained until his death in 1976, an intelligent and seasoned observer who wrote several books on the Soviet Union. Baum, Poerzgen and their colleagues were part of the Moscow scene, and on most points at least as well informed as the diplomats. We talked over everything together, although we naturally refrained from sharing secret information with them, since their duty, after all, was to write for the public.

Most members of the foreign community in Moscow in the 1930s were connected either with the various embassies and legations or with the press corps. During the first half of the decade, however, there was also a large number of Western businessmen, technicians and other visitors who floated in and out of our world but, as a group, left their mark on our life there. Among these, Germans were by far the most numerous. My first assignment under Dirksen was to the consular department, where I busied myself validating Russian commercial documents that had been translated into German. A thoroughly tedious feature of this work was the necessity of signing my name to many hundreds of documents each day, which forced me to abandon my full name, Hans-Heinrich Herwarth von Bittenfeld in favour of simply Herwarth. The good side of this assignment was that I quickly became acquainted with every German businessman or engineer in Russia.

I soon discovered that visitors to the USSR fell into three distinct categories. First, there were those 'experts', who, if put in a good hotel and fed bowls of caviar, were readily convinced that everything was all right in Russia. The second category consisted of those who found the atmosphere so oppressive that they returned home after a few days. Secretary of Legation Herbert Mumm von Schwarzenstein was in this group, and told me that he would rather clean W.C.s on the Unter den

Linden in Berlin than serve as secretary to the German Embassy in Moscow. Mumm's tastes were admittedly exacting, having been accustomed to his family's famous champagne. He later joined the conspiracy against Hitler and was shot after 20 July, 1944. The third group, which was never large, consisted of those who were able to see both the good and the bad without illusions.

Of the Germans in the USSR with whom I maintained close contact, no group was more interesting than the architects and technicians. They numbered well over a thousand when I arrived, the majority of them being employed as engineers or foremen. Some had come with their families, but many others arrived as bachelors and subsequently married Russian girls.

Weddings between German citizens took place in the Embassy according to German law. Pfeiffer, the head of the Consular Section, was an eloquent orator and was always called on to speak at such occasions. He would invariably ask us beforehand whether we would like him to reduce the bride and groom to tears or just the bride alone. Our standard reply was that his fee for ensemble crying would have to be ten marks higher. We always ended such ceremonies by drinking a bottle of champagne.

Prominent among the German experts in Russia was the group of architects working under the leadership of Ernst Mai. One of the best known avant-garde architects of the day and probably the leading city planner in Germany, Mai was highly respected because of his housing projects in Frankfurt and elsewhere. Mai had arrived in 1930 with great ideas, vast hopes, and a group of about twenty young architects to help him implement them. One could never doubt his competence, but it was his idealism that was most striking. There were German engineers whose motives for coming to Russia were less altruistic; the possibility of earning money there at a time when jobs were scarce at home appealed to many. Mai, by contrast, was genuinely committed to helping human beings live better lives, and thought that this could be achieved better by architects than by anyone else.

Though Mai was considered in Germany to stand on the left, his idealism struck me as being non-political in character. Indeed, he seemed obsessed with the technical aspects of his profession, to the point that at the time of his arrival he was blind to many of the difficulties that were evident to others from the outset. Mai's plans for new cities in Siberia and elsewhere grew more and more grandiose, but only in the privacy of his mind. As he became aware of realities, he grew frustrated, a process that was going on at the same time among most of his younger aides.

Through my position, I was able to observe Mai's disillusionment from day to day. At the time of his arrival, the German Embassy was concerned over his poor preparation for life in the USSR and what we believed to be his naïve expectation that he would be greeted with open arms. This might in fact have happened five years earlier; now both he and his Soviet sponsors were overwhelmed by the realities of the First Five-Year Plan. Mai and his young colleagues had read enough about the Plan in Germany to conceive it as a magnificent, even Promethean effort; hence they were the more disappointed when they perceived its one-sided concentration on heavy industry, at the expense of most other fields of activity. Beyond that, they were stunned by the formidable obstacles to accomplishing anything in Russia. They reported to the Embassy on the impediments facing them in their work, on the lack of necessary materials, and on the sharp differences in conception between them and the Soviet architects with whom they had to work. Above all, they found the difficulties of dealing with Soviet bureaucrats virtually insurmountable.

As Mai and his colleagues confronted these problems, their relations with the Embassy grew more intimate. First Mai's young aides began to seek our advice on various questions; then after a while Mai began to come as well. They led me to understand that none of the group had ever considered emigrating permanently, but all had expected to stay in Russia for a long period – much longer than they actually did. The Russians also expected them to stay and their departure marked the culmination of a long process of disenchantment.

When the persecution of Jews began in Germany a few German Jews fled to Russia. Fortunately, their number was not great. In every instance which came to my knowledge, they soon ran foul of the Soviet authorities. The first group with whom I had contact arrived in Moscow in 1936. Their visit had a personal character, since they had been recommended to me by an old friend from my *gymnasium* days, Gerhardt Holländer. Members of the group were not at all pleased with what they saw in the USSR, and I advised them to get out as quickly as possible. None of their German passports was valid any longer so they could not expect to cross the border into some third country after leaving Russia. I therefore intervened with Count Schulenburg, asking his permission to revalidate their papers, in violation of our standing order not to renew passports for German Jews. Schulenburg willingly defied his instructions, and did so repeatedly for some years to come.

German Communists also found their way to the Embassy. One night in the spring of 1933, the doorbell rang in the house on Kalachnyi Pereulok where I was living. Going to the door, I found a frightened man who at first refused to identify himself. Eventually, he told us that he was Max Hölz, the leader of the Communist uprising in Saxony in 1923. After the collapse of his revolt, Hölz had fled to the Soviet Union. We had known he was in the Soviet Union and had assumed that he held an important post somewhere, possibly advising the Russians on German affairs. Apparently this was not the case and he, bitterly disillusioned, was now pleading to return to Germany. We reminded him that he would have to stand trial for high treason and would be subject to severe punishment. He insisted, however, and even came to us a second time. In the end, we communicated with Berlin on the issue, and were told that the German government had no interest in his return. Shortly afterwards, on 16 September, 1933, *Tass* issued a short statement that Max Hölz had drowned while on a boating party on the river Oka near Gorky. Our impression was that he had either committed suicide or had been liquidated by the Russians.

In February 1934, there occurred a brief and unsuccessful uprising in Vienna, at the end of which a large number of Viennese socialists emigrated to the Soviet Union. These 'revolutionary heroes' were assigned to work in Soviet factories and within a short time were embittered and causing serious problems to the Russians. As it turned out, the Austrian workers had views on socialism different to those of the Communist Party in Moscow and did not hesitate to propagate their own ideas among Russian workers. On its side, the Soviet government was uncertain how to treat its honoured guests. In the end, some were sent to labour camps, but quite a number of others succeeded in leaving the Soviet Union, although they could not return to an Austria ruled by Dollfuss. I met members of this group in Moscow and found every one of them disenchanted and bewildered. After the *Anschluss* in 1938, many of them came to the German Embassy requesting repatriation; their wish was granted and they were not prosecuted on their return.

Some of the Germans we met in Moscow had had careers of infinite complexity, though few outshone Karl Albrecht, an expert on forestry. He had been a master sergeant with the Royal Württemberg Army in World War I and had received the highest decoration that a non-commissioned officer could be given. Whether because he was a convinced Communist or merely because he could not get a job in Germany, he emigrated to the Soviet Union after the war. Once there, he had a brilliant career, finally reaching the post of Deputy Commissar for Forestry in the Russian Republic.

To our astonishment, Albrecht appeared at the Embassy one day in 1934, asking to be repatriated with his Russian wife and child. He said that his own work had led to nothing but frustration, that he could not comprehend the purges, and that he was fed up with the Soviet Union and wanted to return home, in spite of the fact that the National Socialists were in charge. In the end, we succeeded in getting him out. His Russian wife refused to leave the Soviet Union and divorced him. His daughter eventually came to Germany.

Albrecht's and my paths crossed once more in December 1942, at a meeting of people involved in the administration of the occupied territories of the USSR. Representatives of all the pertinent Nazi Party agencies and ministries filled a large room in the former Soviet Embassy in Berlin. Those from the army distinguished themselves by the blunt language they used in criticizing the civilian officials' stupid tendency to treat the occupied territories as a colony. Amidst this discussion, I noticed Karl Albrecht, the former long-time resident in the USSR, sitting across the table from me in the uniform of an SS officer. My astonishment at his presence there was heightened by his actual statements. Notwithstanding his uniform and his earlier wrath against the Russians, he now showed himself to be strongly in favour of treating the Russian population decently. It was amazing that an SS man should have so openly disobeyed the policy advocated by his own master, Himmler, a devout believer in the notion of the *Untermenschen*.

These Germans demanded a great deal of my time during my first years in Moscow. Gradually, though, my attention shifted to other matters, and particularly to the drama that was unfolding as Hitler increased his pressure on the countries surrounding Germany. As this occurred, the intensity of my contact with diplomatic colleagues increased, to the point that, by 1935, we were all eagerly seeking means of escaping, if only temporarily, from the great pressures weighing down all of us. Sport proved to be the best diversion we could find and we plunged into it with renewed vigour. In fact, no other activity did more than sport, especially tennis, to sustain the younger diplomats and to hold us together as a group. There were tennis courts in several Moscow embassies and we all played. From the technical point of view the German court was the best. We congregated there with shameless frequency and set up tournaments on the slightest excuse. Parties were built around sport and we even had a Tennis Ball. All in all, life was quite gay, considering the circumstances that surrounded us.

The British had a second tennis court located next to the house of their commercial counsellor, G. P. Paton, who lived in a building that is now used as the residence of the German Ambassador. Next door lived Oskar Ritter von Niedermayer, who was the 'camouflaged' or secret representative of the *Reichswehr* in Moscow. Until 1932 he had the job of supervising all the German officers who came over to participate in the joint training programmes with the Red Army. A Bavarian who had made a great record for himself in the First World War, von Niedermeier was really a fantastic character. It was hard to perceive this on a day-to-day basis since his job isolated him completely; naturally, though, everyone knew that he existed, and especially my friend, Paton, his next-door neighbour. As Niedermayer was not permitted to have any contacts with the diplomatic corps on account of his secret mission, he would sometimes deliberately hit a tennis ball from his court over to Paton's neighbouring court. This gave him an excuse to walk over and retrieve it, in the process exchanging a word or two.

Though I had friends in every embassy, there were naturally those with whom I felt particularly close. We always met at the Americans' *dacha*. Some twenty kilometres to the south of Moscow, the more junior American diplomats had rented a small summer house with a tennis court and a stable with horses, and there the younger members of the diplomatic corps frequently convened. The inner circle of the group that gathered there consisted of the Americans, the British, the Italians, the French, and the Germans with at times guests from other legations. This constituted our 'Mutual Admiration Society'.

The *dacha* was a well-run establishment. There was an old factotum, George, who looked after us, and an equally ancient Russian peasant, Panteleimon, who looked after the horses. Since these two have been well described by Fitzroy Maclean and Charles Thayer, I need add nothing more. Life at the *dacha* was thoroughly informal, with every nation contributing something to the maintenance of the place. Our own contribution was made in German wine, beer, and sausages; the British gave scotch, and the Italians more wine. We all contributed to the effort, but the burden of running the *dacha* was on the shoulders of the Americans, to whom I am eternally grateful.

In the British element we had Fitzroy Maclean, John Russell, William Hayter and Noel Charles. Fitzroy Maclean, in spite of great difficulties, travelled all over the Soviet Union. His vivid and precise descriptions of these expeditions showed he was sure to become a good writer. At his famous dinner-parties he excelled as brilliant host and raconteur. His German was excellent as he had studied at the University of Marburg.

William Hayter and I became very close to each other when we travelled with Schulenburg, his daughter and my wife to the Caucasus and Crimea. Visiting the battlefield of Sebastopol we discovered the grave of a Lieutenant Hayter, a forebear of my friend William, killed at the siege in 1855.

The counsellor of the British Embassy, Noel Charles, had much common sense and could by very outspoken. When he was counsellor in Rome, my wife and I dined with him after the *Anschluss*. He left us in no doubt that Great Britain would make war on Nazi Germany if Hitler continued to violate treaties. He proved his friendship in June 1946 when he was Ambassador in Rome. Pussi asked him to intervene on behalf of an Austrian friend who by mistake had been extradited to Yugoslavia. Thanks to his intervention our friend was liberated.

From time to time some of the ambassadors would also visit the *dacha*. Count Schulenburg came on several occasions, as he was popular with the younger diplomats. He earned this popularity by arranging gatherings especially for the more interesting and lively younger people, notably those with attractive wives. Ambassador Rosso from Italy and his charming American wife Frances enjoyed similar popularity and for much the same reasons. The American Ambassadors, curiously, were less frequent visitors to their compatriots' retreat.

Turning to the Americans who were at the heart of the *dacha* group, I should mention George Kennan, Charles Bohlen, Charles Thayer, Elbridge Durbrow, 'Durby', Loy Henderson, and Norris Chipman. These were all my contemporaries and we were close to one another, thanks in part to our unanimous obsession with the Soviet Union. Even today, when any of us get together we discuss Russia, regardless of whether or not we have had anything to do with it during the last few decades.

There were many of our younger group who were expert on Soviet affairs, notably Fitzroy Maclean, and Guido Relli from the Italian Embassy. From the outset we had a particularly high regard for George Kennan. Kennan was especially respected by the Germans since he had studied in Berlin and was as fluent in German as he was in Russian. Even then he was scholarly in outlook and more disposed to discuss basic principles than tactics. By contrast, we always considered 'Chip' Bohlen

to be a more practical man, whose greatest strength lay in his regular
month-to-month reporting. His wife, Avis, was the very spirit of the
dacha and at the heart of its organization. Kennan's high moral character
was obvious to us all, to the point that one felt at times that he should wear
a halo over his head. Anneliese, his charming Norwegian wife, was in
every respect ideal for George. When he was grave and serious, she would
be gay, laughing and nice to everybody. Kennan's basic seriousness was
relieved by his interest in music. He was an excellent guitarist and knew
many Russian and gypsy songs by heart; George also followed Russian
jazz with interest and a nusement.

In sharp contrast to George Kennan was Charlie Thayer, the brother
of 'Chip' Bohlen's wife Avis. He was regarded as a kind of naughty boy.
Not only did Charlie have an outrageous sense of humour, but he was a
formidable observer and a far deeper man than many people realized.
The American who most closely resembled Kennan was Loy Henderson.
Like Kennan, Henderson was serious, concerned more with basic
developments than with details, and highly respected by all.

'Durby' was lively, outspoken, and frequently bursting out with
critical opinions on the Soviet Union. Nobody surpassed 'Durby' in his
sense of outrage at what was going on there. He was especially incensed at
the purges and was revolted when his Ambassador attended the trials and
openly justified them.

Norris Chipman and his wife Fanny were invariably seated next to
Pussi and myself at luncheons and dinners, because we had the same
seniority and the diplomatic corps was small. As a result we became
intimate. Norris had a special gift of analysing and judging the internal
situation of the Soviet Union. Fanny was of Greco-French origin. Her
grandfather was the famous French sculptor, Bourdelle. She was a
Greek classic beauty and herself an artist.

An important difference between the Americans and my own
colleagues stemmed from the fact that the United States at the time was
not deeply involved in world politics. Hence, the role of American
diplomats in Moscow was that of interested bystanders rather than of
central participants. They could take their time in reporting while we
always worked under gruelling pressure. I was jealous of the time they
had to mull over things, reflect, and report more completely and more
elegantly than we could hope to do.

Thanks to their relative freedom from the tedium of daily reports, the
Americans were able to offer hospitality to visiting fellow countrymen.
Because of this, I met John Kennedy in 1938. Kennedy came for a short

visit to the Soviet Union shortly after his elder brother Joe had visited Moscow. 'Chip' Bohlen called me to ask if I would meet his guest and give him some German views on the Soviet Union. I was glad to do so, since Kennedy's father was well regarded by my American friends. We spent quite a bit of time together, and I was deeply impressed by the intelligent questions he asked me, and also by the vivid interest he took not only in the internal affairs of the USSR but also in its position in the world as a whole. After he left, I urged 'Chip' to persuade this bright young man to enter the foreign service. I assured him that he would be a brilliant diplomat.

Much later, when John Kennedy visited Germany as President of the United States in 1962, Adenauer gave a luncheon in his honour, which I attended as head of the Presidential Office under Lübke. Going along the receiving line, I was by mistake introduced as Staatssekretär von Hase. To my astonishment, President Kennedy said, 'No, it's not Staatssekretär von Hase, but Staatssekretär von Herwarth, and I know him from Moscow.' Later, we had a long chat together, and I was again impressed by his avid interest in everything that was going on, and his astonishing memory for the smallest details.

In 1933 I was promoted to the position of personal secretary to the Ambassador, aide to the Ambassador in the political arena, and secretary to the Moscow diplomatic corps. As secretary to the doyen of the diplomatic corps, it was possible for me to arrange various things to make life more pleasant for Moscow's junior diplomats. If anyone was transferred, I would give a party in his honour. I also saw to it that every Wednesday afternoon in summertime the German Ambassador held open house, to which everyone would come. This pleasant custom was faithfully observed by all three of our Ambassadors during the thirties. I could also be of help to close friends in other missions who had to leave Moscow. As was the custom, our Ambassador would issue a report on every experienced diplomat who departed. Since I wrote these, I saw to it that, in the case of members of our inner circle, the reports would be detailed and, of course, thoroughly favourable. By this means, I endeavoured to smooth the path for my colleagues when they arrived at their next posts. For Germany's missions, these reports were naturally valuable because they enabled contacts to be maintained over many years and all over the world.

In March 1948 I visited William Hayter at the Foreign Office in London. We had not seen each other for more than ten years. He was Assistant Under Secretary. When I walked into his room he gave me a hearty welcome. He showed me the report Schulenburg had sent when Hayter was transferred from Moscow to the Foreign Office in London, describing him as a promising young diplomat. By coincidence this flattering report had just come to his desk from Wadden Hall, where a large part of the files of the German Ministry for Foreign Affairs were kept. Laughing, we agreed that Schulenburg's prediction had been correct. Hayter's further career, Ambassador in Moscow and Warden of New College, Oxford, confirmed Schulenburg's judgment

When our group assembled at the *dacha*, we might play tennis, ride, ski, or hike, but most of all we talked over everything occurring in international and Soviet affairs. Like General Staff Officers we discussed all possible developments, even the most improbable ones. Again and again we scrutinized the ambitious slogan of the Soviet Union 'catch up and overtake the capitalist states'. Some thought that Russia would certainly catch up and perhaps even overtake. Fitzroy Maclean and I were firmly convinced that the Soviets would not succeed in catching up, indeed that they would lag behind by several lengths.

It was in these discussions that many of us, myself included, came to the firm conclusion that there would be war. As I will explain later, we reached this conclusion because of our assessment of Hitler's intentions, rather than those of the Soviet Union. In such a mood, one day in 1938 we all decided to make our last wills and testaments. It was agreed that if the Germans had to leave the Soviet Union, the wine cellar would go to the British and Americans. If the British had to leave, however, the Germans would take over their whisky. Such was our grim humour by the late thirties. Again and again we discussed these problems in our own Embassy. My wife remembers a heated argument of 6 April, 1936. The German troops had moved on 7 March into the demilitarized zone of the Rhineland. I maintained that, even though the Anglo-French General Staff talks had taken place, Hitler would still continue with his 'Saturday surprises'. He will annex Austria and overrun Poland,' I said. 'This means World War II.' My older colleagues, who had lived through World War I, said that such foolishness as had occurred two decades before could not possibly be repeated and accused me of being young and inexperienced. I became more and more aggressive and repeated time and again: 'World War II is as sure as the Amen in church.'

The *dacha* circle formed a kind of Masonic lodge, or, as I have said, a Mutual Admiration Society. In fact, we founded such a group; like Great Britain, the Society had no written constitution, but it existed nonetheless. Since our discussions were frank, we were careful to admit only people in whom we had complete trust. There were, of course, top secret matters that could not be discussed. For my part, though, even this limitation was not absolute, since I came fairly early to consider my government to be one that could not be judged by normal standards of morality.

An excellent example of the special relationships that existed among this group was the link between Fitzroy Maclean, Charlie Thayer, and myself. Long before the war we had decided that if the war came we would not stay in the diplomatic service but would join our respective armies. Our reasons were very different, of course. Maclean was guided by the feeling that in wartime one should be in the army and that army life would be, to quote the title of the American edition of his memoirs, *An Escape to Adventure*. It was not simple for Maclean to get into the army, however, since British diplomats were forbidden to join the colours. Fitzroy had therefore to get himself first elected to Parliament. From there he was permitted to enlist. For Charlie, enlistment meant returning to the point at which he had started his professional life. As a West Point graduate he had always retained the outlook of the military man and was eager to serve if the opportunity arose. When I eventually decided to enlist, I did so because I felt that my time had run out in the diplomatic service. Since my maternal grandmother had been Jewish, I was technically non-Aryan, and by 1938 most of the non-Aryans had been drummed out of the diplomatic service. I knew it was only a matter of time before I followed them. Beyond that, I believed from early on that Hitler had to be removed and that the only way to do that was to join the army, where one at least had a weapon in one's hands.

All three of us therefore had decided by 1938 that we would join our armies, which we did, and with dramatically different results.

5

THE GERMAN EMBASSY

The German Embassy during the 1930s was unique, both among German embassies abroad and among the missions of other nations in Moscow. Since it was to be my haven for eight years, I should like to describe it in some detail.

The German Embassy was outstandingly well qualified to deal with the Soviet Union. Down to the lowest clerical staff, nearly every member had a fluent knowledge of Russian, largely due to the fact that most of them had actually been born there. Those who had not been born there had acquired their Russian as prisoners of war or had Russian-born wives. This meant that even at the lowest levels the German Embassy was bilingual. To help my own work in preparing press reviews I had as assistant Fräulein Elisabeth Winckler, a highly educated woman who had directed a girls' school in Moscow before World War I. Another assistant of mine was Alexander Kaempffe, who had been born in Russia and had lived there all his life. Obviously, such people were invaluable in analysing the domestic affairs of the USSR.

The linguistic expertise of our staff was the envy of every embassy in Moscow. It also had a good effect on new arrivals. Confronted with our staff, newcomers were shamed into mastering the language as quickly as possible and immersing themselves in Soviet life. This extended even to the ambassadors. Von Dirksen plunged into Russian lessons and eventually acquired an excellent understanding and good speaking ability. Dirksen's successor, Rudolf Nadolny, was an able linguist, having been vice-consul in St Petersburg before the war. Count Schulenburg, who succeeded Nadolny, was the least adept in Russian of all our ambassadors. What Schulenburg lacked, however, his staff more than made up for, especially those younger members who had contact with Russian girls and had mastered the so-called *grammatica viva*.

The foreign missions in Moscow were much smaller in the 1930s than they are today. Only seven members of our Embassy were drawn from the Foreign Service. Along with these seven were several career officers, the so-called *Konsulatssekretäre*. Our chief officers were the Ambassador; a counsellor who served as his deputy and was also responsible for political work; another counsellor who headed the Economic Section; a secretary in the Economic Section, who at the same time did cultural work; the director of the Consular Section and one assistant; and a representative of the German news agency who assisted in press work. Finally, there was the secretary to the Ambassador, which post I filled after my term in the Consular Section. In addition to my duties as secretary, I took a hand in political work, was responsible for press reporting, served as protocol officer, and, as I have mentioned, was secretary to the diplomatic corps so long as the German Ambassador was doyen.

The most outstanding member of the Embassy's staff was Gustav Hilger, the *Legionsrat* who headed the Economic Section. Both he and his wife were bilingual, having been born in Russia. Before the Revolution he had been in business in Russia, and his wife's family had owned a well-known electrical company. After a brief period of service with the Red Cross in Moscow, he joined the German Embassy as soon as Germany recognized the Soviet regime, and hence followed the development of our relationship with Russia right from the beginning. Though he had lived happily under the old order, he was no great defender of tsarism, perhaps because he and his wife had both been interned in Siberia after 1914. Moreover, he blamed the loss of his own property in Russia on the follies of the tsarist government. Because of all this, he was willing to view the Soviet system with a degree of indulgence. I believe that Hilger would have rejoiced had the Soviet system been a success, for in his way he was proud of Russia and fond of the Russians. Russia was a second home to him. Indeed, he and his wife always seemed to me to be half German and half Russian.

One of Hilger's greatest strengths was that he knew not only the history of Russia, but also the pasts of most of the Soviet officials whom he encountered. He could invariably tell you where a person had been before the Revolution and after the Revolution. I treated him as a kind of living encyclopedia, to be consulted whenever I had to do a report for the Ambassador. In this respect he was immensely helpful. At the same time, I never considered Hilger to be a very astute or critical man. He invariably assumed that people were basically good and therefore had difficulty comprehending what was happening, first in the Soviet Union and later in Germany. This child-like innocence made him hard to deal with but at the same time was responsible for his great amiability. He was well liked, but he was by no means a sophisticated man.

I was never more convinced of Hilger's naïveté than when I observed his inability in 1940–41 to realize that war with the Soviet Union was imminent. He could not and would not believe it. World War I had cut his heart in two, and he simply could not accept that such a war could occur again. His incomprehension endured to the last moment. When the attack was finally launched, he received it as a wholly unexpected blow.

A particularly important person in our Embassy was Otto Schiller, who covered agricultural affairs. Schiller had been well prepared for his job, having served first in the large Krupp concession on the river Manych and later in the Drusag German–Russian Seed Company in the Kuban district. His Russian was fluent, and he spent so much time roaming the countryside that we called him 'the *kolkhoznik*' – the collective farmer. Thanks to his practical training and to the excellent preparation that he had had earlier at university, Schiller was the finest observer of the agricultural scene in any of the embassies. His reports were treated as the Bible; his analyses were quoted and paraphrased by diplomats of many countries. Schiller worked actively down to 1938, at which time he was removed, not at the request of the Russians but due to intrigues within the Nazi Party.

There is evidence to suggest that the Soviets appreciated Schiller's ability as much as we did. The Russians have never hesitated to ask for the removal of any foreign diplomat whose past or present behaviour did not meet with their approval; after the war, however, Otto Schiller was permitted to return to the Moscow Embassy, where he served again for several years as agricultural attaché. Perhaps the Russians realized he was a deeply knowledgeable expert and that he was genuinely fond of them.

Germany's pre-war consulates were situated in Novosibirsk, Tblisi, Odessa, Kiev, Kharkov, Leningrad, and Vladivostok. Each year the consular officials from these far-flung stations would convene for a full week in Moscow, during which time we would review with them all the main issues of the day. We called this their 'blue week', since we kept them in constant motion between various theatres, operas, restaurants, and parties. 'Blue' in German, of course, means 'tipsy'. As is usually the case, the consular officials were critical of the Embassy and accused their colleagues in the capital of not really knowing what was going on in the country. They thought that we lacked a true knowledge of the situation, and accused us of being too favourable towards the Soviet Union in our reporting. At the end of each 'blue week' we liked to think that we convinced them we were not fooled by Potemkin villages any more than they were, but that we, unlike them, had the responsibility of reporting in the most detached and objective way.

The chief problem before the German Embassy in Moscow, after all, was to put the Soviet experience in perspective. On the one hand, we faced many people at home who thought the USSR would collapse; on the other, we faced an even larger number of people, particularly visiting professors and industrialists, who could see none of the problems of the situation. It fell to us to present a balanced picture, avoiding both these extremes, as well as the irritation that crept into the reports from the consulates.

It must be admitted that life in the consulates was often intolerable. In Kiev, for instance, the German and Polish consulates were put under siege in 1937. Their telephones were disconnected, their plumbing cut off, dirty water sent in through the faucets, and sirens blown all night in the street outside. Harassment assumed various forms, including the arrest of staff personnel, but in the end it failed to achieve its objective of closing the consulates. Only much later, on the very eve of war, were the German consulates in the USSR actually closed.

Few weeks passed without some adventure involving our consulates around the country. One of the most amusing of these occurred before my arrival, in the period when Count Brockdorff-Rantzau was still Ambassador. Apparently Brockdorff-Rantzau received from our consulate in Kiev a lengthy report which had obviously been opened en route. To his astonishment, he found inside not only the consul's report but also a rough copy of the Russian translation that had been inadvertently left there by the Soviet secret police. Brockdorff-Rantzau went at once to Grigorii Chicherin, Commissar of Foreign Affairs, to complain vehemently. His indignation, or so it was reported in the Embassy, focused not so much on the fact that the letter had been opened as that it had been done in so primitive a fashion. Then, with mounting irritation, Brockdorff-Rantzau lodged an official complaint about the poor quality of the translation. He sternly advised Chicherin to secure the services of better translators, lest an international incident be inadvertently caused by sloppiness.

Finally I should mention the name of Gebhardt von Walther, who eventually took over my job as personal assistant to Schulenburg. His views on Soviet affairs were to exert a strong influence on our Embassy. As a newcomer in 1936, von Walther looked on things differently, being perhaps quicker than we were to realize the extent of the changes that had occurred in the Soviet Union. Though we had observed the transformations taking place in the economy, political system, and cultural life, we had not, at the time of von Walther's arrival, put them together sufficiently well. He stimulated us to carry out this synthesis and to build a new picture of the Soviet Union based on the notion that one could no longer speak of Communism there, at least in the old sense.

In this respect, von Walther is as good an example as one could find of the need to rotate diplomats frequently, lest they became bogged down in a particular point of view. He showed that we had all become lazy in our thinking and he encouraged me and my colleagues to develop our ideas about the new direction that Soviet developments seemed to have taken. Our new conception, unlike the old, recognized the changes that had occurred under Stalin. But the Nazis, prisoners of their own anti-Communist propaganda, did not realize the impact of these changes. We considered that precisely because the Soviet Union had begun to revise its ideology it was becoming more powerful and productive and therefore a more significant factor in world politics. In the end it was we and not the Nazis who took Russia seriously. I have often thought that someone should erect a monument to Stalin as the liquidator of Communism. Whether he was or not, he vastly strengthened the USSR. He accomplished this not so much through the principles of Lenin as through the application of ideas and techniques that had proven so successful in Russia and many other states for a century or more.

I should touch on the question of security within our Embassy. In retrospect I am astonished that we cared so little about this problem throughout the late thirties. Not that there were no causes for concern. One day in 1937 I discovered that the safe in which all the secret papers were kept had been tampered with. A broken key was still in the lock, though no documents had been taken. Neither at that time nor later were any of us able to figure out who within the Embassy might have been working with the NKVD.

In spite of such incidents, we took few measures to ensure security. To put it bluntly, we hardly cared whether there were hidden microphones or not. We knew full well that our telephones were tapped, but this scarcely affected our behaviour. Generally speaking, members of the German Embassy never felt themselves to be prisoners in Stalin's Moscow. I certainly felt no strong sense of oppression and did not hesitate to speak my mind on virtually any subject. This sense of ease was shared, I think, by most of the other Moscow diplomats as well. We were certainly not paranoid.

After the 1933 attack on our Ambassador that ended in the wounding of von Twardowski, we began to be followed by the secret police. At first they followed only the Ambassador; soon they dogged the movements of lower-placed members of the Embassy such as myself. How was one to deal with the agents assigned to follow us? If one went shopping, they were there, and shopping was one of our principal diversions. It was unnerving to stand at the counter of the hard-currency shop or one of the commission stores and see your 'tail' standing by your side. You could curse him until your vocabulary was exhausted but he would not reply. He followed you, but in a sense you did not exist.

At length this treatment became so irritating that we began playing foolish tricks. We would leave the Embassy by car and drive like madmen through the city, making a complicated series of turns so as to escape our tails, or three or four of us would assemble on Red Square with our NKVD agents behind and then parade around in formation. We realized that such behaviour was childish and ridiculous, but at times our irritation burst all bounds. A prank which particularly delighted me was for several of us to drive out to the American *dacha* in a single car, the NKVD car following at the usual distance. The secret police would wait around until we had finished our tennis or whatever, in order to assure themselves that we all returned. To give them trouble, one of our number would lie down on the floor during the return trip, leaving the NKVD men frustrated and worried that they had lost one of their charges.

I remember well one trip back to Moscow from the American *dacha* during which we devised a particularly droll variant of this routine. I led the parade in my car, followed by the Ford driven by my NKVD agent and, behind him, Fitzroy Maclean in his car. At a pre-arranged point we stopped near a local policeman, to whom Fitzroy Maclean reported that his friends in the car ahead were being harassed by hooligans who were following him in a late model Ford. The policeman went up to the Ford in question and was beginning to apprehend the driver when he discovered to his horror that he was arresting an agent of the NKVD.

For trips outside the capital, it was particularly tempting to liberate oneself from one's NKVD tail. The Poles were especially adept at this. Their practice was to leave in the middle of the night from the back door of their Embassy and drive as far and as fast as they could without stopping or refuelling. They could get as far as the Polish Consulate in Kiev this way, but no further, since the Soviets flatly refused to provide them with petrol. This effectively limited their cruising range.

There was one exception to our hostile attitude towards the NKVD, namely, the good relations that existed between the German Embassy and the secret police whose duty it was to follow the Ambassador. We carefully informed these agents about the Ambassador's movements. The NKVD people assigned to the Ambassador appreciated this, since it meant that they did not have to sit outside the residence in their unheated Ford at thirty degrees below freezing on the off chance that he would emerge. In return, they assisted us in many ways on our trips. Not only did they help with directions and the like, but they would go so far as to assure us good accommodation wherever we went. They came to trust us.

In my own travels I adhered to the policy we had worked out for dealing with the NKVD officers assigned to our Ambassador. If I left Moscow on a trip, I would ask my driver to stop at the first fork in the road and pretend to make an adjustment to our carburettor. Soon afterwards the people following us would pull up. I would greet them and explain precisely where I planned to go, where and when I would be camping, and at what time every morning I would be getting on the road again. Invariably they would treat this with suspicion, but after the first two days they generally believed me and we would travel together like a convoy, helping each other in whatever way was called for.

On one trip during 1938 I found myself stuck in Odessa, my car having broken down there. I informed the NKVD that I would be heading back the next day to Moscow by train, since I could not get the necessary spare parts from Germany. The NKVD officer asked very politely if he could look at the car and find what parts were broken, in the hope that he could locate a similar vehicle somewhere in Odessa and borrow the necessary parts from it. I doubted that he would succeed, but agreed to give him the two days that he asked for. Forty-eight hours later he returned to inform me that our car was in good order again. He asked only that, when I did receive the spare parts from Germany, would I please send them to him so that he might pass them in turn to the owner of the car in Odessa from which he had pirated the parts.

Such cordiality persisted even after the relationship between our two countries took a final turn for the worse. Count Schulenburg told me that, when he finally had to leave the Soviet Union in 1941, the NKVD agents followed him to the Turkish border. When he boarded the Turkish train, they exchanged friendly waves with each other. Such human relations exist in the worst of times. We did our best to foster them, on the grounds that the people with whom we dealt were only trying to do their duty, as were we.

6

SERVICE UNDER THREE
AMBASSADORS

The first ambassador under whom I served was Herbert von Dirksen, the former cavalry companion of my father's who had shown me such cordiality on my arrival in Moscow. Dirksen was highly esteemed by his professional colleagues. He had begun his career not as a diplomat but as a civil servant in Prussia; only after World War I did he enter diplomacy. His preparation for the ambassadorship in Moscow was nonetheless excellent. He served as Deputy and then as Director of the Department of Eastern Affairs of our Foreign Ministry, and had been Consul General in Danzig. One of the midwives of the Treaty of Rapallo, he had also worked closely with Baron Ago von Maltzan, the Permanent Secretary of the Ministry of Foreign Affairs, a most active proponent of good relations with the USSR. Through all these activities, Dirksen became associated with Count Brockdorff-Rantzau, whom he succeeded as Ambassador to Moscow in 1929.

Dirksen was a tall, broad-shouldered man whose expressive head, great brow and spectacles combined to produce the impression of an intellectual, even of a professor. But Dirksen was in fact the prototype of the Prussian civil servant, punctilious, thorough, hard-working and committed to his job. He was a prodigious worker, as I learned even before my arrival, thanks to my friend and colleague in the Foreign Office in Berlin, Albrecht von Kessel, who worked under Dirksen in the years 1927-29. Thanks also to Kessel, I was forewarned of many of Dirksen's idiosyncrasies and especially of his extreme disinclination to express any personal sentiments. An incident that had occurred in 1927 was particularly vivid in my mind as I set out for Russia. One night Kessel had arrived home in high spirits, ready to open a bottle to celebrate. The occasion for his ebullience was the fact that Dirksen, for the first time in the six months that Kessel had been on his staff, had had a personal word for him. Leaving the office at ten o'clock at night, Dirksen had paused to remark, 'You poor child'.

Dirksen's extreme reticence in personal contacts was reflected in his choice of hobbies. Thus, he preferred the solitude of chess to all other games, and he was an enthusiastic collector of rare Chinese porcelain, even when there were few around him who could understand the subtleties of that art. The forbearance he exhibited when the wife of a diplomat exclaimed about his splendid collection of 'modern German chinaware' was evident in all his diplomatic dealings.

It was an unenviable assignment to follow on the heels of the legendary Brockdorff-Rantzau, who had resigned from his post as Foreign Minister and as leader of the German delegation at Versailles rather than sign the treaty. Thrown into a state of shock at the treatment he had received in Versailles, Brockdorff-Rantzau had been virtually hurled into the arms of the Russians. Though he had his critics at home, Brockdorff-Rantzau was highly respected in Moscow, especially by the Commissar of Foreign Affairs, Chicherin, a fellow aristocrat. Both Chicherin and Brockdorff-Rantzau preferred to work at night, and would often be in touch with one another by telephone while the rest of the city slept. Habits such as this endowed him with a certain mystique, both among the Russians and among his own staff, who rarely saw him.

Von Dirksen's task would have been difficult in any circumstances, but it was rendered yet more complex in 1929 because one could already sense that the close relationship that had hitherto existed between the two countries was weakening. Dirksen's assignment was to re-establish these links. His first specific task was to overcome the mistrust engendered among the Russians by the election of Dr Heinrich Brüning as Chancellor in March 1930. From the Soviet point of view Brüning's foreign policy was firmly centred on the West. His overriding concern was to undo those clauses of the Versailles Treaty that were damaging to Germany. The Soviets, of course, viewed this with the deepest apprehension. To counterbalance Brüning's approach to the British and French, the Soviet Commissar of Foreign Affairs, Litvinov, endeavoured to establish his own links with those countries. Brüning understood that the Soviets were doing this, but was not concerned over Germany's Eastern policy to the extent that his predecessors had been.

In this context I have to pay tribute to Brüning and say a few words about his tragedy, which was also the tragedy of Germany. Brüning appeared to me and to many other patriotic Germans as the last bulwark against the Nazi flood. He had a fine record as an officer in World War I and greatly impressed students and other younger people by his courageous speeches against extremists of both Left and Right. By 1932 he had succeeded in partially revising the Treaty of Versailles, was on the verge of overcoming the worst consequences of the economic crisis, and seemed generally to be re-establishing the Reich as an equal member of the community of nations. We considered Brüning the man to solve Germany's problems.

I was delighted that Hindenburg was re-elected president on 10 April, 1932, defeating both Hitler and the Communist Ernst Thälmann. It seemed obvious that this would assure Brüning's continued influence in Berlin. Knowing, further, that Hindenburg despised the Nazis and was ready to use force against the SA and SS, I saw no reason not to rejoice. It was thus a terrible shock to me when Hindenburg dismissed Brüning in May 1932. Obviously Hindenburg, through age and senility, had fallen under the fatal influence of Papen, Schleicher, and his own son, Oscar, who paved the way for the Nazis. The voters had re-elected Hindenburg in the hope that he would continue Brüning's policies and prevent the Nazis from coming to power. Hindenburg betrayed them, though he did not live to see the fateful results of his decision.

During the Chancellorship of Brüning, the question of German trade with the USSR came to the fore. As had long been the case, this trade revolved around the Russians' desire to import machine tools and heavy equipment from Germany. Many people in Germany considered such exports to be risky since, they claimed, one could not be sure that the Russians would live up to their obligations. In fact the Russians were trying hard to maintain the reputation for fair dealing that the capitalist states had already lost. Von Dirksen laboured tirelessly to convince the German public, the German government, and even the German industrialists that trade with the USSR would not be disastrous. His campaign was phenomenally successful, in part due to the conditions created by the stock market crash of 1929 and by the ensuing world economic crisis. During Dirksen's ambassadorship, industrial products valued at several billion marks were sold to the Soviet Union, to the benefit of the German labour force.

Von Dirksen, as doyen of the diplomatic corps, took his responsibilities seriously. Scarcely a month passed in which he did not make some representation to Litvinov, the head of the *Narkomindel*, on behalf of the foreign missions. He complained about living conditions, about provisioning, about supervision, and then he would complain about living conditions once more. Finally, he became so incensed in his campaign that he presented Litvinov with a large volume in German on the reception afforded foreigners by the tsarist court of Muscovy. Handing it to the Commissar, he urged him to read it so that he would realize that nothing had changed.

A major project each year was the preparation of the Ambassador's annual report, a forty- to sixty-page statement covering every aspect of Soviet affairs. Under Nadolny and Schulenburg this became a collective enterprise, with all of us participating in one way or another; under von Dirksen, however, it was largely a solo performance. Unlike his successors, von Dirksen also did most of his own day-to-day reporting, leaving little to his aides. Since Dirksen was so well acquainted with Soviet affairs, my role under him in the political field was little more than that of assistant. I learned a great deal from him, however.

Hilda von Dirksen, his wife, played a significant part in his success in Moscow. She had a sincere interest in the arts, and managed to keep in touch with scores of people who might not otherwise have come within the Embassy's orbit. She maintained these contacts in spite of the fact that she spoke no language but German and was outspoken to the point of bluntness. This quality caused more than its fair share of difficulties among the younger members of the diplomatic corps. It was customary for every new arrival to the Moscow diplomatic corps to pay Hilda von Dirksen a formal visit. These occasions were widely feared, since it was well known that she would not hesitate to lecture young diplomats' wives on the need to wear woollen stockings and underwear, and to tell them that an improvement to their looks would come from wearing no make-up.

Frau von Dirksen had the wisdom of an old shepherd, having been brought up on an estate where she had learned much about nature, weather, and home remedies. She tended to assume that everyone else had grown up on an estate, too, and would normally ask new arrivals at the Embassy where their families' land was situated. My predecessor at the Embassy, Kurt Brunhoff, startled her by replying that his family had no estate beyond a balcony in Berlin, on which they kept a few flowerpots. After a pause, Frau von Dirksen said sadly, 'I am sorry for you.' This reflected more than mere snobbery. She sincerely believed that a self-sustaining estate freed one from excessive dependence upon government service and hence assured a more disinterested execution of one's duties.

Frau von Dirksen's bluntness reverberated throughout the Moscow diplomatic corps. Once I accompanied her on a visit to the wife of the Estonian minister, Julius Seljamaa, who later became Foreign Minister of Estonia. As it happened, Seljamaa himself had pretensions as an art collector. Sitting down to tea, Frau von Dirksen expressed her hostile views on practically every painting in the room. Mrs Seljamaa was delighted, since she did not approve of her husband's gluttonous collecting. She volunteered to call in her husband so that Hilda von Dirksen could tell him face to face what she thought of his paintings. To my horror, Frau von Dirksen did just this; defended it to me afterwards by saying that it was her duty to prevent Seljamaa from buying bad pictures.

In the early thirties, the Finnish government invited members of the diplomatic corps to visit Finland. Dirksen, as doyen of the diplomatic corps, was scheduled to join this party. At the last moment he was kept in Moscow by business, so Frau von Dirksen went alone, I being designated to accompany her. Before my departure, the Ambassador took me aside and admonished me to watch closely that Frau von Dirksen gave no indiscreet interviews to the press that might insult the Finns. Scarcely had his wife arrived in Helsinki when an English-speaking journalist asked her what she thought of the local architecture. After I had translated the question to her, she expressed the view that four and five storey buildings were much too large for such a country, and that they should build smaller structures instead. Translating this to the correspondent, I reported that the Ambassador's wife had been extremely impressed by Finnish architecture. Although Frau von Dirksen knew only a few words of English, she guessed that I had not rendered her sentiments with precision. When she challenged me, I had to tell her that I was under orders from the Ambassador to translate whatever she said in such a way that it would be pleasing to the correspondent interviewing her.

At the end of 1933 Dirksen was transferred to Japan, to his and our surprise. His behaviour in his new post enabled us to see a side of him that had not been evident while he was in Moscow, namely, his readiness to promote the cause of whatever country he found himself in. While in Moscow he had insisted that German foreign policy should hinge on the relationship with Russia; no sooner was he in Tokyo than he began to insist with equal vehemence that it should turn on the relationship with Japan. Just as earlier he had warned of the danger of Japan to the Soviet Union, so now he issued cautionary statements on the threat posed by the Soviet Union in Eastern Asia. In this respect, Dirksen again showed himself the typical Prussian civil servant who, as *Regierungspräsident* for Potsdam, will look after the needs of that district but will vigorously promote the interests of Breslau from the minute he is named *Regierungspräsident* there. Dirksen was still Ambassador when the National Socialists came to power. At first we found little reason to think that this change marked any basic reorientation in German policy towards the Soviet Union. In his Reichstag speech of May 1933, Hitler spoke of the continuation of normal relationships and gave no indication that any storm might be gathering. The situation changed quickly, however, during the period of Rudolf Nadolny's ambassadorship.

Nadolny had been born in East Prussia, and all his interests were concentrated on Eastern affairs. As a young man he had served as vice-consul in Petersburg and had developed a keen interest in Slav affairs throughout Central Europe. He had long wished to be named Ambassador to Moscow, but when his appointment came, it proved to be the termination rather than the culmination of his career.

He had a somewhat exotic cast to his appearance, looking Mongolian or Turk; one might have taken him for a Cossack. He had the reputation of being severe, demanding, ambitious and stubborn. On account of these traits, he had his share of enemies; at the same time, his straightforwardness and strength of character earned him just as many friends. He possessed enormous vitality, and was known to be uncompromising and persevering. His friends were impressed by his loyalty, his astute brain, his capacity for analysing a situation and then working out a constructive policy. His driving power was unique, perhaps unusual for a diplomat. Indeed, he was more politician than diplomat, but a politician who was always prepared to stand up for his convictions.

I was asked to accompany Nadolny from Berlin on his first trip to Moscow, and from the moment I met him and his family I was immediately impressed by his openness and outspokenness. He was the opposite of Dirksen in many respects. He formed his judgments on the basis of what he could see with his own eyes and, having done so, spoke his mind on the subject precisely like an East Prussian farmer, which his ancestors had been.

Great as was the difference between Nadolny and his predecessor, the difference between Frau Nadolny and Frau von Dirksen was even greater. Frau Nadolny was a gentle person, the right wife for such a strong-willed man as he. Nadolny's energetic approach to all problems followed his motto 'Take action!'; Frau Nadolny was a perfect foil – calm, serene, she exuded a patient and even cosy approach to life that could temper his restless nature. His two daughters, one resembling the father and the other the mother, did much to enliven the atmosphere of the Embassy.

Nadolny's character was revealed to the whole Embassy when he first met us as a group. After the usual pleasantries, he expressed his respect for the staff and his strong desire that each of us should feel free to criticize any of his actions or policies. He insisted only that no one had a right to criticize him *after* an event if the criticism had not been expressed before as well. 'You must,' he said, 'have the courage to speak up to your Ambassador.' This earned him universal respect.

Before setting out for Moscow, Nadolny had formulated his views on Germany's policy towards Russia and had written these down. I later learned that his own memorandum had formed the basis for the instructions he received at the time of his appointment. Nadolny was firmly convinced of the need to stop the deterioration of German–Russian relations and to initiate a more positive course, on the grounds that good relations between these two powers were essential. Needless to say, the idea of preparing a war against the USSR was anathema to him. Like many other East Prussians, he laid great stress on the German–Russian relationship and held to the old saying that, when good relations existed between Germany and Russia, both countries flourished, but whenever the links between them weakened, both countries would suffer. In this sense, Nadolny was a direct heir of the Bismarckian tradition in Prussian foreign policy.

I was surprised to see the number of specific plans for improving German–Soviet relations with which Nadolny arrived. They touched on everything from the most petty issues right up to a scheme for negotiating a new German–Soviet pact. But Nadolny quickly ran into serious difficulties on account both of his style and the substance of his views. He was at a disadvantage from the start because of the lack of cordiality that existed between him and the minister in Berlin, Konstantin von Neurath. This coolness was all but unavoidable, since Nadolny was a man of brutal action while von Neurath was one to avoid difficulties if at all possible. Any good ambassador should always be forwarding concrete suggestions to his minister; Nadolny, though, spewed forth proposals like a fountain, even at the expense of implementing those policies which emanated from Neurath's own office.

I have spoken of Nadolny's plan for bringing about a new treaty between Germany and the USSR. As he conceived it, this would have gone far beyond Litvinov's more modest proposal to come to some agreement regarding the Baltic states. Initially, Nadolny tried to work through the Ministry of Foreign Affairs. In one sense, the ground had been well prepared for this effort, since the Treaty of Berlin had been renewed just before he came, but his call for a broad agreement encompassing political, economic, and cultural relations between the two countries fell on deaf ears. When he failed with Neurath, he tried to gain the ear of Hindenburg. Nadolny was on good terms with the old field marshal and, thanks to his help, in June 1934 he was summoned to Berlin, where he argued vehemently with Neurath on behalf of a more positive policy vis-à-vis the Soviet Union.

After presenting his case to Neurath, Nadolny went directly to Hitler in the hope of gaining from the Führer what he had failed to get elsewhere. Before approaching him, of course, he had to convince himself that Hitler, in spite of all of the passages in *Mein Kampf* that pointed ominously towards Russia and the Ukraine, was still open to reason. Though he had no intention of getting into an argument, as had happened on previous occasions, Nadolny soon found himself engaged in a bitter debate with Hitler, who rejected his proposals with the remark that he wanted to have nothing to do with the Russians. Nadolny persisted, Hitler banged his fist on the table, and soon each was shouting at the other. A few days later Nadolny was received for a second time by Hitler. As Neurath was present this time the conversation took a calmer course, but Hitler persisted in his negative attitude. Before leaving for Moscow Nadolny went once more to Neurath, hoping that he might be given new orders. Nothing had changed, and Nadolny realized he had no future in Moscow.

He returned one more time to take leave of the Embassy. All of us were as deeply impressed by this man in his failure as we had been in his success. All his life he had aspired to serve as Germany's Ambassador in the Soviet Union, wanting nothing higher than to play a role in improving German–Soviet relations. In the end he managed to become Ambassador, but within a year he had resigned, in the full knowledge that his career was finished. We deeply admired the courage and steadfastness with which he had pursued his dream, and when he departed from Moscow for the last time, the tragic victim of that dream, I was not alone in having tears in my eyes.

Count Schulenburg arrived in Moscow in the autumn of 1934. He was the very model of a diplomat. He accepted the Soviet–German situation in which he was placed and tried to work within it. On the basis of Nadolny's experience he concluded that the best strategy in Moscow would be to follow Bismarck's dictum that one cannot change things by swimming against the stream as effectively as by swimming with it. Accordingly, Schulenburg waited quietly for the best moment in which to take action.

His cautious professionalism and fair-mindedness made him far more welcome among the Soviet officials with whom he had to deal than most other diplomats in Moscow. This was well known to Schulenburg's colleagues from other missions and roundly resented by some of them. The American Ambassador, Joseph Davies, for example, once complained to Litvinov that Count Schulenburg seemed to be in special favour, notwithstanding the fact that he was the representative of Nazi Germany. To this Litvinov replied; 'Well, we like him and just cannot say no to him.' This was typical. Schulenburg was genuinely liked in Moscow and was considered by the Soviets to be the representative not of Nazi Germany, but of the Germany they liked.

Schulenburg's effectiveness with the Russians stemmed in part from his style of dealing with them. He once went to the Ministry of Foreign Affairs to ask the Soviet government to undo certain measures that it had taken with regard to Germany. I advised him that it would be better if I or another more junior officer went in his place since the mission was bound to end in failure. To this he replied blandly that he would prefer to go himself and that I should prepare a telegram for Berlin informing the Ministry that everything had been straightened out. Thinking that he was pulling my leg, I did not prepare the telegram and instead waited for him to return. When he came back from his meeting with Litvinov he asked me for the telegram, declaring that he wanted to sign it immediately. Amazed, I asked him what had happened. He reported that after a long and rambling conversation about Germany he had casually mentioned to Litvinov that a diplomat from one of the other embassies had told him that the Soviet government was intending to take measures that would be unacceptable to Germany. Schulenburg said he had explained to the diplomat that of course nothing of the sort could happen, since he knew that his close friend Litvinov, being a gentleman, would never approve of it. To this, Litvinov replied: 'Thank you very much, my dear friend, you are quite right and I am glad you spoke for me.' This is typical of the way Schulenburg handled problems and persons.

He was as popular in the Ministry of Foreign Affairs in Berlin as he was in our Embassy or among the Russians. Everybody in Berlin liked him, to the point that he could be sure that his slightest wish would be granted. He was on particularly good terms with Neurath, and because of that was able to get to Hitler when necessary. In contrast to Nadolny, whose meetings with Hitler were frequently interrupted by outbursts of temper, Schulenburg never allowed his feelings to erupt so openly, at least until the outbreak of war with the Soviet Union. Had I been asked in 1936 or 1937 whether Schulenburg would ever become a member of the anti-Hitler Resistance, I would certainly have replied in the negative. He did not strike me as the kind of man to use force against his government, even against a very evil government; he seemed far too passive, far too much the professional observer, to undertake anything so bold. Obviously, I did him a great injustice, for he was to be among those hanged after the attempt on Hitler's life in July 1944.

Schulenburg's chief concern was always with the individual human being rather than with institutions or the principles underlying them. He was far more ready to acknowledge the positive sides of people's characters than their negative traits. Without being unaware of people's weaknesses, he always claimed that he could learn more from their good qualities. This enabled Schulenburg to form and maintain relations with people with whom he might otherwise have had little in common. More than anything else, it enabled him to function as an able diplomat even in the most trying circumstances.

Schulenburg's positive attitude, however, had a negative side, or so it seemed to those of us who were particularly close to him. We would often get upset over what we felt to be Schulenburg's inability to differentiate between the various people around him, with the result that he would show the same unreserved friendliness towards virtual strangers as he did towards his closest friends and his own staff. This was typical of him. I never had the impression that Schulenburg was a regular churchgoer, but I have no doubt that his benevolence was rooted in his religious nature. He took seriously the precept that man is a creature of God, and believed therefore that to abuse any of one's fellow men was tantamount to abusing the Creator.

Schulenburg had entered government service in 1902, when he was not yet twenty-six. Lacking the private fortune necessary for a diplomatic career, he had entered the consular service, which at that time was still separate from our Foreign Service. He was first sent to Barcelona and then assigned to Warsaw, where he served for several years before World War I. During this time in Poland he formed many close friendships, particularly among the aristocracy. His sympathy for the Poles never left him, and I frequently heard him express his deep concern for that country's welfare. After the partition of Poland in 1939 he did much to enable Poles imprisoned either by the Russians or the National Socialists to emigrate to Romania or elsewhere and thereby escape further persecution. I learned of this both when I was stationed near Warsaw during the Polish campaign in 1939 and after my return from the Western Front in 1940. On both occasions, many Poles expressed their gratitude for the efforts that Schulenburg had made on behalf of their friends.

Schulenburg was mobilized into the army in 1914. He served in the front line, and was then sent to Damascus as diplomat, liaison officer and consul and was subsequently posted to the Caucasus at the time of the Georgian Republic, when Germany had troops stationed there. His efforts on behalf of Georgian independence were much appreciated and were recalled with gratitude even by many of the Bolshevik Georgians. When the German diplomatic and consular services were merged after the war, Schulenburg was at last able to launch a diplomatic career. Following six years spent in Persia and two years in Romania, he was appointed to the ambassadorship in Moscow, much to the surprise of many of his colleagues. Neither up to this time nor subsequently did Schulenburg show any of the careerist ambitions that dominated Dirksen and Nadolny.

Unlike his predecessors, Schulenburg had no elaborate programme that he felt obliged to pursue in Moscow. He did, however, share his predecessors' belief that good relations with Russia were essential to any sound German policy. Indeed, every time Count Schulenburg travelled to Berlin, he made a point of visiting Nadolny in order to demonstrate his sympathy for his predecessor. Unlike his two immediate predecessors, however, Schulenburg pursued his objectives quietly and inconspicuously, to the point that my colleagues and I were initially critical of what we felt to be his excessively passive approach.

At the very least, it can be said that Count Schulenburg was the perfect embodiment of patience. The only times that I can recall him losing his temper all involved his dogs. His two Persian greyhounds were very much a part of his life, and he treated them with respect owed to good friends. When one of my colleagues complained to him that his dogs were fouling the tennis court, Schulenburg exploded, telling him that the dogs were free to do what they liked and he could play tennis elsewhere if he would prefer.

Among ourselves, we blamed Schulenburg's passivity on his many years in the Near East and suspected that the 'Persian–Romanian storyteller' whom we liked so much personally had too oriental a cast of mind to be effective as a diplomat. I was concerned over Schulenburg's sense of time, and worried that he had so long a view of history as to make him ineffective as a German diplomat. I recall him telling me once of the problems which his majordomo in Teheran had had under his successor, Wipert von Blücher. Kasem had served loyally in the German Legation since the age of sixteen. An illiterate, he always presented his bills in the form of drawings of sheep or loaves of bread that he had purchased for the legation. When Schulenburg visited Teheran from Bucharest he noticed immediately that Kasem was downcast, and learned that his dour mien was the result of having been punished for returning two weeks late from a pilgrimage to Mecca. When Schulenburg was told this he exclaimed that two weeks was nothing and that Blücher would have to alter his Mecklenburgian sense of time in order to work effectively in the East.

Thanks to his experience in the Middle East, Schulenburg was disposed to see the Soviet Union as being more 'Oriental' than I did. He would point out that where in German 'immediately' was expressed by the phrase 'this minute', in Russia it was expressed by the term 'this hour' (*seichas*). Gradually I came to realize that this gave him a better appreciation than his predecessors had had of the functioning of Soviet bureaucracy, and at several critical moments saved him from seeking to force events in a way that would have been unproductive.

Schulenburg's style of thought penetrated every aspect of his life. He was an early riser, yet he would never arrive at the Embassy before 10:00 or 11:00 a.m. Invariably, when he did turn up he would be in a great hurry, leaving all of us wondering what in the world had occupied him between his early rising and late arrival. In time I discovered his secret. He would take his time shaving and dressing, and spend a leisurely breakfast with the newspapers. Then he would place himself in an armchair and, as he once put it to me, 'think over the problems of the world'. This solitary practice struck me as rather bizarre at first, especially in light of the amount of work to be done at the Embassy. Gradually, though, I came to appreciate the wisdom of Schulenburg's approach, since most of us devote all our time to the small problems that arrive on our desk and leave no time for mulling over the larger issues. What Schulenburg achieved by his solitary thinking in the armchair is done nowadays by the planning staffs of ministries!

After his arrival in the Chancellery each day I would give Schulenburg a short survey of the latest events. Then the daily morning conference would commence. These sessions had an enigmatic aspect, for Schulenburg rarely revealed his own position. Often, the only sign that he was interested in a given subject would be the rate at which he would twiddle his thumbs, an indicator which was consulted faithfully by our personnel. Everyone knew that if Schulenburg twiddled them rapidly he was following the conversation with rapt attention. The moment his thumbs stopped, however, one knew that there was no hope of re-arousing his interest. After the conference he would delegate to others the ensuing work, especially the reports. Even after having had a conversation with Soviet personalities or senior diplomatic colleagues he would brief the counsellors, and me, in full detail. Then one of us or sometimes a team would be assigned to draft the report.

One evening each week the diplomatic bag left by train for Berlin. In the late afternoon I would go over to Schulenburg's residence to submit for his signature all reports to the Foreign Ministry. Even if he did not agree with some detail, he would sign. When I entered his study I would find him invariably sitting at his enormous desk, composing his private letters, which he would type with two fingers or carefully write by hand in his fluid, strong and clear calligraphy. He would work for hours with his coat hanging over the armchair and a glass of whisky standing by the typewriter. His private correspondence was for him an important part of his life. With great diligence and regularity he exchanged reflections with those who were dear to his heart, mostly women.

Schulenburg was a tall, good-looking, baldish man with closely cropped hair and moustache. He looked extremely imposing, which did much to heighten the awe in which he was held by many diplomats in Moscow and by his Soviet contacts. Within the Embassy however, it was his attitude towards the ambassadorial function that most commanded respect. He understood full well that an ambassador's tenure of service is usually far too brief to enable him to achieve all he wants, and he therefore resolved to imbue the younger members of the staff with his own views on people, policy, and the world. His interest extended to all the younger members of the diplomatic corps, as Charlie Thayer, John Russell, and Fitzroy Maclean could attest. His judgment of the younger diplomats was astute, but always very benevolent.

He had been married for a short time, but the marriage had broken up and his one daughter remained with his former wife. His relationship with this daughter was rather aloof, and she had not visited him either in Persia or in Romania. She did come to Moscow in 1935, however, and it was fascinating to watch the battle being waged between them. On her side, the daughter did not want to succumb to the charm of her father. At first she tried to show no interest in his work or in our diplomatic way of life. But as time went on, she gradually appreciated the affection in which

94

her father was held and came herself to share it. In the end, her resistance broke down entirely, and she acknowledged how much she resembled him, though they had been apart for many years. On his side, Count Schulenburg rejoiced in having found a daughter after so long a separation.

Schulenburg was a romantic. His greatest desire was to acquire an old castle to which he could retire. I once joined him on a visit to a ruined castle in the South Tyrol, which he was prevented from buying when the Italians adopted the policy of not selling to Germans. Then he found the ruins of another castle at Falkenberg, near Weiden in the Oberpfalz in Bavaria. The castle was in a wretched condition, and when we visited it I felt bewildered that a bachelor should wish to devote so much attention to this restoration project. Schulenburg, I realized, lived in the past. In his will, he asked to be buried with the sword of the First Guards Field Artillery Regiment on his right, the spurs at his feet, and his entire body wrapped in an old Caucasian rug. This was never to happen. After he was hanged, his ashes were thrown to the winds.

Being a bachelor, Schulenburg relied heavily upon my wife, Pussi, and me for his entertaining. As a result, there was scarcely a luncheon or dinner that we did not attend, a fact which was noted with a tinge of jealousy by some of my colleagues. Once asked why my wife was so often in his residence, Schulenburg answered with a smile: 'I need a person like Pussi who is at any time available to help me, because she has neither the flu, fits of depression, or children, and she speaks Russian and three other foreign languages.' Pussi often visited his daughter Christa, his niece Ursula Schulenburg, or other house-guests. She would look after them and take them out sightseeing, then meet the cook and butler in order to decide on menus, flower decorations, and provisions needed for the household.

My debt to Schulenburg is immense. When in 1955 I was sent as Ambassador to England, I was completely green as a head of mission. More than once I had to explain to incredulous colleagues in London that my highest diplomatic assignment until then had been personal secretary to our Ambassador in Moscow. I could usually calm their fears, though, by assuring them that all would go smoothly in London if I could emulate Schulenburg's example. And so it did.

The motives underlying Count Schulenburg's actions were always simple but powerful. When eventually he joined the Resistance movement he did so not for any abstract philosophical reasons but because he could not bear to see people suffer. What above all drove him

95

into active opposition to Hitler was his realization of what was being done to the local Polish, Russian and Jewish populations after 1939. This insulted him as a Christian and as an aristocrat, but most of all it violated his common humanity. The war brought dramatic changes in the person whom I had hitherto viewed as a lovable but passive Eastern sage. In 1944 he grew immeasurably in stature. Where he had once been a skilled observer and diplomat, he now became a statesman bent upon action. It was the tragedy of his life that the action he undertook proved fruitless.

7

FIRST BRUSHES
WITH NATIONAL SOCIALISM

Right from the beginning in 1933 Dirksen made it clear that the Nazi Party would not be permitted to interfere with the work of the Embassy, a policy that was reaffirmed by both his successors. Dirksen moreover introduced a local regulation that we would not salute with 'Heil Hitler' but instead continue to use the ordinary '*guten Tag*'.

The National Socialist Party had a special organization for Germans abroad, the so-called *Auslandsorganisation*, with a network of head- and branch-offices in many countries. The *Auslandsorganisation* tried to influence and control the work of the German representatives abroad. It expected Foreign Service officers not only to represent their country but also the National Socialist ideology. Since the *Auslandsorganisation* had no clear picture of what a member of the Foreign Service should be and how he should act, there was naturally a great deal of friction.

Because of the exceptional situation of foreigners in the Soviet Union and the incompatability of National Socialism and Communism, Nadolny and Schulenburg succeeded in convincing the Party that it would be impossible to envisage the opening of a branch-office in the Soviet Union. The Ambassadors did agree to accept at the Embassy a trusted representative of the Party (*Vertrauensmann*). He had to be chosen from the diplomatic staff of the Embassy and approved by the Ambassador. Thanks to this arrangement, there were no Party activities in the Embassy or in the consulates; no rallies, no training courses, no campaigns for raising money. National Socialism was effectively stopped at the Embassy's door. This was the easier since the Nazis were not much interested in events in the USSR, the land of the *Untermenschen*. They considered Moscow a hardship post good enough for a non-Aryan like me. I believe this was one of the main reasons why my difficulties as a non-Aryan were not as great as they would have been in any other post. I was grateful that I was posted to Moscow, which for eight years served as my oasis.

The first *Vertrauensmann* of the National Socialist Party within the German Embassy in Moscow was Herbert Hensel, a Baltic German and convinced National Socialist who succeeded Pfeiffer as head of the Consular Section. His knowledge of political questions was sketchy, and he never belonged to the inner circle of the Embassy. Hensel's main interest was collecting old silver and antique rugs. He was a great connoisseur, and a well-educated man. Notwithstanding his Nazi convictions, he showed compassion for my difficulties. After the war he visited me in Munich, admitted to having been an enthusiastic Nazi, but acknowledged that he had been utterly wrong. He realized that his poor judgment in the 1930s made it impossible for him to re-enter the Foreign Service later.

In 1937 Hensel's post as the Party's 'man of confidence' was assumed by Wilm Stein, who had been correspondent for the liberal *Vossische Zeitung* in Moscow and Warsaw before being appointed press attaché to the German Embassy in Moscow. When I first met him as a newspaper correspondent in Moscow in 1931, he gave me the impression of being a thorough democrat. His wife was a cultivated and patriòtic Pole. I was therefore surprised to encounter him later as a *Vertrauensmann* of the Party. To me he was always an enigma, and every conversation with him left me more baffled as to how he had found his way into the Nazi Party.

Hensel and Stein were certainly not militant Nazis. I had friendly, even cordial, relations with them, though I took care never to express my innermost opinions in their presence. I know that every Party member, especially a *Vertrauensmann*, had to report anti-Nazi attitudes or remarks, and that any member failing to do so risked prosecution, so I shielded them from the dilemma of having to choose between their friendship for me as a colleague and their loyalty to the Party.

What is surprising is that Party members who visited the Embassy from Germany did not interfere with our various evasions of Nazi discipline. Their reason for this was utterly practical: they knew that were they to get into trouble in the USSR, we were the only ones who could help them.

There were no strongly ideological Nazis among the Foreign Service officers at the Moscow Embassy, but there were several on the staff, especially among those who were of Russian–German origin. Such people staunchly supported National Socialism because of its uncompromising hostility towards Communism. Having lost their property and position in Russia, they looked to the Nazis to set things right for them. In all fairness, however, it must be stated that these members of our staff had a poor knowledge of National Socialism, having spent little time in Germany. Thus, even if many of them joined the Party voluntarily, it remained for them more an abstraction than a reality, more linked with their Russian experience than with the life of Germany itself.

In this context the example of the Permanent Secretary at the time of the Nazi take-over is pertinent. Bernhard von Bülow was a convinced democrat. Like everyone else in the diplomatic service, he agonized over the question of whether members of the Foreign Ministry could avoid joining the Party. He sought the advice of the former Chancellor, Heinrich Brüning, who later emigrated to the United States. Brüning's advice was that by all means Bülow should join the Nazi Party if they asked him to do so. After all, Brüning argued, it would be better for responsible people to remain in the diplomatic service than to have them replaced by convinced Nazis. Bülow himself did not follow this advice but felt obliged to pass it on to many others.

One German diplomat in Russia who shared Brüning's view and acted on it was Karl-Georg Pfleiderer, who was serving in Leningrad at the time Hitler came to power. When Pfleiderer paid his periodic visits to the Embassy we had heated arguments over whether or not one should join the Party. Pfleiderer thought it essential to do so, since only in this way could one hope to influence Hitler's policies. I could see his point, of course, but had to explain to him that I could not join under any circumstances, since I was a non-Aryan. Later, when Pfleiderer was transferred to Berlin, the Gestapo managed to get hold of the diary that he kept in the USSR and used evidence in it to send him to the camps. The active intervention of the Permanent Under-Secretary, Baron Ernst von Weizsäcker, succeeded in winning Pfleiderer's freedom.

Some members of our Embassy staff joined the Party early, and all those who did not do so were obliged to become members of some sort of affiliated organization. By 1939, 95 per cent of the members of the diplomatic service had joined. Precisely the same situation existed in the Italian Foreign Service.

My colleagues realized that I was non-Aryan and that I therefore could not join the Party in any circumstances. They appreciated my predicament and were full of understanding. I knew that their expression of concern grew not merely from personal sympathy but from basic opposition to Hitler's racial policies, which to a man they considered loathsome. Indeed, in the entire Ministry of Foreign Affairs there were only two or three people who subscribed to the view that non-Aryans should be dismissed; otherwise, the policy was to hold on to non-Aryans

99

as long as possible. If, finally, a non-Aryan had to be dismissed, the Ministry saw to it that he found a good job either in Germany or in a foreign country. The best proof of the sincerity with which that policy was pursued can be found in the fact that, when a new diplomatic service was established in 1949, practically all the non-Aryans who had been on the rolls during the thirties returned to Germany to re-enter the service. As a result, there was a period in the fifties in which the Federal Republic was represented abroad by some half dozen or so non-Aryan ambassadors.

From an early date my friends began making enquiries about what they could do 'to assure that Johnnie is not kicked out'. From 1933, Theo Kordt, the personal assistant to State Secretary von Bülow; Kordt's younger brother, Erich; and Hasso von Etzdorf of the Personnel Office, did everything they could to protect me. Another of my protectors was the Chief of Personnel, Hans Schroeder, who was an old member of the Nazi Party. Schroeder had served as Consular Secretary in Egypt, where he had gained the confidence of Rudolph Hess, through whose offices he was given his post as Chief of Personnel. Surprisingly, I could not have hoped for a better man in this position, for he worked actively and discreetly to shield people like myself. This was no easy task, and certainly won him no gratitude from the Party. His courage is remembered by all of us with immense gratitude.

In 1935, the Nazis passed the racial laws which they had been applying without legislation since 1933. These stipulated, among other things, that non-Aryans were no longer allowed to hold public office. Only non-Aryans who had served in the front line in World War I and those who had been civil servants before 1918 were exempted. On this point the Nazis fell victim to their own propaganda, believing that all non-Aryans were cowards and had surely not fought for their country in World War I. To the Nazis' great astonishment, not only had most Jews fought bravely and shed their blood for Germany, many of them were even highly decorated. A typical case was Robert Ulrich, a counsellor in our Ministry. He had been severely wounded while serving as commanding officer of a unit that had included Rudolph Hess. The result was that other pretexts had to be found to remove non-Aryans from public office. By 1939 I was the only non-Aryan left in the German Foreign Service. When I discussed my plight with Theo Kordt in Berlin in 1933 I had not realized that the exemption for past military service might apply to me. But Kordt remembered that at the age of fifteen I had run away to join the armed forces. This was to be my salvation.

My lot was greatly eased by the fact that all three of my Ambassadors stood up for me. Dirksen made his support clear from the outset, and I had no fears during his tenure as Ambassador. Nadolny, too, was on my side, and strongly urged me not to give up my job. He did this, I believe, out of the optimistic conviction that the National Socialism regime would either have to change or that it would collapse. I was grateful to him for his advice, since it would have been no easy matter for a non-Aryan to find another job in Germany at the time. Most of my non-Aryan colleagues who had left the service emigrated from Germany, and those who did not do so lived under humiliating conditions. Nadolny was by no means naïve, however, and knew that I could be expelled from the service at any time, notwithstanding Hitler's law on veterans. He therefore offered to keep me on as his private aide in the event that I was actually forced to resign.

Before Nadolny's own involuntary resignation, I gave little thought to my own situation. I had assumed that the system was so odious to God and morality that it would destroy itself. I believed in the proverb, 'The mills of God grind slowly, yet they grind exceeding small' (*Gottes Mühlen mahlen langsam aber gut*). Nadolny's departure forced me to consider my own position more seriously. Denied his protection and seeing his tragic failure, I asked myself whether I should not also leave.

I did not, however, largely because Nadolny's successor, Count Schulenburg, made it clear from the time of his first arrival that I could count on his support and protection. These were not empty words. He did not miss any opportunity to intervene on my behalf with important personalities when he was in Berlin on official or private business. In 1934 I was still an attaché on probation, but for a year I had been due to be made a permanent civil servant and appointed Secretary of Legation. The Foreign Ministry did not dare to ask the Nazi Party to agree to such an appointment because they were afraid that this might lead to my dismissal from the service. Only after four years of persistent pressure did Schulenburg succeed in getting my promotion.

With my decision to stay, I finally realized the extent to which I had been cushioned from the full impact of National Socialism by being in Russia. Notwithstanding my frequent visits to Germany throughout those years, I had shared Nadolny's view that Hitler's party must somehow evolve and thus avert disaster. Several of my younger colleagues agreed with me. This hope was fed by our readings in the works of historians and scholars, who pointed out that no movement is able to maintain its ideological zeal for long, and that in any circumstances Nazi ideology provided little of the rigorous structure that Communism could claim in the writings of Marx. For some of us it was also fed by a gloomy understanding of what was occurring elsewhere in the world, a view which made it easier to rationalize events in Germany.

One day late in 1934 I found myself talking to George Kennan about the grim situation in Germany. He pointed out the analogies between what was taking place in Germany and in the USSR and suggested darkly that it could occur elsewhere as well. He saw that this was no consolation to me, but went on to draw a comparison between programmes for economic recovery being pursued in Germany and those advocated by Roosevelt's New Deal in America. He then drew a comparison between the racial ideas of the National Socialists in Germany and of the Ku Klux Klan in America. The difference, he stressed, was that the Ku Klux Klan was not taking over the American government. If it were to do so, though, and if it were to link up with the New Deal, he felt that something similar to National Socialism could emerge in the United States.

Two events combined to bring home my danger to me. First, the shooting of Ernst Röhm in 1934 forced on me the realization that there existed no free courts in Germany and that one could henceforth be arrested without trial. This gave me a terrible shock, the more so since we had come naïvely to assume that such a destruction of justice as had taken place in the Soviet Union could not happen in Germany.

Second, Nadolny's failure to make headway with Hitler convinced me that the policies of the National Socialist government could only lead to war. I realized that the driving force for Germany's economic recovery was the armaments industry, and that war has always been the best means of keeping ideological fires burning. Thus, even as I lamely tried to argue that the crisis had passed, I recognized that a new and greater crisis was being prepared.

Even though I am a Protestant, and perhaps not a very good one at that, I have often felt that I live my life under a protective angel. One could say just as easily that I have been damned lucky, but I would prefer to think that God or some angel has looked after me at critical points in my life. I was to have particular need for such protection during the decade that began in the autumn and winter of 1934.

Between February and May 1935, I returned to Potsdam for three months in order to do my service in the reserve. I did this with the avowed intention of strengthening my position in the event that I should have to leave Moscow at some future point. I had at least a limited success in that I was promoted to the rank of sergeant (*Wachtmeister*). Again, the non-Aryan laws prevented me from advancing further.

I had no doubt that my unit, the Fourth Cavalry Regiment, was on my side. This was a very conservative body, and there was little pro-Nazi sentiment among its members. The uninhibited conversation in the officers' mess showed clearly the extent of their hostility. One evening, conversation turned to the subject of the Nazi hero, Horst Wessel. My neighbour at the table proclaimed categorically that Wessel was not a hero but a pimp (*Zuhälter*). I immediately seconded him with the observation that Horst Wessel was, to say the least, a disreputable figure. At this point the young ADC, Bogislaw von Bonin, stalked in and told us that this was no fit discussion for an officers' mess. For a while it looked as if a crisis was brewing and that von Bonin would report us both. Fortunately, Major York Bötterling stepped in and announced that it was unimportant whether Horst Wessel was a hero or a pimp; the only thing that mattered was comradeship in the Fourth Cavalry Regiment. With this, he ordered a bottle of champagne and commanded us all to drink the health of the regiment.

Later, von Bonin, like Rommel and various other officers, became an opponent of National Socialism. Contrary to the Führer's orders, he commanded the retreat of the German troops from Warsaw, for which he was sent to a concentration camp. At the end of the war he was liberated in the South Tyrol, along with other prominent prisoners.

My fellow volunteers and I had strong political views, but we quickly demonstrated that our military capacities were of a lesser order. We participated in the regimental manoeuvres that spring. When they were completed, the officer in charge, a First Lieutenant von Winterfeld, brought us together for the customary evaluation. Rather than go through the long litany of individual criticisms that was usual on such occasions, he declared to us; 'Gentlemen, I can be brief: the Intelligentsia is shit' (*Intelligenz-Scheisse*). If he meant that we were too clever to use our common sense, I am afraid he was quite right.

The most important event of my service in Potsdam was that I became engaged. Before leaving Moscow I had written to old cronies in Munich to enquire whether any mutual friends happened to be in Berlin at the time. My friends had apparently long since decided that I should marry Elisabeth von Redwitz, but were wise enough to give me three names rather than just their one recommendation. On my first weekend leave I visited my parents, and for reasons that I myself could not explain, began telephoning Elisabeth von Redwitz. After calling every hour for an entire day, I finally reached her at 11:00 p.m., just as she was returning from a skiing holiday. Having not seen her since she was a cheerful girl twelve years old, I was keen to renew our acquaintance. The following Saturday we met, and everything clicked at once. Within one more week we were engaged. I can still see my father's astonished face upon learning of my intentions, but Pussi, as Elisabeth was known to everyone, immediately won his heart as well. After a riotous trip to the Caucasus with Count Schulenburg and his daughter, Pussi and I were married in November 1935, and settled down in Moscow.

When I proposed to Pussi, I felt obliged to tell her immediately that I was in difficulties with the Nazi Party on account of my non-Aryan status and that if she married me she would have to share these difficulties too. This alone was good reason for her to have rejected me, but she did not. Rather, she explained that her family's strong tradition of Catholicism and monarchism – which she fully shared – and its deep ties in Bavaria prevented her from having the slightest sympathy for the National Socialists.

Once again Hitler's racial laws affected my life directly as it became doubtful that we would be permitted to marry. After a period of great anxiety that extended until the last moment, we did get married, but the fact that I had to force this horror on to my future wife was deeply humiliating to me, just as it was humiliating to know that my career was in constant jeopardy for the same reason. Hitler's insult to the German nation was no abstraction for me; with my marriage I had to realize that it would touch my wife's life and the life of every member of our future family.

8

A WATCH ON GERMANY
AND THE USSR

From the time of Hitler's rise to power, Germany's diplomats – or those of us who opposed him – were put in a peculiarly difficult position. As diplomats, we were obliged to defend the position of our government; as individuals we knew that we could not possibly do so. All this was rendered the more difficult by the often inadequate sense we had in Moscow of what was occurring at home. For example, in January 1933, we got news of the Reichstag fire. The official version, of course, was that the Communists had set fire to the Reichstag. From the beginning, the Embassy was suspicious of this version, since it was unconvincingly presented and poorly documented. The doubts were there from the outset, but we were slow to receive sufficient information to permit us to conclude that it had actually been set on fire by the Nazis themselves. In June 1934, we were shocked by the execution of Ernst Röhm and Hitler's actions against the SA, in the course of which several entirely innocent people were killed. Not only did we have to think over such events in isolation, but we were in the embarrassing position of having to respond to questions on them from many of the other foreigners residing in Moscow. The Scandinavians in general and the Danish Minister Ove Engell in particular were especially incensed that so many hundreds of people were being cruelly sent to death without trial. It was useless to repeat the official line about their being dangerous radicals or launching a subversive mutiny against Hitler. The best we could do was to express the hope – albeit one that I had personally abandoned – that following this gruesome event Nazi ideology would weaken and life would gradually return to normal.

The only factor that alleviated the difficulty of our situation was that the increasing brutality of Stalin's practices in the same period distracted Western diplomats from events occurring in Germany. As the purges began in earnest after a brief respite in 1933–34, Soviet citizens, too, showed less concern over the progress of Nazism in Germany. At times this had absurd consequences. In the spring of 1935, I went on a trip of several weeks to the Caucasus. As it happened, my arrival in Georgia coincided with the postponement of the Comintern meetings that were to have been held in Moscow. One evening in Tblisi, seated in a restaurant high above the city with a wonderful view of Mt David and the surrounding area, I found myself confronted by a particularly surly waiter. 'You are probably one of those foreign Communists who came here for the Comintern meetings,' he said. 'Now, with your meeting postponed, you are travelling all over the country getting good food and housing from the Soviet government and not knowing a damn thing about how the poor Soviet citizens are actually living. If I could, I'd send you right to hell. Anyway, I want you to know that I think you are corrupt and useless.'

I assured the man that I was not a Communist. He immediately interrupted me, fuming that in addition to my other sins I was a coward, and that I was hiding the fact that I was a Communist for fear that he would throw me down the terrace. Only when I showed him my passport was I able to convince him that I was a German diplomat. I explained to him that he need have no fear that our government was run by the Bolsheviks, at which point his mien changed entirely and he asked me please to forgive him for his anger; he really had thought that I was one of those wretched foreign Communists.

After Nadolny's abrupt dismissal, I felt an urgent need to go myself to Germany in order to get a first-hand impression of what was taking place there. My life in Moscow was particularly busy at the time, however, so I did not get back to Germany for an extended period again until the summer of 1936, when I accompanied Schulenburg on a visit to Berlin. I had wanted to attend the Olympic Games and actually witnessed the arrival of Jesse Owens and the other American athletes in mid-July. The foreign athletes and visitors, white and coloured alike, received a tumultuous welcome from the German public. Far from taking this as a manifestation of self-confident chauvinism, I saw it as a clear indication that the Germans wanted to show the rest of the world that they appreciated the contact that the Games provided. In the end I did not attend the Games themselves, for I was overcome by the feeling that they were nothing but a fake, a theatrical event devised by the Nazis to pull a veil over everything that was happening in our country.

Having turned my back on the Olympic Games, I then perversely attended the Nazi Party rally in Nuremberg on 8–14 September, 1936. Erich Kordt, to my surprise, had urged me to go to Nuremberg on the ground that it would provide me with the clearest possible vision of Hitler's full impact on Germany. I told him that not only did I not want to go but that I was not permitted to attend since I was not a member of the Party and a non-Aryan besides. Not being a member of the German nation as Hitler had defined it, I had no business in Nuremberg. Kordt responded to this with the proposal that I be sent to Nuremberg disguised as a distinguished foreign guest. With Kordt's help, I arrived at Nuremberg next day, a 'foreign visitor' in my own country.

This was a foolish risk to have taken. I was given tickets to the demonstrations and meetings. I went twice to the mass meetings – first to the rally in honour of the *Reichsarbeitsdienst* and then to the army rally. I must admit that it was most impressive. I was particularly intrigued to hear Hitler orate. As I had known he would, he started his speeches almost muttering, in order to discern the mood of the crowd. Once he had its measure, he began gradually raising his voice and used all his demagogic arts in order to induce them to turn off their brains.

After the war when I heard these same speeches on recordings, I was at a loss to explain how they could have been so effective only a few years before. Hitler seemed nothing more than the caricature portrayed by Charlie Chaplin in *The Great Dictator*. The fact is, though, that the direct impact of the speeches on all one's senses was immeasurably more powerful than the flat scratchings of the recordings might suggest. The rallies, too, were beautifully organized, and even the smaller meetings were choreographed down to the second. One would have had to be exceptionally insensitive not to have been awed by the sense of organization and control which these meetings exuded. For me personally, they were frightening and repulsive, but I had to admit their effectiveness.

In his speech at the Nuremberg rally, Hitler made violent attacks on the Soviet Union and even spoke of the Ukraine and the Urals as being within Germany's sphere of interest. I should have been more upset than I was by this, but by then we had become accustomed to such oratory. One could easily pass over the statements about the Ukraine as mere demagogic outbursts and think instead of the other deeds that were being done by Hitler's government, deeds of which nearly all the German people approved. During the spring of 1936 German troops had re-occupied the Rhineland. Practically every German greeted this with enthusiasm, and I especially, since my first assignment at the Foreign Office had been on the desk of the Occupied Territories. At the same time, though, I could not help but fear that the move might evoke some reaction from the other side.

Much later I learned from Count Schulenberg, who was on good terms with von Neurath at the time of the re-occupation, that Hitler himself felt similar fears. According to Neurath's report, news of strongly adverse criticism in England and France caused Hitler to propose to Neurath that the German troops be withdrawn. To this suggestion, Neurath responded that there was always time to withdraw but now it would be better to wait and see whether we might get away with it. We did.

Hitler's wild outbursts against the Soviet Union were made less fearsome by the progress of German trade with the USSR. Notwithstanding Hitler's abusive attacks, the shipment of German industrial goods to Russia continued. Hitler was fully aware of this, but for the time being seemed willing to live with the inconsistency. This duality continued right down to 1939, when we began negotiating seriously with the Russians for a treaty. Not only did German exports to the Soviet Union continue amidst all the strains in our relationship in the late 1930s, but the German government also continued to approve Soviet requests for credit, often for significant amounts, and even to initiate them. In 1935 when Hjalmar Schacht proposed a generous new arrangement, the Russians not only accepted it but, to our surprise, suggested that it be used to cover the shipment of war materials. In this instance, however, the discussions did not lead to positive results.

Why did the violently anti-Soviet government of Hitler continue such policies? The answer, or so it seemed to us at the time, was that Hitler's officials, and to some extent even Hitler himself, considered the economic recovery of the country to be more important even than its ideological purity. This was certainly the case with Schacht, who was willing to do whatever was called for in order to finance Germany's rearmament. Göring could never be accused of fondness for the Soviet Union, but because he was charged with responsibility for the Four-Year Plan, he and his colleagues could not avoid taking advantage of the benefits offered by Russian trade. Several of his subordinates, who were drawn from the Foreign Ministry, were enthusiastic at the prospect of maintaining good relations with Russia. Indeed, Göring's own cousin, a ministerial counsellor in the Ministry of Economics, was a staunch supporter of trade with the Soviet Union because the Soviets paid in gold. Behind all this lay concern for Germany's balance of payments, which caused Schacht at one point to require foreigners with money in Germany to spend it there rather than take it abroad. Germans were urged to buy German goods. The slogan, 'Germans, buy German cars!' was sarcastically changed to 'Germans, buy German camels!'

Along with these aspects of German–Soviet relations during the 1930s, there were at least two other, less favourable developments that had to be taken into account in evaluating Hitler's diatribes against the Soviet people and their state. First, as early as the chancellorship of Brüning, one could sense in Moscow that the Russians were sending out feelers towards the West, since they could no longer be confident about Germany's attitude towards them. Seeing that the Germans were recasting their relations with France and England, Litvinov and his colleagues in the Soviet government came to fear that the USSR was becoming isolated. To overcome this, they engineered the entry of the Soviet Union into the League of Nations just at the time Germany walked out. Watching Russia's move towards the West, Schulenburg readily admitted that Germany had left the Russians with no alternative. Far from considering this the chance result of reversible decisions in Berlin, Schulenburg considered the Soviet move to be a fundamental reorientation which we would be quite unable to influence.

Second, the mass purges in the USSR had a direct impact on German–Soviet relations, especially as the Soviet witch-hunt gained its maximum fury in 1937. Soviet purges were not new to us. Our first direct taste of the Stalinist terror occured with the trial of Ambassador von Dirksen's would-be assassin in 1932. A Soviet citizen by the name of Stern had tried to assassinate our Ambassador while he was driving through Moscow in his chauffeur-driven car. By mistake he fired at the Ambassador's car in which the counsellor, von Twardowski, was sitting and wounded him in the left hand. Stern was immediately arrested and the Soviet officials issued an apology. At the trial, over which the notorious Kyrlenko presided, an accomplice by the name of Vasiliev was brought forth and accused of seeking to disturb German–Soviet relations and thereby to strengthen his own anti-Bolshevik faction. An attempt was also made to blame the episode on the Polish government, since Twardowski's driver had a Polish name. But the main charges were against Stern, who stunned the courtroom by offering a full 'confession'. Then, having done so, he declared that everything he had said was untrue and had been extracted under duress. At that moment he was taken from the courtroom, only to reappear somewhat later with a fresh confession.

I have noted that we and our colleagues in the Polish Embassy were absolutely certain that there was no truth in this charge. Dirksen immediately handed in a strongly worded protest against the harassment of our driver, a Soviet citizen of Polish origin. To our surprise, the charges against him were dropped, although for some months we were extremely careful not to allow him out of the Embassy except at those times when he was actually driving Twardowski.

After this revolting incident, our staff had avoided Soviet political trials, lest our presence there might in some way seem to legitimize them. I remember well Count Schulenburg's indignation and bewilderment when the American ambassador, Davies, attended the show trials. Day after day he betook himself to the ballroom of the former Noblemen's Assembly as if the events occurring were as innocent as the dances held there in former days. Even worse, Davies managed to convince himself that there existed serious grounds for the charges that the prosecutors were putting forward. 'Chip' Bohlen, George Kennan, and the other younger members of the American Embassy could not have been more deeply disturbed and embarrassed by Davies' attitude.

Though we did not attend the trials, we followed them with rapt interest. Thanks in part to our detachment from the day-to-day horrors in the courtroom, my colleagues and I were the better able to appreciate the careful method that underlay the process. In a systematic way without parallel in the modern world, including the Terror of the French Revolution, Stalin eliminated his enemies on both Left and Right. Many of these belonged to the national minorities, such as Jews, Poles, Latvians, and Caucasians. Such non-Russians had played a central role in both the Revolution of 1905 and the Bolshevik Revolution, having been long suppressed by the tsars. Most were replaced by Russians. Only some Caucasians were spared, Stalin himself being a Georgian.

We had no doubt that this carefully executed series of political murders conformed to a master plan, to which the dramatic changes occurring in the schools and universities, in the army, and in society at large were related as corollaries. Far from snowballing out of control, the purges proceeded according to plan. Far from being irrational, they struck me at the time as being essential steps in the construction of Stalin's form of state capitalism. When Stalin finally succeeded in mothballing the Comintern in 1934 he had completed the transition to his new form of Great Russian nationalism.

The purges destroyed most of the German Embassy's contacts with the Commissariat for Foreign Affairs. Frequently our telephone calls to specific people there met with the response 'Ego nyetu' ('He is not here'). The closest we ever had to an explanation was when we were told that a person had been 'transferred'. Otherwise, they simply dropped out of the picture. The sudden disappearance of men with whom we had worked for months or even years struck terror in each of us. Though we had never considered our Soviet counterparts as personal friends, we had both respect and a degree of affection for men like Yenukidze and Ordzhonikidze, and their fate profoundly disturbed us.

The purges would have adversely affected our relations with Moscow in any circumstances; the fact that many German subjects were being caught in them exacerbated matters. This was not unprecedented, of course, since German engineers (and French and British as well) had been arrested during the 1929 Shakhty trials. But the movement gained new intensity in 1936. Our problems were multiplied by the fact that the Soviets, in violation of our joint consular treaty, did not permit us access to those Germans who had been arrested. As we learned later when debriefing them, every one eventually signed a confession.

The method employed in every case was the same, namely, to insist that the German Embassy had no interest in their welfare and then to point out that a careful investigation of the person's entire past had been carried out. All the now well-known methods were applied, including threats that action would be taken against Russian girlfriends, that trumped-up photographs would be sent to wives back in Germany, and that the interrogation would be pushed to whatever point was necessary to break the victim. The confessions were signed with eerie regularity. Only in one instance did we manage to rescue the victim before he broke. When we finally gained the release of our consular officer in Novosibirsk, Hermann Strecker, he frankly admitted that had another week elapsed he, too, would have cracked.

The Nazi government was frustrated and embarrassed that Germans were breaking under interrogation. It determined to seek revenge. In 1937 there was a strong feeling that Soviet subjects in Germany should be arrested and given some of their own medicine. All of us in the Embassy spoke out against this plan, arguing, on the one hand, that the only Russians in Germany were high officials and, on the other hand, that by arresting them in Germany we would probably earn Stalin's gratitude for doing a job which he himself would want to have done later anyway. We received clear hints from the Russians that it would be vain for us to retaliate.

The German–Soviet rapprochement that was eventually achieved had this welter of contradictory tendencies. Even while Hitler was uttering his wild diatribes against Russia, the staff of the German Embassy in Moscow was daily acting on its hope that a rapprochement could still be achieved. Even as the purges were claiming the lives of thousands of people, several ministries were maintaining quite normal relations with their Soviet counterparts.

The German–Soviet rapprochment that was eventually achieved had been under study for a long time within our Embassy. Von Twardowski, as a matter of routine, assigned 'Winter Tasks' to each younger member of the Embassy. Such tasks usually involved writing a longish paper on a historical topic or on a political, economic, or diplomatic theme. During my third winter in Moscow, I was assigned the task of preparing an essay on Soviet–Italian relations. The purpose of this paper, of course, was to demonstrate the possibility of the Soviet Union maintaining good relations with a Fascist country. As I began my research I quickly discovered that this thesis could in fact be defended without twisting the evidence; from the outset Mussolini had taken care to keep Italy's relations with Moscow on an even keel.

Once I realized this, however, my zeal for working out the details of the project waned. I procrastinated and offered only the feeblest excuses whenever Twardowski pressed me on my progress. As things became more desperate I had the brilliant idea of asking my friend in the Italian Embassy, Micki Lanza, if he had to hand any reasonably detailed analysis of Russian–Italian relations since World War I. Luckily for me he had precisely what I needed. My Italian was not very good, but it was stronger than my academic scruples. I reworked Lanza's document in an appropriate manner and submitted it. Twardowski in turn passed it back to our Foreign Ministry. I expected the paper to die upon submission and was therefore astonished when Twardowski told me he expected a strong reaction from Berlin. To my amazement, somebody actually read it there, and cabled Moscow enquiring whether the author could substantiate his interesting arguments. Naturally I could do so, but was in no position to show my hand. Fortunately, I had also made use of some material from the American correspondent, Louis Fischer, and could cite that with impunity.

The continuing optimism over German–Soviet relations that Schulenburg and the rest of us showed in the face of the counter-evidence made a strong impression among the other diplomats. Indeed, Schulenburg's optimism gave rise to various rumours among other foreign diplomats in Moscow, none of them with any basis in fact. In 1937, at least, there were practically no solid grounds for thinking that a decisive change in German–Soviet relations was in the offing.

Why did such optimism exist? It was based first on our understanding of history. We knew full well that, in spite of the Great War, German–Russian relations had been cordial over most of the previous century. It was hard to believe that a return to such a condition would not be in the natural order of things. Second, we were convinced that it would be in Germany's interest to do so, and that in the long run countries will always pursue their own interests. None of us could conceive that a world power would adopt a policy that amounted to suicide.

The Sino-Japanese conflict of 1936 made a strong impact on the foreign policy of the Soviet Union and on German–Soviet relations in particular. At the outbreak of the fighting between Japan and China we did not fully appreciate how far the Japanese were prepared to go. Most of us in the Embassy assumed that we were witnessing a repetition of the nineteenth-century efforts by the great powers to pry away a harbour or small coastal district from China. It was not long before we realized that the Japanese aspired to control nothing less than the whole of Manchuria and that they were, in fact, seeking the kind of *Lebensraum* that Hitler had advocated in *Mein Kampf* as essential for powerful nations.

In spite of the German–Japanese alliance, my own sympathies and those of practically everyone in the Embassy were with the Chinese. There were many reasons for this, but none was more important in my own mind than the fact that among the many German officers serving with Chiang Kai-shek were several who were opposed to Hitler. At one point the head of the military mission was the famous General Hans von Seeckt, under whom my father served during World War I. Later, during the battle of Shanghai, we all cheered for the Chinese, because their forces had been trained by German officers. Everyone at the Embassy exulted over the stiff resistance the Chinese put up.

A Japanese success would give them a common border with the Soviet Union and thus present the Russians with the nightmare possibility of a war on two fronts. The reality of this threat was borne home to the Russians with great force when heavy fighting broke out between Japanese and Soviet troops on the Soviet–Manchurian border near Lake Hanka. We were intrigued by the Soviets' meticulous refusal to violate the border, although had they done so they would have had a much easier time in attacking the Japanese positions on the high Hanka hills. Through our own sources, we had reports of hard fighting and considerable losses on the Soviet side. The Soviets finally succeeded in throwing back the Japanese assault, and occupied the hills again.

In a related battle in the Mongolian desert, the Soviets tried out their new tanks, thanks to which the later Marshal Grigori Zhukov gained his first real experience in the use of that weapon in battle. He was to apply this with great success in the battles against us at the end of the war. Neither the Soviet nor the Japanese press recorded the event at all; we concluded that the Russians must have won, however, since after a lapse of several weeks the Soviet provincial press made mention of an agreement for the repatriation of the Japanese dead. A third Soviet–Japanese military engagement in 1936 took place on the Amur River, where numerous small battles were fought. These were duly noted in the Soviet press, but not in such a way as to give rise to any expectations that this limited war could expand into a broader conflict.

It was clear that the Soviets were doing everything in their power to prevent a war on two fronts. The Soviet obsession with this spectre (an obsession that recalls Bismarck) led them to support Chiang Kai-shek, who was fighting the Japanese, and to withhold support from Mao Tse-tung and the Communists, who were focusing their attacks against Chiang. Indeed, they urged Mao Tse-tung to desist and join with Chiang in a united fight against the Japanese intruders. The Soviet concern was not so much to secure the victory of Communism in China as to prevent a possible attack on the USSR. Mao Tse-tung and his comrades were never to forget this, which probably goes far towards explaining the open hostility that later erupted between the two Communist powers.

Faced with the possibility of a war on two fronts, the Russians made haste to improve their relations with the West, and especially with Germany. This placed the Commissar of Foreign Affairs, Litvinov, in an extremely delicate position. As a Jew, he could not help but oppose the racial policies being pursued by Hitler's government, but at the same time, he could not escape the logic of the situation that was forcing his country to mend its bridges with Germany. Moreover, like many Russian Jews, he maintained a deep affection for German culture which caused him, in conversation with Nadolny, to remark how greatly he regretted that he could no longer travel in Germany. In his frequent talks with Schulenburg, Litvinov often pointed out that there was no reason why good relations should not exist between a Communist Soviet Union and Nazi Germany.

Litvinov buttressed this argument by pointing to the harmonious relationship between the Soviet Union and Fascist Italy. Had he chosen to do so, he might also have cited Soviet–Turkish relations as an example of two states with radically different ideologies co-existing peacefully. On the one hand, the Soviets raised little objection to the systematic suppression of all Communist activity in Turkey by the Turkish government; on the other hand, the Turks turned a blind eye to the ruthless force that the Soviet government used against all movements for Turkish autonomy within the USSR.

The success of the *Anschluss* of Austria in 1938 upset the Soviet leaders immensely. From various sides, the German Embassy got clear indications that Stalin interpreted this as proof that the Western powers were not sufficiently determined to be good partners. This made the Soviets more cautious than ever not to provoke Hitler. Stalin's caution was probably strengthened further by the terrible bloodletting that he himself had only recently instigated in his purge of the officer corps of the Red Army. Our military attaché, General Ernst Köstring, knew from the outset that the purge was not confined to the generals but reached down to the level of junior officers.

To realize the true character of the Soviet Union's military situation only made our difficulties more acute in reporting on it to Berlin. On the one hand, we could describe the results of the purges as disastrous for the Red Army. This would indicate to many reasonable people in Berlin that the possibility for an accommodation between Germany and the USSR was growing. But at the same time we knew full well that Hitler might read such a report as an invitation to take advantage of Russia's weakness. Yet if we emphasized the extent to which the Russians were still capable of putting up a strong fight, we could be sure that Hitler would denounce us for having been hood-winked. In the end, we decided that our responsibility was to point out the continuing strength of the Soviet Union. This was the drift of innumerable reports which Köstring prepared for the Ambassador's counter-signature. We soon discovered that Hitler interpreted our reports in exactly the opposite way to what we had expected. Learning that the Russians were still strong and were likely to grow yet stronger, Hitler resolved that he had better strike immediately, lest the Russians grow to the point where they could dictate their terms to all Europe.

At the end of 1937, the *Wehrmachtakademie* in Berlin asked Count Schulenburg to deliver a major address on the current situation in the Soviet Union. It was intended for an audience of senior army officers and for high officials from those ministries with which the army maintained the closest ties. They had turned to von der Schulenburg as the best informed and most authoritative spokesman on Soviet affairs in Germany. That they were prepared to bring the Ambassador back from Moscow indicated the importance which the military academy attached to the occasion. With no idea of the immense importance that Germany's conception of the USSR was soon to acquire, Schulenburg agreed to deliver the address and immediately mobilized the Embassy for its preparation.

As the Ambassador's personal assistant and secretary for political work, it fell to me to draft the lecture. I devoted several months to the task, ploughing through the Embassy archives, utilizing an excellent report that had been written in the mid-thirties by Herbert Dittmann, and, of course, conferring extensively with Hilger, Walther, and Schulenburg himself. Walther proved particularly helpful in my labours, for he systematically argued the opposite view to the one I was defending, notwithstanding that in reality we were in substantial agreement and that several of my leading arguments had originated with him.

The lecture was intended to provide a conspectus of Soviet domestic and foreign policies since 1917. Since Hitler's rise to power, much had been said and written about the USSR and Communism, but surprisingly little hard information had been put in the hands of Germany's leaders. Without saying so, I therefore tried at each point to present Schulenburg's statements in such a way as to adjust the generally held assumptions of the day. First among these was the conviction that the Soviet Union was the very embodiment of Marxism;

The unresolvable opposition between the necessities of the state and the doctrines of the Communist Party has revealed itself during recent years in all aspects of the political, social, economic, and cultural life of the Soviet Union. Contrary to the theory that the state would gradually become extinct, the Soviet state is intervening ever more frequently in every sphere of human activity.

The speech then traced the growing centralistic trend in the USSR in fields as diverse as the family, health, education, and the arts. I explained how, after a period of near anarchy during which the whole school system was handed over to the students, a new and more highly disciplined school system was emerging, with the teachers regaining their old prerogatives. 'All of these measures,' I concluded, 'rest on the realization that those trained in the earlier and strictly Marxist educational system were failing in practical life because they lacked the most basic knowledge.'

Most of these changes were attributed to the army's demand for the development of a large and healthy cadre of recruits; hence the new emphasis on the rights of fathers and on parental authority in general.

Hence, too, the renewal of examinations, grades, and discipline in the schools.

Against this background, I then set forth what subsequently has come to be known as the 'convergence theory' of Soviet development, except that in this case the USSR seemed to be converging not with the parliamentary states of Western Europe but with National Socialist Germany. I spoke of:

'... the desire to bring theatre closer to the people, to make it understandable to them ... Some time ago the directors of two Moscow theatres, Tairov and Meierhold, were severely reprimanded because their productions did not correspond to public taste and were staged in an artificial manner. Atonal music is no longer officially tolerated ... Cubist and Futurist paintings have been removed from the Moscow galleries ... and there is a highly visible return to tradition in architecture as well.'

The picture of contemporary Soviet culture that Schulenburg drew must have seemed unexpectedly and sinisterly familiar to a German in 1937. Schulenburg explained how National Socialism and Communism, starting from opposing positions, seemed to move towards one another. Whereas Stalin laid greater emphasis on the role of the individual in society, Hitler stressed the importance of the community (*Gemeinnutz geht vor Eigennutz*: common interest above private interest). Stalin went so far as to abandon the fundamental Communist principle of equal pay for everybody and instead coined the following slogans: 'Equalization is a *petit bourgeois* prejudice. The industrious and well-trained worker must earn more than the lazy and untrained.'

Similarly, the emphasis on reclaiming the Russian past must have been well-known to Schulenburg's audience. The lecture dealt in some detail with the attacks on Nikolai Bukharin, then editor of *Izvestiia*, and on the playwright Demian Bednii, who had had the temerity to criticize Russia's legendary national heroes and to ridicule the Christianization of Russia. I spoke, too, about the new Soviet history textbooks, in which:

even princes like Alexander Nevskii, who defeated the German knights in the year 1241 at Lake Peipus, and Prince Pozharskii, who led the fight against Poland at the beginning of the 17th century, are being presented as national heroes. Peter the Great appears as an 'intelligent and active Tsar' whose reforms are depicted in such a way as to make him appear a predecessor to Stalin. In brief, the material is consciously being shaped in such a way as to direct the thinking of young people into channels that serve the imperialistic goals of the Soviet state.

In the draft of the lecture that I submitted to Schulenburg, I developed this theme of convergence still further. I noted that both the Soviet and German systems were hostile to existing religion, and both regimes used the schools and public media to replace Christianity by a form of civil religion. This tendency seemed less developed in Germany than in the USSR, but it was widely felt that the eventual aim of many Nazis was to abolish religion entirely and to re-establish the ancient Germanic cult in its place. Both regimes, too, insisted that art was central to their activity and that government must ensure that it be positive, elevating, and accessible to the general public. And just as the Soviets were 'Russifying' their administration, the Germans were 'Aryanizing' theirs. Count Schulenburg excised these explicit comparisons, but left intact my general argument that the Soviet Union was gradually assuming a form familiar to non-Communist Germans.

Another central theme of the lecture was that the needs of the army lay behind many of the changes in the USSR:

... It is especially characteristic that the army is being pushed to the foreground at every opportunity and in such a way that the more doctrinaire followers of Marx and Lenin might see in it the embodiment of a hateful militarism. Not only does the expenditure on technical equipment for the army increase every year, but the living conditions of the soldiers and especially of the officer corps are being improved. During the past two years the 'comrade commander' has again become a 'lieutenant', the 'captain' a 'colonel', and the field marshals are more and more evident in public wearing pleated trousers, lacquered boots, and spurs.

Throughout the speech, I attempted to emphasize the dramatic changes that Stalin had introduced in the USSR. Realizing that von der Schulenburg's audience might be sceptical about such a thesis, I relied heavily on quotations from Leon Trotsky's recent book *The Revolution Betrayed*. Trotsky, I pointed out, accused Stalin of having introduced capitalistic methods and of having created a dictatorship solely out of his lust for power. This same motive underlay Stalin's foreign policy:

According to Trotsky's view, Stalin misuses the Comintern in order to get Communist parties of foreign countries to serve the interests of the Soviet Union. Slogans about world revolution and the need to protect the Soviet Union as the bearer of world revolution are now used simply to disguise the selfish goals of the USSR ... Trotsky and his followers denounce the Comintern's advocacy of popular fronts against fascism as a betrayal of the world revolution ... The Comintern has given orders to the French Communists to support the Blum government and its militaristic policies; those supporting Trotsky and the Fourth Internationale see the federation of all Chinese parties in the national front against Japan as a similar betrayal. According to them, Moscow is abandoning the Chinese Communists and supporting the Nationalists in order to build a bulwark against Japanese pressure on the Soviet borders. The strongest indignation of the Trotskyites is saved for Soviet policy in Spain. They reproach Stalin for supporting a popular front government there, a 'Kerensky regime', instead of working with all its might to bring about a genuine Communist revolution . . .

In order to defend himself against Trotsky's highly dangerous accusations, Stalin accused Trotsky of being unpatriotic and betraying his country.

How right Trotsky was in his reproach that Western Communist parties were being used by Stalin for Soviet national aims was most strikingly demonstrated after the signing of the German–Soviet treaty in 1939. Until then the French Communists had supported the French government and its defence policy against Germany. From one day to the next the French Communists were ordered by Moscow to co-operate with the Nazis in undermining the morale of the French population and of the French army in particular. Naturally these instructions were again revoked in 1941 after the invasion of the Soviet Union by Germany.

Throughout the speech, I tried to depict the Soviet Union as my colleagues and I had observed it during the 1930s, however greatly that differed from popular conceptions in Germany. Although Schulenburg softened somewhat my notion of a growing convergence between the USSR and Germany, it was strongly implied in practically every passage. The conversion of the 7 November and May-day festivities into popular feasts, the reintroduction and secularization of Christmas trees in 1935, the reawakening of pride in the Russian past, the strengthening of the national army, and the re-emergence of Russia's traditional great power foreign policy all had their parallels in Germany.

Notwithstanding the similarities in some fields of the development of the Soviet Union and Germany, the *leitmotiv* of Soviet foreign policy was the fear of Germany. Schulenburg pointed out that:

In Soviet eyes, Germany is the most dangerous enemy against whom it must prepare itself through all possible means. In earlier years Soviet propaganda may have deliberately invented the 'German danger' and exaggerated its importance in order to justify armament programmes. It is evident that the Soviet regime has itself fallen victim to this propaganda and is firmly convinced of the aggressive intentions of National Socialist Germany. The population is daily being indoctrinated with propaganda that encourages hatred and distrust of National Socialist Germany. The population is cut off from contact with foreign countries and is unable to form an independent opinion. Thus, anti-German propaganda exercises an increasingly strong influence over significant parts of the Soviet population.

Schulenburg's intention in thus explaining the situation was that Germany should start at once to remove the causes of such mistrust. The thrust of the entire speech was that, thanks to the growing similarity between the two countries, it would be easier than ever before to achieve this. To stress this point, I had Schulenburg begin the speech with the statement that:

I do not need to underline the important role which Russia has played in German history over the last two centuries or how significantly Russia's attitude towards Germany figured in Bismarck's policies at the time of the foundation of the Reich: You also know the important role of economic relations between Germany and Russia down to the World War.

By such statements, Schulenburg placed himself clearly on record as advocating a détente between the two great northern powers.

It is difficult to judge precisely the impact of Schulenburg's speech. It probably strengthened the hand of those in the army and Ministry of Foreign Affairs who were in favour of a serious approach to the Nazis bête-noire, the USSR. On the other hand, it contributed to the eventual tragedy of the Soviet–German pact of 1939 which paved the way for Hitler's attack on Poland.

In the autumn of 1937 I finally received word that I had to leave the Foreign Service. Schulenburg immediately informed the Ministry that he would resign his ambassadorship if I were forced out of the Foreign Service. He did this in his characteristically quiet way, without any uproar in the press or even in the diplomatic service at large. But he made it clear that he was not one of those ambassadors who tolerated the persecution of his assistants. Here, of course, he was referring to Franz von Papen, who did nothing when two of his assistants – Edgar Jung and Herbert von Bose – were shot on 30 June, 1934, and who, after being moved to Vienna, stood by while another of his aides, Baron Wilhelm von Ketteler, was murdered, and another, Fritz Günther von Tschirschky, was compelled to disappear overnight.

Schulenburg's ultimatum succeeded in keeping me in the service. One of the last documents signed by Neurath was my nomination to the rank of permanent civil servant as Third Secretary. This occurred in 1938, only a few days before he was replaced by von Ribbentrop. In the same order, however, the government declared that I could not advance to a higher position or become chief of a post.

Even before this, in the autumn of 1937, I had had a talk with my colleague in the American Embassy, Loy Henderson, and also Dan Lascelles from the British Embassy. I asked each of them whether they saw any possibility of me leaving the diplomatic service and working in some international organization, or perhaps a research institution or university. Both replied in the negative, assuring me that there were no posts available either in international agencies or in research institutes, and both advised me to stay in the German diplomatic service. Emigration from Germany would not have been simple under any circumstances, since I would have wanted to take my parents with me. For all these reasons, I resolved to stay in the Foreign Service for as long as it was possible to do so.

9

THE SUDETEN CRISIS
AND MY INITIATION INTO THE
RESISTANCE MOVEMENT

With the Sudeten crisis in 1938, the Moscow Embassy directed its attention towards trying to anticipate the response of the Soviet Union. Berlin was particularly anxious over the supposed build-up of Soviet air power in Czechoslovakia and bombarded us with countless enquiries about it. General Köstring rejected out of hand the possibility of such a build-up, pointing out that Czechoslovakia was too close to the surrounding German territories to permit the Russians such a ma-neouvre. He predicted that the Russians would do no more than put a few training aircraft into Czechoslovakia. His conviction was based more on intuition than on any detailed knowledge of the situation, but his belief that only a fool would move planes to Czechoslovakia was conveyed to Berlin with utter conviction. He proved to be correct.

It was at this point that I planned a trip to Odessa. I had applied for permission and for the necessary petrol as far back as May, but my permit was delayed for some while, obviously due to the unwillingness of the Russians to permit foreigners to travel through what might become contested territory, and due also to their general suspicion of foreigners, which had been increasing since January 1938, when various foreign consulates had been closed.

It was my impression that this action had been directed primarily against the Poles and then extended to the missions of other nations out of some misguided sense of impartiality. The Poles, after all, had special contacts in the Ukraine which assured Warsaw a steady flow of valuable information. Meeting with our various consular officers as they returned home via Moscow, I was left with the impression that Germany had not lost much through the closing of the consulates. The actions of foreigners were so closely regulated by 1938 that the consulates provided little information of sufficient value to offset the insupportable life that their staff was forced to lead.

The permit finally arrived in late July 1938, and I departed with my driver, Simon, a former Austrian prisoner-of-war who had settled in Moscow with his Russian wife. Although I certainly had not planned it this way, I was able to carry out quite useful research on the trip, thanks to the help of the NKVD. No sooner had we departed than I paused to inform my NKVD 'tails' that I had no intention of getting them into trouble but that I wanted to take tourist pictures so that I would have a record of the journey. I asked them if they would do me the favour of blowing their horn twice whenever we entered a military district so that I could be sure not to take photographs until they signalled to me again. They obliged, and Simon and I carefully marked every beep on the map.

On my swing through the south, I got considerable information on the stationing of Soviet troops but found no indications that they were preparing to move. Indeed, no one in the Embassy thought the Russians would go to war over Czechoslovakia, or that they were in a position to wage an aggressive war of any sort. Thanks to Köstring, we were all reading our copies of Caulaincourt's adventures in Russia at the time of the Napoleonic invasion. We read this like the Bible, and found in it confirmation of our view that the Russians would be as incapable of waging a successful war of aggression as they would be capable of defending themselves at home.

In August 1938, I went to Berlin, where I saw a lot of my close friends Eddie Brücklmeier and Erich Kordt. Since Eddie, Erich and his brother Theo were to play important roles in my life, a word on these three is in order. After Brücklmeier passed his second examination at the end of 1929 he had been transferred to Baghdad and then to Persia, where he served under Count Schulenburg, who was then Minister in Teheran. Brücklmeier was a most elegant young man, flawlessly dressed and the owner of a stable of polo ponies which he kept throughout his period of service in the Near East. During his early years in the Foreign Service, he gave every appearance of being concerned primarily with living an agreeable life. Gradually Eddie became more serious, however, and instead of sports and parties he directed his efforts towards fighting National Socialism and Hitler. He had a keen sense of humour, was quick in his judgments, and was unusually adept at handling crises.

Since the time Theo Kordt had played so important a part in keeping me in the Ministry of Foreign Affairs, I had stayed in close touch with both him and Erich. Whenever we met, we would exchange views on Nazi policies and express quite openly where we thought it was all leading. Erich Kordt had entered the service two years after me but had already made a name for himself. He came to the attention of Bernhard von Bülow, the Permanent Under-Secretary, who, in 1934, assigned him to Ribbentrop, who had just been appointed Hitler's roving ambassador. Kordt's particular mission was to travel everywhere with Ribbentrop and to report back to the Ministry of Foreign Affairs on his views and opinions. Surprisingly, Ribbentrop appreciated this, since he had formed a high opinion of Kordt's abilities and was confident that his reporting to the Ministry would be accurate in every respect. Between 1935 and 1938 I usually went to Berlin at least twice a year, and my first stop was always to visit Erich Kordt. He would regale me lengthily with tales of Ribbentrop, which kept me far better informed on policy matters than my rank entitled me to be.

Erich Kordt's tales would have been amusing had they not been so frightening. One day, for example, Ribbentrop asked Kordt various questions about Japanese–German relations over the centuries. Kordt did the best he could to sketch out the history of this relationship, stressing his view that some of the Japanese misgivings about Germany dated as far back as Shimonoseki. Ribbentrop, wide-eyed, asked Kordt what sort of a man Shimonoseki was, apparently not realizing that this was the name of a Japanese seaport and a treaty, not of a statesman. Such exchanges quickly convinced Kordt that Ribbentrop was utterly unqualified for his job.

When I came to see Erich Kordt in August 1938, he had no time to see me and asked Brücklmeier to brief me carefully on all the points that I was to relay to Schulenburg in Moscow. Brücklmeier, who was serving with Kordt as private secretary to Ribbentrop, went into great detail on the impending crisis in Czechoslovakia. Our conversation turned to the proper steps that 'we' – I was not yet sure who was included in this 'we' – should take so as to prevent the worst from happening. He explained that Erich's brother, Theo Kordt, who was counsellor at our Embassy in London, had orders to urge his British contacts to do everything in their power to resist Germany's moves against Czechoslovakia. Again, I wondered who had issued such orders, and who were Theo's British contacts. As our conversation progressed, Brücklmeier stressed the fact that I had better connections with foreign diplomats in Moscow than anyone else in our Embassy and suggested that it would be extremely useful if I could be in touch with them in order to carry out the same mission there as Theo Kordt was handling in London. At the least, we decided, such a move would help convince the British and French that the message they had received from London was not just the personal démarche of Theo Kordt. We would thus add weight to Theo's arguments.

I made no attempt to seek the origins of the instructions which Brücklmeier was giving me on the orders of Erich Kordt. He did state, though, that Colonel-General Ludwig Beck and General Erwin von Witzleben were prepared to take decisive steps against Hitler if the British and the French were to back Czechoslovakia against Hitler's attack. I thus understood that Kordt was in direct contact with people from the General Staff, but the identity of the other intermediaries remained unknown to me. Nor did I make any effort to find out more about them. Having worked in the Soviet Union, I appreciated perhaps better than most the means to which the machinery of state can resort in order to stamp out opposition. I was therefore the more willing to preserve my ignorance.

This is not to say that I was unaware of the extent of the military opposition to Hitler at the time of my meeting with Kordt. My father had been a close friend of General Werner von Fritsch, who had been removed, along with Konstantin von Neurath, in a most disgraceful way early in 1938. I knew from him of the events leading up to the purge of von Fritsch and had shared my father's sense of outrage.

Returning to Moscow, I reported immediately to my Ambassador on the European situation, dwelling particularly on the impending crisis in Czechoslovakia. I did not, however, report anything to Schulenburg about the possibility of a military coup against Hitler. After leaving the Ambassador, however, I resolved to get in touch with my closest friends among the various embassies in Moscow to tell them the true nature of the crisis that was so rapidly mounting. After careful thought I decided to whom I should make known my views and the highly confidential information on which they were based. My choice obviously lay among the various members of our Mutual Admiration Society. At the British Embassy, the member of the Society who seemed to me most likely to report fully on any statement I might give him was Fitzroy Maclean. Being on close terms with him, I felt able to be explicit.

Our first discussion took place on 22 August; the conversation Maclean reports in his memoirs as having taken place on that date actually occurred somewhat later. I tried to brief Fitzroy as fully as possible, and at the end I was left in no doubt that a full report would be made to London. After the war, when the British government published certain of its diplomatic papers relating to this era, I learned the precise character of my friend's report. Apparently, the British Ambassador,

Viscount Chilston, wasted no time, and despatched immediately the following message to Mr Collier, head of the Northern Department in the Foreign Office:

British Embassy, Moscow, August 23, 1938

My dear Collier:

Maclean had a not uninteresting conversation yesterday with the German Ambassador's Private Secretary, with whom he is on quite intimate terms and who had asked specially if he might come and have a talk with him.

Our German colleague began by saying that his Ambassador, who has just returned from leave, had been to see Litvinov and had told him that Germany would only invade Czechoslovakia in the event of an act of provocation on the part of the Czechs. To this Litvinov had replied that an act of provocation on the part of the Czechs was unthinkable and that the Germans would certainly be the aggressors in any conflict which might arise. If Germany were to invade Czechoslovakia, the French would undoubtedly mobilize and Great Britain, however much Mr. Chamberlain might dislike it, would be obliged to come to their assistance. The Soviet Union 'would do its best to help Czechoslovakia'. The Ambassador had duly telegraphed Litvinov's remarks to Berlin.

The German secretary went on to say that Dircksen [sic], in his reports from London, had given it as his considered view that Great Britain would certainly go to war if Czechoslovakia were invaded and France went to her assistance. He had also expressed the view that, if his Government wanted an understanding with Great Britain, now was the moment, as they could never hope to find a British Government better disposed towards Germany than that now in power and if nothing was done relations between the two countries could only deteriorate. Unfortunately however little attention was paid in Berlin to Dircksen's reports, or, for that matter, to those from other missions abroad. To the Führer it was quite incredible that the British should fail to understand that, in invading Czechoslovakia, Germany, in whatever circumstances the invasion took place, would simply be rescuing three and a half million Germans, who were hers by right. Whatever his Ambassadors reported, he simply could not believe that, when, as it seemed to him, it was so clear that Germany was in the

126

right, Great Britain would be prepared to go to war on behalf of Czechoslovakia. Ribbentrop shared, or affected to share, the Führer's optimism and the certainty that Great Britain would in no circumstances move and that Germany would be able to invade Czechoslovakia with impunity was reflected with alarming clearness in the dispatches and instructions which went out from the Wilhelmstrasse. This, our informant said, was very disturbing to professional diplomats like his Ambassador, who saw their country about to involve herself in a war in which the odds would in their opinion be heavily against her. The recent panic on the Berlin bourse was entirely due to fear of war in well-informed circles. The blame, they felt, would lie to a certain extent with His Majesty's Government who, as in 1914, had failed to make their position sufficiently clear. The only hope in their opinion would be for a representative of His Majesty's Government to inform the Führer himself quite categorically that in certain circumstances Great Britain would quite certainly go to war in defence of Czechoslovakia. This might well have the necessary deterrent effect.

I may add that Cholerton of the *Daily Telegraph* was recently spoken to in the same sense by the *D.N.B.* correspondent here, who is practically attached to the German Embassy and has access to the confidential dispatches. Cholerton says that he seemed very much depressed by the insane optimism prevailing in official circles in Berlin with regard to the Czech problem.

Yours ever,
Chilston[1]

The reference in Chilston's letter to similar reports received by the *Daily Telegraph*'s correspondent, Cholerton, from his counterpart, Ernst Schüle from the German News Agency, also originated with me, in the hopes that a report in the *Daily Telegraph* might serve our cause.

Chilston's account was accurate and complete in all but one point, attesting to my friend Fitzroy's diligence as a reporter. Years later, in a letter of 3 June, 1978, Maclean recalled an important issue that I had raised with him but which unfortunately was not included in Chilston's report to London:

[1] *Documents on British Foreign Policy*, 1919–1939, E. L. Woodward, Rohan Butler, editors, third series, Vol. 2 (London, 1949), pp. 140–41.

My recollection is that you also emphasized most strongly the need for the British to take a firm line with Hitler over Czechoslovakia. You said that the Czechs' will to resist would depend very largely on the attitude of the French and ourselves and also told me that there were a number of German generals who would be more inclined to stand up to Hitler if we adopted a really resolute attitude.

Later on the same day, 23 August, Chilston sent off a second message based on my discussions with Maclean. In this message he passed on the details of Schulenburg's conversation with Litvinov, along with my own observations on the matter:

It appears that after Litvinov had told the Ambassador that, in the event of a German invasion of Czechoslovakia, the Soviet Union 'would do its best to help Czechoslovakia', he went on to say that, if Germany were only democratic, the Soviet attitude towards the Czechoslovakia question would be completely different, as the Soviet Union 'had always been in favour of national self-determination'. Our informant told us that the Embassy had not yet telegraphed this remark of Litvinov's to Berlin, as they felt that it would only enrage the Führer. They themselves took it as a clear indication that the Soviet Government were by no means opposed to the idea of a Soviet–German *rapprochement*. Any such *rapprochement* was, however, unfortunately quite out of the question owing to Herr Hitler's passionate and unreasoning hatred of what he imagined to be Bolshevism.[2]

A third telegram a few days later reported the contents of a further conversation that I held with Maclean on 28 August:

We understand from the German Embassy that contrary to rumours published in the Press, the Ambassador has made no formal *démarche* at the Peoples' Commissariat of Foreign Affairs concerning Czech problem. Our information is that, following on his conversation with M. Litvinoff on August 21 reported in my letters to Mr. Collier of August 23, the Ambassador saw Commissar for Foreign Affairs on August 28, when in the course of conversation he again referred to question of Czechoslovakia and expressed view that hostilities between Germany and Soviet Union were unlikely, if only because neither Poland nor Roumania would allow the passage of German or Soviet troops across their territory. To this M. Litvinoff replied that he was not so sure about that, as at the moment Roumania seems 'much alarmed'.[3]

I should perhaps stress here that in leaking information to Maclean and various other foreign diplomats in Moscow, I acted on Brücklmeier's and

[2] *Ibid.*, p. 141, fn. 3.
[3] *Ibid.*, p. 179.

my own initiative and without the knowledge of anyone else in the Embassy, least of all Schulenburg;[4] leaking official secrets and publicizing one's private dissent from the policies of the government for which one worked were not viewed with favour in Berlin. Not wishing to lay others open to the charge of high treason, I preferred to act on my own.

With my first conversation with Maclean on the 22nd, I knew that I had crossed the Rubicon. Having once violated my oath to maintain the confidentiality of my Ministry's affairs, as well as the normal rules governing contacts with other diplomats, I knew that repeated transgressions would not put me in any worse light than I was in already, and yet could substantially help in my campaign to strengthen the forces of opposition to Hitler. I therefore turned to my closest friend at the French Embassy, Baron Gontran de Juniac, then a Second Secretary. Like many good French aristocrats, de Juniac's father had been an officer and de Juniac himself had served in the cavalry. An extremely clever man, he had a typically French wit, sometimes caustic. Also typically French, he thoroughly appreciated good wine and good living. De Juniac was part of the society of young secretaries in Moscow, and even joined some of the parties in which only people from North European countries participated. He did this in part out of love for German wine, which he drank by the bottle. He was alone among members of the French and Italian Embassies in joining these parties, but if there was any principle of exclusion it operated against those who would drink fewer than three glasses. De Juniac always fitted in perfectly.

Gontran de Juniac was also among those who frequented the American *dacha*. Knowing that I would find him there, I set out by car for an afternoon of tennis. Arriving at the *dacha*, I saw de Juniac with his colleague, Baron Maurice Dayet, then First Secretary at the French Embassy and fortunately also a trusted friend of mine. While my own recollection of the conversation that took place on that late August day in 1938 is quite complete, de Juniac's own account, as he set it down in a letter of 28 February, 1976, may be of interest:

At that moment (Dayet and I) were getting ready to return to Moscow. Just as we reached the garden gate, you signalled from afar that we should wait for you there. You ran to join us and the things you told us then struck us deeply. 'I don't speak to you solely as a friend

[4] Karl E. Schorske, 'Two German Ambassadors: Dirksen and Schulenburg', *The Diplomats, 1919–1939*, Gordon A. Craig, Felix Gilbert, editors, 2 vols. (New York, 1974), II, p. 491.

of peace or as a good European,' you told us, 'but also as a good German.' Hitler is preaching a foolish form of politics that can only lead us directly to a general war. He will provoke a world coalition against Germany and we will suffer a worse defeat than in 1918. He must be stopped while there is still time. There is but one way to accomplish this: to show oneself to be firm and to talk to him with utter brutality if necessary. The dismemberment of Czechoslovakia cannot be passively accepted. Hitler must be made to understand that if he decides to try to resolve the issue by force he will have to reckon with the resistance of the French army and England.

You added that you had taken the step of speaking to the British as well. You reported to us that you had told them to send their most capable man to Berlin, someone who expressed himself in an energetic and imposing language that would enable Hitler to feel Britain's resoluteness. 'Send Churchill there!' you had said. 'That will be your last chance. If nobody stops him now, Hitler will persist in bringing off his audacious coup and a general war will break out.'

Did my French friends succeed in reporting back to Paris? Only in 1976 did I learn from de Juniac that my views had in fact been communicated to the then Permanent Under-Secretary at the Quai d'Orsay, Alexis Léger, better known under his pen name St John Perse. Here are de Juniac's recollections on this point:

Returning to the Embassy we decided – Dayet and I – that he would send a personal letter to Léger to tell him what you had just reported to us. This message went out by pouch the next day over Dayet's signature. At the end of his letter Dayet wrote that he had a very favourable opinion of you and that this led him to emphasize that your arguments, in his opinion, warranted the most serious consideration. This letter must have reached Léger but I have no confirmation of it.

The reason Dayet's letter is not extant today, in all likelihood, is that it was burnt along with most of Léger's other papers on the eve of the German occupation of France. Very few papers remain today in Léger's archives.

Only much later did I learn that Maurice Dayet also reported our conversation by cable to the Quai d'Orsay, on 30 August, 1938. His cabled report was more concise and guarded than the letter:

In this report I am relying on a person who is supposed to be accurately informed and whose sincerity cannot be doubted. This person reports that there exists a great divergence of view between high ranking members of the German diplomatic corps, on the one hand, and the National Socialist leaders on the other, over what attitude France would assume in the event of German military intervention in Czechoslovakia. He says that the leaders of the Nazi party would persist in under-estimating the importance of the warnings that we have given them in spite of opinions to the contrary from senior officials on the Wilhelmstrasse. The Nazi leaders are especially persuaded that France would shy if the Germans were to claim 'Czech provocation' as their excuse for their incursion into Czechoslovakia.

My interlocutor predicted that only direct and very serious warnings coming from prominent French and British statesmen and politicians would be able to dissipate the feeling that we are equivocating and to lead the National Socialist leaders to revise their views of the risks that a military movement into Czechoslovakia would entail.

Did this have any effect? When in 1953 Dayet gave me a copy of this cable, he also told me that his report to the Quai d'Orsay was circulated throughout the Russian Department in Paris, and also through other departments, thanks to Léger. But one will look in vain for any evidence that it changed anyone's mind as to the course of action to be followed.

Even as I was presenting my arguments to my British and French friends, I was asking myself what would happen if their governments would not heed the warnings and persisted in what struck me as a spineless and ultimately fatal course. The alternative would eventually be war – a war waged by Hitler against all Europe that remained outside his power. I had no doubt that this 'unthinkable' outcome was daily becoming not only conceivable but likely. Yet by pressing my case with the British and the French I felt that I had already done everything that could be achieved from my lowly position in Moscow to turn the course of events.

This was the hardest thing to accept. For days I had brooded over my inability to do anything to affect the thinking of the National Socialist leaders in Berlin. Finally, on 29 August, I decided to resort to a more direct form of action, namely a cable to Berlin warning of the likelihood of French and British resistance to a German coup in Czechoslovakia. I had no evidence that any resistance would be forthcoming; certainly neither Fitzroy Maclean nor Gontran de Juniac had said anything to justify such a belief. But my conversations with these friends had carried their own risks. I reasoned that a report on them to Berlin could have the double benefit of covering my indiscretion in meeting Maclean and de Juniac in the first place, and, more importantly, of forcing the Nazi leaders to consider the *possibility* that Britain and France might oppose their moves in Czechoslovakia. I therefore had the following memorandum sent to the Wilhelmstrasse by cable on the 29th:

Moscow, August 29, 1938

On Sunday, 28 August, 1938, Reuter and Havas representatives spoke to me about the Tass report from Prague which had appeared in the Soviet press, according to which the German representatives in London, Warsaw, Bucharest, Belgrade, and other places had, on official instructions, announced that, in the event of further delay in solving the Sudeten German problem, Germany would have to take active steps. They asked me whether the Ambassador, Count Schulenburg, had also made such a *démarche*. I replied in the negative, and pointed out that the People's Commissar, Litvinov, had likewise given a *dementi* to an American journalist. I was not aware of alleged *démarches* by German representatives in a number of other capitals.

A French Secretary of Legation, who was also present, stated to me later that, according to their information received from the Rumanian Government, the German Minister had in fact made such a *démarche*. He wished to tell me quite frankly that the situation was very serious. France had given Czechoslovakia her word and would keep it. It was indisputable and unalterable that France would at once intervene in the event of a German–Czechoslovak war. It was equally certain that Great Britain would stand by the side of France. To my objection that France would surely not attack Germany in the event of a conflict arising from provocation by Czechoslovakia, the French Secretary of Legation replied that that was an entirely useless, but all the more dangerous *jeu de mots*. It was out of the question that little Czechoslovakia could ever provoke powerful Germany. He then repeated once more that we should not indulge in illusions, for France would, in any circumstances, come to the assistance of Czechoslovakia in case of war. Neither could authoritative personages in Berlin delude themselves, for some ten days ago General Vuillemin had stated France's above-mentioned attitude frankly to Field Marshal Göring.

A British Secretary of Legation, who on former occasions had frequently emphasized that France would intervene in any case in the event of a German–Czechoslovak war and that Great Britain would just as surely follow, again expressed the same opinion, and added that Sir John Simon's recent statements should not be interpreted in any other way. If it came to war between Germany, France and Britain, the only ones to benefit would be the Soviets. In the event of war the Soviet Union would expose herself as little as possible. To my question whether there was not the possibility of the Soviets sending troops through Rumania, he replied that the Rumanian Government had officially informed them that they would never permit the transit of Soviet troops.

As I pointed out in the course of the conversation that, after all, Great Britain

132

would not wage war against us in order to hinder $3\frac{1}{2}$ million Germans in the exercise of their right of self-determination, he objected that unfortunately German claims in the Czechoslovak question had never been precisely formulated. When one concession was made to us we always demanded fresh concessions. Germany had always evaded making a concrete statement of her demands.

The Hungarian Chargé d'Affaires asked me whether the Ambassador, Count Schulenburg, had made a *démarche* with Litvinov in the Czechoslovak matter. He had received a corresponding inquiry from Budapest. I replied in the negative.[5]

In the same vein, on August 21, I gave Schulenburg a second memorandum in which I reported a conversation that I had had with the French Chargé d'Affaires, M. Payart. Here I tried once more to weave a few casual remarks by my French colleague into a fabric that would appear in Berlin to support the view that France would act with great resolve in the event of a German attack on Czechoslovakia. Again, it was necessary to create this impression through my own literary fancy rather than on the basis of actual reports from the French Embassy. In actuality, Payart was no more sanguine about the likelihood of France putting up any real resistance than were his younger colleagues. Here is the memorandum as it was received in Berlin from Schulenburg on 2 September:

On the evening of August 30 the French Chargé d'Affaires spoke to me about the Czechoslovak question. I took the opportunity of denying the rumours of Reich Government *démarches* in the Czechoslovak question, particularly in Bucharest and Belgrade, by referring to my conversation on the same subject with another member of the French Embassy a few days ago ....

M. Payart emphasized that France had a treaty with Czechoslovakia. There was no point in discussing whether this treaty was good or bad. It existed and France must keep her word, otherwise she would cease to be a Great Power. In case of war the Soviets would have the last laugh. Having no common frontier they had no need to expose themselves to any great danger. They would assist the Czechs as much as lay within their power, namely, in the supply of war materials, primarily aircraft, and by sending technicians. The possibility of air attacks on East Prussia could not be excluded. He thought it improbable that the Soviets would bomb Berlin, as in such an event the losses in aircraft would be too great.

When I remarked that the Soviets could not carry out an air attack on Königsberg without having to fly over neutral territory, he said that the Soviets would not scruple to fly over neutral countries.

[5] *Documents on German Foreign Policy, 1918–1945, Germany and Czechoslovakia*, Washington, 1949, pp. 656–657.

133

In this connection I would like to mention that a member of the Italian Embassy here told me that forty Soviet aircraft had flown to Czechoslovakia over Polish territory at a great height some time ago. This had been reported to him by an absolutely reliable informant. The Poles had noticed the flight of the Soviet aircraft too late to take practical measures against it.[6]

It did not take long to see how utterly all my efforts had failed. Daladier and Chamberlain went to Munich after Chamberlain had visited Hitler at Bad Godesberg. Hitler got the Sudetenland, as he desired, though he was apparently disappointed at not having gained the whole of Czechoslovakia. Daladier and Chamberlain were convinced that they had preserved peace, and most of the German population shared their conviction. The man in the street in Germany considered Chamberlain a hero, for he did not want war. That same man in the street believed Hitler's affirmation that there would be no World War II.

Theo Kordt's efforts in London to urge the British towards a more resolute position on the eve of the Sudeten crisis also failed completely. Whether the British did not understand what Kordt and I were telling them, or, as seems likely, were not able fully to admit to themselves that there existed a Resistance movement within Germany, they ignored both his and my overtures. There was no response to either of our entreaties.

My disappointment at the failure of the plan into which I had entered with such high hopes was profound. I was to experience this disappointment again and again, particularly after the failure of each of the various attempts to get rid of Hitler, but never afterwards was my sadness so wretched.

With the incorporation of Czechoslovakia into the Germany Reich, orders were given that we should take over the Czech Legation in Moscow, just as we had earlier taken over the Austrian Legation. With the exception of the Minister, Zdenek Fierlinger, most of the Czech diplomats were given posts in our Embassy. In arranging this, Schulenburg showed his characteristic decency and kindness. Not only did he take pains to see that all the Czechs were given worthy positions, but he made sure that they were reinserted into the diplomatic list at once with their former ranks intact.

Our military attaché, General Köstring, was particularly concerned to help Colonel Frantisek Dastich, the former Czech military attaché. When Dastich was finally ordered to return to Czechoslovakia, Köstring gave a party in his honour and presented him with a couple of bottles of

[6] *Ibid.*, pp. 666–667.

fine wine, with the request that Dastich remember him when he drank it after the war. In 1946, while I was working at the Bavarian State Chancellery, I received a telephone call from the Czech Consul General Ernest Steiner, who was trying to arrange a meeting between his guest, the head of the Czech military mission in Berlin, and Köstring. I was delighted to discover that this official was our old Moscow friend, Dastich. I managed to get hold of Köstring and both he and his wife, a Sudeten German from Reichenberg, arrived in Munich soon afterwards. Dastich awaited Köstring on the doorstep of Steiner's residence and, saluting, asked if he might embrace him. At dinner, Dastich expressed his heartfelt gratitude to Köstring for his kindness during Czechoslovakia's darkest hour and told how he had drunk the wine in his memory at the end of the war.

10

MEMEL, 1938–1939

In the autumn of 1938, to my great surprise, I was appointed to the Consulate General in Memel. For several reasons my transfer to this contested corner between Germany and Lithuania terrified me. First, it came in the wake of the Czech crisis, and tension was running high. Second, I know nothing about the consulate itself. Third, I knew full well that Memel was one of those territories which Hitler intended to bring back into the German Reich, having been part of Germany for centuries and being still populated almost wholly by Germans.

With all this in my mind, I took the train from Moscow to Memel, where I was met at the station by a good friend of mine. Ernst Günther Mohr, who had been serving as deputy Consul General but was to depart that evening for Berlin. I told him of my apprehensions, and asked if he had a moment to give me some advice on my new responsibilities. He declined, explaining that elections had just brought the German majority back into power and a new government was being formed at the moment. Given the uncertainty that these changes occasioned, he advised me simply to keep my eyes open. He then invited me to his farewell party, to be held that same evening.

Being in a rather gloomy mood, I decided to drink my whisky straight and, with its help, to make the acquaintance of as many people as possible. In this I was fortunate. Ottomar Schreiber, who played a leading part in German politics in Memel, was friendly to me, as were Martin Kakies, the editor of the *Memeler Dampfboot*, Gerhard Schmaeling, a local ship owner, and the mayor of Memel, Wilhelm Brindlinger. All in all, it was a satisfying evening, and I succeeded in delivering Mohr to the station in time for his train. I walked back to my hotel with Baron Karl von Dreihann-Hollenia, a former Austrian diplomat with a tremendous sense of humour. We were both quite drunk, and when a group of good citizens of Memel saluted me with a rousing 'Heil Hitler', I told them, 'Get your arse off the sidewalk and greet your consul in a proper way!' I can't myself verify the wording, but this is what Dreihann-Hollenia reported to me the following morning over coffee. He had not the slightest doubt that I would be withdrawn from Memel that day, or by evening at the latest.

To my amazement, nothing happened. Far from being thrown out of town, I noticed immediately that I was cordially received on all sides. I was anxious to learn what was happening, and finally met one of the men I had encountered on that first evening. They told me that they had taken an immediate liking to me at Mohr's party and then again on the street, at which time, as they put it, 'I had greeted them in so intimate a way'.

Reinhold von Saucken, the Consul General in Memel, had the reputation of being a difficult man to work with. Upon his return, I let him understand that I was not competing with him and in fact had no ambition but to return to Moscow as soon as possible. On this basis we got on splendidly, the more readily because he was so frequently out of town. I next had to contend with the staff of the consulate. Most were Party members, many of them convinced Nazis. Upon first meeting them, I made it clear that I would expect them to follow my orders to the letter, as precisely as in the Prussian army in which I had served. I considered this particularly important in the light of the peculiar challenges we faced in Memel. Not being a Nazi, I was firmly convinced that this was the only way that I could maintain my authority among them. This heel-clicking stratagem succeeded, and they worked loyally for me.

Memel turned out to be full of surprises. For one thing, the town is situated amidst a lovely region. The Memel district as a whole is rightly renowned for its delicate beauty, the unspoilt charm of a sparsely populated coastal zone with deep lagoons and dark forests rich in game of all sorts. Unaccustomed to human beings, the elks would often wander right down to the Baltic seashore and watch us as we strolled by.

Several people whom I met were no less attractive than the land. Kakies, the editor of the *Memeler Dampfboot*, was a particularly intelligent man who presided over one of the more interesting newspapers in Germany. Notwithstanding East Prussia's reputation as an ultra-conservative region, Kakies and his paper were thoroughly liberal. His circle of friends included a number with whom I would gladly have formed close ties had I stayed longer. Other Memel residents were less pleasing, though tolerable. One might have expected nothing but trouble from the Gestapo official responsible for Memel, a man named Gräfe, whose office was at nearby Tilsit. Mohr had reminded me of the importance of maintaining correct relations with Gräfe and I managed to do just that, thanks both to my own efforts and to his. The other German official responsible for the affairs of Memel was the infamous *Gauleiter* Erich Koch, the *Oberpräsident* of East Prussia who had his headquarters in Königsberg. To put it mildly, Koch was a thoroughly unattractive character. Both the Consul General and I came into constant contact with him on account of his desire to exercise his authority directly in the Memel district. It was again the local Gestapo official, Gräfe, who intervened every time to keep Koch out. It was to Gräfe that I directed my pleas on behalf of the Jews after the re-absorption of Memel into the Reich. I begged him not to permit the kind of atrocities against Jews that had already taken place elsewhere. As long as I remained in Memel, Gräfe succeeded in this, proving himself a most unlikely ally.

I had expected that Gailius, the Lithuanian governor of the Memel district, would treat us with coolness, if not outright hostility. On the contrary, he was an extraordinarily pleasant man, with whom I had the best relations from the first. I explained to him that I was fresh from Moscow, where I had become a good friend of the Lithuanian Minister, Jurgis Baltrusaitis, and of his counsellor, Richard Rabinavicius, and that my major concern now was simply to become acquainted with life in the *Memelgebiet*. He asked me how long I expected to remain in Memel, to which I replied that I did not hope to stay beyond 1 April, 1939. This visibly gave him a shock. Not realizing that I had merely stressed my personal wish to leave within four months of my appointment, he immediately assumed that 1 April was the date on which the Memel district was to be incorporated once more into the German Reich. Only later did I realize the cause of his confusion. Unfortunately, I never had the opportunity to apologize for my gaffe, since on 22 March, 1939, Hitler forced the Lithuanian government to hand Memel back to Germany.

The Nazis considered the re-absorption of Memel into the Reich as a signal victory, a worthy successor to the acquisition of Czechoslovakia. The actual takeover occurred when the First Infantry Regiment marched in from Königsberg, accompanied by a bicycle battalion from Tilsit. A huge St Bernard dog drew the great bass drum which led the Königsberg band. Hitler also came to celebrate the occasion, which took place only a few days after the Sudeten crisis. It was a sparkling clear day and the Führer arrived by sea on a destroyer, stepping from the ship like Lohengrin disembarking from his swan.

Under the circumstances, and with the memory of Hitler's

Nuremberg speech fresh in my mind, I expected to hear a typical example of Hitler's demagogic oratory. To my surprise, he gave a talk that was notably moderate, both in content and form. His performance testified eloquently to his canny ability to adapt himself to his audience. He understood that he was addressing East Prussians who felt themselves to be German, notwithstanding the fact that many were ethnically Lithuanian. At the same time, he understood that they were not accustomed to Nazi rhetoric and therefore he struck just the right tone in his address. He thanked the people of Memel for their patience under Lithuanian occupation and offered a few general remarks on the future, none of them particularly extravagant.

All this, I should stress, took place within twenty-four hours of the so-called 'agreement' being signed. Although there had been some minor incidents involving Germans and Lithuanians prior to the take-over, the German population gave little evidence of being impelled by chauvinism. The Lithuanian government had resisted all moves towards self-government within the Memel district right down to the time of my arrival, with the result that the re-incorporation of Memel into Germany was genuinely popular. This contrasted sharply with the situation in Czechoslovakia when that country was absorbed into the Reich. This saved me from what would otherwise have been an insupportable task, since I would have refused to participate in the take-over of a hostile and alien population.

In spite of the expressed desire of the population, I had no illusions that, in rejoining the Reich, the people of Memel and especially their leaders were getting into a situation that would be far less agreeable than they expected. Even before the *Anschluss* I had explained this carefully to Ernst Neumann, the leader of Memel's German population, and now I repeated it again. A quiet, good-looking man with all the best features of the East Prussian, Neumann heard me out. I warned him that Germany was no longer what he supposed it to be and told him that he should not blame me when he discovered this for himself. When I finally left Memel, Neumann was among those who accompanied me to the train. As I boarded, he recalled our conversation and acknowledged that I had been right. Subsequently, Neumann was killed in action fighting for the country which he had helped Memel to rejoin.

I I

THE NAZI–SOVIET PACT, 1939

As my days in Memel drew to a close, there were suggestions in the Ministry of Foreign Affairs that I should be transferred to Bucharest. I resisted this vigorously, knowing full well that my having escaped harm in Memel was due more to luck than design and that I could not count on that luck continuing in another post. Typically, Schulenburg intervened in my behalf, with a letter to the Personnel Office. Schulenburg argued that my stay in Memel should not be prolonged any longer than necessary and that I should be reassigned to Moscow so as to assist him in dealing with the many chicaneries that the Soviet Foreign Ministry had concocted in its dealings with the diplomatic corps, of which he himself was doyen. This letter did the trick and I was posted back to Moscow. Just at the moment when I was passing through Berlin on my way to Moscow, Count Schulenburg was departing for Teheran to take part in the festivities in honour of the marriage of the Crown Prince Reza Pahlevi to a very beautiful sister of Egypt's King Farouk.

Schulenburg had already formed his party, but he invited me to join him, thinking the trip would provide a welcome break after Memel. Two air force planes were assigned to the delegation, one, a Junker 52, to carry the people, and a second, a Heinkel, to carry the luggage. Thanks to these plans, we had a wonderful trip to Persia via Belgrade, Athens, Rhodes, Beirut, and Baghdad. Typically, Schulenburg reasoned that the fortnight we had saved by getting the aircraft was now ours to spend sightseeing.

This trip showed Schulenburg at his very best. He knew all the places through which we travelled and was known everywhere in return. In Athens he took me out to Salamis to show me where the Greek and Persian ships had been arrayed, and from Beirut we took an excursion to Damascus. News of Schulenburg's arrival had travelled ahead of us wherever we went, so that when we reached Damascus the best antiquarian dealers were already waiting for him.

Each nation had been invited to send a small military detachment to the wedding, but Hitler, with characteristic arrogance, proposed to send an entire air force squadron. The old Shah resisted this, rightly wanting the various military contingents to be of roughly equal size. Hitler took umbrage at this and refused to send any soldiers at all, but this ridiculous episode was not permitted to dampen spirits at the festivities. I stayed in royal splendour with our Minister, Wolfgang Smend, at his residence near Teheran. After the wedding, Schulenburg announced that he was taking us all on a private expedition to Isfahan and Persepolis. We commandeered the air force Junker 52. The two crew members had no accurate maps, but Schulenburg told them not to worry; he knew the country well and would direct them from the cockpit. He did this magnificently, even to the point of directing them to the best spot for landing on the open plain at Persepolis, where there was no proper airstrip.

At Persepolis, British army tents were pitched directly in front of Xerxes' great staircase. I stayed in a tent with my old school friend from Potsdam and colleague in the diplomatic corps, Werner von Holleben, certainly not imagining that the next British military gear I would attempt to use would be a bomb intended for Adolf Hitler. All of us assembled and spent a long, thoughtful evening under the stars. The complete tranquillity of that sparkling evening contrasted starkly with the events taking place in Europe. I could not help but think that this might be the last moment of peace that I would know for some while.

This feeling had been eating at me through the month following the seizure of Czechoslovakia. Like many others, I had expected that we would begin immediately to step up pressure on Poland in order to get back Danzig and the Corridor. Since both Britain and France had by this time signed treaties with Poland, it seemed inevitable that such pressure would lead to a general conflagration. This realization gave the wedding festivities an atmosphere of strained pathos, in which everyone strove to savour the joyful moment. A side-trip to the Caspian, the numerous receptions at legations, and the countless personal contacts, all became suffused with this desperate desire to make every minute count.

In the first days of May, Count Schulenburg received orders to report back to Berlin for consultations with the Ministry and with the Führer. He therefore flew directly to Berlin and left me to take his baggage overland to Moscow. The long trip first to Baku and thence by train over several days to Moscow gave me ample opportunity to think over my situation. All my calculations were seriously out of date, however, since I had left Moscow in October 1938 and a very different situation was to greet me upon my return in May 1939. It did not take me long to realize how thoroughly German–Soviet relations had been altered within a brief period of time.

Rather than review in detail all that was occurring in those days – a story that has been retold many times already – let me touch only upon some of the highlights. In retrospect, it is easy to conceive the transformation of our relations in terms of a series of milestones that were passed.

One minor but revealing episode occurred just as I was departing for Memel, when Schulenburg had gone to Litvinov with the proposal that they reach a gentlemen's agreement to prevent personal attacks in their national presses on Hitler and Stalin. At three month intervals for several years prior to this, Litvinov and Schulenburg had been presenting each other with the collected insults gleaned by their staffs from the German or Russian press. This had become so routine an event that after a while they would simply show each other the outside of the folders and agree that each had protested; both considered it ludicrous for grown men to go through such an exercise. I considered that the agreement to prevent such personal attacks reflected a fundamental shift in our relations with the Soviet Union.

Another milestone was passed on 10 March, 1939, when Stalin delivered his famous speech in which he avowed that he was not prepared to take the chestnuts out of the fire for Great Britain and France. By claiming that there were no visible grounds for conflict between the USSR and Germany, and by making that claim at so important a forum as the 18th Party Congress, he did much to enhance the better relations which he considered existed already.

Yet another significant milestone was passed on 3 May, when Litvinov was removed from office and replaced by Molotov. Unlike the other two events, we did not fully appreciate the significance of this at the time it occurred. Later we realized that, with Litvinov's dismissal, the policy of collective security and undivided peace had come to an end. (Litvinov's slogan was 'peace is indivisible'.) I had always assumed that Litvinov would be willing to enter into better relations with Germany were he permitted to do so by his leader. Stalin apparently thought differently, perhaps because Litvinov had never been a part of the Kremlin's inner circle, and, unlike his successor, was not a Politburo member. A further factor in Stalin's mind might have been that Litvinov was a Jew, one of the few who had not already been removed from office. It may be that out of some perverse respect for Nazi ideology, Stalin considered Molotov a more appropriate person to negotiate with the Germans. One thing was certain: Stalin was by now prepared to do whatever was necessary to avoid being drawn into a war with Germany.

Even before his appointment as Minister of Foreign Affairs, there was a consensus among the younger diplomats that Molotov was a hard-working and rather bland man. We could not imagine him other than sitting stolidly in his chair behind a massive desk. He lacked all humour, but was reliable and gave the impression of being a good stodgy German civil servant. Though it was impossible to admire him, Molotov was held in some respect by our Embassy because we knew that he did not hesitate to speak his mind where another might be silent. In his negotiations with Schulenburg, he never hid the fact that our former policy still led him to distrust Germany. Such candour earned Molotov high marks among us. On the other hand, we knew full well that he had no authority of his own. On even the most trivial point he had to wait for orders from the Kremlin, thus causing the negotiations with Schulenburg to bog down utterly whenever Stalin was not actively pulling the strings.

In this new climate, the German government entered into negotiations to revive commercial relations with the USSR. Representing Germany in these talks was Karl Schnurre, a contemporary of mine who had served for several years as a judge before entering the Foreign Service. He fully shared the view that German–Soviet relations should be put on an even keel as rapidly as possible. The Soviets welcomed our initiatives, but Molotov was naturally cautious. In meeting after meeting he insisted that, before commercial talks could progress further, some form of political basis would have first to be agreed upon. He knew that the Soviet negotiations with the British and French were imminent, and he did not want our commercial discussions to compromise anything that might happen in that quarter unless firm assurances from the Germans were in hand. As in the German proverb, he did not want to give up a sparrow in the hand for a pigeon on the rooftop. Yet the fact that Molotov pressed so hard for a political understanding gave us to understand that the Soviets really wanted to proceed as rapidly as possible in the talks with Germany. Under such favourable conditions. Schnurre was not long in achieving his goal.

The Russians were now going all out to impress their various visitors from the West. A major exhibition mounted in 1939 lauded Soviet achievements in agriculture; achievements which, in the opinion of all of us at the Embassy, were modest to say the least. Nonetheless, the Soviets

143

were extremely clever in presenting the exhibition; not only was it mounted effectively, but every road leading to it was repaved, and the houses lining the roadside were given a fresh coat of paint. It was a splendid Potemkin village. A large delegation from the Ministry of Agriculture in Berlin toured the exhibition and was greatly impressed. As their opinion rose, our estimation of the group declined.

At the same time, the Soviet representative in Berlin, my old friend from the Caucasus, Georgi Astakhov, entered upon a period of intense activity with a view towards expanding the relationship into other areas as well. Astakhov was regarded by our Ministry as a first-class diplomat with an independent mind unlike the average Soviet official; this helped him in his effort.

What Astakhov probably did not realize was the seriousness with which Hitler was pursuing his attempts to get back Danzig and the Polish Corridor. This was the objective towards which all Hitler's cordial moves involving the Russians were directed. I had no illusions about the perils of the situation, and by now had lost all doubt that German pressure in that quarter would inevitably lead to war. For my part, I understood that the sole purpose of Hitler's rapprochement with Stalin was to secure Soviet neutrality in the event of a German attack on Poland.

This was the more necessary on account of the Anglo-Polish treaty. Until the signing of that agreement, Hitler was convinced that the British would meet a German invasion of Poland in much the way they had met the *Anschluss* of Austria, and the occupation of Czechoslovakia. It is a sad irony that one effect of the treaty was to cause Hitler to consider seriously his relationship with the USSR. Yet the treaty itself did not impel Hitler to action. No German diplomat whom I knew felt that Hitler really took seriously Britain's guarantees to Poland, since Britain was too far away to intervene effectively even if it wished to do so. The British guarantees might have caused Hitler to think twice about an actual invasion but they certainly did not rule out a campaign of pressure. It was the opening of direct negotiations between Britain, France and the USSR that galvanized Hitler into action, for then he saw the possibility that Russia might somehow be enlisted in the campaign to block Germany in Poland. In my opinion, the Franco-British initiative made Hitler genuinely nervous and convinced him that he must come to a political agreement with Stalin; even make far-reaching concessions, if necessary, so as to assure Stalin's acquiescence in the dismemberment of Poland. In the end, of course, Stalin was no less eager than Hitler to get the job done.

It was fascinating to see how Hitler and Ribbentrop and, through them, Schulenburg, began exerting pressure on the Russians to bring their negotiations in Moscow and Berlin to a successful conclusion early enough to permit the attack on Poland, which was planned for late August. This pressure on Schulenburg from Hitler and Ribbentrop was not daily but hourly. They forced Schulenburg again and again to ask that Ribbentrop be received in Moscow at the earliest possible date.

As I observed the persistence with which Berlin was pursuing its aim, I became convinced that Hitler was on the brink of reaching an agreement with Moscow. The British and French faced great difficulties in their negotiations with the Soviets over an agreement to stop German aggression against Poland. The Poles did not want to accept help from the Soviets since they remembered all too well the three partitions of their country in the eighteenth century in which Russia had participated. Also, it was known that Stalin desired to reintegrate the three Baltic states with the Soviet Union. It would have been incompatible with the democratic conscience of France and Great Britain to allow him to destroy the freedom of three independent states. On the other side, I was convinced that Hitler would have not the slightest remorse in handing these states over to Stalin if by so doing he could secure Soviet co-operation. The sole possibility for preventing Poland's fall was for the Western powers to move vigorously and quickly in their negotiations with Stalin so as to beat Hitler to the mark.

In these circumstances I resolved to make one last-ditch effort to prevent Hitler's plan. There were two possibilities open to me. First, I could attempt to convey information about the Soviet-German negotiations to Italy, from which they had carefully been kept secret. It was Mussolini after all who, by convening the Munich conference in autumn 1938, had succeeded in preventing Hitler from invading Czechoslovakia outright. Second, I could try to convince the Western powers of the danger of the situation and thereby encourage them to act more resolutely. In the end I decided to do both at once.

Before plunging into this risky activity, I again asked myself whether I should not inform Schulenburg of my intentions. I decided against doing so, since I was not convinced that he was prepared to go as far as I was. Moreover I knew that by involving him in conspiracy and high treason I would be endangering his life. This I was not prepared to do.

In May 1938 I began warning my closest friends that it was not the British and French but Hitler who would sign an agreement with Stalin. As I realized that they would not believe my Cassandra-like message simply because it came from me, I decided on a different tactic, i.e. to

145

prove the truth of my gloomy forecast by giving them detailed information about the progress of the secret negotiations.

In my effort to mobilize the Italians it was natural that I should turn to Guido Relli, my good friend in the Italian Embassy. Relli was a highly competent expert on Soviet affairs. He was born in the Austro–Hungarian Empire. In the summer of 1914 at the age of sixteen he went on an Austrian ship to the Black Sea. At the outbreak of World War I the ship was captured by the Russians and he was interned. During his internment he worked in different capacities and acquired a profound knowledge of Russian life and language. After the war he was permanently attached to the Italian Embassy in Moscow as expert and interpreter. In some ways his position was similar to that of Hilger in the German Embassy. I was confident that Relli would convey my reports to Rome with accuracy, and that Mussolini or his advisers would give them a careful reading. I therefore arranged to meet him on 6 May, immediately after my return from Persia.

I briefed Relli the way a General Staff officer would have done. I made it clear that, in my opinion, the British and French would never be able to come to an agreement with the Soviet Union, but that Hitler, being constrained by no moral compunction, would be quite willing to sacrifice the independence of the Baltic States, of Finland, and perhaps even of Romania for the sake of an agreement with Stalin.

Apparently I succeeded. Relli returned at once to his Embassy and reported my entire conversation to Rosso. The Italian Ambassador was astonished at Relli's tale, but probably at the same time suspicious of the motives behind my action and hence sceptical about the truth of the information I was leaking to him. He was not yet prepared to pass on my revelations to the Palazzo Chigi. Since I had no way of knowing for sure whether Rosso was reporting back to Rome, I had to rely on the fact that Relli seemed to accept my story at face value.

Over the next weeks I continued to meet Relli frequently. I reported to him on Schulenburg's talk with Molotov on 20 May, in which Molotov had held out the Soviet government's interest in building a 'political basis' before entering into detailed economic negotiations with Germany. I also reported Schulenburg's impression, as of 25 May, that the grounds for an improvement of Soviet–German relations were increasing rapidly, and would continue to do so if only Germany managed to prevent Russia's relationship with France and England from taking on a more binding character. More important, perhaps, I spoke of Ribbentrop's view of the matter, as expressed in various instructions that we had received in the Embassy. I all but quoted Ribbentrop's message of 25 May that, if Germany could be confident that the USSR had no designs to subvert it through Communist revolutionaries, there need be no further clash of interest between the two countries. In his message Ribbentrop had gone as far as to declare that:

If, contrary to our desire, we should be dragged into military involvement with Poland, this need not necessarily lead to a clash of interests with Soviet Russia. We can already say today that in the settlement of the German–Polish question – in whatever way it should come about – we will take into account Russian interests if possible.

Gradually my reports found their way into the cables from the Italian Embassy to Rome. By 12 June Rosso was passing on to the Italian Foreign Minister, Conte Galeazzo Ciano, practically my entire talks with Relli. On that day he informed Rome that Mikoyan had taken the decision to sign a commercial treaty with Germany and, more important, to come to the political agreement that could alone provide a sufficient basis for Russia to enter the partnership with Hitler in other spheres.[1]

On 12 June I again met Relli, this time for over an hour. Relli seemed excited by my news, and I began to wonder whether my efforts might finally lead to some concrete effort by Mussolini. Rosso's cable on 13 June filled in all the gaps in my previous reports:

Count von Schulenburg left the day before yesterday for Berlin, where he will be joined by the commercial attaché of the German embassy, Mr Hilger, who is planning to depart from Moscow this evening. The return of the ambassador and his colleague was decided upon as a result of a recent conversation between Hilger and Mikoyan, the Commissar for Foreign Trade. According to the confidential information furnished by the embassy of Germany, Mikoyan had called Hilger and declared to him that the Soviet government, having accepted the recent German proposal, was now prepared to re-open commercial negotiations. Mikoyan suggested that the German government promptly despatch Schnurre to Moscow. He also gave assurances that the Soviet side would honour the various conditions advanced during the previous winter. To this, Hilger replied that at the same time the German government would agree to concessions, analogous concessions would have to be made by the Soviet government. Mikoyan insisted again that he still had certain reservations but in the end let it be understood that the possibility of an agreement with Germany was not to be excluded. This led to Hilger's decision to return to Berlin in order to review the situation with the pertinent organs there. He was principally concerned to

[1] These cables are extracted by Mario Toscano, *L'Italia e gli Accordi Tedesco–Sovietici dell'Agosto 1939*, Florence, 1952, pp. 46, ff.

discuss the situation regarding certain raw materials, such as manganese and petroleum, which Germany sought from the USSR but which the Soviets seemed not to have the capacity to provide. On its side, [the USSR] would insist on payment in cash or finished goods. In his conversation with Hilger, Mikoyan had again returned to the question of a political basis for their further discussions. This convinced von Schulenburg that he himself must also go to Berlin in order to confer at the Wilhelmstrasse. As best I can understand, my German colleague [e.g., Schulenburg] would personally be inclined to give the Moscow government certain concessions even in the political field, and has certain ideas on this subject that he intends to advance to Ribbentrop. He is prepared, among other things, to give the Soviet government formal guarantees that Germany has no aggressive designs against the USSR. Von Schulenburg also sees the possibility of a public declaration by Germany that would confirm the full vigour and friendly spirit of the Treaty of Berlin, which is still in force. I suppose that my colleague has in mind a deal that is analogous to the Polish–Soviet agreement that Moscow and Warsaw made last November. Von Schulenburg asks himself, finally, if it would not be possible to propose to the USSR a German–Soviet naval pact covering the Baltic and eventually some kind of agreement involving a guarantee to Poland by the two countries (excluding the question of Danzig), and also to Rumania.

Naturally, in the mind of my German colleague, the proposals that would eventually be made to Moscow would be conditional upon the Soviet government's renouncing the agreement with England and France that is being negotiated at the present time.

I must now note that all I am reporting was entrusted to me through a most confidential channel – not from von Schulenburg himself, who has already departed for Berlin, but from one of his collaborators. On account of this, I cannot guarantee the absolute exactitude of the intentions that I have here attributed to von Schulenburg . . .[2]

Over a decade after the above cable was sent by Rosso to the Italian Foreign Ministry I was to discover that it, and indeed, the entire series of cables stretching back to mid-May 1939, had not been designated as Secret, and hence had been distributed to the political officers at the Palazzo Chigi as ordinary despatches.

Unfortunately, my hopes regarding Mussolini's reaction to the news of the impending German–Soviet pact were not fulfilled. Mussolini was obviously surprised to learn of the secret German–Soviet discussions, but, as he claimed next day to our Ambassador in Rome, they did not particularly alarm him.

[2] *Ibid.*, pp. 47–48.

148

Telegram
Rome, June 14, 1939 1:40 p.m.
Arrival: June 14, 1939 5:40 p.m.

No. 252 of June 16

Very secret.

In the course of a general political discussion which lasted approximately half an hour and followed the ceremonial presentation of the Manesse manuscript to the Duce, Mussolini had Ciano read me a telegram that had just arrived from the Italian embassy in Moscow. The embassy's report, based on a conversation with Count Schulenburg, communicated suggestions which the latter wanted to make in Berlin in regard to certain steps that might be taken with the Moscow government. I assume those suggestions have reached Berlin by now. The Duce welcomed this with the remark that Schulenburg's suggestions concerning our rapprochement with Russia bordered on, but did not exceed what was possible without risking being misunderstood by our own people. He said he was also thinking of the [reaction of the] Spanish people. Possible [Schulenburg's] suggestions will come in time to prevent the Soviets from entering into an alliance with England and France. Such a pact, according to Ciano's opinion, could hardly be promoted by the trip [to the USSR] of Mr Strang. The Russians could scarcely be flattered that the English were sending a second or third rate person to Moscow to deal with such important questions. When Ciano was questioned, he explicitly agreed with this evaluation.

According to the Duce, more and more voices opposed to an alliance with Russia will become audible in conservative England, because the British recognize that such an alliance would not long be without the strongest repercussions in their own internal affairs. He said he also believes that the Soviets would take even greater advantage of a pact with France and in the more or less near future intervene in the internal affairs of that partner by demanding that the Communists participate in state business not only through a Popular Front but by direct involvement. This danger doubtless does exist for France, but less so for England, where the Communists play a less important role. Ciano based his opinions on remarks by the highly intelligent Russian ambassador here, Helfand, an extreme Communist who fanatically hates the bourgeoisie of the western democracies.

Concluding this part of his remarks, the Duce stated that even if an [Anglo–Franco–Soviet] pact were concluded it would not be too great a misfortune since one could be quite sure that the Russians would not enter into military actions beyond their borders.

A few days later, our Embassy received a further notice from Berlin relating a chilling incident that had occurred in Rome. Our Ambassador,

Mackensen, had seen Mussolini again who was now eager to discuss with him the Soviet–German rapproachement. Mussolini made it clear that he was raising this question on the basis of reports which he had received from his Embassy in Moscow. These were attributed to Schulenburg, although they had all come from me. Mussolini expressed his view that Germany would be going too far if it offered the Soviet Union all three Baltic republics and a part of Bessarabia, and suggested that perhaps the offer of one of the Baltic states would be sufficient at the beginning of the negotiations.

The fact that in both conversations Mussolini showed himself so well informed on a matter that Hitler had kept secret from the Italian government, and that he expressed doubt, albeit obliquely, about what he understood to be Hitler's position, caused a considerable stir in our Foreign Ministry. Schulenburg, who had stayed on in Berlin, was immediately called in and asked to explain how the Italians might have come by their intimate knowledge of his own confidential views and those of the Ministry. During this interview, they presented Schulenburg with every shred of evidence with which Mussolini had confronted our Ambassador and asked him to shed light on their origin. Needless to say, Schulenburg had to plead ignorance. His absence from Moscow removed any possibility of his knowing what had been going on there.

By this point our Foreign Ministry was sufficiently aroused to make enquiries in Moscow. As our Chargé d'Affaires, Werner von Tippel-skirch, had not the slightest clue, he asked me if I could imagine from what source the Italians had got their information. I said that I had absolutely no idea. My session with von Tippelskirch alarmed me greatly and I set about covering my tracks as best as I could.

I went immediately to Relli and informed him what he had triggered off, telling him in detail what had happened as a consequence of Rosso's reports. I told him bluntly that I had given him the details about the German–Soviet negotiations on my own responsibility, without any authorization from my superiors. Furthermore I stressed that my forecast, that Hitler would sacrify the Baltic states, was my personal guess which I had never talked over with Schulenburg. I implored Relli to be very careful in reporting our conversations and not to mention me or the German Embassy as the source. We understood one another.

Next I drafted a memorandum listing the rumours circulating among Moscow diplomats and journalists, in order to make it appear that the Italians, far from tapping some secret source in our Embassy, had simply drawn on these rumours.

Tippelskirch accepted my report as a plausible explanation and sent it to Berlin with the following cable which I had drafted:

To the Foreign Office
Berlin

24 June, 1939

Content: rumours about a German–Soviet rapprochement in Moscow

Because of the long duration of the English–French–Soviet negotiations as well as the lack of information to the public about these negotiations, a favourable atmosphere for rumours, assumptions and inventions has been created. The fantasy of the foreign journalists, especially the English and French, seems to deal intensively with the possibility of a German–Soviet rapprochement.

In the enclosure the rumours going around Moscow last week are listed.

von Tippelskirch.

Report

about rumours on alleged German–Soviet rapprochement circulating in Moscow.

1. On 20 June, 1939, Cholerton, a reporter for the *Daily Telegraph* and *Express*, received a wire from London inquiring if it was true that a German business delegation was staying in Moscow at present to make a deal re. the exchange of Soviet fats, oil and wood with German goods and also to negotiation about a credit for 800 million marks. Mr Cholerton, on the basis of information given to him by the German Embassy, sent a negative answer to London.
2. On 22 June American and English correspondents received inquiries from their editorial offices asking if it were true that a delegation of German economists would be going to Moscow to make a business deal there with a credit of 60 million pounds. The inquiry was based on a report of the British radio. This rumour was also denied as not true by members of the German Embassy.
3. On 23 June the Moscow representative of Havas was informed from Paris that, according to a report of the Havas representative in Berlin, a delegation of German economists – seven persons – would be travelling to Moscow for business negotiations and he was asked to find out what was going on in Moscow. Inquiries into this matter were negated by the German Embassy.
4. On Thursday, 22 June, rumours were going around amongst American journalists saying that the representative of the Führer, Rudolf Hess or another high-ranking German was present in Moscow. This rumour was also denied by the Embassy.

No sooner was Schulenburg again *en poste* than Hilger was summoned to Berlin, whence he was immediately flown to Obersalzburg in order to give a full report on the Russian situation to Hitler. Upon his return to Moscow, Hilger told me about his conversation. He had tried to give Hitler a balanced picture of Russia's strengths, neither exaggerating nor minimizing them. Apparently, this did little more than leave Hitler wondering where the loyalties of this russified German lay.

As I observed Schulenburg during June, 1939, I realized that his conception of the negotiations was so different from Hitler's that further meetings between them could only have had the effect of bringing their disagreement to light. Schulenburg saw the establishment of good relations with the USSR as an end in itself, while Hitler viewed it simply as a means of assuring Stalin's quiescence in the face of a German attack on Poland. Schulenburg was acutely aware of this difference, and one could sense that it disturbed him profoundly, but on a day-to-day basis he was no less upset by the erratic nature of the signals he was receiving from Berlin. These inconsistencies arose from the differing timetables favoured by Ribbentrop on the one hand and the Ministry of Foreign Affairs on the other. Finally, though, Hitler's impatience won the day and Schulenburg was urged to press forward as quickly as possible.

This again stung me to action. I was by no means pleased that my earlier contact with Relli had led to such unexpected and, for me, dangerous results, but having long since crossed the Rubicon, I decided to resume my little campaign to strengthen the will of the Western powers. I considered an approach to the British to be particularly important in view of the negotiations between them and the French and the Russians. With this in mind I reviewed my possible contacts. I had no hope of approaching directly the chief British negotiator, William Strang, in spite of the fact that I had known him well from the time he had served as counsellor at the British Embassy in Moscow. Nor could I meet my old friend Conrad Collier, another member of the delegation who had formerly served as air attaché with the British Embassy in Moscow. I did meet Strang and Collier socially during their visit, but we all understood the inappropriateness of entering into more serious discussions at the moment.

The one Briton whom I decided I could alert to the possibility of a Soviet–German agreement was my friend Armin Dew, who had just succeeded Fitzroy Maclean. In the course of a conversation with him during the second week of July, I made the same point as I had already stressed with Relli, albeit now in more cautious tones. I also sought out my old friend at the French Embassy, Baron Gontran de Juniac. Again I reported what I had earlier passed on to Relli, namely, that it would not be France or England that would make the treaty with the USSR, but Germany. Unlike France or Great Britain, Germany was in a position to make concessions to Stalin in the Baltic, concessions which would seal our rapprochement. This conversation took place at the American *dacha*, but I do not recall the precise date, since it was impossible for me to keep a diary of such conspiratorial activities.

It goes without saying that during these critical days I talked with only one member of each of the various foreign embassies. To have maintained illicit contact with more than one person would not only have imperilled the confidentiality of my reports but would have diluted their impact, since I made a point of informing each person that I was passing information to no one else at his Embassy. It was important that each of my contacts act in the knowledge that he alone was responsible for transmitting my reports to his government.

After his return from Berlin, Schulenburg maintained close contact with his good friend, Rosso. There could be no doubt that, thanks to Schulenburg's diligence, Rosso and his Embassy were far better informed on the ominous developments between Berlin and Moscow than was Rosso's counterpart in Berlin, Attolico, notwithstanding the fact that Attolico had served for many years in Moscow and had an excellent grasp of the situation. Knowing that Schulenburg and Rosso were in such regular communication, and sensing already that Mussolini was not about to stand in the way of a pact between Hitler and Stalin, I made no further confidences to Relli.

Once the British and French began to negotiate in earnest for a pact with the USSR against Germany, it was obviously more difficult for me to meet my French and British colleagues so frequently. In addition to the problems posed by the negotiations, the various arrangements connected with them demanded every minute of my friends' time, making it more difficult for me to see them. In view of these obstacles and of the disquieting results of my conversations with Relli, I decided that it would be best now to focus my efforts on the American Embassy. There were several reasons for this change in tactics. First of all, the Americans had time enough to be in contact with me, their role being more that of observer than participant in the unfolding drama. Second, I was pretty sure that by informing the Americans, word would reach Paris and London, since I knew that their Foreign Offices both maintained confidential contact with Washington. Moreover, I had every reason to

153

believe that my previous conversations with Bohlen had been passed on faithfully to the State Department. For these reasons I again turned my attention to 'Chip' Bohlen.

Actually, my 'reports' to Bohlen had begun on a modest scale a while earlier. I first spoke to 'Chip' Bohlen about the impending change in German–Soviet relations on 16 May, 1939. 'Chip' himself has described our conversations in some detail, so I need not retell the whole story here. I was at first somewhat less forthcoming with Bohlen than I had been with the others. This reticence gave rise to a thoroughly unsettling scepticism on the part of 'Chip' which I had to overcome by providing further data. Even then, I parcelled out my information to him gradually, and only as a means of overcoming what struck me as excessive doubts.

As usual, 'Chip' and I met at the American *dacha*. Since he was a good rider, I arranged that we would ride together. Once we had got away from the fields nearest to the *dacha*, I told him that a series of unexpected discussions on German–Soviet relations had been taking place in Berlin, and that the result of these discussions could constitute a major shift in German policy. I told him that, earlier in May, a series of discussions on the military strength of the USSR had taken place in Berlin. The object of these was to determine whether the Russians were in any position to respond militarily to a German invasion of Poland. While I did not cite Schulenburg's lecture at the *Wehrmachtsakademie*, I did say that expert opinion was agreed that the Soviet Union was in no condition to wage an offensive campaign. I knew that Hilger had made this point in Berlin and assumed that Schulenburg would also be willing to do so now, in the event that he was asked. Finally, I revealed to 'Chip' that the Foreign Ministry in Berlin had asked me to arrange for Schulenburg to meet Molotov as soon as the Ambassador returned to Moscow from Berlin.

Two days later, I was at the *dacha* again. Bohlen now seemed even more sceptical than he had been on the 16th, so I told him that Schulenburg would soon arrive back in Moscow carrying orders from Ribbentrop that he was to determine whether the Russians were prepared to enter into closer relations with Germany.

I had no way of being certain that all this would be reported back to Washington, although 'Chip's' interest in my narrative indicated that he would not keep its contents to himself. In his memoirs, Bohlen confirmed that he reviewed my report with the new American Chargé d'Affaires and that they cabled the following report to Washington on 20 May:

On his return to Berlin from Teheran the German Ambassador was told by Ribbentrop, obviously reflecting Hitler's views, that in the opinion of the German government, Communism had ceased to exist in the Soviet Union; that the Communist International was no longer a factor of importance in Soviet foreign relations, and that consequently it was felt that no real ideological barrier remained between Germany and Russia. Under the circumstances, it was desired that the Ambassador return to Moscow to convey very discreetly to the Soviet government the impression that Germany entertained no animosity towards it and to endeavor to ascertain the present Soviet attitude towards Soviet–German relations. Ribbentrop impressed upon the Ambassador the necessity of exercising the greatest caution in the premises, as any appearance of a German approach to the Soviet Union would alarm Japan, which in view of the special relationship existing between Germany and that country would be very undesirable.

In reply to the Ambassador's query as to whether in view of the Soviet–British negotiations some more specific and direct approach would not be desirable, Ribbentrop replied that the German government was not alarmed at the prospect of an agreement between Great Britain and the Soviet Union as it was not convinced that England and France would be disposed to lend extensive or wholehearted military assistance to any country in Eastern Europe. Ribbentrop then told the Ambassador that Germany desired mediation to settle the question of Danzig and the auto-road across the corridor to East Prussia and that even in the event of a conflict with Poland, Germany had no intention of attempting to occupy the whole of that country. Ribbentrop's instructions were oral and they left to the Ambassador's discretion the manner of bringing the foregoing to the attention of the Soviet government. The impression, however, was received that without committing the German government to any line of action vis-à-vis the Soviet Government, he was to convey an indication of the change in attitude on the part of the higher circles in Berlin towards this country [the Soviet Union] as well as the assurance that Germany was in favour of the maintenance of an independent Poland. Despite Ribbentrop's statement to the contrary, it was believed that the purpose of this approach was not unconnected with the Soviet–British negotiations.

In conveying the above information it was emphasized that the Ambassador's instructions were general in nature and could not be taken as a definite German proposal to the Union of Soviet Socialist Republics, although a possible first step in that direction, and that future developments along this line would depend upon the reaction encountered by the Ambassador in his conversations here. In this connection it was stated that officials of the Soviet Embassy in Berlin, especially the Counsellor, Astakhov, have intimated recently to members of the German Foreign Office that Soviet foreign policy was now on a new basis, a statement which has been repeated here to a German correspondent by the new Chief of the Press Section of the Commissariat for Foreign Affairs. . . .

Bohlen records in his memoirs that he handled my reports with considerable care, drafting his cables in longhand rather than dictating them, fearing their interception by Russian bugs. They were then coded and cabled to Washington, bearing the highest security classification. The cables were passed directly to the Secretary of State, Cordell Hull, who was then responsible for handling their contents. According to Bohlen, Hull at once met the Ambassadors of Great Britain and France and shared with them the contents of my reports on the German–Soviet pact. Bohlen, of course, had no way of knowing that both the British and French had already been tipped off independently.

The Ambassador, after commenting on the more favourable atmosphere in regard to the Soviet Union which he had found in Berlin, inquired of Molotov as to the possibility of continuing the economic negotiations which had been in abeyance for some months. In reply, Molotov expressed doubt as to the feasibility of the development of economic relations between the two countries in the absence of a 'political base', and requested the Ambassador's views on this subject. The Ambassador, it was stated, replied that since as an Ambassador he did not determine policy, he could not offer any authoritative opinion on this matter, but that perhaps Molotov as Foreign Minister of the Soviet Union would be in a position to explain exactly what the Soviet government envisaged by a 'political basis'. Molotov, however, evaded the question by a vague reference to the necessity of giving the matter further consideration.

In his conversation with Potemkin, which consisted largely of an exchange of courtesies, the Ambassador again referred to his belief in the possibility of an improvement in Soviet–German relations at the present time.

In general the impression was received, and I understand reported to Berlin, that Molotov was purposely reserved in regard to the general question of an improvement in Soviet–German relations and that only a definite proposal from the German government would be seriously considered here. Consequently, it was believed that any further developments along this line would depend upon whether the German government was prepared at the present time to make a clear and definite approach to the Soviet government, and the personal opinion was offered that in light of Ribbentrop's concern over the possible effect on Japan, such a step was doubtful, at least pending the outcome of German–Japanese conversations which it was stated are now being carried on.

I realized full well that the minute my efforts in Moscow came to light, the Nazi authorities would have every right to charge me with high treason. This was somewhat disturbing, though I tried to console myself with the thought that my leaks were far more likely to escape disclosure in Moscow than they would have been had they taken place in Berlin. This did not allay my concerns, however, and my position became increasingly uncomfortable. It was made worse by the fact that I had acted on my own, without the reassurance of Schulenburg, Erich Kordt, or any of my other Berlin friends.

To be sure, Schulenburg was aware that I was in constant contact with other young diplomats in Moscow and had no objection. But I was not yet sufficiently confident of Schulenburg's attitude to tell him my thoughts on the events of the moment, let alone my efforts to thwart a German–Soviet agreement.

As Hitler's impatience grew, Schulenburg increased his efforts to come to terms with the Russians. Once more, I reported all this in considerable detail to Bohlen. Bohlen's report on our conversation was contained in a further cable of 1 July:

The Ambassador told Molotov that, following his visit to Berlin, he could assure him that Germany entertained no aggressive designs against the Soviet Union, and in confirmation thereof pointed out that the German press had ceased entirely the publication of any anti-Soviet views or articles; that acquiescence in the Hungarian annexation of Ruthenia could be regarded as proof that Germany entertained no designs on the Ukraine; and that furthermore the conclusion of nonaggression pacts with the Balkan countries was additional proof of the absence of any German intention to attack the Soviet Union. In respect of the nonaggression pacts with the Balkan states, Molotov remarked that these treaties were with third countries and not with the Soviet Union. The Ambassador then remarked that the nonaggression treaty of 1926 between Germany and the Soviet Union was still in existence. To this Molotov replied that he was interested to hear the Ambassador say so inasmuch as the Soviet government had had certain doubts as to the continued validity of that treaty in view of subsequent agreements entered into by the German government. The Ambassador said that if Molotov referred to the German–Italian Alliance, he could assure him that this was in no way affecting the treaty. Molotov then stated that the denunciation of the nonaggression treaty with Poland had raised doubts of the value of such treaties at the present time, to which the Ambassador replied that the situation with respect to Poland was somewhat different in that the German government felt that Poland by joining the 'encirclement' policy of Great Britain had in fact contravened the nonaggression pact with Germany.

The subject of the new commercial negotiations was then discussed, and Molotov informed the Ambassador that as he was not familiar with the details of this matter it would be better for the German Commercial Counselor to continue his discussion with Foreign Trade Commissar Anastas I. Mikoyan. Upon departing, the Ambassador inquired whether he was correct in assuming that the Soviet Union desired normal relations with all countries which did not transgress Soviet interests and whether this was equally applicable to Germany Molotov replied in the affirmative.

By this point Bohlen's keen interest in our conversations left me fully confident that he was reporting them to Washington. We always met in the most informal conditions, and I regret that 'Chip's' professional duties prevented him from enjoying the summer days more fully. But I knew he was doing his job and therefore continued to feed him information. I reported to him in great detail about the various commercial negotiations that were under way, and let him know about the USSR's huge order for German turbines practically before the ink was dry on the agreement. In addition, I spelled out in some detail the political implications of the Soviet Union's agreement to purchase various machines for military production from Germany, emphasizing that such purchases reflected the understanding that was growing between the two countries.

I was appalled that the British and French governments did not seem to perceive the importance of these negotiations. Had they done so, they would have sent higher ranking officials to meet the Russians in Leningrad at this time. I did not hesitate to regale Bohlen with the pleasure that Berlin had derived from the Allies' seeming lack of concern. Bohlen had by now abandoned his sceptical posture and was seeking me out at every opportunity. This satisfied me that my reports were reaching their target in Washington, but also caused me to worry about the possibility of my being exposed. Fortunately, Bohlen's personal loyalty and professionalism combined to protect me.

By early August it was clear that Schulenburg would reach an agreement with Molotov. On 5 August, Schulenburg told me that his most recent discussion with Molotov had convinced him that the Russians were prepared to enter into more formal negotiations. By this point Schulenburg had calmed the Soviets' suspicions regarding the possibility of German expansion into the Baltic, and had even indicated that Germany would respect the region as a Soviet sphere of influence, i.e., that Hitler would not oppose the annexation of the three Baltic republics by Stalin. With this and other assurances, the Russians apparently were convinced of the desirability of pushing forward in their talks with us, even though their discussions with the British and French were still proceeding, albeit without great zeal on either side. Once convinced that Germany's position was growing stronger, Schulenburg let Molotov know that Berlin did not look with favour on the continuation of the Anglo-French-Soviet discussions in Moscow. This prompted

Molotov to refer once more to the Soviet desire to put their defence on a completely secure basis, which we understood to mean on the basis of political agreement.

On 15 August the two met once more, and Molotov expressed the Soviet Union's readiness to move to direct negotiations leading to an agreement. As usual, I reported this to Bohlen shortly after it occurred. In fact, as I later learned, I moved faster than Schulenburg, who waited until the following day, 16 August, before cabling to von Weizsäcker in Berlin that, 'At this point it actually looks as if we will achieve the desired success in our negotiations here.'

My reporting also took a new turn on the 16th, thanks to a ball that was held at the German Embassy and was attended by most of the younger diplomats in Moscow, including nearly every member of the Mutual Admiration Society. Schulenburg was the host, but was not able to receive his guests, having been called once more to the Kremlin to discuss the proposed German–Soviet pact with Molotov. My friend Migone, first secretary of the Italian Embassy, noticed Schulenburg's absence at once and came over to me to ask the reason. I replied that I would tell him later, at the end of the ball. After several hours of dancing, we sat down to the light meal that had been prepared, the champagne having already begun to flow earlier. Between the dinner and the confusion of guests leaving the Embassy an hour later, I found the opportunity to chat privately with both Migone and Bohlen. I told Migone exactly what was occurring in the Kremlin, and said that the agreement was so far advanced that Ribbentrop had already indicated his readiness to come to Moscow for the signing. Eager for Migone to report this to Rome, I nonetheless took the precaution of asking him not to disclose in his report that the information had come from Moscow. Migone wasted no time. By one a.m. on the 17th the Italian government received a telegram from Migone's Ambassador, Rosso, containing everything that I had passed to my friend. The Rosso telegram had no impact in Rome; indeed, the Italian foreign minister did not so much as mention it in his diary! Independent of me, Admiral Canaris, head of German counter-intelligence, had been informing the Italian military attaché in Berlin of Hitler's plans and had been urging the Italians to inform Hitler that they would not accept his proposed action against Poland.

My leaks to Bohlen did not bring about their desired results, either. At the ball and in a further meeting the next day I was able to brief 'Chip' fully on the dramatic turn of events. When the American diplomatic papers were published after the war, I learned that he had cabled the following message to Washington, apparently after due consultation with the Ambassador:

The German Ambassador saw Molotov last night for an hour and a half and under instructions from his government made to Molotov the following statement in respect to Germany [sic] policy towards the Soviet Union which it is understood emanated from Hitler himself:

After reiterating that the German government had entertained no aggressive intentions whatsoever against the Soviet Union and that there was no conflict of interest between the countries from 'the Baltic to the Black Sea', the statement continued that the German government was prepared to discuss in advance with the Soviet government 'any territorial question in Eastern Europe'; that the German government felt that serious conversations between the two governments should begin soon, since events might otherwise develop which might adversely and unnecessarily affect Soviet–German relations. The statement concluded that the German government was prepared to send a high-ranking official to discuss the question in Moscow. The Ambassador, I understand, left no written memorandum of this statement but his remarks were taken down verbatim by a stenographer. The Ambassador added that Hitler had requested that the contents of his statement be brought to the attention of Stalin himself.

Molotov in reply, after promising to bring the contents of the statement immediately to Stalin's attention, added that for the first time the Soviet government was convinced of the seriousness of Germany's desire to improve its relations with the Soviet Union and he informed the Ambassador that the Soviet government would 'welcome' the continuation of the political conversations but only if there was reasonable assurance that they would lead to definite and concrete results. As possible results, Molotov mentioned: (1) the conclusion of a non-aggression pact between the Soviet Union and Germany; (2) the cessation of any direct or indirect encouragement on the part of Germany to Japanese aggression in the Far East; and (3) regulations of mutual interest in the Baltic. Molotov felt that these three subjects should be discussed in preliminary conversations before the question of sending a German emissary to Moscow should be definitely decided. The results of the Ambassador's interview with Molotov were telegraphed to Berlin last night and a complete account is going forward by special courier from the German Embassy on Thursday ...

Although it is possibly too soon to speak of a definite German–Soviet rapprochement at the present time ... a steady progress can be noted in the conversation which the German Ambassador here has had with Molotov during the past two and a half months. Furthermore I have every reason to believe that the Soviet government has not in connection with the present negotiations informed the French and British governments of these developments in its relationship with Germany.

This, then, is Bohlen's account of my contact with him. It is accurate on all major points. The only note that should perhaps be added is that I mentioned to Bohlen that I was quite sure Ribbentrop would be named as Germany's negotiator. Since this could not yet be firmly established, however, Bohlen judiciously did not include it.

The only near miss that occurred in his otherwise careful handling of my reports had nothing to do with 'Chip'. As it happened, this cable was passed on from the Secretary of State, Hull, to the British Ambassador who cabled its contents to the British Foreign Office just before a German spy was discovered in the cipher room in London. There was considerable fear that this spy might have deciphered the messages from Hull and identified the source of Hull's information. Fortunately this did not happen and, in fact, the deciphering was delayed until after the spy had been replaced.

It was easier to pass on my information to 'Chip' than it might otherwise have been, since I asked nothing in return. Being firmly convinced that the British and French negotiations with the Russians would come to nothing, I had no need to ask him to see that pressure was exerted in that quarter; and since his own government was more an observer than a participant, there was nothing further that I could have gained through him anyway.

In reviewing these conversations with 'Chip' Bohlen, I must distinguish between my visceral feeling that Hitler intended to go to war against Poland and my day-to-day reporting of events. Whereas my daily reporting was based scrupulously on confirmed facts, my conviction regarding Hitler's military intentions came from within me. This made it the more difficult for me to convince 'Chip' that war was inevitable. I hammered away at him as hard as I could but he stubbornly resisted my arguments and I could only be proved right by the outbreak of war. Nor did I think that he was merely adopting a tone of scepticism in order to get more information from me. In the face of his obstinacy, I insisted over and over that Hitler was prepared to sell out the Baltic States and perhaps even Romania and parts of the Balkans in order to get the Soviets to acquiesce in his project. In Bohlen's eyes, however, all this seemed to amount to little more than Cassandra-like cries, and from a lowly second secretary in the German Embassy at that – scarcely material for a formal report to Washington!

Given what seemed to be Bohlen's deep scepticism, one might wonder why I did not reveal to 'Chip' that there existed a Resistance movement in Germany bent on preventing Hitler from starting a war. I realized that such news would carry considerable weight with his superiors, but did not report it since I had no way of knowing for certain that a larger movement really was active. During my months in Memel and Teheran I had been out of touch with my Berlin friends, nor did I dare contact them now, since all our communications with Germany were closely monitored. Being incompletely informed myself, I therefore remained silent.

Over the years, Stalin's motives in promoting the pact with Hitler have been hotly disputed. I have not followed these debates closely, and can only report what I then believed to have been the case, namely, that Stalin was not seeking merely to gain time. To be sure, his Machiavellianism was profound, and he never doubted that the ends justified the means, but there was near unanimity among the Western embassies in Moscow that Stalin had a higher regard for the Germans than for the other Western powers, and that he certainly trusted them more. The speech which Stalin delivered in March 1939, revealed these feelings directly. Later, in a cable to Hitler of 8 August, Stalin spoke of a non-aggression pact as a 'basis for liquidating the political tension' between Germany and the USSR – far more than he need have said had he been merely playing for time. Schulenburg, too, had come to the opinion that Stalin was genuine in his approach to Germany.

With the way now open for the final agreement between Stalin and Hitler, I had to admit to myself that my modest efforts at obstruction had failed. I had played my last card and could henceforth not expect to influence events, even marginally, from my lowly position in the diplomatic service. I was disgusted with diplomacy and with myself as a diplomat, and wanted nothing so much as to join the army. The centre of action was there, I realized, and with a rifle in my hand I could surely accomplish more than with a pen or cocktail glass. I therefore resolved to return at once to Berlin to explore the possibility of joining the army. I asked Count Schulenburg's permission on 16 August. He at once said I could go, and I left immediately for Berlin, pausing only to visit friends briefly in Stockholm.

In Berlin I telephoned the former assistant military attaché at our Embassy, Colonel Hans Krebs, and told him that I wanted to leave the diplomatic service and join the army. Krebs knew my difficulties. He understood that a non-Aryan such as myself was banned from serving as an officer in the German Army. To get around this, he advised me to contact my old regiment (the Fourth Cavalry, which had now become the Sixth Armoured Car Regiment), without going through the normal channels.

Following Krebs' advice, I tried first to reach Lieutenant Heinz von Twardowski, the son of my former counsellor and ADC to the Sixth Armoured Car Regiment. But the regiment was already on manoeuvres in East Prussia. I realized at once that the preliminaries to the mobilization of German forces against Poland were already in progress. Failing to make contact with Twardowski, I went to the *Wehrbezirkskommando Ausland* (Registry Office for Reservists Living Abroad), whose commanding officer, Major Bochow, informed me in a matter-of-fact way that my case presented not one but several problems. First, Ribbentrop had forbidden members of the Ministry of Foreign Affairs to be mobilized without his explicit consent. The reason for this was that at the outset of World War I junior members of the Ministry of Foreign Affairs' staff had been called up with the result that the Ministry had been crippled for several weeks until it managed to reclaim its staff. Second, as a non-Aryan, I could not serve as an officer or non-commissioned officer. The only alternative, then, was to bring me into the army by demoting me to the rank of Private First Class (*Gefreiter*). Bochow ruled this out, on the grounds that it would be a dishonour to the German army to demote anyone bearing the name of so illustrious a figure in Prussian history as Field Marshal von Herwarth.

Having eliminated every possibility, Bochow gave me his personal advice on how to solve my problem – the same advice as Krebs had given. I should try to make direct contact with a colonel who was in command of a regiment, because he would be free to recruit whomever he wanted, even if it violated the racial laws. I was grateful for this advice and acted on it at once. Curiously, the daughter of Bochow later married my cousin, Captain von Haber, a descendant of the same Jewish family as my grandmother's.

Returning to my home in Berlin, I took care not to report all this to my parents, who were always ready to take offence at any hindrance to my career. Shortly after my arrival I received a summons by telephone from the office of Ernst von Weizsäcker, Permanent Under-Secretary since the resignation of Bernhard von Bülow and Hans Georg von Mackensen. Weizsäcker was a close friend of Schulenburg's, a staunch foe of Hitler and one of the many civil servants who stayed on in order to do everything within their power to prevent the outbreak of war. I reported to Weizsäcker's office. Scarcely had I entered than he asked me whether I thought there would be a treaty with the Russians. I replied that I was convinced that there would be, since Hitler, unlike the British and French, was in a position to make the concessions to Stalin that he had so strongly desired. Weizsäcker, of course, was well informed on events and knew that the German army had already been mobilized against Poland. Nonetheless, he heard my views with obvious distress, realizing what the treaty would mean for Germany.

I returned home with a long face. Later that same day, I was summoned once more to the Ministry, this time to the Protocol Section. There I was told that on the following morning, 22 August, Ribbentrop was flying to Moscow and that I was to accompany him on the trip, which was to be interrupted for one night in Königsberg. I was selected to accompany Ribbentrop because of my acquaintance with the officialdom of East Prussia, dating from my time in Memel. It was Schulenburg who had nominated me for this assignment.

Before setting out, I telephoned *Oberregierungsrat* von Plötz, who was on the Königsberg staff of *Oberpräsident* and *Gauleiter* Erich Koch, asking him to make all necessary arrangements for Ribbentrop to pass through Königsberg and to spend the night at the Park Hotel – all top secret. Also, in order to forward my own plans, I told Plötz to order Major Ritter and Edler von Dawans of the First Army Corps to report at the lobby of the Park Hotel at 11:00 p.m. Plötz began to complain about the difficulties in doing this, but I cut him off sharply, saying that I didn't want to hear anything about difficulties and that Dawans must be there without fail at 11:00 p.m. Within a couple of hours, I called back to check on Plötz, and he again began complaining about the difficulties. Once more I ordered him to bring Dawans to the Park Hotel without fail.

Shortly before 11:00 p.m. that same evening, I arrived at the Park Hotel with Ribbentrop and his suite. Dawans was sitting in the lobby. Immediately, he rushed over to me and asked: 'What the hell did you order me to come here for? We are no longer in Königsberg.' In my haste, I had forgotten that the army had been mobilized and that Dawans was now at Mohrungen, 120 kilometres from Königsberg.

I apologized as best I could and explained that I had wanted to see him desperately as an old friend. First, I gave him some news – hot news – to pass on to his Army Corps Commander, General Georg von Küchler. I told Dawans that Ribbentrop was on his way to Moscow to sign a treaty, and I informed him about the actual details of the agreement. He thanked me heartily for this information and agreed to pass it on. Then I came to the main point. I explained that I wanted to leave the diplomatic service but was prevented by the Aryan laws from joining the army with my rank of *Wachtmeister*. He assured me that a place would be found for me, and that he was prepared to take action in spite of the legal difficulties. He asked me to be sure to get back to East Prussia quickly and to report to him in Mohrungen no later than 25 August, because their orders were to start hostilities on 26 August.

When Ribbentrop arrived in Moscow to negotiate the treaty with Stalin, a group of Soviet officials and senior staff of our Embassy were there to greet him. Disembarking from the plane, I found myself standing next to my old friend, Gebhardt von Walther. He greeted me with a nod and we watched the show before us. Amidst the bustle, Walther grabbed my arm and said: 'Look how the Gestapo officers are shaking hands with their counterparts of the NKWD and how they are all smiling at each other. They're obviously delighted finally to be able to collaborate. But watch out! This will be disastrous, especially when they start exchanging files.'

During my last days in Moscow, I took no interest in the negotiations, since I knew that the treaty was by now a *fait accompli*. The fact that so high-ranking a figure as the Minister for Foreign Affairs had been sent to Moscow for the negotiations all but assured that the knot would finally be tied. The Nazi–Soviet pact, dated 23 August, 1939, was signed at two o'clock on the morning of 24 August. Moments later, photographers were invited into the room where the ceremony took place in order to record the momentous event. The German photographer Helmut Laux was among those thus honoured. He later told me how he had taken a shot of Stalin and Ribbentrop together, the Georgian's champagne glass raised in a toast to the health of the Führer, and Ribbentrop's glass raised to Stalin's health. Seeing him at work, Stalin remarked that it would probably not be a good idea to publish the photo, lest it give the Soviet and German people a false impression. Laux immediately began to take the film out of his camera in order to turn it over to Stalin. Stalin stopped him with a wave, assuring him that he trusted the word of a German.

On the night the treaty was signed, I was sitting in the residence of our Ambassador maintaining telephone contact between Moscow and Berlin. At one point I had to get Hitler's approval for a slight frontier adjustment. It was surprising to me to see how rapidly Hitler gave his assent to this and every other request that I passed on by phone. In each case he acted within less than three quarters of an hour, thus indicating clearly how eager he was to conclude the pact.

Once these final details were ironed out, I spent the rest of the night telephoning Germany trying to discover the whereabouts of my wife. Pussi had been taking the waters at Karlsbad. After several calls to the

Ministry and to my parents, I finally got word to her that she should come to Moscow as quickly as possible, so that she would not be crossing Poland at the moment of invasion. She achieved this by flying over Stockholm, but arrived in Moscow just after my own departure with Ribbentrop's party later that same day.

Promptly at nine on the morning of the 24th I went to Schulenburg. Events had so disrupted his accustomed routine that he was already in his office. I told him of my wish to leave the diplomatic service at once and join the army. As usual, I addressed him not in the second person plural *Sie*, as would have been normal in the diplomatic corps generally, but with his title, *Herr Botschafter*, the anachronistic usage which the Nazis had forbidden but which we preserved in Moscow as if it were a password symbolizing our distance from Hitler's rule. Schulenburg's response was typical of him. 'My dear Johnnie,' he said, 'why are you in such a rush? This war will last a long, long time, just like World War I. Even if you wait a few months, you will have plenty of time.'

In one way, I was grateful to Schulenburg for his advice. Pussi was still en route to Moscow, and I realized that a delay might enable me to see her before leaving, as I very much wanted to do. Yet I knew that such an arrangement would only postpone the inevitable. Admitting this to myself, I said: 'Mr Ambassador, I think my time has run out. I no longer want to be in the Foreign Service and would like to leave as quickly as possible to join the army.' Schulenburg sat there quietly, his thumbs twiddling. After a long pause he said: 'Well, you may be right. I worked hard for good relations between the Soviet Union and Germany, and in one sense I have achieved my goal. But you know perfectly well I did not really achieve anything. Up to now, the brakes which keep the train of Europe from plummeting down the track to war have held. With this treaty, they will be released. Nothing now exists to prevent Europe from plunging into war and Germany from hurtling into the abyss.' Schulenberg's tragedy was that he understood fully what his own achievement had helped to bring about.

I decided to stick to my original plan and leave with Ribbentrop by plane late that morning. The only foreigner to whom I said goodbye was 'Chip' Bohlen. So angered and depressed was I by now that I felt no hesitation in revealing to 'Chip' the secret contents of the Nazi–Soviet pact, presenting them as a lurid sort of going-away present. Unlike my earlier leaks, this could have no purpose beyond confronting the Western powers as soon as possible with the result of their neglect of Hitler's actions. My conversation with Bohlen is reported in his memoirs. Except for the fact that Ribbentrop was staying at the former Austrian legation rather than the German Chancery, his account is accurate in all details:

In the morning, Johnnie called and asked if I would go to the German Chancery to see him. While Ribbentrop was upstairs sleeping off his long night of successful negotiations and festivities at the Kremlin, my friend gave me the details of the ten-year pact. He told me that 'a full understanding' had also been embodied in a secret protocol whereby eastern Poland, Estonia, Latvia, and Bessarabia were recognized as spheres of Soviet vital interest, while western Poland would fall under German hegemony. Finland was not mentioned. The secret protocol also provided that the Soviet Union would be given territorial compensation if it so desired for any territorial changes that Germany might make in the countries lying between them. A provision of the basic agreement prohibiting each of the contracting parties from joining any group of powers directed against the other precluded Soviet adherence to the Anglo–French association as well as a German alliance with Japan ....

Johnnie said that the negotiations had been conducted personally by Stalin, who did not disguise from Ribbentrop that he had long been in favour of a Soviet–German rapprochement. When the treaty was concluded, Stalin drank a toast to Hitler, saying, 'The Germans love their Führer,' and called Hitler 'molodetz', a Russian slang expression meaning a 'fine fellow'.

Johnnie was depressed by the pact. As he sat in his dark, panelled office, he clearly foresaw that this would mean war against Poland. He told me that he was going back to Germany to rejoin his regiment.[3]

It was a moving moment. I knew the snug world of diplomatic Moscow was collapsing, and that after nearly a decade there I was being set adrift. I had no idea whether I would ever see 'Chip' again. But now I was in a terrible hurry. I had only a few hours in which to pull together my belongings and to settle my affairs. I finally arrived at the airport, just in time to see Ribbentrop's plane taxi down the runway. With some difficulty I got myself a place on the second plane, which was already on the runway, its doors closed and engines running. The engines stopped, the door re-opened and I jumped aboard. We flew directly to Stettin, from which I proceeded alone to Königsberg.

[3] Bohlen, pp. 82–3.

12

POLAND AND THE WESTERN FRONT, 1939–1940

After equipping myself in Königsberg, I went directly to Mohrungen and reported to Dawans, who showed me on the map which regiments were under the command of the Third Army. He offered to attach me to any regiment I wished, and I chose one of the two cavalry regiments stationed there. Immediately he sat down and wrote a letter of introduction to Lieutenant Colonel Helmuth Wachsen, the commander of the First Cavalry Regiment. After checking in briefly with General Georg von Küchler, to whom I gave a full report on what had occurred in Moscow, I hurried to my regiment so as to be there before the start of hostilities about 4.00 a.m. on 26 August.

On my way I stopped at Brigade headquarters and reported to the General Staff, Major von Collani, who offered to send me on by jeep to my regiment. Tension was already high. Collani spoke of a border incident that had occurred earlier that day when one of the non-commissioned officers of the First Cavalry Regiment had crossed the German–Polish frontier by mistake and had been killed.

Lying down for a short rest, I was immediately awakened by the telephone in Collani's room. Grabbing it, I was astonished to hear orders that the planned hostilities against Poland were to be suspended. I awakened Collani, who was also trying to rest. Half awake, he fumed that some mistake must have occurred in transmitting the order. Checking it for himself, he confirmed that the message was correct and therefore sent me at once to Wachsen to report to him. Apparently, Mussolini had tried at the last moment to convene an international conference. He did succeed in gaining a delay to 1 September but he did not achieve his larger objective, namely, to avert war by a new conference.

I reached Wachsen by midnight on the 25th just as he was issuing orders that the attack was not to be launched. Reading the letter from Dawans, Wachsen immediately welcomed me to the regiment and, after an hour, we sat down for a conversation. Assuring me that I could trust him as a fellow cavalry officer, he asked me for my honest assessment of the situation as I had seen it unfolding in Moscow. I told him that the attack against Poland could not be forestalled at this point and that, once launched, it would call forth a response from Great Britain, France, and eventually the United States. Any housewife keeping her accounts could see that against such odds Germany stood little chance. Such a war was bound to end, I concluded, exactly as World War I had ended.

Wachsen pressed me for my reasons for thinking that Great Britain and France would enter the war. I told him what I knew of the opinions of our Ambassadors, Dirksen in London and Welczeck in Paris. Both had reported to the Wilhelmstrasse that Britain and France would definitely go to war in the event of a German attack on Poland. Hitler had rejected their warnings because he was convinced, as a consequence of British and French passivity in the case of Czechoslovakia, that neither country would come to the help of Poland. I told Wachsen that my British and French friends in Moscow had left me in no doubt that this time Hitler would not get away with it. It is worth mentioning that when Britain and France did declare war, Hitler was so much taken by surprise that his reaction was to ask, 'What shall we do now?'

Wachsen was much moved by what I had said and, after a long pause, admitted that it was probably all true. He added that between the signing of the Soviet–German treaty on 23 August until the morning of the 25th, when orders were given to attack Poland, he had expected that the crisis would be solved peacefully, as at the Munich conference in the autumn of 1938. This hope had been shared by the regiment. With the new orders not to open hostilities as a result of Mussolini's intervention, this expectation had been briefly revived.

Wachsen sadly recalled his experience in World War I. He could well imagine, he said, the terrible and useless bloodshed that would occur. After another long pause he began again: 'Yes, Herwarth, I can find no grounds for disagreeing with your analysis. I therefore ask only one thing of you: do not discuss this with the other young officers. Most of them will go to their graves in the course of this war, and one can only hope that they will be able to die with their illusions intact.'

Once more Wachsen paused, and then continued: 'At the end of this, if we survive, you will probably be back in the Foreign Ministry and I perhaps will be selling newspapers or shoelaces outside the Friedrichstrasse station in the centre of Berlin. When you pass by, I hope you will remember to say a word to your former colonel.' I made a grim bet with him: if we won the war, I would give him a hundred bottles of fine French champagne; if we lost, however, he would give me nothing, because he would have nothing to give.

After the war, Wachsen was finally released from an American POW camp in France, where he read in the newspaper of my appointment to the Bavarian State Chancellery. He wrote me a postcard saying that he would arrive in Munich in a trainful of discharged prisoners. I went to see the Bavarian Prime Minister, Wilhelm Hoegner, to tell him about Wachsen and to get his permission to meet my friend at the station. He told me to use his car, and to bring Wachsen to the Presidential Office so that he could shake hands, with him. I found my former colonel at once, wearing an American uniform with the letters 'PW' on his back. I reported to him: 'Captain von Herwarth at your orders!' He was evidently much touched. I had also to report that his spot at the Friedrichstrasse Station was in the Soviet sector of Berlin but that I would help him find a better place for his newspaper and shoelace stand somewhere in the West.

On 1 September, 1939 the invasion of Poland began. The idea of regaining Danzig and the Corridor was not unpopular in the German army, especially not in an East Prussian regiment such as mine. The regiment reflected the feeling in Germany as a whole, particularly in the army, that both territories were properly Germany's and had been handed over to Poland only because of the spirit of vindictiveness that had prevailed at the Versailles Congress in 1918. Yet we crossed the frontier without a single 'Hurrah!' from the ranks. What a difference from 1914!

When we first made contact with the enemy, the three platoons of the Third Squadron of the First Cavalry Regiment were led by Lieutenant Egbert von Schmidt-Pauli, Lieutenant Count Friedrich Solms, and myself. The father of Schmidt-Pauli and an uncle of Solms had both served with my father in the Third Uhlan Guards Regiment, and when my father was captain of the Third Squadron, Schmidt-Pauli's father had been his lieutenant. It was, therefore, a striking coincidence that the three of us should have come together at this moment.

Far more bizarre, however, was the discovery in the course of conversation that we all had Jewish blood in our veins. When we first attacked, our unit had to capture a small hill. According to the lessons learned in World War I, German officers were not to march in front of their troops, lest the officer corps be needlessly destroyed. Nevertheless, at the height of the attack, I glanced to left and right and spotted Solms and Schmidt-Pauli moving along fifteen to twenty yards in front of their soldiers, who were understandably frightened at their first exposure to battle. I could not help but smile at the fact that we were all out there, disproving Hitler's theory that non-Aryans were incapable of being good officers.

In the first few days, we encountered practically no resistance and fought only one fierce night battle and a few minor skirmishes. Soon we found ourselves besieging Warsaw. I was stationed with my men by the railway line from Moscow, on the outskirts of the Polish capital. The signalman's wooden house close by was already well known to me, for I had always noticed it on my trips back home, knowing that when the train passed it I would soon be in Warsaw.

At this spot I met Colonel General Werner Baron von Fritsch, formerly the Supreme Commander of the German Army. Fritsch and my father had served in World War I under Field Marshal August von Mackensen. Because of this link, Fritsch had befriended me and been of great help over my difficulties as a non-Aryan.

His own history reflected the worst tendencies of the era. In February 1938, the Nazis had used a trumped-up charge that Fritsch was a homosexual in order to remove him from his command. Later, at the insistence of the army, he had been rehabilitated, although not given active command. The charges against him as well as the developments in Germany had left a deep mark upon Fritsch. At the outbreak of the war against Poland, he had joined the artillery regiment of which he was an honorary colonel.

When he saw me, Fritsch greeted me cordially, sent his warmest regards to my parents and rode off. Within half an hour I learned that he had been killed. Apparently, he had moved right to the front line. Violating orders, he stood erect, scanning the enemy lines with his field glasses until, a few seconds later, he was cut down by machine-gun fire. It was clear to us all that this brave man had committed suicide.

Shortly after the siege began, Lieutenant Count Solms was ordered to lead a cavalry patrol to determine whether we could get over the Vistula bridge in the suburb of Praga, to the north of Warsaw. A patrol from our brigade's bicycle battalion had been sent out on the same mission. I was part of Solms' group. We watched as the bicyclists advanced on the exposed road and were shot down. Thanks to our horses, we could go over the fields and thus avoid drawing fire. Soon we reached a village. In order to learn whether it was still held by Polish troops, our patrol approached as near to the settlement as possible, close enough for me to try my Russian on an old villager whom we encountered. As we were talking, our horses suddenly bolted and at the same instant the Poles in the village opened fire. Not being trained to shoot at mounted cavalry, however, they made the old mistake of aiming at our bodies rather than at those of the horses, and hence missed us. Our patrol did not accomplish its mission, but the ancient strength of the cavalry twice saved it from sure disaster.

The Poles, too, had mounted cavalry. One day, a patrol of cavalrymen from my unit was returning through a small wood when it stumbled into a Polish cavalry patrol only fifty yards away. There would certainly have been a battle had it not been for the fact that the Poles were equipped with lances, which we lacked. Since there was no time to dismount and to start shooting, the leader of the German patrol rightly decided to retreat. They turned heel and galloped away through the woods, the Polish horsemen in hot pursuit and gaining ground. Only when the Poles caught sight of the entire German regiment on the horizon did they back off. It is hard to imagine that a war which began with medieval lances could have ended with atomic bombs!

Warsaw fell after a brief resistance. The German army's record up to this point was good but by no means splendid. We had discovered just how raw and inexperienced our troops were; our better leadership and superior equipment barely compensated for this.

I took the opportunity to enter Warsaw. I was finally able to send a message to Pussi from there by telegraph and to assure her that I was not injured. Immediately after this my regiment was sent off to the East, pushing steadily forward until we got orders to make contact with the Soviet troops which had invaded East Poland as a consequence of the Hitler–Stalin Treaty. On our way to meet the Russian troops we occupied a Polish estate whose owner, an elderly countess, expressed great and rather pathetic relief at having been taken over by the Germans rather than by the Soviets. I wondered whether this would actually make much difference in the long run.

Because I spoke Russian, I was sent across the lines in order to establish contact with the Soviet troops. According to German military regulations, I was required to wear helmet and gloves for the occasion, since one had always to be thus equipped when reporting to his superior. I made my way to the Soviet lines with no difficulty, but was received by the commanding officer with extreme coldness. He bluntly let me know that if I did not remove my gloves he would consider it an insult to the Red Army. I realized that on this point German and Soviet military regulations were diametrically opposed. Once I explained this to him he

172

immediately changed his mood and, after reviewing in some detail the respective positions of the two regiments, invited me to an impromptu dinner which his officers were holding that evening.

The dinner was a lively affair, the Red Army officers taking great pains to congratulate me on the successes of the German army. After drinking to the health of Stalin and Hitler, the Soviet officers asked me when I thought our army could attack England and France. They wished Germany success in this, and expressed their warm desire that soldiers of the two armies should be comrades-in-arms in such an undertaking. I was astonished, and in a strange way heartened by such expressions of pro-German feeling. Under the circumstances, I hadn't the heart to explain to them that I considered an attack on France and Britain would be a catastrophe.

Soviet–German conviviality was the order of the day. In the autumn of 1939 Ribbentrop went again to Moscow in order to sign a second treaty with the Soviet Union. Stalin gave a party in honour of the visiting German delegation. Just as the group was about to start eating, Stalin came round to Köstring and heartily told him: 'General, you must forget that we attacked you during the trials.' He was referring to the fact that at the Radek trial in the winter of 1936–37 they had cited Köstring as the German with whom the accused had been in contact and that, as a consequence, the Soviets had demanded his recall. Stalin was not usually in the habit of apologizing for anything that went on during his show trials.

Since I was not in Moscow at this time, I must rely on my wife's experience to document the extraordinary cordiality that sprang up between Germans and Russians at this period. Trained as a secretary in industry and already having worked for Count von der Schulenburg, Pussi was a natural addition to the Embassy staff after I left. She was one of a large number of new people who had been taken on by the Embassy to handle new work in the political, economic, and military fields. Meanwhile, the Soviet authorities had lifted the ban on contact with Germans that had been in effect since 1932. Since most of my Soviet friends did not know that I had departed, they – or at least those who had survived the purges – invited us to dinner and theatre parties. Pussi sometimes went to them alone.

On 7 November, 1939, Pussi attended a reception at the 'Spiridonovka' in honour of the Soviet Revolution. As usual, it was a huge affair, with abundant buffet, liveried servants and numerous guests; among them, of course, the entire diplomatic corps. Pussi was much impressed by the great cordiality which the Soviet officials lavished upon the Germans. The atmosphere had changed overnight, as a conversation between my wife and Anastas Mikoyan attests. She had been talking to Guido Relli, my old Italian friend. Mikoyan joined them and affably opened the conversation by asking how long Pussi had been in Moscow. She in turn enquired about his family. With a radiant smile the forty-eight-year-old Armenian answered: 'I have five sons ... and I could produce some more!'

Gradually, the talk shifted to politics. With his Armenian expansiveness, Mikoyan praised the virtues of the German people. He spoke of German accuracy, thoroughness, and punctiliousness, and explained that the only thing Germany really lacked was the boundless raw materials of the USSR. The combination of Soviet natural resources and German know-how opened prospects that simply took his breath away. Mikoyan declared enthusiastically that the treaty marked one of the most important moments in all history, and that the alliance that it brought into being was unbeatable. Not realizing that Relli was an Italian, although he was wearing the lictor of the Italian Fascist party, Mikoyan then proceeded to contrast German thoroughness with southern slovenliness and *Schlamperei*. Relli, who was standing at Mikoyan's elbow, took it all with good humour.

Pussi took the opportunity to tell Mikoyan that between mid-September and mid-October she had been in Murmansk. She knew, of course, that it was Mikoyan who had developed Murmansk from a fishing station to an important ice-free port with huge industrial and military installations. She described to him how, with two other members of the Embassy, she had taken care of the crews and passengers from some twenty of our ships that had taken refuge in Murmansk in order to avoid seizure by the British navy. Pussi praised the co-operativeness of the Soviet officials in Murmansk, who helped to get some two thousand passengers back to Germany and who provided our ships and crews with everything they needed.

The German ships departed singly in the dead of night under a faint new moon, so they could reach German ports unnoticed by the British. For three days after their departure, the Soviet authorities did not allow ships of other nations to leave Murmansk, lest their wireless reports might enable the British to learn the position of our vessels.

The conversation with Mikoyan continued for some while, and ended with his expressing the hope that from now on we might meet more often. Over the next few months he was to dine frequently with Schulenburg and a small group of guests, to whom he evinced the same enthusiasm over the prospects of German–Soviet friendship. It is interesting to note that Mikoyan was one of the first high-ranking Soviet officials to come to Germany after relations were renewed under Adenauer in 1955.

In contrast to the cordial atmosphere that now existed between Russians and Germans was the enforced coldness between the diplomats of Germany, France and Great Britain, who, as belligerents, ordered their respective diplomats to avoid all fraternization. This was especially depressing for my wife, since our most intimate friends were suddenly declared enemies. Through looks and signs exchanged in secret, they assured each other of their mutual friendship. Once Pussi found herself at the Bolshoi sitting next to our best friend, de Juniac. When the lights went out, they took the chance to talk with all their usual openness. The moment the lights went on, they had to ignore each other.

Once our troops had established contact with the Red Army, my regiment was pulled back to Garwolin, south-east of Warsaw, where our stay was brief. At the end of November 1939, my regiment was transferred to Westphalia, where we remained until the outbreak of war on the Western Front in 1940. We arrived by train at Kloppenburg station, only a few miles from the villages in which we would be billeted Disembarking from the train, we were greeted as heroes of the Polish campaign and offered schnapps by the local populace. Some of the men were soon quite tipsy. Ordinarily, this would have presented no particular problem, but we had to make quite a journey that same evening, and a good number of the men were incapable of climbing into the saddle. By an enormous effort we got everyone mounted and set out on the icy roads. The horses slipped constantly and the men were falling from the saddles at every turn. It was all we officers could do to keep these heroes of the Polish campaign astride their mounts.

In the following months we moved nearer and nearer to the Dutch border. We had no doubt that the so-called 'Phoney War' would soon be replaced by the real thing. My regiment viewed the possibility of war in the West with the greatest apprehension. Practically every soldier had at least one relative who had been killed on the Western Front during World War I. Almost to a man we were convinced that the outbreak of war there would seal our fate as it had done theirs. These apprehensions were shared by the higher-ranking officers and also by the generals – a fact that I learned during some brief days in Berlin.

Once the regiment had been moved West, it became easier for me to get back to Berlin for short leaves. During one such visit to my parents, I made an effort to meet every commanding officer I knew. From them I gained the impression that there was no enthusiasm for the campaign against France and Britain. I also checked with Brücklmeier, Kordt, and Etzdorf. Kordt and Etzdorf were by now on constant call, so my visits to them were brief and hurried. I was able to spend more time with Brücklmeier, but recent events had placed him in an extremely delicate position that made him a less useful source of information than he would have been earlier. It seems that Ribbentrop had discovered that Brücklmeier was harshly critical of his policies and had charged him with disloyalty. In October 1939, Brücklmeier was arrested and interrogated and on 1 January, 1940, was dismissed from the Foreign Service. Thanks to the intervention of his military friends, who also belonged to the opposition, Brücklmeier became counsellor for war administration. When the Nazi security police chased him from that post, too, the General Manager of 'Nordsee,' a big fishing concern, employed him to liaise with the reserve army headquarters in Berlin. Thanks to these developments, Brücklmeier was for the time being detached from the informal network in which he had earlier played so central a role.

From these conversations I learned that several generals of the highest rank considered an attack on France and England to be a disastrous project and therefore had joined in an effort to dissuade Hitler from opening a Western Front. I had only the most general information on all this, but understood from Brücklmeier, Kordt, and Etzdorf that, as in August 1938, plans were being worked out to remove Hitler from power by force. I learned that it was Colonel General Franz Halder who had given the order to do this, and that the plan had been underway since October 1938. Etzdorf was much involved, through his role as the representative of State Secretary von Weizsäcker in the office of the Chief of the General Staff. In this post, he was in close contact with Colonel General Halder and Lieutenant Colonel Helmuth Groscurth, the latter being known to me already as one of the key figures in the military conspiracy to prevent the outbreak of war with France. Hitler insisted vehemently that the attack on France must start, going as far as to call his generals cowards, but the invasion was nevertheless postponed several times. Unfortunately, though, Halder also postponed his plan to remove Hitler. Every time the coup was about to be carried out, Halder found a new excuse for not issuing the final orders.

While in Berlin I made contact with various of my foreign friends who were still connected with the embassies there. Micki Lanza, my old friend from Moscow, had moved to the Italian Embassy, and we had a long and frank conversations on New Year's Eve 1939.[1] I told him of my experiences in Poland and reported my fears over the way the SS was coming increasingly into the picture, ruining whatever good relations might have been established by the army. I passed on to him information about incidents between soldiers and SS personnel and indicated that the SS was getting the upper hand. We also discussed the mood among our troops in the West. I explained that, while the younger soldiers were in good spirits, those whose memory reached back to World War I were uneasy, convinced that an invasion could only lead to unnecessary slaughter and, in the end, to a catastrophe for Germany. The fatalism of these older soldiers seemed to me to be unshakable. Summing up, I expressed my own view that Germany could never win in the West. Even if a violent offensive enabled us once more to occupy Belgium and part of France, we would be bogged down in a stalemate, as in 1914. Our government had to recognize that such an attack would result finally in rebellion within Germany and the ultimate accession to power of the Bolsheviks. Our only hope, I argued, was to be content with the situation as it was, and to negiotiate at once on this basis. I knew, though, that this would never happen.

Shortly after this conversation, on 10 January, I bumped into 'Chip' and Avis Bohlen in the lobby of the Adlon Hotel. In the course of a long and sombre meeting, 'Chip' told me that he wanted to return to the United States as soon as possible since Avis was pregnant. He intended to travel across Belgium and Holland that same week. I considered it my duty as a friend to warn him that Germany might attack these countries and that the fighting could be under way on the very days he intended to be crossing them. 'Chip' followed my advice and left at once. To my surprise, the attack did not take place on the 17th as planned, having been postponed yet again.

Among the other Americans whom I met at this time were George Kennan, Alexander Kirk, whom I knew well from Moscow, Jacob Beam, and Sam Edison Woods. With Kennan and Kirk especially I was forthcoming, since I trusted them as old friends. Sammy Woods showed great friendliness towards me and we had a number of far-ranging conversations. Unknown to me, Woods was apparently on the American intelligence staff and filed reports about our meetings which later gave rise to certain legends regarding my own supposed links with American intelligence. Granted that I had done the Americans a favour by my

[1] An account of this conversation is in Leonardo Simoni (pseud. of Michele Lanza), *Berlino ambasciata d'Italia 1939–43*, Rome, 1946, pp. 47–48.

earlier revelations to Bohlen and that my reports to Woods may also have been useful, I cannot flatter myself that I played the cloak-and-dagger role assigned to me after the event.[2]

I arrived back with my regiment on 13 January. At the end of the month we were moved up almost to the Dutch border, at the town of Lingen. The regiment settled into the modern artillery barracks there, which included a fine officers' mess. Our officers were granted special permission to use this facility, although the elderly mess officer warned us that we would have to pay for any damage we inflicted. By this time we had waited several months for the order to attack. Having cooled our heels through January, February, and then March, we finally concluded that the invasion had been cancelled. In our pleasure at having escaped a repetition of the ordeal of 1914, we decided to have a feast. As was customary in German cavalry regiments, the officers by late evening were all mounted on stools, which we rode like horses in review before our colonel, who was mounted on the shoulders of one of the tallest officers. Quite a few glasses had already been broken by the time the mess officer closed the cellar. Several of the younger officers took exception to this order and went immediately to the mess officer's room to object. The old man was asleep by then, and only the sound of several pistol shots fired through his door succeeded in arousing him. Reluctantly, he dug up something more for us to drink, but was careful to render a precise reckoning the next day. Among other items, his bill showed 'one bottle of mouthwash, consumed by Lieutenant So-and-so', presumably from the mess officer's washstand.

A regimental reunion was held on 8 May. It was a splendid day, the band was playing, and our colonel, a lover of music, finished the festivities by beating the bass drum. We finally got to bed at 3:00 a.m. At 3:30 my orderly burst in on me with an order to report to regimental headquarters. I told him to go to hell and went back to sleep, at which point he went to Captain Otto von Sauken, a reserve officer from East Prussia. Von Sauken also tried to awaken me, but I barked at him as well. This was the less excusable because I was a mere NCO while von Sauken was quite a bit older and considered a kind of benevolent uncle; our old-fashioned nickname for him was 'Uncle Kunibert'. Only when 'Uncle Kunibert' threw a pitcher of cold water over me did I finally arouse myself to the point that I could focus on the news that the attack was imminent.

I reported to regimental headquarters. There I was given orders to join a patrol under the command of Lieutenant Count Solms that was setting

[2] See William Stevenson, *A Man Called Intrepid*, New York, 1976, pp. 224–25.

178

out at once towards Coevorden on the Dutch border, so as to be able to cross at 3:45 a.m. the following morning. All day on the 9th we rode towards the border, reaching the frontier by nightfall. Soon the sky reverberated with the roar of German bombers, which we later learned were on their way to destroy the city of Rotterdam. By 3:30 a.m. the artillery fire had been unleashed.

As cavalrymen, my colleagues and I viewed the invasion of Holland with particular trepidation since we knew that when the Dutch opened the dykes anyone on horseback would be lost at once. They did not open the dykes, though, but blew up their bridges instead. It was an impressive and terrifying sight to see the horizon lit by the flames of the bridges exploding simultaneously. This action slowed our advance, but at length we succeeded in engaging the Dutch troops in battle. They were well camouflaged and managed to inflict heavy losses on our unit before we finally overpowered them. One by one they emerged from their bunkers and surrendered. At this point a remarkable but in its way characteristic event occurred.

A group of us – Dutch and German soldiers – went to a neighbouring café and had a coffee break together. The Dutch reproached us for having fired on them, to which we replied lamely that we did so as soldiers under orders, just as they would have done. The only scant consolation that I could offer was that for them the war was over, while for us it had only begun.

This softened the mood in that Dutch café but it did not ease my own conscience. I was quartered near the Zuyder Zee with a Dutch priest, who with great persistence pointed out to me how great a sin it was for a Christian to do what I had done. I heard him out in silence, admiring his courage and recognizing the truth of his argument. In general, the Dutch population was deeply shocked by the attack but, like this priest, treated us soldiers with decency.

During our brief stay by the Zuyder Zee, my unit was ordered to commandeer some of the large flat-bottomed boats used on the inland waterways and prepare them for an attack on Amsterdam. Knowing that we would be assigned to the assault, we took a dim view of the idea of a seaborne cavalry charge. In our initial experiments the cumbersome craft were nearly swamped in the open water. Fortunately for us, Holland surrendered just as our nautical skills were about to be tested. The regiment was transferred by train first to Germany and then into Belgium and France where we followed up the forces that had led the invasion.

Against all our expectations, we met with little resistance from the

French. One colonial unit that we attacked was made up of blacks, who put up a fierce fight with bush knives until the last moment. The strength of their resistance was exceptional. We captured several white officers and NCOs from this unit. Our men asked these officers reproachfully why they had led these blacks into a European fight which in no way involved them.

By no means all aspects of the invasion of France were carried out with Prussian efficiency. My own laziness was responsible for one of the many lapses. While in France, I was assigned to carry some messages from headquarters to our first and second battalions. After reaching the first battalion, I should have returned to headquarters and then gone from there to the second. Being clever, I decided instead to travel directly between the two battalions, thus saving a few miles. It was pitch dark and I was being driven in a motorcycle with a sidecar, again to save effort. Moving slowly through the black night, we suddenly crashed into a solid mass, which turned out to be a French tank. My driver coolly announced, 'Lieutenant, we seem to have made a mistake.' Turning rapidly around, we roared off, and by the time the French soldiers realized what had happened we were beyond the reach of their guns.

We encountered some opposition before Paris but succeeded in moving quickly across the Seine and to the south of Bordeaux, where we were stationed for some while. Being close to Biarritz, we could go there often. Even better from the standpoint of cavalrymen, the great Boussac stables were nearby as well. We took excellent care of the horses and exercised them daily. One morning as we were engaged in this pleasant task, it was announced that the horses were to be taken away. We adamantly refused to permit this, arguing that they were private property and that we were taking care of them in their owner's absence. Shortly afterwards we received another order, this one impossible to resist. It turned out that the horses were destined for the use of Ribbentrop, which hardly endeared him to our unit.

One morning as I was leaving my hotel in Biarritz, a small detachment of soldiers led by a non-commissioned officer passed by. According to regulations, the NCO had to order his men to do the goose step as they passed me. Just as he reached me, however, I found myself being embraced by a very lovely woman, much to my own and his consternation. The soldiers goose-stepped by with grins on their faces, and I turned to see Frau Basseches, the Russian wife of an Austrian–Jewish reporter who had been stationed in Moscow. To my astonishment, I learned that this elegant former ballerina was living with her daughter and poodle in Biarritz, without work and without money, while her husband had fled across the border to San Sebastian. She was in despair and on the verge of suicide. We went for a meal together. I assured her that the daughter could manage without her but that her poodle could not and that she should therefore hold on until work could be found for her. Within a few days, she had a job in the officers' mess and her daughter was working on the German military switchboard.

We were quartered just south of Bordeaux in the small town of Salles, where the local populace at first received us with understandable reserve. The fact that we were replacing SS troops caused the atmosphere to improve rapidly, for the SS had caused quite a bit of friction. In fact, an incident between a local boy and an SS man had taken place on the very eve of our arrival. Our First Lieutenant, Valentin von Dietmann, intervened at once on behalf of the French boy, an act appreciated by the inhabitants.

Throughout our stay, we made a point of quartering as many of our soldiers as possible with the local peasantry. Not only did this guarantee that our horses would be well cared for, but the work the men were ordered to do on the farms kept them out of trouble and built up good-will. In the same spirit, our regimental band performed every Sunday afternoon in town, carefully avoiding all military marches. After a short time the concerts were considered a pleasant pastime by the populace.

At the end of the French campaign I got my long overdue promotion to the rank of second lieutenant. This promotion was fraught with difficulties, since non-Aryans were not allowed to be officers. It was only made possible through the intervention of my friends Schulenburg and Etzdorf. Even then, the promotion was only temporary, final confirmation having to wait until after the war was over.

By mid-August our summer holidays in France were over, and my regiment was sent back to Poland. For some time letters were exchanged between our men and the French families with which they had been billeted.

However little our regiment had suffered during the French campaign, and however salubrious our stay in the French countryside, the German army's easy victory in France had catastrophic results. It seemed to prove that Hitler had been right in predicting a swift victory and his generals utterly wrong in their anticipation of heavy fighting. From this point on, Hitler considered himself to be the greatest field marshal of all times. Buoyed up by his vindication in the French campaign, he was no longer prepared to take advice from anyone.

13

ON THE EVE OF 22 JUNE, 1941

In the middle of August 1940, I was ordered to report to General Staff Colonel Bernhard von Lossberg, a cousin of mine who was working in the *Wehrmachtführungsstab*. As such, he was under the direct command of Field Marshal Keitel and Colonel General Jodl. Lossberg wanted to have a heart-to-heart talk with me on the possibility of a war with the Soviet Union. In the strictest secrecy he informed me that Hitler had given orders to work out an over-all plan for the invasion of the USSR. He said that only a very limited number of high-ranking officers in the General Staff knew about the project. According to Lossberg, Hitler gave his orders on the following assumptions: first, that the Soviet Union was getting stronger every year, and would finally be a mortal danger for Germany; second, that Hitler's reading of the laws of history indicated to him that anyone who would succeed him would be a weaker man than himself. He therefore concluded that the best and probably the only opportunity to destroy the Soviet Union and the Communist system was at hand. Under the onslaught of the German armed forces, the Soviet Union would, he believed, collapse politically and militarily within six weeks. All Soviet territory up to the 'A-A line', e.g., the north-south line between Arkhangelsk and Astrakhan, was to be occupied in order to secure the necessary *Lebensraum* and raw materials for the German people. Hitler was convinced that this area could be secured by mobile troops alone. After securing the area, these forces would then be replaced by German military settlements similar to the old Austrian military colonies that had held that country's frontier against the Ottoman Turks for centuries. Lossberg wanted my opinion on all this.

I told him that we would have the greatest difficulty in reaching the A-A line at all. Even if our army could get that far the Russians would still have a sufficiently broad industrial base behind the A-A line to enable them to continue waging modern warfare against us. I reminded

Lossberg of General Köstring's frequently stated view that the USSR was incapable of a major offensive campaign but eminently capable of waging a sustained defensive war. Further, I argued that the notion of reaching the A-A line within six weeks was absurd, given the problems of provisioning an army at such distances and in so hostile a climate.

Lossberg agreed with everything I said but had to admit there was nothing he could do about it, since Hitler considered himself to be his own best general. On this note we parted. I saw Lossberg again at the end of September 1940, when he told me that the plan had been called off for the moment. This did not mean, however, that military preparations on the Eastern Front had been stopped. They were actively continued as a sort of preventive measure; intended, so it was said, to discourage a Soviet attack. But upon my return to Poland I was able to see with my own eyes that none of these measures was of a defensive nature.

After my visit to Lossberg I made a brief trip to Moscow to see my wife. It was no simple matter to arrange this expedition. According to our regulations, I should have petitioned headquarters for permission to go abroad, which I certainly would not have received. Fortunately, Colonel Wachsen was willing to sign for me when I promised to bring him information on developments in the diplomatic world and also a load of caviar. I obtained the German exit permit throught the good offices of my friends in the Foreign Office. Since I had never handed in my diplomatic passport, the task of getting a Soviet visa was simpler than it might otherwise have been. In the end I got it through my old friend Astakhov, now Stalin's Chargé d'Affaires in Berlin. Thus prepared, I drove in a regimental jeep from Biala Podlaska to Warsaw, where I boarded the train. Well before reaching the Soviet border I had changed into civilian clothes and prepared myself to proceed to Moscow.

In Moscow I had long conversations with Schulenburg and also with General Köstring, in the course of which I passed on to them everything I knew about the build-up of arms in Poland. I made a point, also, of telling both Schulenburg and Köstring the details of my meeting with Lossberg, on the grounds that as Ambassador and military attaché they ought to have full knowledge of everything that was occurring. They were flabbergasted at my report of a possible attack on Russia. Both wavered between viewing these preparations as an exercise in contingency planning or as one more lever by which Hitler could press the Russians to increase their deliveries of grain, manganese, and other raw materials. Neither of them could believe that Hitler would do so foolish a thing as to destroy himself by attacking the Soviet Union. By that time everyone in the Embassy had read Caulaincourt's famous book on Napoleon's campaign in Russia, which had just been newly edited in a German translation. Was Hitler really intending to repeat Napoleon's mistakes? Our experts found it unthinkable.

During my stay in Moscow, I also visited my American friends and the American *dacha*. Charlie Thayer, an avid horseman and polo player, pumped me on my cavalry adventures over the past year. The American military attaché was amazed at my stories of cavalry actions in Poland, and at the way we had managed to build up our meagre brigade to division strength by the time we reached France. I had to explain that we were no more than infantrymen who used horses to get to the scene of the battle, and that, in fact, there were a number of ways that cavalry could be put to good use in modern warfare.

I immediately fell into my old habit of talking over every possible development with my closest friends, and they reciprocated with their own visions of the future. In the light of what happened only a few months afterwards, it is surprising that not one of the American group in Moscow considered that an all-out invasion of Russia would be launched. Such an invasion was hard for those in Moscow to conceive, since the 1939 agreement had placed Germany once more in the status of 'most-favoured nation' and created an atmosphere of friendship between Germany and the USSR that had been absent since 1933. For my own part, I was by now firmly convinced that our preparations in Poland could only culminate in an attack on the USSR.

Charlie Thayer asked me if I did not want to see John Russell from the British Embassy. Russell, a friend of mine from several years before, was by this time Second Secretary. His father was the renowned Russell Pasha, a distinguished colonial administrator and linguist who had long served in Egypt. I told Thayer that I would like to see Russell, knowing full well that for a German officer to meet a foreign diplomat from an enemy country was cause for court martial, even without the Nazis. Charlie organized a secret rendezvous at the stable at the American *dacha*. I was supposed to go to inspect the horses and Russell was to meet me there soon afterwards.

Everything went according to plan and I was able to spend some time with Russell reviewing every aspect of the military picture. We considered the possibility of a war between the Soviet Union and

Germany and were both convinced that otherwise the war would develop into a stalemate.

I also reviewed with Russell the prospects of German success in North Africa. Russell made the obvious point that the Allies were operating on safe and short supply lines and we were not, and that if we crossed the Libyan border we would probably be too weak to capture the whole of Lower Egypt. We agreed that it would be necessary for the Germans to establish a foothold in Malta in order to secure their supply line. Hitler had in fact trained paratroopers for this mission, and they were apparently set to move at the time of the outbreak of the war in the Balkans in the spring of 1941. By this time, however, they were needed elsewhere and the plan against Malta was dropped.

Forty years later, in 1978, Russell told me that he had at once reported our conversations to London.

I returned to my regiment in mid-October 1940, weighed down by the many kilos of caviar that I had promised to bring back with me. This, plus my news from the diplomatic world, made quite a stir and earned me the title of the regiment's Foreign Minister. Scarcely had I settled back into the regiment's routine than Molotov made what turned out to be his first and last trip to Berlin. At Schulenburg's request I was detached from the army and placed at his disposal during the meetings. Arriving in Berlin, I reported at once to the old Hohenzollern palace Schloss Bellevue, which was now serving as a Nazi guest house. Since Schulenburg had not yet arrived from Moscow, I reported to *Staatssekretär* Hans-Otto Meisner. Meisner was an old civil servant who had earlier served as State Secretary and head of the Presidential Office under Friedrich Ebert and Hindenburg. He was among those officials who had stayed on under Hitler. Thinking that I was a career officer, Meisner received me most cordially with champagne and caviar and we had a pleasant talk, in spite of our vast difference in age and rank. I was much impressed by his kind, almost paternal attitude. At Meisner's orders, I was equipped with a dress uniform and also with formal diplomatic evening dress, so that I could take part in all the events connected with the Molotov visit.

News that Molotov was coming to Berlin had caused a great scare among my friends. They were all confident that the USSR had no desire to risk a great war, certainly not one against Germany. This point, which I had stressed in 1937 in my draft of Schulenburg's lecture at the *Wehmachtakademie*, had been developed again by Walther in an excellent review of the situation in the Soviet Union which he wrote for Etzdorf on 18 October, 1940. Now, however, the argument carried a sharper and more blatantly seditious political stamp, because 'Barbarossa', the attack on Russia, was already in preparation.[1]

Etzdorf and I agreed that we had reached a potentially disastrous situation. We mulled over all possible outcomes of the forthcoming meetings on the eve of Molotov's arrival, not knowing what Hitler really had in mind. We knew only that planning for the invasion of the USSR had been called off only weeks prior to Molotov's trip. This led us to conclude that the Molotov visit might well be a preliminary to a higher-level meeting between Hitler and Stalin. It was this which we most feared. Molotov, after all, could do nothing on his own and had constantly to refer back to Moscow for guidance. But if Stalin himself were to negotiate with Hitler, he could do so with full authority. I conjectured at the time that if Stalin and Hitler were to meet, they would get on very well with one another and could easily come to an agreement which might provide the basis for some combined offensive action. This in turn could lead to the joint domination of the Mediterranean by Germany and the USSR, which even the Allies might not be able to resist successfully. Etzdorf and I were terrified by the vision of a world dominated by Hitler and Stalin.

As Schulenburg's aide, I was near him at all the negotiations. I did not take part in the discussions themselves, which were attended only by Schulenburg, Hilger, who did the interpreting, and Paul Schmidt, who wrote the records, but since all three were good friends of mine, I followed the progress of the negotiations closely. Their course quickly revealed Hitler's true intentions to me. No sooner did Molotov raise the subject of Finland, the Dardanelles and Bulgaria than Hitler tried to convince him that the Soviet Union should instead advance in the direction of the Persian Gulf. Molotov should have understood the implication of this. For his part, Hitler had no sympathy for Molotov and resented his lack of power and his preoccupation with details. He did not view the meetings as crucial, nor did he see them as a prelude to a session with Stalin. After the meetings, the Germans made no effort to renew the political dialogue, a fact which alone should have warned Stalin about Hitler's intentions. When the Soviets eventually submitted their political proposals in writing, Hitler did not even deign to reply. Shortly after the visit, he gave orders to continue preparations for an invasion of Russia.

[1] See 'Opposition gegen "Barbarossa" in Herbst 1940', *Vierteljahrshefte für Zeitgeschichte*, 1975, No. 3, pp. 332–40.

In December, 1940, after the visit of Molotov had taken place, I returned to my regiment in Poland. This time I had scarcely unpacked when, to my great surprise, I was seconded to the Air Command. Returning to Berlin, I discovered that Colonel Engineer Dietrich Schwencke, head of the *Auswertungs Abteilung* (Reconnaissance Division), had asked that I be attached to him for two months. Schwencke had served as Deputy Air Attaché in London. He became famous for an excellent paper he wrote on the British air force in June 1939. The Battle of Britain proved that his reporting on the impressive strength of the British air force was right and Goering's evaluation had been wrong. In December 1940, Goering ordered him to prepare a study on the strength of the Soviet air force and aircraft industry in the context of the general political, economic and scientific situation of the Soviet Union.

At the start of our work, Schwencke assembled all the papers that had been prepared on this subject. We quickly perceived that these papers were entirely inadequate in that they failed to represent any of the strengths – particularly the defensive strength – of the country. I was greatly impressed by Schwencke's thoroughness and did everything in my power to help him. I believe that he succeeded in correcting the false impressions left by many of the earlier studies.

Why had the German administration so badly underestimated Soviet strengths? Schwencke complained bitterly that the SS and the Party organizations had relied heavily on the superficial analyses of an institute in Berlin that tended systematically to underestimate the potential that the Soviet Union had at its disposal. As I went through the reports commissioned by German officers I was also struck, as was Schwencke, by the fact that many of them had been prepared by Germans who were born in Russia, or who had lived in the Soviet Union but were later expelled. Naturally, such people had an axe to grind. Like émigrés everywhere, they underestimated the strengths of their former place of residence and overestimated the animosity of the people against their government.

Schwencke soon saw the need to examine the situation in the Soviet Union at first hand, which he did at the end of our work. At the start of his tour there, he was confined to Moscow and shown very little. Then, suddenly, he was permitted to see a number of important factories where the production of aircraft engines and bodies was going forward. It was not until after the war that I learned why this dramatic change had occurred. As Schwencke later explained to me, the office next door to his in the Ministry was occupied by First Lieutenant Harro Schulze-Boysen, a leading member of the *Rote Kapelle* resistance group that co-operated with the Soviet Union. Apparently, Schwencke's first cables reporting on his mission to the USSR came to the desk of Schulze-Boysen, who immediately transmitted them back to Moscow, where they were seen by the highest officials. Though he had not yet been shown much, Schwencke's reports had been reasonably positive. The Soviets concluded that, if he had been this positive on the basis of such slim evidence, he should be permitted to see everything in the hope that he would emphasize yet more firmly the Soviet strength. As a result, he and his two fellow officers, accompanied by some eight representatives of German industry, saw four aircraft body factories, three engine factories, and a plant for light metalworking – all within a month.

Schwencke was greatly impressed by the factories and reported that the equipment going into production was far superior to that which was actually in service in the Soviet air force. He observed, also, that Soviet aircraft designers followed the usual Russian practice of constructing machines as simply as possible. They knew that their technicians were not competent to handle complex equipment and wisely resolved to work within this restriction. The resulting airframes struck Schwencke as being unsophisticated but durable, which confirmed the conclusions he had reached in his earlier report.

In February, 1941, I went for a second time to Moscow and stayed until mid-March. I reported immediately to Count Schulenburg that military preparations on the Eastern Front were now in full swing. Schulenburg confided in me his conviction that Hitler had definitely chosen war, since he, Schulenburg, had not received any instructions for continuing the political dialogue with the Soviet Union. Schulenburg was the more profoundly upset because on 10 January, 1941, a far-reaching economic treaty had been signed between Germany and the Soviet Union by Mikoyan and my old friend Karl Schnurre. The treaty not only guaranteed the delivery to Germany of raw materials which were badly needed for continuing the war against the Western powers, but also of goods bought by the Soviet Union in the Far East, such as rubber and non-ferrous metals. The Soviet Union expected in return to receive industrial equipment from Germany.

This agreement enabled Germany to circumvent the British blockade. Since Hitler was thus able to obtain all the raw materials he wanted by peaceful means, it was all the more incomprehensible to Schulenburg that he should have decided on war. Schulenburg was resolved to do anything in his power to change Hitler's mind, though he feared he would fail in the attempt. He was to get his chance at the end of April, when his pessimism proved justified.

I met my other friends as well, but by this time the direction of events was clear to all of us. I saw Charlie Thayer, but neither he nor I was in any mood to philosophize, or even to joke in our usual manner. All in all, this final visit to Moscow was a sombre experience for me, calling to mind all the events that I had witnessed over the past decade. I reviewed those years in my mind as the train carried me Westward once more on 15 March.

However unpleasant an experience for me, my trip to Moscow was a godsend for my regiment, since I returned with the usual cargo of caviar. They ate it all within a few days of my return. The caviar gone, the regiment quickly settled once more into a grim mood. During those days, there occurred two incidents which revealed clearly the atmosphere at the time. We had among us a First Lieutenant Walter-Kunibert Frick, the son of the Nazi Minister of the Interior who had been a loyal follower of Hitler from the beginning. Frick had broken with his father when the latter had divorced his mother and, by the time I met him, was as outspoken an anti-Nazi as one could find. One evening shortly after my return from Moscow, the officers held a dinner to which we invited the Nazi Party official responsible for the county in which we were encamped. He seemed a decent enough person, more civil servant than Party functionary, but by some mishap, he was seated next to Frick. Wanting to say the appropriate thing, the Nazi functionary made various complimentary allusions to Hitler, the Party, and Reichsminister Frick. I watched as Frick grew more and more nervous and finally jumped up and threw a tankard of beer into the official's face. I took the poor man to the bathroom and did my best to smooth things over, assuring him that Frick had simply had too much to drink. Fortunately, Frick had the good sense to apologize next day.

Another event that took place immediately before the beginning of the Russian campaign was equally telling. A Party propagandist was sent to our division to fire our ardour for battle. I must admit that he gave a well-constructed speech. He spoke of the Teutonic knights moving Eastward long ago, and implied that one day it would fall to us to launch a similar crusade. After he finished, there was absolutely no applause. A group gathered around the speaker to engage him in conversation. Lieutenant Colonel Wachsen was there, and Lieutenant Hans-Heinrich Schlenther, a tall, extremely good-looking East Prussian

189

who was very lively and outspoken. The speaker turned to Schlenther and asked him why there had been so little enthusiasm, to which Schlenther replied: 'There can be no talk of enthusiasm, but if the First Cavalry Division attacks, it will do its duty.' I will never forget Schlenther's words, for they summed up the situation exactly.

We had one or two frontier incidents at this time, due largely to our soldiers getting drunk and crossing the lines. In every case, the Soviets treated them correctly, sending them back without having interrogated them. German aircraft also frequently violated the line of demarcation, but they too were never fired at. Evidently the Red Army was under orders to avoid incidents at any cost, but their orders on the Far Eastern front were the opposite. Red Army troops on the Mongolian and Chinese borders were ordered to shoot at the slightest violation of the frontier.

Stalin himself gave the most dramatic proof of his intentions. On 13 April, 1941, he unexpectedly appeared at the railway station to see off the Japanese Foreign Minister, Yosuke Matsuoka, who had just signed a pact of neutrality with the Soviet Union. Seeing Schulenburg standing on the platform, Stalin put his arm on Schulenburg's shoulder and whispered some words into his ear. As far as Schulenburg, with his restricted command of Russian, could understand, Stalin assured him of his friendly attitude towards Germany and asked Schulenburg to work for the continuation of this friendship in Berlin. Some minutes later Stalin turned to the acting military attaché, Colonel Krebs, took Krebs' right hand in his two hands, pressed it strongly and said: 'We will be friends, whatever may happen.' Krebs answered in a loud and clear voice: 'I am convinced of that.'

A few days after this historic moment, Schulenburg went to Berlin, accompanied by Walther, who had taken my place as secretary to the Ambassador. The purpose of this trip was to see Hitler and to convince him of the Soviet Union's peaceful intentions towards Germany. At about the same time Pussi left Moscow. Schulenburg wisely insisted on her departure because she was expecting a baby in late autumn and he was afraid that at any moment war might break out between Germany and the Soviet Union. Pussi spent a few days in Berlin visiting her mother, my parents, and me. I was there attending a brief course on military interpreting in Russian. During this tense period, Schulenburg, Walther, Pussi and I took most of our meals together and discussed the imminent conversation between Schulenburg and Hitler, now scheduled for 26 April. On the evening of the 25th the four of us dined at Schnurre's house. He was doubtful about Schulenburg's success, in view of the experience he himself had had with Hitler at the end of January. In the course of a conversation, Hitler had categorically denied to Schnurre that he was planning war against the Soviet Union, but the Führer's further remarks had made Schnurre suspect that this was not true.

Schulenburg and Walther stayed at the Hotel Adlon, just around the corner from the Reichs Chancery and the Foreign Office. My wife still remembers the tense atmosphere of 26 April. She was sitting in the lobby of the Hotel Adlon with Schulenburg and Walther just before they left for the Chancery. All three were terribly excited, realizing that this was perhaps the last chance anyone would have to dissuade Hitler from waging war against the USSR. Schulenburg asked Pussi to wait for their return. Preparing herself to wait patiently for the entire afternoon, Pussi was astonished when Schulenburg and Walther returned in less than an hour, their faces marked by deep disappointment and sorrow. The account confirmed the bitter truth of her first impression. According to them, Hitler had not even read the memorandum which Schulenburg had sent him previously. Schulenburg set forth again his views on the state of Soviet affairs, emphasizing his conviction that the USSR would do its best to prevent being drawn into war. He stressed the importance of maintaining the 'positive neutrality' of Russia. Finally, he assured Hitler that the Russians could be trusted to honour any agreement that Hitler could make with them. Hitler listened to all this in silence. When Schulenburg had finished his report, Hitler stood up, put Schulenburg's memo into the drawer of his desk, shook hands with Schulenburg and Walther, and said: 'Thank you, this was extremely interesting.' No questions, no discussion, not the slightest allusion to his intention of attacking the USSR. Hitler's silence left Schulenburg convinced that his earlier suspicions were justified and that the fatal decision had long since been taken.

A few days after Schulenburg and Walther had returned to Moscow, Pussi and I met my former boss Colonel Engineer Schwencke. We discussed the German defeat in the Battle of Britain and he remarked bitterly that his report on Britain's air strength had been disregarded. Goering had counted merely the British planes above ground and not those hidden or underground. Schwencke told me privately that he had given a full report on his visit to the USSR to General Hans Jeschonnek, the Chief of the General Staff of the Air Force. Jeschonnek heard him out, and then advised Schwencke to keep his conclusions to himself as the final decision had already been taken. Schwencke was disappointed that for the second time his report had not been heeded.

My course on military Russian completed, I returned to my regiment. When Schulenburg arrived once more in Moscow, all he could do was await the inevitable results of all he had seen and participated in. Since I was not there myself during the last months before the German invasion, it is fortunate that he set down his own impressions in a series of letters to my wife. After Pussi left Moscow she and Schulenburg entered into a correspondence which was to continue virtually without interruption until the time of Schulenburg's arrest in 1944. Considering the extreme risks involved in his saying anything of substance in letters passing through the mails, it is surprising how much he was able to communicate, albeit in somewhat veiled language. Thus, when he spoke of the dismissing of the generals in September 1942, he was careful to refer to the 'surely false' rumours on the subject, just as he made reference to non-existent newspaper reports as a means of alluding to the battle of Stalingrad. Nonetheless, he succeeded in communicating his concerns, however elliptically.

On 11 May, 1941, Schulenburg wrote:

There is no longer much work to be done. Everyone here in Moscow is speaking about Stalin's taking over the Presidency of the Council of Ministers. Among his first acts was to discredit news from American sources that the Soviet Union was taking steps for military preparedness by sending troops to the western frontier, and so forth. Shortly afterwards, the legations of Belgium, Norway, and Yugoslavia were expelled from Moscow. The awesome silence appears to us frightening: is it the lull before the storm?

Beginning in this letter, Schulenburg began documenting the steady departure of foreign diplomats from Moscow – of which the Soviet government was, of course, fully aware but from which it seemed hesitant to draw the obvious conclusions.

Schulenburg was quite direct in reporting that 'the matter of great interest to us is still as threatening as ever. We expect the crisis to come to a head around the end of June. Therefore, I'm hoping that in one way or another I can get to Germany in July to take care of the furnishing of the castle [Falkenberg, Schulenburg's new residence].'

While others may not have had Schulenburg's knowledge of the precise timetable, the other diplomats were in no doubt what was impending. By the 24th Schulenburg was spending more of his time giving farewell soirées for departing diplomats than communicating with Berlin. 'It seems strange to us that we have no delegations here at present, and no special negotiations under way. We receive few requests through our couriers and those that do come in can be seen to in a few minutes. In brief, we have little to do and aren't used to it.'

Shortly afterwards, on 28 May, Schulenburg again wrote: 'There isn't much going on here. We are floating amidst positive and negative rumours. No one knows anything for certain, but I personally feel that all that we expect to occur will finally happen.' He also referred to 'a certain restlessness here'. Among Russians this was caused by the fact that the Soviet government refused to acknowledge what was happening. Among diplomats the restlessness was deepened by such measures as the Soviet government's edict closing much of the territory of the potential war zone – including Leningrad – to foreigners. This measure was occasioned by the general situation, but also, as Schulenburg wrote, by the over-eagerness of some of our colleagues, especially the Japanese and Finns, who found it necessary to travel in the ticklish regions. 'It was,' he concluded, 'an unpleasant atmosphere.'

Two months before the start of hostilities, I was seconded to the LIII Corps command in Radom, where I was assigned to the General Staff officer who was gathering intelligence on the enemy. Immediately I received orders to lecture on the Soviet Union to the officers. In this talk, I repeated many of the same points that I had developed earlier in my lecture for Schulenburg. I mentioned the poor offensive capacity of the Red Army but stressed as strongly as I could the ability of the population at large to fight a successful defensive campaign. I was careful not to make any mention of the possibility of Red Army troops defecting to the German side, although Köstring had figured from the beginning that this was likely. We knew full well that few families in Russia had been untouched by the collectivization and the purges, and that millions must be harbouring resentment against the regime. I followed Köstring's example in making no mention of this, since we were both convinced that to speak publicly of the possibility of mass defection would play into the hands of those Nazis who were most zealous for a campaign against Russia.

The audience listened with rapt attention and, when I had finished my talk, asked me many perceptive questions. What was most striking though, was that not one person there gave any indication that he sensed an attack was imminent. To be sure, anyone mentioning this top secret matter would have been shot at once, but even taking this into account, I could detect nothing to suggest that anyone present realized what was impending.

It is curious how successfully Hitler managed to keep those around him in the dark. I am convinced that nearly all our generals on the Eastern Front believed that the sole reason for the large build-up in the spring and summer of 1941 was to press Stalin to continue his deliveries of raw materials to Germany. Until the last moment the majority of our generals refused to accept the possibility of war.

The secret of the attack was guarded with fierce jealousy. My wife later told me of a conversation that took place just before she left the USSR, involving her, our close friend Walther, and Colonel Krebs, who filled in for Köstring when the latter was on leave from Moscow. Walther obliquely alluded to the impending campaign and Krebs immediately cut him off, stating that if anyone were to mention the attack he would have to report him at once.

Krebs' extreme loyalty in this situation anticipated his later fate. He and I had become good friends when he was an aide to the military attaché in Moscow. His wit, his intelligence and his clear judgment attracted me to him. He did not lack courage in defending his opinions, even when they were critical of National Socialism, as they often were. Later, when I met him as Chief of the General Staff of the Army Group Centre on the Eastern Front he shared my pessimistic assessment of the future. By the end of the war he had risen to the rank of Chief of the General Staff of the Army, a hopeless position, as he fully realized. In the last days of the war Krebs had the misfortune of being with Hitler in the bunker in Berlin, where he committed suicide.

Upon learning of my assignment to Radom, I had immediately requested a transfer back to my regiment, on the grounds that I had resigned from the diplomatic service in order to join the army, not to serve in another staff position. This request was granted two weeks before the fateful day of 22 June, 1941. By now tension was mounting everywhere. On 17 June – only five days before the outbreak of war – Schulenburg wrote my wife:

This is probably the last courier by which I can write to you from here. I will therefore report to you as much as possible.

We still don't know anything, but the famous rumours are reaching Himalayan heights. The Soviet government published a communiqué five days ago, in which it claimed that the USSR would never attack

Germany and that one should not expect an attack by Germany on the USSR. All the rumours collapsed. Everyone believed the communiqué had been issued with our agreement. But then there was no response from Germany. We don't know if the Soviet communiqué was even published in Germany! This caused the diplomatic corps to lose the little composure it still had! Yesterday, today and tomorrow the English and Italian women and children, as well as the Hungarians, departed or will depart. The Americans are staying put. But Steinhardt [the Ambassador] has rented a *dacha* 'somewhere' for his office 'just in case of emergency'. He has also bought a bus for some incomprehensible reason and stocked up on petrol. As you can see, dear Pussi, there is much going on here. But we are watching developments calmly.

It was no longer possible to keep the impending attack under cover. On 20 June the General Staff officer of the First Cavalry Division assembled one officer from every battalion in the division and announced Hitler's decision to crush Communism once and for all by invading the USSR. He explained that this drastic step would not only guarantee the Reich all the essential raw materials that it now lacked but it would provide Germans themselves with *Lebensraum*. In his speech, the officer cautioned us that we might encounter Germans in Soviet uniforms whose assignment would be to commit acts of sabotage in the rear of the Soviet lines and that we should take care not to shoot at them. I asked rather impertinently how we would be able to distinguish between these German soldiers and the genuine Russians. The officer had no answer except to suggest that they might try to signal us. I then enquired how we would recognize their sign, but again he had no reply. I doubt if many of those officers present shared the High Command's naïve illusions.

Continuing his address, the officer ordered us to execute all captured Soviet commissars. Most of my fellow officers were twenty to twenty-five years old, and had only recently had occasion to acquaint themselves with the rules of warfare governing prisoners. They knew that once a man had given up fighting and was in our hands, we were obliged to preserve his life. With one voice, we refused to carry out such an order. The senior officer obstinately stuck to his line, and told us that, if we sent back commissars from the front line, they would immediately be returned to us with orders that they be shot. Again, we told him that we would refuse to do so. After all, as one of my

195

younger colleagues remarked, we *were* Christian officers.

I then told the officers present that as far as my regiment was concerned there was no problem. If any commissar were captured by units of my regiment he would be sent to me and I would interrogate him in order to confirm whether he was indeed a commissar. If that was established, we could simply tear off all distinguishing marks and take the man's papers; then, having destroyed the evidence, I would order him to deny that he had ever been a commissar. In this way, we would circumvent the order.

We could not have been more blunt in informing this major of our intentions to ignore the command. He made no response and with the benefit of hindsight I suspect that he agreed with us. His attitude suggested that he felt he had done his duty by informing us of the command, rather than by gaining our compliance with it. By taking this easy way out, this man epitomized the shortcoming of many of our generals, who blithely passed on orders which were immoral and which, in fact, placed their troops under an obligation to commit crimes.

I often asked myself at the time why none of them had the courage to resign and why instead they chose to place so heavy a burden on their inferiors. Would Prussia's generals of the time of Wilhelm I have done this? My impression is that they would not and that their refusal would have arisen from their stronger Christian principles. I doubt if our generals who so conveniently shirked their moral responsibilities during the war lost much sleep over the Ten Commandments or had the Bible for bedside reading.

14

THE RUSSIAN CAMPAIGN

My regiment advanced into the USSR before dawn on 22 June, 1941. Before crossing the river Bug we unleashed an artillery barrage for forty-five minutes. Against the darkened sky, the artillery fire stood out boldly, making an awesome impression. For several hours the Soviets did not reply. We had caught them unprepared, and, as many Russians told us later, not even dressed for the day. Furthermore, there were practically no regular Soviet troops on the border itself. We were astounded that the Russians had not anticipated the attack and had made no preparations to meet it.

Other parts of the front confirmed this impression. When German troops began the bombardment of Lemberg in the Western Ukraine, the local Soviet commander could not believe that they were attacking, and hence did not return the artillery fire. This commander was later taken prisoner and explained his strange reaction by saying that he believed the German artillery was practising and had fired across the frontier by mistake. As he had strict orders to avoid any frontier incident, he did not return the fire until the German infantry attack made clear that war had actually broken out.

Was Stalin pursuing a policy so subtle that we all failed to appreciate it? Quite the contrary. So complete was his failure to anticipate the attack that Soviet deliveries of raw materials continued to cross the frontier by rail right up to the beginning of Operation Barbarossa. I myself witnessed the passage of such shipments by rail at the bridge at Brest-Litovsk and Theodor Oberländer, who commanded the Ukrainian 'Nightingale' (*Nachtigal*) Unit at Lemberg, reported that shipments were proceeding in that region practically to the moment of the invasion. Stalin flatly refused to believe that Hitler would attack a country from which he was getting such benefits. When the attack came, he therefore felt deeply disappointed and betrayed.

As the campaign began, even our common soldiers were nervous, because no one could imagine what our objectives could or should be, or where the campaign would end. The soldiers were prepared to do their duty, but without a trace of enthusiasm. The difficulties we encountered in crossing the Bug only intensified the pervasive fear and anxiety. We immediately ran into fierce resistance from units of a frontier-guard regiment of the NKVD. They were excellently camouflaged, with many of them in positions in the tree tops linked by wooden planks. It was impossible to break their resistance, so we had to cross the Bug elsewhere.

The soldiers' spirits sank even further when we were attacked by low-flying aircraft with bombs and machine guns. Marching on a road through the swamps, we found ourselves in chaos amidst panicking horses. Fortunately for us, this successful attack was an exception. The Soviet air force was obsolete and its new planes had not yet been deployed in sufficient numbers. It made only a few appearances and these were quite ineffective. The fighting spirit of the Soviet infantry could not have been lower. If they put up any stiff resistance it was only because of the difficulty of deserting at that particular moment, due, for example, to the temporary stabilization of the front line. Captives later reported that they had been driven forward by the political commissars and officers.

We quickly broke through the Soviet lines. No sooner had we done so than the soldiers of the Red Army abandoned all resistance, throwing away their weapons, and waiting to be taken prisoner. Cavalry patrols sent out on reconnaisance collected hundreds of Russian soldiers. Since the cavalrymen had to get on with their assignments, they would detach one of their number to lead the Red Army troops back to our lines. The prisoners followed without resistance, often trudging in long lines behind a single German soldier.

I was assigned to interrogate the many Soviet soldiers who had crossed the lines or been taken captive. As the only officer in my regiment who spoke Russian, this interrogation work was quite intensive. Our objective was to identify the units against which we were fighting, to learn something of the numbers and equipment of the fighting men, and to ascertain the state of their morale. The Red Army prisoners were uniformly co-operative, and, equally important, the information they gave us was precise and reliable.

One of the first officers I encountered was a young and very pleasant man from the Soviet artillery, whose insignia and red piping on his trousers indicated that he was a captain. To my astonishment, he

198

implored me to tell him where our artillery was situated. I had to inform him that this was no longer a concern of his, since he was a prisoner. 'No, no,' he retorted, 'I am not interested in knowing for myself, but for you, so that I can show you how to direct your artillery so as to hit our emplacement – they're now hitting a few hundred metres short of our battery.' I was more than a little surprised by this.

Among the Soviet officers whom I interrogated was an ex-diplomat who had served in Copenhagen together with my former Moscow colleague, Herbert Hensel. With this basis for contact, we had a most interesting discussion. I pointed out to him that the Soviet troops had put up a poor resistance and the local populace was greeting the Germans as liberators. He acknowledged this, but reminded me that the Germans were only at the border and that the Soviets had been taken by surprise. He seemed confident that resistance would develop, and that in the long run events would take a very different course than seemed likely at this point. I have no idea whether the man survived the war, but was deeply impressed by the views he expressed during this outspoken conversation.

Many of the Russian soldiers who crossed the lines or were taken prisoner showed an amazing fatalism. I remember well the reaction of a group of Russian soldiers as I interrogated them during a bombardment. Shells were whizzing through the air and crashing into trees all about us. I was anxious to move, but the Soviets kept their ground until I finally told them that I was going to protect myself and that they should do likewise. Their attitude towards death was quite different from ours.

Shortly after this incident we captured a young boy of about fourteen or fifteen, who was brought to me for interrogation. This brave lad had crossed the front lines and penetrated into the German rear. He explained his actions by his desire to visit his parents. This lie soon collapsed, and he admitted that the purpose of his trip was to see what was going on behind the German lines. I asked him why he had done this. He replied that he felt it was his duty to do so. I lectured him sternly, telling him that a boy of fourteen had no such duty, and that he had best get back to school as soon as it re-opened. To add weight to my words, I told him that if he were caught again, I could not guarantee that he would not be shot.

Within two weeks, he had been caught again and brought to me once more for interrogation. This posed a terrible problem. I had great sympathy for the boy, but at the same time had to be mindful of the safety of my regiment. After some hesitation I decided to give him a good thrashing and send him back. Was I right to have done this? Fortunately, by next day we were advancing so rapidly that I knew it would be impossible for him to follow us.

First Lieutenant Frick, the member of our regiment who had earlier bathed the visiting Nazi official with beer, was killed on the main road leading from Mogilev to Gomel. In the early stages of the war it was customary for regimental commanders to write to the family of any officer killed in action. Such letters noted the circumstances of the soldier's death, mentioned that he had died in the service of his country, and stated that the nation could be proud of him. It will be recalled that Frick's father was a prominent Nazi and Hitler's Minister of the Interior. I drafted the letter to him from our commander, Colonel Wachsen. In it I spoke warmly of young Frick's heroism and generally reproduced the form of such letters from World War I, mentioning that he had lived up to the traditions of his regiment and had died for his Fatherland, but saying nothing about Führer and Reich. This was intended and received as a double insult to the Nazis. Within a few days Hitler's Minister sent us a reply, in which he expressed his pride that his son had been killed fighting for Führer and Reich and offering to send the regiment a signed picture of himself. Wachsen responded immediately with a letter stating that he did not want a signed picture of the Minister but that he would be most grateful for a photograph of young Frick, who had lived up to the finest traditions of his regiment. No further reply was received. After several such incidents, the Nazi Party finally insisted that all deaths be reported to the local Party Office, which would then inform the family in the suitable Nazi phraseology.

Shortly after Frick's death I found myself in a foxhole under heavy artillery and mortar fire for hours. There were four of us, frightened and depressed. In order to overcome our fear we invented a game. Each of us had to describe an evening in a smart hotel for a dinner-dance. We discussed the menus, the wine, described the dresses, the jewellery and the looks of our wives, and our favourite music. Before this pleasant pastime had run its course the artillery barrage ceased and we were able to move forward once more.

Our fears would have been greater at the outset of the campaign had we encountered partisan activity. German troops had been warned of this possibility and expected to be plagued by guerilla activity practically from the first day, but during the first months of the Russian campaign we encountered no partisans at all. On the contrary, we heard of partisan groups working within Soviet-held territory, obviously using the general confusion to settle old scores with local officials and with the regime. Our own intelligence unit, Wally II, took advantage of this to infiltrate spies and agitators behind the Soviet lines. Later, when the Russians and Ukrainians became thoroughly disillusioned by the German civil administration, they started a partisan movement behind the German lines. By their oppressive and criminal methods, Hitler and his henchmen thus succeeded in driving large parts of the population back into the arms of Stalin.

The reception we received from civilians was astonishingly cordial. Entering the villages we were greeted as liberators. Except for officials of the Communist Party, practically no one fled. The Soviet government's efforts to evacuate the population from the areas under German threat were widely obstructed and generally a failure. The only areas in which the Soviet government succeeded in evacuating the personnel and machinery of industrial plants were all at a considerable distance from the front lines. Nor did the peasants heed the orders of the Soviet government to destroy the harvest and all grain reserves, or to drive off their cattle. Stalin's order to leave the occupied territories to the German invaders as scorched earth was viewed by the peasantry as an act of despair and only served to intensify their hatred of the dictator.

The local population showed genuine kindness towards the German troops and pinned great hopes on our arrival. Everywhere we went we were greeted with bread and salt, the traditional Slav symbols of hospitality. Even in the poor villages where provisions were in short supply, the peasants generously offered to share their cucumbers, yogurt, and bread with individual soldiers as a sign of friendship. Again and again we were told by the villagers: 'Now, thank goodness, we will be treated as human beings and will be given back our rights as men.' At this point they still believed strongly in the Germans' sense of justice and humanity.

In one village that had just been evacuated by the Red Army, we rode through a main street lined with peasants who, to our surprise, were shouting and gleefully waving at the sky. I dismounted and looked overhead just as a squadron of German fighters encountered a group of Soviet planes. In the ensuing battle all the Soviet planes were shot down. As each crashed to the ground in flames, the villagers clapped their hands, shouting that soon Stalin, too, would fall.

The feelings of the average Soviet citizen with which I had contact were guided more by economic considerations than by ideological or even patriotic concerns. They did not care which government ruled, provided their standard of living improved. Ukrainians and Russians often told us that they would have no objection to a strong German influence on their administration. This attitude, of course, was the product of the incredible privations which the Soviet system had inflicted in the course of the Revolution, Civil War, and Stalin's Five-Year Plans. The masses had no realization that, for all the suffering, Stalin's 'Great Leap Forward' was bound to lead the country to a certain prosperity. Their scepticism was justified, because to date the prosperity of the elite had been built on the peasantry's toil, just as it had been under the tsars. The average citizen had no confidence that things would ever improve for him under Soviet rule.

The welcome given to the German soldiers was all the more surprising in view of the virulent anti-German propaganda from 1933 to 1938, renewed with the outbreak of the war. It seemed not to have impressed the Soviet population at all. For many, Hitler was a saviour who was expected to redeem the poor Ukrainians and Russians and secure them a brighter future. There was an element of anti-Semitism in this enthusiasm, and many had believed the Nazi propaganda that Stalin was married to a daughter of his Jewish-born henchman, Lazar Kaganovich. They were unaware of the fact that Jewish influence in Moscow had been greatly reduced, and that a new policy of Soviet chauvinism had taken its place. But the deepest concern of those Soviet citizens with whom I had contact seemed to spring always from their economic aspirations.

Scarcely had we arrived in a village than we would be asked what would happen to the collective farms. Even the meanest peasant expected to get back his property and perhaps to end up with more than one cow. The peasants' hatred of the collective and *Sovkhoz* farms was boundless. They did not realize that their low standard of living was due at least as much to the extremely high indirect taxes on agricultural production as to collectivization *per se*. Nor did they themselves put forward specific ideas as to how to divide the land. Their confidence in the German talent for organization was so boundless that they assumed the invaders would cope with such problems with ease.

We would assure them that private property would be restored, and that we would permit the villagers themselves to decide what they wished to do with the collective farms – a policy that often gave rise to wrangling. We insisted only that the harvest be collected, lest yet more grave difficulties presented themselves in the autumn. They accepted this.

Artisans and shop-keepers in the towns hoped for the re-opening of individual enterprises and the restoration of property, and were willing to collaborate with the Germans to achieve it. Such Soviet citizens were prepared to contribute to the overthrow of Stalin's system by fulfilling even the most far-reaching German demands. They were aware that Germany in time of war would not be capable of satisfying their strong demand for tools, clothing and consumer goods, but were convinced that Germany would supply these goods after the war and that light industry would be developed in a liberated Russia.

A recurrent development whenever we stayed in a village for more than a few hours was the appearance of individual peasants or of whole delegations seeking to meet us. In every case, they arrived with lists of the most active local Communist Party members, against whom they wanted us to take action. More often than not, these first comers would be followed by a second group anxious that we should arrest the earlier arrivals. Such occurrences are inevitable for any occupying army, but they still posed tremendous difficulties. In practice it was impossible to sort out the good villagers from the bad. I therefore advised my fellow officers not to get into such political questions for the time being and instead to tell the local population to get back to work.

How did our soldiers view the peasants? During the first days of fighting we captured a village and were resting there when Soviet artillery fire broke out. A number of the farmhouses caught fire, particularly those with thatched roofs. A strong wind arose and the separate fires swelled into a conflagration that we were helpless to stop. As we were abandoning the village to find a safer spot for the night, our soldiers noticed the peasants climbing to the rooftops. Perched high astride the roofbeams of those farmhouses which were not yet burning, the peasants held aloft their icons and prayed to God to calm the wind and keep the fire away from their homes. When our soldiers laughed at them, I tried to explain that at this point praying was the only thing left for them to do.

Further contact with the local population soon changed the German attitudes towards the enemy. To the surprise of the soldiers, who were naturally under the influence of Nazi propaganda, the Russians and Ukrainians who came over to our side or were captured turned out to be ordinary people like themselves and far cleaner than our troops expected *Untermenschen* to be. It may seem trivial, but the discovery that in every village there were schools and *banias* (a kind of sauna) struck a mortal blow at Nazi theories about our enemy. The village *banias* came to be much frequented by German officers and men and provided occasions for much conviviality.

The German soldiers also came to be much impressed by the high morals of the Ukrainian and Russian girls. The village girls were prepared to be perfectly polite to the German soldiers, but for the most part they were unwilling to go further. The soldiers could not help but contrast this to the attitude of German girls. It was understood that these Ukrainian and Russian girls wanted marriage and nothing else.

Many of the first prisoners we took asked immediately whether we did not have work for them and proclaimed their readiness to go with us. Opportunism may have played a part in this, but most seemed genuinely desirous of doing what they could to destroy the hated system that had collectivized their farms and brutalized their lives. They had no idea yet what might happen to them as prisoners of war.

Spontaneously, and without any orders from above, the army had begun to accept such co-operation. The rank-and-file soldier knew instinctively that it was a necessity. At first, the prisoners of war rendered precious service as scouts, helped in the military kitchens, drove carts, and worked in military workshops. As our losses began to mount, the prisoners were promoted to carrying ammunition and machine guns and then even to manning the guns themselves. This took place on an informal basis, but it was widespread. Hence, long before the question of whether former Red Army soldiers should be permitted to serve as volunteers in the German army was posed at the official level, it had already been answered in practice. Against this background, Hitler's view of the volunteers as *Untermenschen* to be kept in minor supporting functions was the more absurd. The volunteers were already in German service, thanks to the co-operation that arose naturally between them and our common soldiers on the Eastern Front. The army High Command could neither start nor stop this phenomenon. In creating the volunteer units as it did later, it was simply ratifying actions that had already occurred. I doubt whether it had any alternative but to give its approval to what had long since taken place.

Near Pinsk, we captured a group of Turkestani who were serving in Soviet labour battalions. Their strong Mongol features and the quilted jackets in which they were dressed baffled their German captors. The German soldiers, most of whom had rarely, if ever, encountered foreign peoples of any description, jumped to the conclusion that here, finally, they had encountered true *Untermenschen*. The poor Turkestani had the devil of a time convincing the German soldiers that they were not part of the Soviet fighting units. Finally, they held their fingers before their faces in such a way as to look like bars, thus communicating to their captors that they were serving time as forced labour in the Red Army but were not actual fighting troops. This entitled them to better treatment than they otherwise might have received, yet it is still pitiful to think of these poor souls, who had only recently left one forced-labour camp, so eagerly putting themselves in another. What we could not know at this early stage of the war was that many Turkestani and peoples of the Caucasus were to be executed by the SS because of their exotic appearance. Many Mohammedans were shot as Jews for the simple reason that they were circumcised.

The task of the First Cavalry Division was to secure the vast Pripet Marshes. Armoured divisions had been assigned to cross the Pripet swamp on the famous *Rollbahn*, a well-built East-West highway. Meanwhile, our cavalry division had been ordered to move through the territory to the right of the *Rollbahn*, usually through open land. To the astonishment of the commanders, the cavalrymen crossed the swamp as rapidly as the motorized divisions on the *Rollbahn*. This was possible in part because we did not encounter the fierce Russian resistance that we had anticipated and were able to move unimpeded.

The greatest difficulty which the German advance encountered in my area was caused by the deployment of the Soviet T-34 tanks. This tank was an excellent machine, superior to our own and quite impervious to our artillery. The German 3.7 anti-tank shells would hit the T-34 and bounce off into the air, while even the more powerful '5' anti-tank shells frequently failed to incapacitate them.

The damage inflicted by the T-34s was mitigated by the poor judgment of the Soviet commanders in deploying them. They could easily burst through our lines, but rather than plunge forward as the German tanks had done in France, the T-34s were usually ordered to turn back after only a few kilometres, their assignment being to accompany the infantry and to stay near it rather than to advance boldly into new territory. Since our artillery was ineffective against the T-34s, the German troops would hide themselves in hastily dug pits or wherever else they could get cover and wait until the tanks had passed. Then they would leap on them from behind, open the hatches, and throw in hand grenades. Until we began using 8.8 mm anti-aircraft guns against the Soviet tanks, this was the best we could do.

Another surprise was the quantity and the quality of Soviet artillery and mortars. Contrary to the experience of World War I, when a high percentage of the imperial Russian army's shells did not explode due to their poor quality, the ammunition now functioned perfectly.

Soviet resistance was rendered more effective by the excellence of their camouflage. The Red Army troops had been thoroughly trained, but I believe they also possessed a natural feeling for such work that stemmed from the peasant soldiers' close links with nature. A second area in which the Soviet soldiers showed superiority from the outset was their ability to construct defensive positions and bridges in no time at all. I recall at one point we were resting confidently with a river in front of us, only to find that during the night the Russians had bridged the same river three miles to the west and moved around to our rear. Such work confirmed the old proverb that, if you drop a Russian peasant in the forest with only an axe, within the week he will be resting comfortably in a fully-furnished house.

In his wisdom, Hitler had not bothered to equip the troops for a winter campaign. With the outset of autumn we began to suffer heavily, both from rain and cold. Even before the snows set in, the hardship inflicted by rain and mud was worse than the actual battle losses. The Russian peasants called that part of the year 'the time without roads' and stayed at home. For our troops it was utterly demoralizing. The deepening cold also wreaked havoc with the engines of the tanks and trucks, which were still running on summer-weight oil when the snows began, for the simple reason that, once more, the need for winter weight oil had not been anticipated.

By the time we reached Briansk, the rain gave way to snow and we had to battle in a heavy snow storm. It was at this time that my unit, having encircled a large force of Russians, was in turn encircled by a second Russian unit. For a while we were pressed from behind and in front and it looked as if the inner Russian unit would break through to the outer ring. Since the forces that had encircled us were also trying to break through to the centre, chaos ensued. I am sure that nobody on either the Russian or German side had the slightest idea of the shape of the battle as a whole, especially because it all happened at night. Fortunately, we succeeded in containing the Russians, and the forces that had encircled us retired.

By this point, our condition had become bitterly difficult. We were all but frozen, had little food and, of course, nothing to drink. One day in late October I returned from a mission, feeling absolutely miserable. To my amazement, I was handed the bottom half of a double boiler, in which members of our staff had brewed up a kind of chocolate brandy from alcohol and chocolate that had mysteriously appeared. Exhausted as I was, I downed the entire potful and immediately fell asleep. Within the hour I was rudely awakened and told to report at once to Colonel Wachsen. I vaguely remember him speaking to me and someone touching my jacket on the left side, to which I responded by trying vigorously to brush the hand away. Then I passed out. Next morning I woke up and fished about for my jacket, which was missing. The only one to be found had an Iron Cross, First Class, which I knew could not be mine. My friends roared with laughter as I stormed about and finally explained to me that this was indeed my jacket, and that Wachsen had awarded me the Iron Cross at the 'ceremony' which I could only vaguely remember. Receiving it, I apparently exclaimed only *'Hopla! Wir leben!'* – 'Well, well! So there we are.'

After Briansk, we received orders to assemble the First Cavalry Division behind the front lines and then to march to Gomel in order to pass in review before Field Marshal Fedor von Bock. We were appalled at the order to cover so many miles in so brief a time, knowing full well that our horses could not manage it. Indeed, on that long bitter march we lost many of our best animals. Decimated by battle and bedraggled by the march, we finally arrived at Gomel in late November 1941. There the entire division was paraded before its commander for the last time. It was an impressive ceremony, and also deeply moving, for we all understood that the day of the mounted cavalry was past, and that a new and harsher era of warfare was upon us.

Yet for all the nostalgia evoked by this historic review, the performance of the German cavalry was far more significant than one might have expected in so highly motorized a campaign. The reason for this good showing was that the terrain in which the German army was fighting differed little from what it might have been centuries earlier. The horse was perfectly adapted to such conditions. Whether on sand, wet earth, or in the large wooded regions through which we had to move, the horses were able to move readily and without the problems that even the best-engineered wheeled and tracked vehicles encountered.

Why then was our division disbanded as a cavalry unit, despite our great successes in the Russian campaign? All of us knew that Hitler detested the cavalry. It may be apocryphal, but it was widely rumoured that he had been bitten by a horse in his youth, thus giving rise to his phobia. Besides which, the anti-Nazi mood of the cavalry must have been well known to the Führer. While the transformation of our cavalry division into an armoured car division was under discussion, offers were received from the SS to take us over lock, stock, and barrel. We refused these outright. Then the SS began directing its appeal to individual officers. It was a subject of pride among us that not one of us yielded to the SS's blandishments and changed his uniform.

Viewed from a Nazi point of view, the cavalry was undeniably and proudly a subversive force. It is noteworthy that the only unit on which the anti-Hitler conspirators could rely was the *Kavallerie Brigade Mitte*, and perhaps two other cavalry units on the Eastern Front. The stubborn and old-fashioned cavalry officer was perhaps more inclined than his colleagues in the other services to express his hostility to Hitler's policies.

The parade completed, we put our remaining horses on railway cars and went west with them. As we were loading, I noticed columns of Soviet prisoners moving past at a distance, marching arm-in-arm but reeling like drunkards. I thought nothing more of it at the time, but the following morning one of my men woke me up to point out the corpses of Russian soldiers strewn along the tracks. They had apparently not been fed for days, and their 'drunkenness' was the result of sheer fatigue. Many died in the railway cars, and were hurled on to the line by the dwindling number of survivors who did not want to live with corpses.

When our train paused for several hours at the frontier town of Wirballen-Eydtkuhnen, I was able to walk to the nearby station and put through a call to my wife in Kitzbühl. I had been anxious for some weeks to know whether our child had been born, and she was able to tell me that a daughter, Alexandra, had arrived on 8 November. Like any proud father, I was eager to learn the baby's weight – six and a half pounds – which I immediately reported to my fellow officers as six and a half kilos. We had only a bottle of Cointreau with which to celebrate the birth of this prodigious child, which we did with some gusto. My fellow officers immediately baptized her 'Cointrine'. When she was baptized with her real name, Alexandra – in memory of happy times in Russia – Schulenburg was her godfather.

After the First Cavalry Division was withdrawn from the Soviet Union, we were sent to a manoeuvre ground at Ohrdruf near Erfurt in Thuringia. Our unit was so much larger than the population of the village of Ohrdruf that we were forbidden to go to the local pubs or cinema, lest the town be over-run with cavalrymen. We were confined to our barracks, which featured a dreary barn-like officers' mess that had been constructed prior to World War I. Boredom set in. The building desperately needed decoration, and since it bore a certain resemblance to a railway station, we decided that every time one of us travelled by rail he would steal signs from the various stations and bring them back. Before long, the building resembled a conglomeration of all the major German railway stations.

This failed to relieve our boredom. At one point we held a party, which brought together the entire officer corps of the division. The sense of release at this occasion was so great that there was dancing on the tables, singing, whistling, and general pandemonium. Captain Schlenther particularly distinguished himself by simultaneously dancing and whistling. At the end of this gathering, someone suggested that we hold a horse show, including a jumping competition. Pieces of furniture were immediately transformed into obstacles and our horses were saddled up. Before long we were jumping some of the larger tables in the room, a dangerous procedure rendered less so only by the good sense of the horses and by the Lord's well-known protection of drunks.

Our division included one motorcycle battalion, whose members had been confined to the sidelines while we held our cavalry manoeuvre. Naturally, they felt cheated and on the same evening declared a motorcycle race. The roar was thunderous, and some of the machines slipped from under their riders. Miraculously, no one was badly hurt, although in the course of the evening we did manage to do considerable damage to that dreadful Wilhelminian barn. In due course we were presented with a bill, which we dutifully paid, grateful for at least this degree of diversion.

About this time my cousin, Colonel von Lossberg, ordered me to report to him. This was our first meeting since the outbreak of the war and the German army had already been forced to retreat before Moscow. Again he agreed with me that Germany's hopes in the East were illusory, and that Hitler's famous Arkhangelsk-Astrakhan line was unattainable. By this point Lossberg was convinced that Hitler was essentially lacking in courage. He had reached this conclusion on the basis of his own experience during the invasion of Norway. After the initial successful attack, the German forces had met fierce resistance and counter-attacks from the British and Norwegians. Soon they were in danger of being wiped out. At this point Hitler had argued for a retreat, and only Lossberg's insistence on the need to follow through stiffened Hitler's will to the point that he did not call off the attack.

Having prepared operation 'Sea Lion' Hitler, like Napoleon at Boulogne in 1812, did not take the risk of ordering the invasion of Great Britain. The attack on Russia was no proof of his courage, either, since he had managed to convince himself that the German army would sweep away all resistance within six weeks.

Blindly convinced of the simplicity of the task, Hitler forged ahead. Even when the six-week dream crumbled and trouble set in, he refused to follow the advice of the General Staff to draw back the front line and consolidate for a new offensive in the spring of 1942. As a result, the German army was denied the possibility of a more or less orderly retreat when the Soviets successfully counter-attacked. Instead it was put in the almost untenable position of surviving a brutal winter with inadequate supplies and equipment. It must be admitted, however, that Hitler's order not to give ground under any circumstances prevented the disaster of a chaotic retreat.

Bravado became a surrogate for bravery. Goebbels issued several radio announcements claiming that the bulk of the Red Army had been destroyed. Our officers responded to this self-delusion with sardonic humour. I recall a comrade at Briansk who showed up one day with a bottle of cognac and proposed a celebration. Astonished, I asked him what in heaven's name there was to celebrate. He replied that he had just heard on the radio that we had destroyed our minus-100th Soviet division. We drank to our success.

What a pity that Hitler never had the chance to be enlightened by such humour! Somehow, though, he did become aware of our regiment's disrespect towards him and his policies. Early in 1942, Hitler was told that the officers of our First Cavalry Division were a gang of old-fashioned anti-Nazis. He cynically replied that, as long as we were willing to die while performing our duties, he would postpone the question of our ultimate fate until the end of the war. It was a characteristic answer and a clever one, too, in that it went to the heart of the dilemma of those officers who opposed Hitler but remained loyal to their duty. Exploiting his perception of this, Hitler soon sent the division back into the fray, now in the new role of an armoured division. The commander of our regiment, Colonel Wachsen, was transferred to another post. We greatly regretted his departure, as it had always been his goal to spare the lives of his men, rather than to gain military distinction and award. Perhaps this humane attitude was the cause of his transfer.

15

THE FORMATION OF THE VOLUNTEER UNITS: SCHULENBURG, STAUFFENBERG, AND KÖSTRING

Just as my old cavalry division was being transformed into an armoured division, I was seconded as an officer to the so-called Department Thirteen of the Ministry of Foreign Affairs. Department Thirteen was responsible for all the Ministry's affairs in the Soviet Union, which for all practical purposes meant that part of the Soviet Union that was under German rule. It was soon to become painfully evident how limited was the Ministry's role even within those territories, but I had no idea of this when I left my division for Berlin on 3 March, 1942.

Schulenburg headed Department Thirteen and it was he who was responsible for my transfer. In order to bring me on to his staff, he intervened with Field Marshal Keitel, as I later learned from a letter he wrote to Pussi. At the time I joined Schulenburg's staff, he was embroiled in a major battle to gain for the Ministry some voice in the administration of the occupied territories. His chief opponent in this effort was Alfred Rosenberg, who, as head of Hitler's notorious *Ostministerium*, was responsible for Party policy in all occupied territories. In addition to Rosenberg, he had also to contend with Fritz Sauckel, who was in charge of extracting labour from the Soviet population; with the infamous Erich Koch, now *Reichskommissar* for the Ukraine; and with the SS, which was already intervening in the captured territories in its characteristically brutal and capricious manner.

Schulenburg came into frontal conflict with this ruthless crowd over the competence of the Ministry of Foreign Affairs in the occupied territories of the East. His view was that Rosenberg's *Ostministerium* should have only a transitional role and that the Ministry of Foreign Affairs should hold full responsibility for all matters affecting the future of the USSR and its relations with Germany. In pursuing his campaign, Schulenburg found himself in the bizarre position of promoting the claims of Ribbentrop, the Nazi in charge of the Ministry of Foreign

Affairs. Ribbentrop remained the perfect yes-man, ever ready to ingratiate himself with Hitler, but his ambition rendered him amenable to Schulenburg's campaign.

Amidst the day-to-day jockeying for power, Schulenburg had to remain guarded about his own programme, lest he be overwhelmed by a tide of Nazi opposition. One can search the archives in vain for a full statement of Schulenburg's views at this time, but he had thought through the matter carefully, and arrived at a programme that was almost totally at odds with what was actually happening.

First, Schulenburg wanted Poland to be re-created as an independent state, and the autonomy of the three Baltic republics to be restored. His long association with Poland and his close personal links with many leading Polish personalities made it impossible for him to consider seriously any other policy than this. Between 1939 and 1942 Schulenburg had helped many of his Polish friends leave their country by intervening constantly with the German and Soviet governments on their behalf. Second, he advocated the establishment of independent states of Georgia and Armenia in the Caucasus. Again, his earlier contact with Georgia at the time of its brief independence and his realization that such a state would, in all likelihood, be well disposed towards Germany, reinforced his commitment to this policy. Unlike the Nazis, he would have extended this same policy of self-determination to the Russians themselves and to the Ukrainians.

Schulenburg was convinced that the Soviet Union could only be defeated with the help of the Russians themselves and that the war had therefore to be transformed into a civil war. In his opinion, Germany had to sponsor local self-government in the occupied territories and to favour the formation of an anti-Soviet Russian government and of such governments among the minorities. Germany had to recognize these governments as allies, to treat them accordingly and to declare solemnly that she had no territorial claims on Russia. It had to help the different Soviet nations, including the Great Russians, to build up their own independent states by applying a policy of self-determination and by enabling them to join a European union based on equality and free collaboration under German leadership. If, in the course of time, the centripetal forces in Russia should prevail over the separatist, he went so far as to envisage a new Russian federal state with far-reaching autonomy for the minorities. In opposition to Hitler's and Rosenberg's opinions, he was persuaded that the Great Russian nation had to play a leading part in the new Russia.

The idea of helping the minorities of the Soviet Union to build up their own states was less utopian than it may seem today. Most of these minorities had been subjugated by Russia only during the last two centuries and many had tried to win back their independence after the Revolution of 1917. Some of them had even succeeded in forming independent states; the three Baltic states, however, being the only ones which had succeeded in defending their independence against the Red Army. Certainly national feeling was not equally developed among all the different minorites, but the torch of nationalism had been lit, and in the hands of capable nationalist leaders, might have led to similar results as in nineteenth-century Europe.

As a matter of fact, the percentage of deserters from the minority races was very high. Enquiries among the population of the occupied territories and prisoners-of-war elicited that the minorities were not satisfied with the fictitious rights with which Stalin's constitution had endowed them. They especially resented the recently intensified Great Russian propaganda and grip on their local governments, which they saw as a renewal of the old tsarist methods of suppression. The number of people in favour of the status of the minorities under the Soviet system was relatively small and consisted mostly of those who had benefited personally by Soviet rule. Neither the tsars nor Stalin had yet succeeded in welding the different nationalities into one nation or a federation. The minorities therefore hoped for Germany's support in their struggle for independence.

These were Schulenburg's long-term goals. His more immediate concern was to ensure that the population was treated in a decent and humane manner. He was deeply upset by the reports of the brutal treatment being meted out to the people of the occupied territories and knew that such behaviour would utterly discredit Germany, not only among the leaders of the national minorities within the USSR but, even worse, among the population at large. Were it to continue, he knew it would lead directly to the collapse of all his own hopes and to the stiffening of Soviet resistance.

I could not help but be impressed with the humanity with which Schulenburg approached his work in Department Thirteen, but I could also see just how limited a role he, the Department, and indeed, the Ministry of Foreign Affairs as a whole, could play in any issue pertaining to the USSR. Schulenburg's ideas contradicted Hitler's own colonial plans so completely that no compromise between the two was possible. Hitler decided that the Ministry of Foreign Affairs could not be trusted to protect Nazi interests, and decided to back the very agencies against which Schulenburg had struggled in vain.

It was obvious to me that the Ministry offered even fewer opportunities to influence the situation now than when I had left it in 1939, and that, for me, Department Thirteen was little more than an observation post. I therefore resolved to return to the army. No sooner had I reached this decision than Ribbentrop again entered my life. Studying a protocol in which I was cited, Ribbentrop took sharp exception to practically every point I had made. He immediately announced that the author of such a memorandum should not be permitted to serve in the Ministry of Foreign Affairs.

Before leaving, I donned my dress uniform and made an appearance at the personnel office of the Ministry of Foreign Affairs. My request for a transfer back to the army was granted without delay. The personnel officer from whom I took leave spoke warmly on how valuable it must have been for a young officer like me to have seen how the Ministry of Foreign Affairs worked. I rather flippantly replied that I had observed the Ministry of Foreign Affairs over twelve years and had deliberately resigned in order to join the army. Later in the year, after this same personnel officer had joined the army, he appeared at a staff meeting in the Caucasus. I congratulated him on having left the Ministry of Foreign Affairs to become a decent soldier. He obviously remembered our earlier conversation and did not find my remark amusing.

After leaving my post with Schulenburg, I was transferred to 'Spala', a former hunting lodge of the tsars in Poland, where I was assigned to the staff of the *Wehrmacht befehlshaber im Generalgouvernement*. There I served under General Baron Curt von Gienanth, a cavalry officer and a close friend of both Köstring and Schulenburg. Gienanth had just been named to replace Colonel General Johannes Blaskowitz, who had been relieved of his command because he had dared object to the treatment the Poles were receiving at the hands of Governor General Frank. He had also dared to defend those Jews assigned to work in factories against Hitler and Himmler's desire to send them to concentration camps. Blaskowitz had tried to cast his defence in terms the Nazis could accept, pointing out that the extermination of these Jewish workers would damage Germany's war production and that all their places would then have to be filled by Germans or Poles, who were urgently needed elsewhere. His tactics failed. When Gienanth replaced him, he too made great efforts to shape his arguments on behalf of the Jews in terms the

Nazis could understand. In spite of a cautious start, however, he soon offended the Party and was dismissed.

My specific task under Gienanth was to give advice on how to set up special battalions of former Soviet soldiers from Georgia, Azerbaijan, Turkestan, Armenia, the North Caucasus and the Volga Tatar areas. At first, some German officers were sceptical whether these former Soviet soldiers would fight vigorously for the German side, but they demonstrated such toughness, such a capacity to endure the hardships of the Russian winter and to muddle through, that by the early spring of 1942 it was clear they had passed the test. Soon whole units were being formed, with former Soviet officers offering their services. The eagerness of these former Red Army officers and soldiers immensely simplified our work. The battalions were quickly set up and Schulenburg came out from Berlin to inspect them.

My work in Poland and with Schulenburg gave me a reputation as an expert on the problems of integrating former Red Army troops into the German army. I was therefore assigned to the army's General Staff, and was posted to the Organizational Division at the headquarters in Vinnitsa and later in Mauerwald, near Angerburg in East Prussia. This assignment had been engineered by Major Count Claus von Stauffenberg who, as head of Section II of the Organizational Division, was responsible for organizing into units all former Soviet soldiers who had volunteered to serve in the army. Stauffenberg wanted to have someone on his staff who was knowledgeable about the Soviet Union.

I had known of Stauffenberg for a long while, since he was a cousin of my wife, but I had never met him until now, in the spring of 1942. Our relationship was warm from the outset. We were both extroverts and easily made friends, even amidst the hectic pace of our work. Stauffenberg had a great sense of humour and could laugh like a boy with little provocation. Moreover, we had many interests in common. We both read voraciously and shared a love for English literature. I constantly fed him English novels and the works of such historians as Macaulay. On this basis, our collaboration flourished.

The great Field Marshal Gneisenau was among his ancestors, and Stauffenberg was a worthy heir in every respect. Over the next two years I frequently attended meetings with Claus at which higher-ranking officers were present. According to the usual practice, the most senior officer would be in the chair. Regardless of who presided, though, Stauffenberg invariably managed to take charge. What most surprised me was the manner in which those who surpassed him in rank recognized his natural superiority and yielded to it.

As a young man, Claus von Stauffenberg had participated actively in the German Youth Movement. I learned from him that he had initially been quite impressed by Hitler's accomplishments – the re-arming of Germany, the reoccupation of the Rhineland, and so forth. He had been particularly attracted by the fact that all this had been accomplished without armed conflict. By the time I met Stauffenberg, however, he had already become thoroughly alarmed over what was taking place. At our first meeting, he indicated that he was especially outraged at the treatment given to Soviet soldiers who had surrendered or been captured; he spoke about this openly and with passion.

Stauffenberg had had no prior contact with Russia. It is true that his father-in-law, Baron Lerchenfeld, had served as Consul General in Kovno, and that his mother and mother-in-law were of Baltic origin, but I never felt that these links were a factor in Stauffenberg's strong reaction against the ill-treatment of Soviet prisoners. Rather, as he made clear to me, his objections rose from his strong Christian beliefs. He was a devout member of an old Catholic family, and very strict in his moral views.

Stauffenberg brought to his work an unusually sensitive perception of human nature. When I arrived to work for him, he had before him an order that would have required all Soviet prisoners to be branded on the seat with some sort of identification mark. He quickly telephoned the general who was in a position to reverse the order. Stauffenberg set forth the perfectly sound military arguments against so odious a scheme. I listened in amazement as he pressed his case by assuring the general that, when next they met on Unter den Linden, the royal avenue of Berlin, he, Stauffenberg, would challenge the general's identity and require him to drop his trousers to prove he was not a Russian captive. The order was rescinded, although the story did not end there. The Russians somehow got a copy of the order and published it, with the consequences that could have been expected.

Along with this fine sensitivity to human nature, Stauffenberg possessed a rigorous sense of organization. I recall his pointing out to me Hitler's technique of appointing two or even three officials or agencies to handle the same problem. Besides forcing them all to com-pete with each other, this method had the advantage, in Nazi theory at least, of providing a kind of surrogate for more democratic forms of controlling a bureaucracy. It also ensured that no group would acquire too much influence and thereby threaten the Führer, who never had cabinet meetings. On the other hand, the absence of a clear hierarchical chain of command all but guaranteed that chaos would prevail. Thus, Stauffenberg fully appreciated the confusion and duplication of effort that lay behind Hitler's apparently monolithic regime.

Stauffenberg also directed his incisive managerial sense against the army, and with withering results. I once watched with bitter amusement as he tried to explain the organization of our military command to a group of young captains who were training for service with the General Staff. He spoke of the *Generalstab des Heeres*, which was responsible for operations in the Soviet Union and Poland, and of the *Wehrmachts- führungsstab* which was in charge of the action in France, Scandinavia, Africa and the Balkans. He pointed out that, in World War I, there had been a single command rather than two, and that this had assured a degree of co-ordination that was utterly lacking now. He then went on to list a series of anomalies, such as the fact that the *Generalstab des Heeres* retained responsibility for quartermastering in both the East and West, though its battle responsibilities were confined to the Russian Front, and that the *Wehrmachtsführungsstab* nonetheless maintained a small and unco-ordinated quartermaster corps of its own. As he spoke, Stauffenberg moved to the blackboard and tried to chart the hopelessly tangled organization. Before long his diagram looked like a confused work of abstract art. Stauffenberg paused. Finally, in despair, he asked his audience if any organization so constructed could possibly win a war.

No sooner did he direct his attention to the organization of the volunteer units than he found himself face to face with the same staggering problems of conflicting authority, misrule and outright brutality that had stymied von der Schulenburg. From the outset he had to contend with Alfred Rosenberg, the confused and basically insignificant head of Hitler's *Ostministerium*. Raised in the Baltic and trained as an architect in Moscow before the World War, Rosenberg was driven by a hatred for the Russians more profound than can be explained even by tsarist Russia's chauvinistic pan-Slavism. But his hatred was far stronger than his personality. He was not even a strong negative figure in the sense that Goering or Koch were. Though head of the *Ostministerium*, he had no great influence with Hitler. He considered his unreadable book, *The Myth of the Twentieth Century*, to be the embodiment of truth, although even his immediate subordinates ridiculed it and considered him a fool.

It is therefore not surprising that former *Gauleiter* and now Com-

217

missar for the Ukraine, Erich Koch, came so prominently to the fore. The sinister Koch whom I had dealt with earlier in Memel, had not the slightest doubt that Russians and Ukrainians were true *Untermenschen*, and he treated them accordingly. Using all his authority, he excluded Ukrainians from leading posts and, in order to prevent the formation of a new intellectual class, abolished all education in the Ukraine beyond the first four grades. When he became alarmed at the rapid increase of the population, Koch repealed all measures aimed at the protection of children and pregnant women and stopped the construction of housing and sanitary facilities. Koch's officials treated the Ukraine as a slave colony with no other function than to produce cheap raw materials and agricultural products for Germany. Koch's flunkies did everything they could to obstruct the promised transformation of the collective farms into co-operatives and the gradual restitution of property to the peasants.

It was an absurd psychological blunder that the German officials in the occupied Soviet territories were given the title 'commissar' after the German propaganda had denounced the Soviet commissars as tormentors and vampires. The *Ostministerium* did not realize that the word 'commissar' reminded the population of years of oppression under Stalin and must have been odious to the people. They soon discovered that the new commissars were no better than the old ones; even worse, indeed, as beating was now introduced. The Bolsheviks shot people as a punishment but never punished by beating.

Beyond Rosenberg and Koch, Stauffenberg had also to contend with *Gauleiter* Fritz Sauckel, whose job it was to mobilize the local population for labour for the Reich. Initially, Sauckel had the immense benefit of tens of thousands of people who genuinely wanted to contribute to the German campaign against Stalin. Rather than let them volunteer, he commandeered them, placed them behind bars and shipped them off as forced labour. When the supply of recruits began to dwindle in response to this outrageous treatment, Sauckel resorted to more barbaric methods of recruitment, even to the point of sending police to surround worshippers in church and herd them into waiting trucks or trains at gunpoint.

Finally Stauffenberg had to cope with the inhuman ideas and policies of Heinrich Himmler and his SS. In the early summer of 1942 Stauffenberg learned just how far Himmler's fancy could carry him. One evening in May, an officer arrived at the mess hall of the Organization Division and told us in a trembling voice that he had witnessed SS troops rounding up the Jewish population of a Ukrainian village, leading them to a nearby field, and after commanding them to dig graves, shooting them down, young and old alike. This was the first time that Stauffenberg or any of us on his staff had heard of the mass execution of Jews, and the impact on us all was overwhelming. Hitler refused to permit Soviet prisoners-of-war to enter Germany. So millions of prisoners were crowded in the Soviet Union and Poland. As a result hundreds of thousands died of starvation in 1941–42. Hitler cynically declared that this decimation was desirable as it would weaken the biological potential of the Soviet people. Though in one sense separate from the problem of the volunteers, such savagery on the part of the civil authorities became a kind of albatross around our necks impeding our own efforts on the volunteers' behalf.

In the course of almost daily meetings in the late spring of 1942, Stauffenberg frequently expressed to me his belief that a more humane treatment of the population could be brought about if only the more sinister members of Hitler's retinue were removed. He was equally convinced that it would be possible for Germany to enter a new era in its relations with France after the initial victory. In this latter view, Stauffenberg agreed with Hitler's own Ambassador in France, Otto Abetz. Like many people who believed they could influence Hitler, however, Abetz failed. Similarly, Stauffenberg was soon to abandon his optimistic belief that only the influence of Hitler's advisers blocked a change in policy. Step by step, each one taken on the basis of what was happening in Germany and the German-ruled parts of Europe, Stauffenberg moved towards his final decision to assassinate Hitler as the only cause of the evil.

Stauffenberg's character was never more clearly revealed than in his refusal to give up in the face of the havoc wreaked by Hitler's civil administration in the USSR. On the contrary, he redoubled his efforts on behalf of the former Red Army volunteers in the German forces. By the spring of 1942 there were already some quarter of a million volunteers in the German army. Moving with caution and finesse, so as not to provoke a counter-stroke from Hitler and his henchmen, Stauffenberg undertook a number of measures that dramatically improved their chaotic situation.

First, he subjected all volunteers to standard regulations. Up to this time they had been paid at whatever level the local officer might fix, clothed with whatever uniforms might be at hand, fed however much or little it suited the German officers to give them, and assigned whatever tasks needed to be done. To regulate this, Stauffenberg gave orders to draft a single Regulation covering every aspect of the volunteers' lives. In drafting Regulation 8,000 we made every effort to bring the status of the volunteers up to the same level as that of the German soldiers. At this stage the gap was still enormous, and evident in matters as diverse as uniforms, medals, and provisions. Regulation 8,000 accomplished one thing of considerable importance, though; it established the principle that the army was empowered, indeed obligated, to regulate the conditions of the volunteers. Once established, this principle could then be broadened so as eventually to reach the point where there was full equality between the former Soviets and their German colleagues in arms.

In this connection the question arises whether the recruitment was voluntary or not. Originally an overwhelming number of volunteers consisted of civilians and deserters. Later on, the levying took place also in the prisoner-of-war camps. Strict orders had been given that the recruiting had to be carried out on a voluntary basis as the army itself was anxious to form reliable troops which did not desert at the first opportunity. The prisoners-of-war could choose if they wanted to enter a combat or a supply unit or if they preferred to remain prisoners. Many prisoners-of-war probably volunteered not so much because they were eager to fight. They rather wished to be free again and to escape the camps.

In summer 1942 the building up of volunteer units was in full swing. When Hitler was informed about what was going on in the army he was infuriated and immediately forbade the formation of new Russian and Ukrainian volunteer units. Stauffenberg secretly informed the army that in three weeks' time an order would be given forbidding the formation of new units. The army understood the hint and took the opportunity to increase the number of volunteer units before the order came into force.

As Hitler ignored the importance of the volunteers enlisted in purely German units as so-called auxiliaries (*Hilfswillige*), the General Staff gave orders that every division on the Eastern Front had to contain about fifteen per cent volunteers. The formation of small Caucasian and Turkestan units, however, went on thanks to Rosenberg's idea of dismembering Russia.

A second area in which Stauffenberg made great advances was to exploit the prejudices of Rosenberg in order to help the volunteers. So deep was Rosenberg's hatred of the Russians that he was quite prepared to enlist the help of the non-Slavic peoples of the USSR against them. Thus, while he shared Hitler's conviction that the USSR must be eliminated as a great power, he differed radically in the means through which he was prepared to accomplish this. He fostered a plan to build up a chain of border states around Russia, a kind of *cordon sanitaire* under German suzerainty including Estonia, Lithuania, Latvia, the Ukraine, a Tatar state in the Volga basin, a Caucasian federation, Turkestan, and a Cossack preserve. His ideas about the status of these border states were influenced by dim notions of how the British Empire was organized. With this model in mind, Rosenberg stopped short of proposing full independence but spoke in veiled terms of autonomy under German control. More important, his views permitted units of non-Russian people to be formed without violating Hitler's injunctions against the use of 'Russians' in the German army.

So far as Cossacks were concerned, SS ideologues had convinced themselves that they were not Russians or Ukrainians but a nation of their own. To establish their erroneous point, they even published a lavishly produced volume on the subject. Making use of the 'discovery' the SS that the Cossacks were an independent people, Stauffenberg gave orders that they were exempt from Hitler's ban. We in our turn saw to it that the exemption was widely publicized. As a result, thousands of POWs – many of them Russians – took the hint, identified themselves as Cossacks and left the camps.

Scarcely had I begun working with Stauffenberg than he realized that he could not see to the needs of the volunteers and at the same time keep abreast of his other responsibilities. With volunteers now serving in practically every German unit, the task of communicating with the German officers responsible would alone have filled Stauffenberg's day. We discussed what could be done about this. Finally, he proposed to assign to me the major responsibility for the volunteers. I declined at once, arguing that only a person with considerable military experience could fill the bill. I reminded him of the many departments and agencies involved indirectly with the volunteers and the division of authority among them. It would be impossible for someone like me to exert any decisive influence. I encouraged Stauffenberg to seek someone of high standing in the German army who could wield sufficient authority to act in all spheres and who would at the same time command the respect of the volunteers themselves. In my opinion, the only person who had these qualities was General Ernst Köstring, the former military attaché in Moscow.

Köstring had been born and educated in Russia. He had been ADC to General von Seeckt, who had initiated German–Soviet military co-operation. Köstring combined the good traits of the Germans and Russians. He was generous, broad-minded, a good observer and excellent speaker in German and Russian. Being modest he never over-estimated himself. He personified the maxim of the Prussian General Staff '*Mehr sein als scheinen*' (be more and seem less).

Once Stauffenberg had accepted that only a senior figure with real authority could carry out the task, I had little difficulty convincing him that Köstring would be the most appropriate person. He sent me immediately to Berlin to speak with the general. I found Köstring in his flat, where he had been living in quiet retirement since his departure from the USSR. His involuntary idleness arose from a disastrous interview with Hitler. As Köstring told me, he had stopped off in East Prussia on his return from Moscow in order to report to the Führer. Hitler had questioned him closely on the prospects for the German invasion, and had offered him a key position in the administration of the occupied territories. But Köstring strongly disagreed with Hitler's view that the war would be over in six weeks and told the Führer as much. He argued that the first German blows had merely succeeded in waking the Russian bear from its slumber, and that before long the bear would be fighting back fiercely. Moreover, he dared to draw Hitler's attention to the fact that Russian winters are very cold and that the Soviet Union does not end at the Urals. So displeased was Hitler at this impertinence that he relegated Köstring to the Reserves.

I told Köstring that Stauffenberg wanted to see him and set forth the general outlines of our proposal. I spoke of the brutality with which the Nazis were treating the former Soviet troops and the necessity of his intervention to alleviate further suffering. I also told him about the widespread feeling on the front that Germany could not expect to defeat the Soviet Union alone, but would have to make use of the strong desire of the people of the USSR to overthrow Stalin. In my presentation I sought to make a case for Stauffenberg's view that a German–Soviet war was hopeless, but that a civil war within the USSR was not. This last point I developed in detail, for it was one on which Stauffenberg's feelings were strong.

At first, Köstring refused to have anything to do with the plan. He had spent many years trying to establish good relations between Germany and the Soviet Union and to avert the present war. Hitler had systematically ignored his counsel. He had no desire to serve in a war which he had so strongly opposed and which he considered to violate all the laws of humanity.

I argued as forcefully as I could that Köstring alone was in a position to alleviate the suffering of many millions of people, not only those Red Army soldiers who had come over to the German side but also the civilian population of the occupied territories. If he did not help, he would be personally responsible for the loss of thousands of lives. At length, Köstring changed his mind and consented to join Stauffenberg in his endeavour.

Leaving Köstring, I went at once to Schulenburg, who was delighted at the prospect of his old friend being reactivated for so worthy an effort. 'He is absolutely the right man in the right place,' Schulenburg exclaimed, and promised to do whatever he could to assist us. Within a few days, Köstring and I were on our way to meet Stauffenberg at Vinnitsa. It was a historic meeting. The three of us were alone in the room. Stauffenberg and Köstring greeted each other warmly and turned at once to the issue at hand. I could immediately sense that the spark was passed. Claus Stauffenberg, the embodiment of radiant youth, and Ernst Köstring, the incarnation of the Wise Old Man, agreed at once to collaborate with one another. After Köstring had left the room, Stauffenberg turned to me and exclaimed, 'What a splendid chap!'[1] He was entirely correct.

During their meeting, Stauffenberg had had to tell Köstring that the specific areas of his future responsibility could not be precisely defined until the Army High Command had reviewed the matter, but that it was his, Stauffenberg's, hope that he would be given control of the entire force of Soviet volunteers serving in the German Army and also of all military occupied territories in the East. As it happened, Köstring was not to be given so wide a responsibility, largely because Hitler still remembered his unpleasant advice at the outbreak of the war. Keitel and Jodl also opposed Köstring's appointment, although I do not know the origin of their disapproval. His range of activity was restricted to the Caucasus.

The title that Stauffenberg and I invented for Köstring was 'General in Charge of Caucasian Affairs'. This seemed suitable in view of the fact that our offensive in the Caucasus was just opening and that Stauffenberg had every hope of reducing the role of the Nazi and German civil authorities there to a minimum. His ally was Lieutenant Colonel

[1] Cf. Joachim Kramarz, *Stauffenberg: The Life and Death of an Officer*, London, p. 101.

Hans von Altenstadt who, under the Quartermaster General, Lieutenant General Eduard Wagner, was responsible for the military administration of the occupied Soviet territories. Altenstadt, supported by Stauffenberg, went in for a large-scale political experiment in the North Caucasus. He intended to prove that, by an administration based on equality, voluntary collaboration of the inhabitants and local self-government, much better results could be obtained than by the colonial methods of the civilian authorities.

Having settled the question of a title, Stauffenberg then asked me what sort of staff Köstring would need. I told him that it should be kept as small as possible, because our effectiveness would only be hampered by a retinue of assistants, chiefs of staff, etc. He readily agreed, and Köstring and I ended up with what was probably the smallest staff in the German army – a clerk-secretary and a driver. We were often to rejoice at the speed of movement and flexibility this afforded us.

Köstring's appointment had not struck all the officials who had to confirm it as so obviously a good thing as it seemed to Stauffenberg and me. Final confirmation was delayed for some months, during which time Köstring and I undertook an extended inspection tour of the volunteers in the *Generalgouvernement* and in the Ukraine. In Poland we inspected several units that were soon to see action in the Caucasus. They made a strong impression on us, and further convinced us that the army was fully capable of handling such outfits in a decent and professional manner.

Only one unit formed in the Polish *Generalgouvernement* at this time gave cause for alarm, and in this case the army took swift action. But the story of Major Meyer-Mader's Turkestan battalion did not end there. Meyer-Mader had been one of the first to form a volunteer unit within the regular army, having been recruiting volunteers from prison camps as early as November 1941. From the outset he supported the humane treatment of all volunteer soldiers, as well as of prisoners. Meyer-Mader had considerable experience in commanding foreign troops. After World War I he had joined the Chinese army of Chiang Kai-shek as a training officer and later he had served with the National Chinese puppet government in Nanking.

Meyer-Mader formed his battalion of Turkestani in Poland. The battalion that was sent under his command to fight partisans in the Soviet Union proved efficient in action, but this efficiency was more than counterbalanced by the looting and raping in which the troops indulged. Discipline in his battalion grew more and more lax. When word of this reached his army superiors, Meyer-Mader was summarily removed from his post.

It was then that he offered his services to the SS who commissioned him to form a Turkestani SS regiment. At the end of 1943, Meyer-Mader again toured the prison camps in Poland to recruit for his new unit. He also visited the Turkestani units of the army and proposed to various of the volunteers that they join the new SS regiment, promising them higher pay, quicker promotion, and so forth. The army tried to stop this but many Turkestani volunteers deserted the army for the SS. Meyer-Mader handed out commissions to his old cronies among the Turkestani, did not enforce discipline, and generally allowed them to do whatever they pleased. When the SS-sponsored Turkestani regiment was sent into action, Meyer-Mader again lost all control of his troops, who engaged in looting and rape on a large scale. Finally, even the SS admitted that Meyer-Mader and some of the leading Turkestani officers had to be removed and that the whole regiment should be disbanded. As Meyer-Mader was exceedingly popular among the Turkestani, the SS simply shot him, along with many of his officers, in order to deprive the regiment of its leaders. They reported to the Turkestani that Meyer-Mader and his officers had fallen into an ambush and had been killed by partisans.

While in Poland, Köstring and I based ourselves at Spala, the tsars' former hunting lodge where I had been posted only a few months before. It was a wonderful Victorian pile festooned with hunting trophies and possessing an enormous balcony that opened out on to the peaceful forest. General von Gienanth was headquartered there, and Schulenburg came from Berlin to join us. I vividly remember an evening in July, when the group of us retired to the balcony for a long conversation under the moonlit sky. The three *grand seigneurs*, Köstring, Schulenburg and Gienanth, had over a century of active service between them and had commensurate gifts as *raconteurs*. I sat in delight and listened to their stories. That long summer evening was one of those magical moments in which the terrible developments taking place around us were temporarily forgotten. Within a year Gienanth was to be dismissed, and within another Schulenburg was to be hanged.

From Spala we moved on to the Ukraine and eventually to Mirgorod. During our inspection tour there we paid numerous calls on senior German officers in charge of volunteer units and even took our case directly to Reichsmarshal Hermann Goering. The meeting took place out of doors, with Goering and Köstring at one table and Goering's ADC and me sitting within earshot at another.

Köstring began the conversation by explaining as best he could the sort of people the Russians and Ukrainians were. He argued that one could rely on them as soldiers, and that the notion of their being some kind of *Untermenschen* simply did not correspond with the facts. Goering listened without interrupting, but then unleashed his usual rhetoric. He spoke with contempt of the Ukrainians, and expanded on the need to send his SS stallions into the Ukraine to create a new race of people. At this point, Köstring stood up. He told Goering that he himself had had a Russian wetnurse, and that Goering would be well advised to check with the troops before instituting his scheme to create a new race, since any German could tell him that the morality of Ukrainian women was higher than that of most Germans. Then he abruptly took his leave. Over the next years, Köstring and I were to pay countless visits to Nazi officials with the aim of improving the treatment of former Soviet troops fighting in the German army. Never again was I to see Köstring in such a rage.

On 1 August we conferred with one of the most colourful figures ever to be associated with the volunteers, Oskar Ritter von Niedermayer. Von Niedermayer, whom I had met in Moscow before 1932 while he was the *Reichswehr*'s unofficial representative to the Red Army, was a kind of German Lawrence of Arabia, at once a soldier, scholar, and adventurer.

As a youth, Niedermayer had studied Persian, Turkish, and Arabic, thanks to which he had been sent to Afghanistan during World War I to foment an anti-British uprising. He did not succeed, but became a Muslim while trying, and eventually made a pilgrimage to Mecca. During the thirties he had directed the Institute of Strategic Studies in Berlin. Because of these qualifications he was appointed commander of the 162nd Turkic Infantry division. It was the task of this division to set up mainly Muslim volunteer battalions from Turkestan and the Caucasus. By 1943 he finally succeeded in realizing his dream of going to the front with his own division. He and his division were transferred to Yugoslavia to fight the partisans. When they were later moved to Italy he was no longer permitted to lead the division since the high command considered him lacking in experience.

I last saw him on the Rhine at the end of 1944, at which time he was confidently claiming that the Russians would do him no harm if he was taken captive. General Köstring vehemently disagreed, arguing that they would both be hanged, but von Niedermayer slightly lower than Köstring because he was only a major general. Köstring was wrong about himself but correct about von Niedermayer, who, after having been court-martialled by the Germans in 1944 for defeatist attitudes, died in a Russian prison.

During the same week as we saw von Niedermayer, Köstring filed the report on our inspection tour with Colonel General Halder. In the document, which I drafted, he took note of the fact that about eighty per cent of the 100,000 Turkic soliders of the Red Army who had crossed the lines or been captured during the first year of war had not survived the winter due to poor clothing and inadequate provisions. In spite of this, Köstring still saw the possibility of improving the situation. He could not conceive that German officials and soldiers would not accord better treatment to the former Soviet troops if they only knew more about them.

On 10 August, 1942, Köstring's appointment was finally confirmed and we received orders to report to Army Group A, which was already moving forward into the Caucasus. There we were to participate in the army's controlled experiment to demonstrate that an administration based on equality, voluntary collaboration of the inhabitants, and self-government would achieve more than could be obtained by the brutal colonialist methods employed by the Nazi civil authorities.

16

THE CAUCASUS

Shortly after the German troops entered the Caucasus, the First
Mountain Division approached Mount Elbrus, the highest mountain
in Europe. A small group was assigned the task of climbing Mount
Elbrus and planting the German flag there. The commander of that
division, Lieutenant General Lanz, got wind of the fact that an SS unit
was trying to accomplish the same feat. He therefore wired ahead with
strict orders to his group to get there first. The troops made a great
effort to scale the peak as quickly as possible, but only the commanding
officer and one soldier got all the way to the summit. There they found
a hut. Opening the door, the Germans were greeted by a room full of
Red Army soldiers. Immediately the Germans cried out 'Hands up!
You are our prisoners!' The Soviets obeyed. After three quarters of
an hour, the Soviets realized that they were the prisoners of only two
men, and declared in turn 'Hands up! You are *our* prisoners.' Then
a discussion ensued, in which the German officer let it be known that
at any minute he would be joined by his whole unit. That settled the
matter. The German army officer regained control and after a few more
minutes he was reinforced by the rest of his detachment. In this case,
the army managed to stay on top of the situation. In the German occupation of the Caucasus as a whole the army was similarly fortunate, for
a while at least.

Köstring and I left Vinnitsa in the second half of August 1942. Before
our departure we were told of the progress of the military operations
to the south. The advance had proceeded smoothly as far as the
mountains at Sukhumi and the area around Ordzhonikidze, but Field
Marshal Wilhelm List had incurred Hitler's wrath by not pressing the
offensive further. This failure led eventually to List's replacement by
Colonel General Erwin von Kleist.

We arrived at the Army Group Caucasus, where we reported to Field
Marshal List. After conferring with him, it was decided that Köstring

228

should move closer to the field of action. We therefore advanced to Piatigorsk, the headquarters of the First Panzer Army led by Colonel General Erwin von Kleist, a long-time friend of Köstring's. They shared an affection for the population of the occupied territories. On Kleist's staff were several other good friends of both Köstring and mine, which greatly helped our work.

According to the rules for occupied territories that had been worked out before the war, each newly seized region was to be placed initially under military control. Then, as soon as the front moved on, captured territories were to be transferred to the authority of Rosenberg's *Ostministerium*. Rosenberg was then to appoint *Reichkommissare* for each territory. By the time we arrived in the Caucasus, Rosenberg had already appointed such an official for that area, a man by the name of Arno Schickedanz. We had no idea what policy Schickedanz would follow, but we were optimistic on account of Rosenberg's belief that the Caucasian people should be well treated so as to win them away from the control of Moscow.

Schickedanz never arrived on the scene, and the North Caucasus remained under military administration. The representatives of the *Ostministerium* for the time being were Gerhard von Mende and Otto Bräutigam. Bräutigam had been seconded from the Foreign Office to the *Ostministerium*. During his diplomatic career he had served at the Soviet desk in the Ministry and in Moscow, Kiev and Tbilisi. As liaison officer of the *Ostministerium* to the military authority he co-operated closely with Altenstadt and Stauffenberg. Mende too was knowledgeable about the Soviet Union, being a specialist on the Caucasian and Turkish people. The presence of these two seasoned experts, sympathetic to the people of the Caucasus, was a great help for Köstring.

This rapport had reached something of a peak in August 1942, when Köstring, Schulenburg, my old friend Pfleiderer from Moscow, and I were appointed to an inspection commission that toured the various installations where prisoners bound for slave labour in Germany were quartered. The commission was painstaking in its work, and reported both on the conditions in the camps, which were wretched, and on the need for an overall plan for the establishment of federated but autonomous political units in the Caucasus. Meeting a group of Party officials after we had completed our research, we managed to make a most unfavourable impression by our bluntness. One of the Party officials whom we met reported back to his chiefs:

The worst that I encountered was a statement by Herr Herwarth von Bittenfeld that there are gentlemen in the *Ostministerium*, notably Bräutigam and Mende, who share the Foreign Ministry's point of view.[1]

Köstring discussed the treatment of the local population in great detail with Kleist, urging that German soldiers be ordered to act towards the native population as they would towards the locals while on manoeuvres in Germany. Köstring was the more emphatic because he knew the disastrous effect the brutal colonial policy of the early phases of the Russian campaign had had on the Ukrainians and Russians. He stressed the vital importance of treating prisoners-of-war decently, and pointed out that the starvation of prisoners at the beginning of the war had been a flagrant violation of the Geneva Convention and did not cease to be a violation simply because Hitler declared the Convention suspended with regard to the Soviet Union because the latter country had itself not signed the Convention. Not only was it a crime, but, as Köstring pointed out, it drove the Soviet people back into the arms of Stalin.

Köstring's efforts with Kleist were entirely successful, in that the Field Marshal gave orders that the prisoners-of-war in camps in the North Caucasus should be treated humanely.

Thanks to the support provided by Kleist and his subordinates, Köstring succeeded in implementing the orders for a friendly treatment of the local population which had been given by Altenstadt. Civilian officials were forbidden to interfere, and Sauckel was prevented from carrying out his forced recruiting there. German soldiers got strict orders to respect the customs and property of the population. Leaflets and articles in the army newspapers informed the soldiers about the geography of the region and the customs and habits of the population, about their anti-Soviet attitude and their readiness to co-operate. The soldiers were reminded that the population expected the German army to treat them as human beings on the basis of complete equality. Local self-government was immediately introduced, with Germans only in advisory roles. The private initiative of craftsmen and shop-keepers was encouraged. Adequate measures for the re-opening of the high schools were taken.

Otto Schiller, the former agricultural attaché of the German Embassy in Moscow, had worked out detailed plans for converting the Soviet

[1] US National Archives, Document NG-1657.

collective farms into co-operatives. His land charter satisfied the peasants' ardent desire for private property by returning the land to them, and retained the obvious advantages of co-operative use of modern technology and machinery. These plans were fully realized in the North Caucasus.

In the regions under civil administration Schiller's plans were often obstructed. Hitler and the Commissars considered Stalin's slave collective system to be the best instrument to get hold of the largest possible share of agricultural production.

The new policy in the North Caucasus had striking results. There were no partisans and no sabotage. The country was appeased. The collaboration of Kleist and Köstring had borne fruit.

All of this was going on within weeks of our arrival. Köstring became deeply involved in seeing that the volunteer units functioned on a similar basis. The units in question were made up of Georgians, Armenians and North Caucasians, and were the ones whose formation I had witnessed while on the staff of General von Gienanth in Poland. These units had been intended not only for work behind the lines but also for the front line itself and for occupation purposes later. It was our feeling that by having local troops with native leaders stationed in the area, we would speed up the establishment of good relations between the civilian population and those in uniform and give to the inhabitants confidence that we had indeed come with good intentions.

Scarcely had we settled in, though, than Köstring learned that many German officers and non-commissioned officers had only scant knowledge of the people they commanded. We at once cabled a complaint to Stauffenberg, who issued orders that the German personnel should encourage native leaders wherever possible, and turn over their role to them. This took many months to implement, but the decision was a sound one, and beneficial results almost immediate. Our main problem was the poor quality of much of the German personnel and the often unsatisfactory performance of the volunteer officers.

We were never able to find out whether our assumptions about the native troops were valid, since the occupation was so brief. The first of our volunteer units saw action while General Köstring was in the Caucasus, however, and did not discredit themselves. Naturally, there were some deserters, but in cases where German soldiers disappeared, there was a natural tendency to assume that they had been captured by the Soviets, whereas when volunteers disappeared, it was all too easy to assume that they had deserted. It was in these early encounters that

Caucasian volunteer companies of the *Bergmann* unit found themselves facing Armenian and Georgian troops on the other side. In such cases, there were many soldiers from the Red Army who deserted to our side, and practically none of ours who fled to the Soviet lines. Von Kleist and Köstring sent men of this unit to the prisoner-of-war camps and asked them to report any instances of treatment that violated our standards.

The excellent performance of this unit in the North Caucasus that had been created by special order of Admiral Canaris in his capacity as head of the *Abwehr* gave us reason to think that others might have succeeded as well. It was led by Captain Theodor Oberländer, and was formed from Caucasian prisoners-of-war and from other men from the Caucasus who had emigrated from the USSR earlier. On 10 June, 1942, I had paid a visit to this unit at its quarters near Mittenwald in Bavaria. It was an unusual formation in every sense, even to the point of taking its oath not to Hitler but to the German *Wehrmacht*. While *Bergmann* included Armenians and other Caucasian peoples, the bulk of its members were Georgians, among them a number of former officers in the Red Army. During my visit I was fascinated to see the way in which Georgian émigrés and former officers of the Red Army amalgamated to form a new and cohesive unit. It was also instructive to see how well organized the Georgian émigrés were. This was no doubt helped by the fact that a short-lived Georgian Republic had flourished briefly under German protection at the end of World War I.

Oberländer was himself a curious phenomenon in the history of National Socialism. I first met him in Moscow in the mid-1930s when he came in his capacity of professor and head of the East European Institute at the University of Königsberg. Wilhelm Baum, our press attaché, a staunch anti-Nazi, knew Oberländer and thought well of him. Knowing that he was a Party member, though, I had handled him rather carefully. When I next met him in 1942, I saw an entirely different side of the man and we got along extremely well. One day, while visiting a company exercising in the mountains, we happened to come upon a doe just as she was giving birth. This somehow gave rise to a conversation on the prospects for the war. I told Oberländer quite bluntly that I considered the war in Africa to be finished and the larger war to be unwinnable and virtually lost already, notwithstanding the enthusiasm that had been shown by those parts of the Soviet population which we had liberated. Oberländer still hoped that Hitler would adopt a realistic policy regarding the Soviet people and that such a policy would open the way for a German victory over Stalin. Only events during the German occupation of the Ukraine in 1942 had made Oberländer critical. No longer was he a true believer. Had he been so, he surely would have reported me.

Köstring and I kept in close contact with Oberländer and his unit, visiting him about two dozen times in the course of the years 1942–43. We constantly exchanged experiences and opinions with him. Oberländer had a remarkable gift for understanding the Caucasians and dealing with them on the basis of equality. His German officers and NCOs followed his example and his volunteers loved him and had full confidence in his leadership.

Oberländer got more and more upset by the crimes being committed in the occupied territories by the civilian administration. He hated Koch, who he knew well from his Königsberg days, when Koch was *Gauleiter* there. In 1942–43 Oberländer finally wrote two memoranda about the Ukraine, in which he denounced Koch's methods and called for radical changes. In June 1943, he summed up his ideas on the future of the volunteers and on German policy in the East. His arguments were fully in line with the convictions of Köstring and the rest of us who worked with the volunteers. Oberländer's action in writing this tract was most courageous and, predictably, it gave rise to an effort to court-martial him. Köstring and the General Staff swung into action in his defence but their success was only partial. In the end he was dismissed from the army. Only at the end of the war was he again given a commission in the Air Force, where he once more worked on behalf of the volunteers.

Kleist's headquarters were at Piatigorsk, a splendid town on the plain adjoining the foothills of the Caucasus, with Mt Elbrus in the distance. The fertile plain produced more than enough food for the population and the other necessities of life existed in abundance there as well. The town was little damaged, and the population was completely open and friendly towards the Germans. Social life around the historic springs revived during the occupation, and cultural activities of various sorts sprang up. Many local people who I met openly stated that life had returned to what it had been before Stalin, and they were glad of it.

At Kislovodsk life also returned to normal, and even a degree of gaiety was seen. On 11 October the Muslim holiday of Beyram was celebrated and Köstring gave a speech in Russian. His assurances regarding the establishment of local self-government within a federation and the dismantling of collective farms were greeted with wild enthusiasm. Gifts were presented to him, and a spirit of great warmth prevailed.

Well before this time Köstring had begun to work like a travelling preacher, lecturing groups of officers wherever he could on the best way of treating the local population. Here he had to contend with the confusing impact on German troops of pre-war Nazi propaganda about the *Untermenschen* who were said to inhabit the USSR, and with the *Ostministerium*'s policy of treating favourably the non-Slavic minorities while meting out the harshest treatment to the Russians themselves. Köstring had to justify the favourable treatment he advocated for the conquered peoples of the Caucasus without implying that one had a free hand to ill-treat the other peoples of the USSR.

It was during these tours that I witnessed Köstring's rapport with the local people. Once, when the oath was being administered to a group of Armenian volunteers of the *Bergmann* unit, General Köstring delivered a speech to the men in Russian. After he had finished, I noticed the enthusiasm among the volunteers and was somewhat at a loss to explain it. The answer seemed to be that Köstring had a large nose and could easily be mistaken for an Armenian. The Armenian volunteers had apparently concluded that, if one of their number could even become a general, everything would be all right for them too.

General Köstring also paid a visit to Nalchik, the capital of the Kabardians in the foothills of the Caucasus. There was great rejoicing at his arrival and all the elders of the small Kabardian nation came together to celebrate. Oberländer's *Bergmann* unit was stationed there as well, and joined in the feast. Köstring first met the local officers and then went to the open-air meeting grounds and delivered a speech to the large assembly. He declared that the Kabardians were free to manage their own affairs and that collectivization would be abolished. So jubilant were the tribesmen at this news that they tossed him high into the air several times. They also offered one hundred of their famous Kabardian horses to the German army, and declared that the riders wanted to stay with the horses in order to join the fighting on the German side. Then the Kabardians roasted several sheep. When they were placed on the table, everyone moved in with his own knife. My neighbour at the table, a Kabardian elder, cut out one of the best pieces and presented it to me.

When we arrived in the Caucasus, we were still quite inexperienced. Köstring had developed the notion of giving back to the various nationalities their own languages and of doing whatever was necessary to revive their indigenous cultural life, and had considered extending

234

such cultural autonomy even to such smaller tribal groups as the Kabardians, Ossetians, and Cireassians. The elders of these tribes made it clear that, in their view, it would be a great mistake to attempt to build purely on their indigenous roots, since they had no literature of their own beyond an oral tradition. They told him bluntly that if he tried to transform their language into a written tongue, he would cut them off from higher education and hence from world civilization. They urged him instead to teach them Russian, or preferably, German. In any circumstances they insisted on acquiring a language known throughout the world. They considered the contact with the outside world that they had gained through their knowledge of Russian to be one of the few genuine gains they had made under Russian rule.

During the preceding decade, there had been a basic change in the Soviet attitude towards the non-Russian nationalities. Lenin's slogan had been 'National in form, Communist in content'. Under Stalin's nationalistic form of State Socialism, the slogan was changed in practice to 'Great Russian in form and Russian nationalist in content'. This had led immediately to the substitution of the Cyrillic alphabet for the Latin, into which the native languages had been transcribed only a decade or so before. This did not apply to the Georgians, Armenians, or Azerbaijani, but it did affect the Turkestanis and smaller groups.

During the occupation of the Caucasus we encountered various small groups of Jews. According to Hitler's prescripts, they should have been the object of persecution of the worst kind. Köstring, however, took the position that the fact that they were of the Jewish faith did not mean that they were ethnically Jewish, as Hitler conceived it. He could point to the existence of several mountain peoples who had adopted the Jewish faith but were otherwise indistinguishable from the rest of the population. Köstring also made frequent use of the argument that since some of these 'Jewish' mountaineers had served as officers in the tsar's army, in which no Jew could be an officer, they were surely acceptable to the *Wehrmacht*. Of course, he knew full well that he was engaging in casuistry, but he did so readily in order to save human lives. Braütigam and Oberländer followed the same policy, like Köstring applying it so as to protect large numbers of Jews in the Caucasus. Oberländer was particularly successful in protecting those Jews in the ranks of his own unit, who were in fact Jews by nationality as well as faith. However heavy the losses among the Jews in the Caucasus, they would surely have been far worse but for the stand taken by those three men.

While all this was occurring, heavy fighting was going ahead on all the major passes: the Sukhumi Military Highway, the Ossetian Military Highway, and the Georgian Military Highway. The German army failed to force any of these, however, with the result that we never succeeded in gaining control of the shores of the Black Sea.

Once the German offensive had been stopped, and when, after Stalingrad, it became clear that a new offensive was out of the question, the situation for the Caucasian units became particularly difficult. We had to explain the situation candidly to our volunteers and could not soften the blow by kindling the false hope that German forces could regain their position in the Caucasus. It was all the more important that we made every conceivable effort to gain full equality within the German army for those Caucasian troops who chose to retreat with us. Having cut themselves off from their homelands, these loyal soldiers became entirely our responsibility.

During the late autumn of 1942, I went briefly to the Seventeenth Army under Colonel General Ruoff. The Chief of Staff was Lieutenant General Vincenz Müller, who later acquired a certain renown by siding with the East German government and helping to build up its military forces. A Bavarian by birth, Müller was already at this time sharply critical of official policy. I remember well one evening when a group of us, consisting of Müller, Colonel General Ruoff, Colonel Wetzel, Captain Pfleiderer, Colonel von Lewinski, and Ruoff's young nephew, a first lieutenant, were chatting informally. I was asked my opinion of Ribbentrop and stated it without ornamentation: he was no good whatsoever, had not the slightest idea of foreign policy, was a 'yes man', and his dearest hope was to anticipate Hitler's own views. As I was holding forth, First Lieutenant Ruoff interrupted me and informed me that, as a member of the German Foreign Ministry, I owed allegiance to Ribbentrop. I retorted that I had left the diplomatic service and that these were my honest opinions. Young Ruoff stated that he considered my attitude inappropriate for a German officer. This situation had grown quite tense when Colonel General Ruoff interrupted his nephew and ordered him to stop the conversation. The following day, I was quite nervous to learn what had happened, since I knew full well that it was Lieutenant Ruoff's duty to report me. To his credit, he did not do so.

The retreat from the Caucasus began in the early weeks of 1943. Before leaving Stavropol and moving east to the Kuban bridgehead, I looked in at a special shop for officers that had been opened there.

Having completely worn out the shirts I had with me, I was pleased to get replacements, even without the necessary coupons. While at the shop, I noticed a young lieutenant ordering, of all things, a sword. When I asked him whether he intended to use it for bread or for sausage, he replied that he had just been promoted and was buying the sword to celebrate. I could not help but wonder what this eighteen-year-old would do with that fine sword after the Russians marched into Stavropol.

In February 1943, the last group of officers of Army Group Caucasus was evacuated from the Kuban to the Crimea, where a new headquarters were established. We were moved to the Crimea in gliders towed by engine-powered craft. As we floated above the Sea of Azov, Soviet aircraft attacked the convoy and one of the gliders was disconnected from its tow-plane. Watching it crash land on an icefloe, I realized that the situation was extremely perilous. Fortunately, we had all provided ourselves with a bottle of brandy and a kilo of chocolate before departing. Those down on the icefloe had a second piece of luck – one of the group had brought a flare-pistol with which to attract the attention of passing German aircraft. In the end they succeeded in this, and were picked up and delivered safely to the Crimea.

After my arrival in Simveropol I reported to Field Marshal von Kleist and told him all that I had observed during the retreat. I described to him in some detail the ill-treatment of prisoners-of-war and said bluntly that prisoners who were physically incapable of marching were being shot by their guards. I pointed out to Kleist that this violated the Geneva Convention, and that, since it was occurring under his command, he would inevitably be held responsible. To reinforce my point, I passed on to him specific reports on excesses that I had learned of from members of Oberländer's *Bergmann* unit. Oberländer's officers had done everything they could to prevent the worst from occurring, but they had failed. Kleist was infuriated that his orders to treat the prisoners-of-war humanely had been so flagrantly disobeyed, and he gave immediate orders to stop such crimes.

Kleist abruptly changed the subject. Mentioning the news that Gustav von Steengracht had been named as Weiszäcker's successor as Permanent Under Secretary of the Ministry of Foreign Affairs, Kleist asked me my opinion on the appointment. I knew Steengracht well. He was a decent man, though he had chosen to make his career through the Nazi Party. In spite of his lack of diplomatic experience, I held him in a certain esteem that he did much to justify later when he refused to take part in the crimes that other Nazis were perpetrating.

Being in a grim mood, though, I flippantly asked Kleist what he would think if I were appointed chief of the General Staff of Army Group A. I assured him that, while my knowledge of military affairs was minimal, it was certainly greater than Steengracht's knowledge of diplomacy.

Again, the subject changed, but the conversation carried on as if Kleist himself wanted to continue it. He dwelt at length on the disastrous military situation and concluded that the war could no longer be won on the battlefield. I expressed my view that it was high time that Hitler realized the army's situation and was told to end the war. Kleist agreed, but instead of declaring his own readiness to take this step, unexpectedly proposed that I be sent to meet Hitler. This proposal, astonishing in itself, was the more amazing since Kleist, as a Field Marshal of the German army, was precisely the person for the task. As we talked further, it became clear that Kleist felt it to be inappropriate for a military man to raise so 'political' an issue and that he was serious in proposing that, since I had diplomatic experience, I should be the one to tell Hitler the situation was hopeless. It is scarcely surprising that this never occurred, though I was soon to become involved in other activities that were intended to affect Hitler even more directly.

While it was a great relief to be able to retreat to safety in the Crimea, this made more urgent the need for Germany to develop a policy for ruling that territory. At one point, Hitler had the idea of evacuating the population of the Crimea completely and turning the peninsula into a kind of German Gibraltar. He presumably had no idea that the place was densely populated and that its population was mostly Tartar. This Black Sea Gibraltar never came into being, but the fact that it could even be considered demonstrates what fantastic notions could germinate in the heads of Hitler and his henchmen.

The difficult task of determining how to treat the local Tartar population fell to Field Marshal Erich von Manstein, who had commanded the German forces that conquered the Crimea. Being Asians, the Tartars were in real danger of being treated as *Untermenschen*. Major Werner von Hentig, the Ministry of Foreign Affairs' liaison officer to Field Marshal von Manstein, knew the Eastern peoples well, having served in Iran and Afghanistan during World War I and being himself a close friend of the *Mufti* of Jerusalem. It was Hentig who explained to Manstein just who the Tartars were. Manstein learned his lesson well, thanks to which the Tartars received special treatment at the Germans' hands. Even the SS commander of the region, who was

238

stationed at Simveropol, accepted this reasoning and respected their special situation.

Unfortunately for them the Tartars were frequently assigned positions as auxiliary policemen in the region. Their functions were not extensive, being confined largely to peace-keeping at the neighbourhood level. The worst that could be said of them is that a few were trained to do service in the event of partisan activity in the Crimea. Their more usual function was to patrol bridges or stand guard at supply depots. After the war, though, the Soviet government chose to believe that they had all collaborated with the SS. With this excuse, Stalin uprooted the Tartars and sprinkled them throughout the USSR. The same fate awaited the Volga Germans, the Kabardians, the Karachai, and the Volga Tartars.

At Kokosi I visited the *Bergmann* battalion on the former estate of Prince Yusupov. There I had long conversations with Oberländer and also with a group of experts on the Caucasus, all on the *Bergmann* staff. I also renewed acquaintance with a number of Georgian officers whom I had first met at the Luttensee. I remember well the clear day when 'Givi' Gabliani, Oberländer and I took a long walk in the mountains above Yalta. Surrounded by such beauty, I opened my heart to my Georgian friend, telling him that I could not imagine that we could possibly win the war. I told him that I had no choice but to accept whatever treatment I would receive at the hands of the Allies, but that he, a Georgian officer serving in the German armed forces, could still exercise some choice if he cared to do so. He replied simply: 'I will stay with you. Your fate will be my fate.'

Contrary to my expectations, 'Givi' survived. After the war we met again during Adenauer's first trip to America. I was secretary-general of his delegation. We stopped briefly in Chicago on 14 and 15 April, 1953, where we stayed, incongruously, at the Hotel Bismarck. While there, I received an unexpected telephone call from 'Givi', now a doctor in the United States. He told me that he wanted to see me, and also wanted to meet Chancellor Adenauer, whom he considered to be a great man. When I mentioned this to Adenauer, the Chancellor seemed delighted and within the day these two figures from such different phases of Germany's recent history shook hands.

Under German rule in the Crimea an effort was made to re-open the churches and mosques that had been closed by the Soviets. The local population warmly approved of this. I remember well being in Simveropol at Easter and seeing the large crowds that assembled for mass there. During my visit to Oberländer's *Bergmann* unit I discovered that he had permitted the mosque at Kokosi to function again. By the time of my arrival there, the mullah of Kokosi was back in his former place in the minaret, calling his faithful to worship.

17

THE RESISTANCE

My involvement with the military Resistance against Hitler began with my first conversations with Schulenburg, Köstring, and particularly Stauffenberg in the spring and summer of 1942. Our common interest at that time was to do whatever we could to undermine Hitler's decrees on the treatment of the conquered peoples of the USSR. This interest bound us together for the remainder of that year but it did not yet lead me into more extensive conspiratorial activity.

During my time in the Caucasus, Köstring and I had kept in constant touch with Stauffenberg. Our telephone communications with the General Staff Headquarters were excellent, but we were cautious in using them. We preferred instead to pass reports through officers travelling to and from headquarters. There was a steady flow of such travellers whom we could trust, and hence we were able to stay in direct contact at all times. To such people we could entrust reports on our efforts to counteract official policies in the occupied zone that we would never have risked by telephone.

Thanks to such communications, we were well informed about the conference held at Vinnitsa in October 1942, at which Stauffenberg had so vehemently condemned German policy towards the East. This meeting of some three dozen civil and military officials had been convened by Hans Schmid von Altenstadt to consider Germany's policies regarding agriculture in Russia. Stauffenberg's passionate argument that we were sowing hatred that could only be reduced by a policy of decency and sympathy was echoed throughout the officer corps. That he did not suffer serious consequences from his speech was due only to the fact that the organizer of the event, Altenstadt, was himself in the Resistance. Altenstadt, incidentally, had long been a close friend of mine. He had also served in the Fourth Cavalry Regiment in Potsdam, and was a frequent visitor to my parents' house, where he met his future wife.

Direct contact between Stauffenberg and me was renewed in the winter of 1942. I was still in the Caucasus in November, the retreat to the Crimea still being two months in the future. In December, though, I was invited to participate in a conference on the occupied areas of the USSR held in Berlin. I travelled to Berlin via Mauerwald in East Prussia, where the General Staff Headquarters had been moved from Vinnitsa. The purpose was to meet Stauffenberg, who had cabled ahead to say that he wanted me to bring him up to date on events in the Caucasus. As it turned out, he also wanted to chat about the state of affairs generally.

In order to set my discussions with Stauffenberg in their proper context and to explain why they were to have so great an impact on my future, I should relate several conversations that I had had with him back in the spring and summer of 1942, on the eve of my departure for the Caucasus. At that time we had discussed Germany's situation from every conceivable point of view. I tried to convince Stauffenberg that the source of all evil in Germany was Hitler, and that as long as Hitler remained in power we could not hope for change. Stauffenberg's position at this time was somewhat different. He believed that by eliminating the leading Nazis around Hitler one could alter the policies of Hitler's government. He still held to the view that, if Hitler could be liberated from the influence of the likes of Himmler, Sauckel, and Koch, it would be possible to impose on him the views of more moderate members of the Nazi Party and of the officer corps.

Given this, I was astonished to see the enormous change that had taken place in Stauffenberg's attitude when we next met in mid-December 1942. By now he was convinced that Germany was doomed and that a catastrophe was inevitable. He knew all too well that it would be impossible to remove the men surrounding Hitler and realized that the root of the problem was Hitler himself. Yet having come this far, he did not take the step that followed naturally from his own argument. Hence, I was heartened by Stauffenberg's analysis but depressed by the fact that it did not go further. At the conclusion of our conversation the two of us took the twelve-hour trip by train to Berlin, arriving just in time for the conference on the 18th.

The conference had been convened in order to bring representatives of the army together with officials of Rosenberg's *Ostministerium* and the SS, and took place in the *Ostministerium*'s quarters in the former Soviet Embassy. In addition to Stauffenberg, many other future leaders of the conspiracy against Hitler were there, among them Lieutenant

Fabian von Schlabrendorff, Lieutenant Colonel Schmid von Altenstadt, General Eduard Wagner, and Major General Henning von Tresckow.

The purpose of the conference was to oppose the brutal policies being pursued in the occupied territories of the Soviet Union. The army officers were the driving force behind this effort, but they got support from Mende and Bräutigam from the *Osterministerium* and even from such representatives of the SS as *Obersturmbahnführer* Gräfe, whom I remembered from Memel, and Albrecht, the former deputy commissar for forestry in the Russian Republic of the USSR. In spite of my subordinate position I did not hesitate to speak out in support of those who decried the savagery of what had been going on, and in favour of a policy of alliance with the people of the USSR against Stalin's rule. My experience in Moscow gave my comments a weight in the discussion that they might not otherwise have possessed. The slogan that I introduced, 'Russia can only be defeated by Russians', became the theme of the conference and was elaborated on every side. As I had intended it, the slogan was to have justified more humanity towards the local population and equal treatment for former Soviet soldiers now serving as volunteers with the *Wehrmacht*. I firmly believed that the only way we could win the support of the Soviet population was first to rid ourselves of Hitler and the policies he represented. Only then could a free Germany hope to ally itself with anti-Communist forces in Russia.

I doubt if I had the intention of speaking out so bluntly when I arrived at the conference, but the session with Stauffenberg only two days earlier, not to mention my long apprenticeship at not holding my tongue, had prepared me well. Stauffenberg expressed his agreement with my remarks and, after the conference, proposed that we continue our earlier conversation as soon as possible. I explained that I was on my way to Kitzbühl for Christmas but promised to meet him in Mauerwald immediately after the holiday. After a flying trip to Kitzbühl, I therefore arrived back in East Prussia by the 27th.

By now Stauffenberg knew that he would soon be leaving his present post in order to join the campaign in Africa. He was acutely aware of his impending departure, scarcely a month away. Even more than during the previous week he was filled with despair, and his mood of gloom could not help but infect me. Once more we reviewed in detail all the possible steps that might be taken to restore sanity to the country's leadership.

This meeting plunged me into even deeper gloom than our earlier conversation. Both of us had by now fully acknowledged the cause of Germany's troubles, yet without having come up with any course of action that was sure to be effective.

In this mood I hastened back to Kitzbühl, arriving just in time for New Year's Eve. In retrospect I am astonished at the amount of travelling I did, but it was simple for an officer to do so and I had all the energy needed for such adventures. No sooner did I reach Kitzbühl for the second time than I received orders from Stauffenberg to report back to the Caucasus as soon after the New Year as possible. On New Year's Eve, I was therefore determined to celebrate, knowing full well that there would be scant cause for levity in the coming months. Some enterprising ladies of Kitzbühl had had the inspired idea of arranging a ball in the tennis club to which all the local people and officers on leave were invited. Pussi and I were glad to be together, and did not decide to attend the party until 11:00 p.m. on New Year's Eve. I donned my dinner jacket and, since it was a very cold evening, my officer's fur overcoat and officer's cap and belt, with its pistol. In this half-military, half-civilian costume I left for the party. We had a wonderful time until early next morning, when someone in the hall shouted that police had surrounded us and we were under arrest. Pussi and I climbed out of a window and strode deliberately towards our home. Scarcely had we started than we were hailed by a policeman. Before he could get out a word, I commanded him to go to hell and also to stand at attention. Others managed to escape as well, and we soon reassembled at the home of a Persian friend. This second group was smaller than the first but in equally high spirits, and we celebrated until 5:00 a.m. As I recall, our fellow revellers included two Austrian Grand Dukes, one of whom was serving in the navy and the other in the army.

The aftermath of the evening was grim. Within a few days, all those elegant ladies at Kitzbühl who had organized the ball were sent to factories to work.

What with the conference, the sombre meeting with Stauffenberg, and my adventures in Kitzbühl my 'vacation' was anything but relaxing – a suitable preparation, as it turned out, for my final months in the USSR. This period was the more bleak for me because I was no longer working under Köstring. After the retreat from the Caucasus, his mission had ended. On 22 January, 1943, he married the widow of an ambassador, settled at his new wife's home in Bavaria, and waited for a new assignment.

Within three months of Köstring's departure, I, too, left the Crimea. In late April 1943 I was again assigned to the Organizational Division of the General Staff Headquarters at Mauerwald in East Prussia, the place where I had met Stauffenberg the previous winter. Stauffenberg himself had been in Africa for three months, during which time his post was filled by Lieutenant Colonel Bernhard Klamroth, a man with whom I was soon to have much contact as a member of the conspiracy against Hitler. Klamroth was later to be executed after the assassination attempt of 20 July, 1944.

Scarcely had I arrived in Mauerwald than I was appalled to learn from Klamroth that Stauffenberg had been gravely wounded in Africa. Klamroth told me that he had lost his left eye, his right hand, and several fingers of his left hand, and that a leg had been badly wounded as well. Anxious to see Stauffenberg and to check on his condition at first hand, I arranged at once to visit him at the hospital in the Lazarettstrasse in Munich, where he had been sent to recuperate.

When I arrived in Munich on 1 May, 1943, I found him in even worse shape than I had expected, and still fighting for his life. Several operations had already been performed and it seemed that others were still in store. But I immediately sensed that he was concentrating all his energies on recovering as quickly as possible. He had seen with his own eyes the impending catastrophe in North Africa and was already aware of the defeat of German forces in the East. We were not able to talk for long, but I was left with the impression that Claus Stauffenberg's fierce resolve to recover was connected directly with the plans that he was even then formulating for the future. His body had been mangled, but a flame seemed to be burning within him, the hard flame of a person utterly set on carrying out his mission in life.

At the beginning of May I returned to Mauerwald, where I continued my work in the Organizational Division. Once more I picked up the old pattern of life that I had formed while working under Stauffenberg early in 1942. Since reports came in both in the morning and late at night, we had to work an extremely long day. After rising at seven, we would work until noon, break for lunch, and then take a brief nap. After a full afternoon, we would dine and then work until 2:00 a.m., when the last reports were filed from the Front.

My most intimate colleague at Mauerwald was Captain Joachim Kuhn. In August 1943, I received a telephone call from him. 'My friend,' he said, 'I would like to talk over something with you.' I saw nothing unusual in this, since we communicated frequently with one another about the affairs of the volunteers. I went to see him at once, and we took a long walk in the beautiful woods surrounding Mauerwald. After five or ten minutes, he asked if I recalled my conversations with Stauffenberg in the spring of 1942 and at Christmas-time of that year. I did, of course, and instantly understood the purpose of our meeting. Kuhn told me that Stauffenberg had originally pinned all his hopes on the possibility of the Field Marshals and Generals initiating action against Hitler. It had taken very little time after Stauffenberg's final recovery and his return to Berlin for him to realize how vain this hope had been. He had now concluded that the younger officers would have to take the lead in eliminating Hitler. The time was already late, and much had occurred that should have been averted. There was therefore a great need for speed. Kuhn asked me if I was prepared to live up to what I had told Stauffenberg in 1942. I was about to reply when Kuhn cut me off, saying that I should think it over and tell him my decision on the following morning.

My conversation with Kuhn left me deeply confused. My first reaction was to blame myself bitterly for having been so outspoken. I cursed myself for having allowed this to become a habit, one that had endangered many besides myself. I accused myself of recklessness in having proclaimed to so many people that Hitler should be eliminated. I was acutely aware at that moment of the gulf between mere talk about eliminating a national leader and actually joining an organization for that purpose – in wartime too. I asked myself if I had any right to do that, not in any legal sense, but in that I would be daring to take God's work into my own hands. I also reviewed the oath that I had taken and which I was now proposing to break. Finally, I wondered whether any such action against the government would do anything to prevent ultimate disaster for Germany.

For a moment I thought that I had best return to my regiment and do my duty as a front line officer in the expectation of falling in action for 'Führer and Reich'. I admitted to myself that this was a cowardly solution. Most of my fellow officers in the regiment had fallen at Stalingrad and others had been taken prisoner. If I were to die, as seemed all but inevitable, it would be far better to do so in a worthy cause, since it mattered little whether one was shot in action or hanged.

I also had to consider the possible fate of my family in the event that I joined the military Resistance. I was fully aware that I would be endangering the lives of my parents, my wife, and my child; that participation would not affect me alone. On this point a death on the front line offered certain practical advantages, since my family would receive all the benefits and honours due to the relations of a hero of the Fatherland. The wives and children of anyone convicted of treason would certainly be annihilated. But even with so harrowing a prospect before me, I reminded myself that I had long since crossed the Rubicon. To pull back now was bound to fail – not to mention the fact that I would have betrayed my own convictions.

I then had to consider the problem of my oath. I argued that Hitler had violated his oath to the German people by committing millions of crimes and that no oath could bind me to such a monster. I recalled, too, the instructions I had been given as a young recruit: that one was obliged to fulfil all orders unless the person giving them was insane or had commanded one to commit a crime. Both situations existed now. This relieved me, for it enabled me to consider what my real duties were. I told myself that both my obligations as a Christian and my family tradition required that I did not hold back, and that I take part in this awful mission.

Next morning I reported my decision to Kuhn with a quaking heart. I had known, of course, that there was an organized Resistance movement within the Foreign Ministry. I had been in touch with Erich Kordt more or less regularly since our meeting in Berlin in 1938, and I had also been close to Brücklmeier, another member of the Resistance within the Foreign Ministry. Furthermore, I had kept in touch with Etzdorf. Through these friends, I had already become part of a loose network of like-minded people. Through them, I had known that senior army officers had planned action against Hitler in 1938, and that on the eve of the war against France further action had been contemplated by the group linked with Lieutenant Colonel Hellmut Groscurth, of which Etzdorf had been a part.

Etzdorf himself had further implicated me in the Resistance during the late spring of 1942, immediately before Köstring was appointed General in Charge of Caucasian Affairs. At that time, Etzdorf had asked me to fill his place for several weeks while he was on leave in Germany. He did this so as to ensure that nobody would be sent from the Foreign Ministry to take his job and possibly find out what he was up to. He asked me not to be too active, but told me that I could use the opportunity to get in touch with our various mutual friends. I did this, and kept in close contact not only with those in Berlin but also with the several members of the Resistance who were on the staff of General Eduard Wagner, the army's Quartermaster-General. Wagner,

I knew, had been among those who collaborated with Halder in 1939 in his attempt to eliminate Hitler. He was to commit suicide in order to avoid arrest after 20 July, 1944. In this way, I was also in regular touch with Hans von Altenstadt, my old friend on Wagner's staff responsible for building up the military administration of occupied territories, who was already an active figure in the Resistance.

Because of these contacts, extending over many years, I felt that by accepting Kuhn's proposal, I was not entering into something alien but rather that I was becoming formally part of a network that I had been near to for several years and in which I had already played a part, both through my activities in Moscow and through the Resistance within the Foreign Ministry. I at once began working with Kuhn.

At the end of November Stauffenberg ordered me to report to him in Berlin, officially to discuss the problems of the volunteers in the reserve army. That evening I telephoned my mother in Berlin to tell her I was coming. When she answered she told me: 'Our house has just been hit by incendiary bombs. It is burning. I have no time to speak to you, but I am very happy that you are all right.' Although she had spoken in a calm voice, I felt miserable and helpless, not knowing what had happened to my parents. I took my orderly with me to Berlin. Stauffenberg had kindly sent his car to the station and I went at once to our house. I found myself standing in front of the ruins of our home. A refrigerator was hanging in space from the fragment of a wall on the second floor. I found a note with information about my parents' whereabouts. After the bombing they had both left Berlin and taken refuge at the Silesian country estate of my mother's sister, Elisabeth von Falkenstein. I still remember my orderly's cold remark: 'It's just as well that we don't have to search the rubble, since every-thing has been destroyed.' I finally got in touch with my parents in Silesia and learned that they were safe, although none of their belongings had been saved.

Then I went to see Stauffenberg. In the course of our conversation I realized that he was now 'Chief of Staff' of the military Resistance. He was well aware that time was running short. Too many attempts to eliminate Hitler had failed. In 1943 Colonel Henning von Tresckow had organized military resistance in the Army Group Centre of the Russian front. Perhaps the most promising attempt had been that made in March 1943, when Hitler paid a visit to the Smolensk headquarters of this Army Group. A member of Tresckow's staff was Lieutenant Fabian von Schlabrendorff, a reserve officer and active member of the conspiracy. Various schemes had been hatched to assassinate Hitler during the visit but none of them came to anything. Finally, when Hitler was returning from Smolensk to Rastenburg, Schlabrendorff and his friends placed in his Focke-Wulf 'Condor' aircraft a bomb disguised as a couple of bottles of Cointreau, addressed to an officer of the General Staff of the Army. The British-made bomb hidden inside the parcel had to be triggered by a simple fuse mechanism. As luck would have it, the fuse failed to detonate and the bottles of 'Cointreau' arrived safely in East Prussia.

This was by no means the only effort to lure Hitler into a position where members of the conspiracy could strike him down. A whole series of efforts was mounted, each more ingenious than the last. The task was made fiendishly difficult by the fact that the Führer refused to be pinned down by any precise commitments. This, along with his unerring sense of danger, brought each of these attempts to nought.

Another promising scheme was devised by Tresckow. The decisive role was assigned to a cavalry unit whose officers were known to be unflaggingly loyal to the conspiracy. The brigade in question had actually been established in January 1943, under the command of Lieutenant Colonel Baron Georg von Böselager. Böselager was a highly decorated officer who was considered to be 'bullet-proof'. After our First Cavalry Division was disbanded, three new brigades were formed in recognition of the fact that cavalry could still play a useful role on the Russian front. Böselager's group was intended by Field Marshal von Kluge, who authorized its formation, to be a flexible unit that could be shifted to any point at which the special characteristics of the cavalry would be useful to Army Group Centre. The great virtue of Böselager's brigade was that every officer in it was fully prepared to shoot Hitler down like a mad dog. All opposed Hitler out of deep convictions, but they also resented him as a man known to be hostile to the cavalry. At one time it was hoped that Hitler could be persuaded to visit the brigade, at which moment the officers would have been able to fall upon him and kill him. As so often happened, he refused to put in an appearance, however, and the plan died. Yet another plan of action came to fruition immediately after this discouraging attempt. Hitler had committed himself to attending the Heroes' Memorial Day ceremonies, scheduled originally for mid–March 1943, and then postponed to 21 March. The idea for his assassination was simple but effective. Like the Roman emperors, Hitler enjoyed producing captured enemy arms on public occasions (his actual captives fared worse than the Romans). A member of the conspiracy in Army Group Centre, Colonel Baron von Gersdorff, was put in charge of the exhibit since the new commander of Army Group Centre, Field Marshal Model, wanted to be sure that there would be someone at hand competent to explain to Hitler in detail the various trophies that were to be shown. Hitler put in his scheduled appearance at the armoury on Unter den Linden and Gersdorff was there, festooned with a bomb and a grenade under his clothes. Hitler delivered a short speech, but then, as if smelling the danger by some sixth sense, he all but ran through the exhibition and out of the armoury, leaving Gersdorff bewildered and furious.

Through Kuhn, I quickly became acquainted with the unwritten procedures of the movement. Absolute discretion was obviously of the utmost importance; indeed, it can fairly be said that practically everyone in Germany was more free to express his hostility to Hitler than were those conspiring to take his life. At every phase of my involvement with the plot, I was to be struck by the manner in which seemingly innocent acts could have the most dire consequences. Often a complete outsider could trigger off a conversation that would unintentionally put the whole conspiracy in jeopardy. For example, Major General Hellmut Stieff, an active member of the Resistance who served as Chief of the Organizational Division, was of a voluble temperament and therefore especially prone to indiscretions. Having known him since my days in the Fourth Cavalry Regiment (he was then in the artillery) I frequently dined with him at the officers' mess. Scarcely a day went by on which we were not joined by at least one officer passing through from the front. On several such occasions Stieff became quite worked up and made statements strongly critical of Hitler. His feelings simply burst to the surface. Each time this occurred, we would all be plunged into hair-raising speculation about whether those who had heard our conversation would keep its contents to themselves or denounce us.

Stauffenberg's own exuberance more than once aroused my concern, lest he unwittingly violate his own rules. On one of my visits to his office in Berlin in early 1944, I noticed Ambassador Ulrich von Hassell standing at the end of the corridor outside Stauffenberg's office. I knew that Hassell had been a strong force for a change and that he was part of the diplomatic wing of the conspiracy. In fact, even more than Schulenburg himself, he was the likely choice for Minister of Foreign Affairs in a future government. I had no fear of meeting Hassell in the privacy of Stauffenberg's office but was concerned lest a chance meeting in the corridor lead to unanticipated consequences. I therefore ducked into the lavatory and waited there until Hassell had gone on.

Among the procedures that we observed, none was more important than the age-old precept of conspirators that no single member should know too much. One had to carry out one's own responsibilities without asking too many questions about other parts of the operation. Indeed, a person could have played a central role in the project to assassinate Hitler without having any idea of the structure of the larger operation of which he was a part. To my knowledge, the only person besides Stauffenberg who was fully abreast of every phase of the conspiracy was my friend Hasso von Etzdorf. As Permanent Under Secretary of the Foreign Ministry's representative to the Chief of the General Staff, he was ideally situated to contact the widest variety of people without arousing suspicion. Hence, he knew everything concerning both the military and the civilian side of the conspiracy. But in this he was exceptional. Whatever criticism one may have of the Resistance as a whole, one of its undeniable strengths was that its complex mechanism was put in place and maintained with only a few people apprised of *all* its component elements.

I knew from Stauffenberg that Schulenburg was involved with the plot. The full extent of his involvement I only learned later, however, after he was hanged. Given the close friendship that existed between us, it is surprising how well each of us managed to conceal from the other his involvement in the Resistance. The last time I met him was on 8 June, 1944, only two weeks before the attempted coup. We were both at the Imperial Hotel in Vienna, where we were attending the Turkestani Congress. Though we talked about every conceivable subject, neither Schulenburg nor I disclosed our position in the Resistance. Only a few weeks later this man so dear to me was to be hanged.

In his official work, Schulenburg tried hard to promote a sane policy towards the occupied areas of the USSR. He followed carefully everything that took place there and became increasingly upset at the starving of prisoners and the sending of Jews to concentration camps. His deep affection for Poland made him react all the more strongly to the way the Poles were treated in the *Generalgouvernement*. As he watched these awful developments, this kindly man found his humane feelings so violated that he became an active conspirator. I cannot fix a date for his conversion to the cause, for it did not happen suddenly. It was a gradual process which unfolded with each fresh revelation of the crimes that were being committed. I learned of his conversion with the deepest pride.

Even Schulenburg was not brought in on the military plans. His activity in the Resistance was confined to the diplomatic side of things. Naturally, I could have no contact with him in his capacity as a member of the diplomatic Resistance, for to do so would have been to mix the deliberately isolated elements of the movement. As for my other old diplomatic friends, it would have been difficult for me to keep in touch with them, even if I had wished to do so. By 1941 Kordt had been assigned first to Japan and then to China, Brücklmeier had been ousted, and my good friends Albrecht von Kessel and Gottfried von Nostitz were in Switzerland and at the Vatican, respectively.

My sole written contact with von Nostitz during the war was through one of those lapses that can destroy any conspiratorial movement. Late in the autumn of 1943 von Nostitz sent me a letter from his post in Switzerland. He blithely advised me to get into contact with Adam von Trott zu Solz. I was appalled. I knew full well that Trott was one of the leading figures in the Resistance within the Foreign Office. I knew, too, that Nostitz's letter to me had travelled from Switzerland to the Foreign Ministry in Berlin via the diplomatic bag and thence via a second bag to the General Staff Headquarters, from which it was delivered to me by hand. In short, there were three points at which the link between the diplomatic and the military branches of the conspiracy could have been exposed. Realizing this, I stated in my reply to von Nostitz that I had already been in touch with Trott and that he had been of immense assistance to me. I emphasized that the purpose of my correspondence with Trott had been to explore the treatment given to officers of Indian extraction serving in the British army, which offered certain parallels to the Soviet officers in our ranks.

Except for such incidents, I was completely isolated from the diplomatic Resistance and from the civilian Resistance as well. Helmuth von Moltke, Goerdeler, and their friends on the civilian side of the Resistance were already meeting regularly by the time I entered the movement, but for me to have attempted to get in direct touch with them would have endangered both their group and my own colleagues. Being in the military sector, I had to do my job there; and for the military, the task at hand was to eliminate Hitler. There were those in the military Resistance who, in moments of frustration, might declare that their civilian counterparts were engaged in a kind of tea party, and it is true that the civilians' work – that of planning Germany's future – could only be accomplished when the 'dirty work' of eliminating Hitler had been successfully seen to. But apart from such occasional pangs, members of the military Resistance appreciated full well the importance of what the civilians were doing.

The significance of this order of events can scarcely be over-emphasized. Only by taking it into account can one appreciate the roles of General Köstring and Count Schulenburg in the Resistance. Stauffenberg told me that Köstring would be given responsibility for administering Soviet territories under German rule and that Schulenburg was earmarked to carry out negotiations with the Russians immediately after the assassination of Hitler. Both, in other words, were central figures in the conspirators' planning. But neither I nor anyone else thought it necessary to initiate them into any further aspects of the plot. To have done so would have increased the danger of discovery. Our concern in this area was great, as we knew through Canaris that Himmler, who had long since known of the existence of the Resistance, had had intimations that the level of activity was increasing. Apparently, Himmler was waiting in order to find out more about the conspiracy before taking action.

As my involvement with the conspiracy deepened, I got to know a number of people in East Prussia who were playing a central part in the project. All were old cronies of Köstring. Among them was General Fritz Lindemann, an extremely good-looking and intelligent artillery officer who would have played a decisive role had the attempt on Hitler's life succeeded. After the attempt of 20 July, 1944, Lindemann somehow escaped the first round-up of conspirators but was eventually captured in Berlin after several months in hiding. Another trusted member of the conspiracy in East Prussia was Major General Count Heinrich von Dohna-Tolksdorf. A learned and discrete man, this scion of one of the great families of Germany was somebody to whom we could speak with complete frankness.

Such men formed the outer and more senior circle of activists in the area. Closer to the centre were Klamroth, Albrecht von Hagen and, of course, Kuhn. Soon after my initiation into the conspiracy my relations with Klamroth had become as close as they had been to Stauffenberg before his departure for Africa. Klamroth had been initiated into the plot at the same time as I was, also by Stauffenberg. Since he was head of the Organizational Division that was responsible for building up the volunteer units, there was no problem about seeing him regularly. For the same reason, I could maintain regular contact with Lieutenant Albrecht von Hagen, a member of Klamroth's staff and a most valuable member of the conspiracy.

Köstring's position as Inspector General for the Turkic and Caucasian units and later General for the volunteer units enabled me to speak to practically anyone at headquarters or in the front line. I was thus in a unique position to serve as a kind of one-man communications network.

For a time after my first involvement with Kuhn and his colleagues, some hesitation persisted about proceeding with the assassination. After all, innocent people might be killed, not to mention members of the conspiracy. In the end, everyone who involved himself with explosives reached the conclusion that such a chance had to be taken. It is worth noting that, when Stauffenberg placed a bomb under the table at Hitler's barracks, he knowingly risked the lives of some of his own friends. Indeed, on 20 July, 1944, Colonel Heinz Brandt of the General Staff was killed and Lieutenant General Adolf Heusinger wounded – both sympathized with the conspiracy. There was no way of avoiding this, but the possibility of killing innocent people along with Hitler bothered the consciences of everyone involved.

The decisive argument for action was the general conviction that German troops would never be willing to accept a different command so long as Hitler lived, but that news of Hitler's death would instantly bring about the collapse of the myth that surrounded his name. Hence there was no way of gaining the support of large numbers of German troops without eliminating Hitler. I was to use this argument with Stauffenberg during one of my last conversations with him, in the early spring of 1944.

The twenty-eight-year-old Kuhn and I began our work by considering every way in which the elimination of Hitler could be promoted in our region of East Prussia. Himmler, Goering and Ribbentrop all spent much time at their retreats in the area around Mauerwald, so there was work to be done plotting schedules, learning about facilities, and the like. It was not long before we were face to face with the difficulty that beset all the participants in the conspiracy, namely, the absence of any convincing cover for our activities. There were to be many efforts to circumvent this problem, but not until the creation of the so-called Project Valkyrie was it really solved. Project Valkyrie was initially conceived by the high command of the army as a plan for mobilization in the event either of mutiny within Germany or of major difficulties of any sort to the rear of the fighting forces, such as the appearance of enemy parachute-troops behind the front lines. Since the project was designed for implementation within Germany, and since it involved the simultaneous mobilization of diverse military forces, it was ideally suited as a cover for our own designs.

Stauffenberg was the first to hit upon the clever idea of exploiting this cover, and it was he, too, who set down the general outline of the plot. His own position after his return to activity in August 1943, provided him legitimate grounds for working on the Valkyrie plans, and he did so with a vengeance. Between August and October 1943, the conspirators at Mauerwald devoted much time and energy to the East Prussian end of this crucial project.

The job of those of us working at General Staff Headquarters was to elaborate the Valkyrie plan for our region and to co-ordinate all its various aspects there. The general plan for the mobilization of the Replacement Army had been prepared some months earlier and issued in great secrecy at the end of July. Supplementary orders were issued in October, thus providing us with a highly specific framework within which to work, and an organizational structure that reached into each military district. As I have noted, the particular task of those of us at Mauerwald was to observe the situation at the headquarters of Hitler, Goering, and Himmler in order to discern what type of action would be most appropriate against each of them. Then we were to determine which units might be suitable for each task.

This was our greatest problem: there were no units whose reliability we could absolutely count upon so long as Hitler was alive. Even if we had believed such units to exist, it would have been impossible to determine their reliability with any degree of confidence. After all, we could not hope to know every officer involved, still less could we have any idea of the attitudes of each individual soldier.

It would have been difficult in any circumstances to identify among the tens of thousands of troops those upon whom we could count. The task of locating them became more vexatious as we realized that few, if any, were likely to fit that category. This, I believe, was one of the main difficulties in planning the operation against Hitler. We never had any troops upon which we could rely one hundred per cent. Lacking them, it was necessary to devise all sorts of complicated and risky substitutes.

It has been claimed that Stauffenberg intended to mobilize the volunteer units for the coup against Hitler. This is untrue. First, Stauffenberg and all of us believed firmly that the elimination of

255

Hitler was a German problem that could only be handled by Germans. Second, it was out of the question to tell the volunteers that they had not only to fight against the dictator Stalin but also against the tyrant Hitler. In reality, the tactics regarding the volunteers were far simpler. It was expected that the removal of Hitler would usher in a new policy towards the USSR. We anticipated that any new German government would be in a position to call for a genuine war of liberation within the USSR, a war in which the volunteers would play a direct and central role. This, at least, was the theory. In retrospect it seems possible that, even at the time of Köstring's appointment as Inspector General for Turkish and Caucasian Units, it may already have been too late to implement the dreams that had led to his appointment in the first place. But in spite of Stalingrad, we still held out the faint hope that the elimination of Hitler would create a completely new situation.

The search for fully reliable troops ended in failure, but we did feel that at least one division was a strong prospect. The newly formed 18th Artillery Division had only recently arrived in the East Prussian area and was not due to spend much time there before being reassigned to the field. Among the staff officers of this division was Major Ewald von Kluge, son of the Field Marshal Günther von Kluge. Klamroth knew the younger von Kluge personally and concluded that he at least could be relied upon, although we could never be sure that the mass of officers and soldiers in the division had any sympathy for the project. I vividly recall Klamroth's despair as he spoke of this problem, saying that we were walking on a thin layer of ice over an unknown sea.

Even this thin ice soon melted, when the division was transferred to the front. By the time the final attempt on Hitler's life was made, on 20 July, 1944, the only unit in the region that could conceivably have been mobilized in support of the coup was an Artillery Assault Battalion stationed in Lötzen. Whether the assassination occurred in Berchtesgaden or Mauerwald, we desperately hoped that this unit would obey the follow-up orders issued by the Resistance. But we had no certain knowledge of the attitudes either of its officers or its soldiers.

All the work surrounding Project Valkyrie was demanding, and not merely intellectually. Because our work had to go forward under conditions of strictest secrecy, we could not avail ourselves of the secretarial help that would normally have been at our disposal. Absurd as it may seem in this era of instant reproduction, we had the devil of a time making copies of the drafts, or even getting our ideas down in legible form. We all had handwriting so atrocious as to rule out that method of communication. Fortunately, Hagen turned out to be a *bravura* performer on the typewriter, capable of turning out sheet after sheet of local plans for Valkyrie with great speed and accuracy.

While we were pursuing this research during the autumn of 1943, we were simultaneously making plans for more direct action against Hitler. At the headquarters of the General Staff there was a bomb that we had been carefully preserving for use against the Führer. It was not a large bomb and could easily be carried by one man. It contained a chemical ten-minute fuse, and was one of a number that had been captured from the British. Nearly all the others had been consigned to the use of our army and were kept under close guard; but this one had been secured by Colonel Henning von Tresckow and Stauffenberg in Berlin, and reached Colonel (later Major General) Hellmuth Stieff in early October 1943. We were enormously proud of its explosive power, which was reputed to be far greater than those of domestic German manufacture.

Most of the time, this prize was kept under the bed of Colonel Stieff. Stieff had long been critical of Hitler, but became actively involved in the conspiracy only during the late summer and autumn of 1943. From that time onward he was a central figure in all questions involving the co-ordination of all the details of the conspiracy in the various offices in Mauerwald.

In late October 1943, Stieff went on leave for a brief period. He recognized the possibility of his orderly or someone else rummaging through his belongings and accidently coming across the bomb and wisely concluded that it should be removed for the duration of his absence and replaced under his bed upon his return. Stieff therefore dismantled it and hid the various parts in different places. It fell to me to act as host to the explosive materials, which I kept under my bed while Stieff was away.

During the autumn and winter of 1943 we went through such manoeuvres several times. At length, we all came to the conclusion that it was simply too dangerous to carry on in this manner. It was decided, therefore, that the bomb had to be removed from the premises and hidden more securely. After much debate it was decided that we should dig a hole in the forest near headquarters at Mauerwald and bury it until such time as it was needed. We decided to seal the orders that we had drafted for Project Valkyrie and bury them as well. Two separate holes were therefore dug near the quarters of the Organizational Division and the bomb and papers disposed of. The burial went off without a hitch.

We had barely had time to enjoy our relief when Kuhn called in great agitation to report that a catastrophe had occurred. Apparently the secret military police had seen Kuhn and Hagen hiding the bomb and, with the help of their dogs, they had managed to uncover it. We had no evidence that they had yet come across the second hole with papers for Project Valkyrie, but could not rule out the possibility since the two burial sites were not far from each other. We were plunged into the fear that the entire plot would be exposed and all of us summarily executed for treason.

Kuhn reacted with characteristic coolness. Upon learning that the military police claimed to have seen soldiers in caps in the vicinity in which the explosives were discovered, Kuhn advised me to wear my more formal hat. Meanwhile, he acted on Stauffenberg's order that, in the event of the plot being discovered, Lieutenant Colonel Schrader should immediately be contacted. Schrader had been in the Resistance since 1939, and after 20 July, 1944 was to commit suicide rather than let himself be captured. Kuhn went to see Schrader to tell him that the bomb had been uncovered by secret military police who were under his orders.

Schrader had a large forehead, upon which beads of sweat now formed in great profusion. With the sword of Damocles hanging over the entire conspiracy, Schrader finally managed to compose himself and inform us that he would take action immediately and keep us posted in as discreet a fashion as possible. He then went to see Colonel General Kurt Zeitzler, Chief of the General Staff, the only man with the authority to prevent a full investigation by the Gestapo. He told Zeitzler about the bomb, and said that the British had evidently reached the conclusion that he, Zeitzler, was one of the top figures in the German war machine and, as such, had to be eliminated. Zeitzler was able to examine the bomb and confirm that it was of British manufacture. Continuing the preposterous tale, Schrader told Zeitzler that, given the importance of the investigation to Zeitzler himself and to the section under his command, it was best that it should be carried out by qualified military authorities rather than by bringing in the Gestapo. Zeitzler was so flattered by the compliment which he thought the British had paid him that he saw no reason to question the veracity of the tale as a whole. He therefore turned to the conspirators to carry out the investigation. Needless to say, the investigation led nowhere.

At times our efforts at Mauerwald took on the character of a tragi-comedy. When our bomb was discovered, the dogs belonging to the secret military police picked up a wrong scent at the excavation and raced to the living quarters of General Eduard Wagner. Like Schrader, Wagner had been close to the Resistance for several years and was later to commit suicide after 20 July. In spite of his close involvement with the conspiracy, however, he knew nothing about the various hideaways that had been devised for the bomb, nor did he know that the plans for Project Valkyrie had been sealed up and buried for safety. Wagner was a large and energetic man whose vigorous, uncompromising, and punctilious nature had earned him the affectionate title 'Nero'. The troop of dogs and the secret military police stormed into Wagner's quarters but failed to find him there. In an instant, the dogs led the whole group directly to 'Nero' himself: sitting in an outhouse which had a window looking out on the Mauersee. True to his title, Wagner flew into a rage and threw out the whole group. Wagner, incidentally, more than once carried out his conspiratorial activities in unusual places. Etzdorf told me that several times he and Wagner, in order not to be detected, had held their conversations in the sauna bath.

Fortunately, when the military police discovered the bomb, they did not also come across the papers that set forth details of the coup against Hitler. For some time, however, we lived in terror that one day the dogs would find these papers as well. Our fear was the more acute because we knew that it was impossible for us to go out to the woods and recover the papers since the area had been placed under constant surveillance by the military police. In the end, the police and their dogs failed to discover the papers, nor did we succeed in exhuming them ourselves. In all likelihood they are still buried there today, in that part of East Prussia belonging to Poland.

After the capture of the explosives, our arsenal had to be renewed. The task was not a simple one, in spite of the fact that explosives abounded in the area. If an approach to anyone aroused the slightest suspicion, we could have placed the entire conspiracy in jeopardy. At length we made contact with an officer in the Engineers whom we could trust and I was supposed to pick up the explosives from him. All the necessary arrangements were made, but on the intended day of departure I was unable to get away from my office and Kuhn had to go in my place.

On his return, Kuhn sent a telegram asking me to meet him at the station, so that he could drop off the explosives en route to his official destination, which was Rastenburg. Kuhn's telegram was delivered to the headquarters of the volunteer units, where it naturally passed through the hands of our Chief of Staff, Colonel Heinz Herre. Although I was on intimate terms with Köstring, I was only his ADC, while Herre was technically next in command. My relations with Herre were therefore somewhat delicate, the more so since he had never quite been able to work out what I was really doing there. Not being himself connected with the conspiracy, Herre had no idea of the real purpose of this request. He therefore told me it was unnecessary for me to go to the station. I had no choice but to obey. This created great difficulties for Kuhn, however, since he was forced to take the explosives with him right into Hitler's headquarters at Wolfschanse near Rastenburg, before bringing them back to safe-keeping at the General Staff Headquarters. In the end, Kuhn managed to get the explosives safely in and out of the lion's den at Wolfschanse and then back to Mauerwald, where he deposited them at their destination.

Once more we began our work of hiding the bombs at the General Staff Headquarters. Our efforts were more successful this time. The explosives remained in hiding until they were eventually removed from Mauerwald. These same explosives eventually returned to East Prussia in Stauffenberg's briefcase on the morning of 20 July, and were detonated in the briefing hut at Wolfschanse early that afternoon.

In spring 1944 Kuhn came up for transfer. His promotion and reassignment had been due for some while. His staying too long at Mauerwald would have given rise to suspicions. We therefore had no choice but to accept his transfer to a front-line *Jaeger* Division as a First General Staff Officer.

To some extent the suspicions that we sought to avoid regarding Kuhn arose whenever an individual stayed too long in one place. The same problem would have existed for any troops upon whom we might have chosen to rely. Important as it was to have reliable people near the General Staff Headquarters, it would have raised suspicions were they to have stayed there too long.

Kuhn's transfer, although regrettable from one point of view, protected him for the time being from any suspicion. It did not finally remove the doubts of the authorities, however, least of all those which arose after 20 July. It was known that Kuhn had had close ties with Stauffenberg, Klamroth and the like. As part of the general purge, Kuhn's divisional commander, General Gustav von Ziehlberg, was therefore ordered to arrest him. Ziehlberg was decent enough to let

Kuhn know what was afoot and deliberately give him enough time to take action, probably expecting him to commit suicide. In fact, Kuhn escaped to the Russian lines. When it was discovered that this had occurred, von Ziehlberg himself was arrested, given a lengthy sentence and then, at Hitler's insistence, executed.

Kuhn returned from Russia after the war, but remains incommunicado to this day. This is the more regrettable since he probably knows more about the early phase of the military conspiracy than practically anyone else. His silence is perhaps understandable, since at the time of his flight to the Russians he was widely criticized for having endanged the life of his commanding general. Having known him well, I have never doubted that, under the pressure of the moment, Kuhn simply did not realize that by choosing flight rather than suicide he might place von Ziehlberg's life in jeopardy.

18

VOLUNTEERS, GENERALS, AND CONSPIRATORS

By the beginning of 1943 the number of volunteers had become so large (around 800,000) that the resistance of those who opposed their use in the German army began to dwindle. In January 1943 Klamroth could at last realize Stauffenberg's old plan, the creation of an office responsible for all volunteers from the Soviet Union under the General of the *Osttruppen*. Klamroth would have preferred Köstring in this position, but opposition from influential circles was too great, so Lieutenant General Heinz Hellmich was appointed. A typical Prussian officer, Hellmich had no special knowledge of the Soviet Union and no command of the Russian language, but he was a decent man of strong feelings, which guided him in his work. Two of his sons had already been killed in action, and later, when Hellmich was again commanding a division, he too was killed. Hellmich shared Köstring's views on the volunteers and on the proper treatment of the occupied territories. He handled his job responsibly, and was particularly successful in choosing excellent staff officers who approached their work with enthusiasm and energy. They were to fight for their volunteer comrades with the same devotion as Hellmich showed.

After long discussions with me, Klamroth came to the conclusion that we could not do without Köstring's unique knowledge of Russia. On 13 June, 1943, he was appointed Inspector General for Turkic and Caucasian Units. Köstring's new designation was again a compromise, we would have preferred him to have full authority over all volunteer units.

The responsibilities of Köstring and Hellmich overlapped, but their co-operation was to work out extremely well; with Hellmich working at the headquarters of the General Staff and Köstring as a roving general on every front, caring not only for his Caucasian and Turkish units but also for the Russian and Ukranian volunteers. Each respected the other and his sphere of activity. Many volunteers owed the improvement of their position to the close relationship that these fine men maintained. On 1 January, 1944, Köstring finally took over Hellmich's position after changing its name to *General der Freiwilligenverbände*. The name *Osttruppen* was considered derogatory by the volunteers, because their relatives serving as labourers in Germany had to wear the *Ostabzeichen*, a badge identifying them as second-class.

In part because of Hitler's well-known hostility towards the volunteer units, there were to be many arguments about their usefulness. Certainly the volunteer battalions engaged in provisioning and construction work did yeoman service on behalf of the German army. Beyond this, there were many battalions which distinguished themselves in actual fighting. Indeed, some of these battalions were even singled out in the German *Wehrmachtsbericht*, the daily report from the various fighting fronts; such mention alone was considered high decoration. The brave stand of the *Bergmann* unit in the defence of the Crimea near Perekop was one such noteworthy instance. Another volunteer battalion was applauded for doing its duty up to the bitter end in the battle of Stalingrad, while the Georgian battalion No. 795 was commended for its bravery in the defence of Cherbourg.

Köstring tried to explain to anyone raising doubts about the usefulness of the volunteers that their willingness to fight with our army depended in large measure on German policy towards them. For example, the failure to equip volunteer units adequately was bound to cripple their effectiveness. There were Italian, Rumanian and Hungarian divisions also fighting with us from 1941 onwards. Not only were they poorly equipped for a winter campaign, but their armour and equipment was inferior to ours. When such units were overrun, as they were in the battle of the Don, one did not need to search further than this for an explanation.

A remarkable group of officers emerged from the ranks of the Red Army troops in the German army. It is difficult to generalize about these men, so great were the differences between them, but one can say that they all genuinely hated Stalin and his system, that they wanted to construct a new future for their people, and that they hoped Hitler and the Nazi regime could help them in their efforts. They had all lived for years under Soviet rule and had been bombarded by intensive anti-Nazi and even anti-German propaganda until 1939. This seems to have had no impact on them. Like so many of the average citizens whom I had known during my years in Moscow, they discounted totally whatever emanated from their government. This immunity to propaganda did not exist in Germany, where most people believed what the government told them.

Many Red Army officers who joined the volunteers arrived with enormous hopes about National Socialism. They did not realize that the treatment meted out on their territories by Hitler would be as bad as anything Stalin had done and even worse. Still less could they imagine that it might be preferable to suffer under one's own dictator, rather than a foreign one. But they could not help but understand what people like *Gauleiters* Koch and Sauckel were up to when they witnessed the forced emigration of their people to work in Germany. Had they been mere mercenaries, their disillusionment would have been less. They were idealists, however, and hence their disenchantment was the more profound.

In spite of this, they retained their faith in those German officers whom they understood were opposed to this colonial policy. In fact, their trust in the German military authorities grew as their faith in the civilian, i.e., Nazi, authorities was eroded. It was this that accounts for the peculiar intimacy that existed between volunteer officers and those German officers who tried to win concessions for the volunteers. In hundreds of cases this friendship remained intact until the end of the war.

Köstring understood well that the fighting quality of the volunteers would never be great unless the German army treated them fairly and maintained them well. To this end he and his staff promoted a long series of measures – some of symbolic importance, others practical – that brought the volunteers to full equality with their German colleagues-in-arms.

When Köstring took up his new command, he quickly discovered that troops in volunteer units were not permitted to receive the Iron Cross. The few cases in which it had been awarded to non-Germans could all be traced to the action of local commanders unacquainted with the regulations. We immediately launched efforts to change the rule. When these were blocked, we managed to create a special 'Badge of Gallantry for the Peoples of the Eastern Nations'. This decoration was conferred in three classes: bronze, silver, and gold; and could be conferred more than once. Though it was certainly not what we would have preferred, we thought the medal was at least an improvement and were therefore surprised when the volunteers complained about it, on the grounds that the decoration could not be awarded to the Germans with whom they served. They accused us of practising arbitrary inequality. Accordingly it was decreed that German personnel serving with volunteer units would receive the same decoration. Thanks to this, I was later to receive the 'Badge of Gallantry' in silver. Eventually Köstring even overcame the opposition to decorating volunteers with the Iron Cross, which was to find many recipients. At the end of the war we had the '*Untermensch*' in

German general's uniform decorated with the Iron Cross.

A similar point of honour was raised later, when Hitler came up with the idea of having special uniforms for our volunteer units. He wanted to be sure that the fabric would be of a different shade to the German army's traditional field grey. Köstring immediately set out to reverse this decision, which the volunteer troops could not help but take as evidence of their second-class status within the *Wehrmacht*. In the end, two arguments changed Hitler's mind: first, that German industry should not be called upon to provide fresh uniforms for so many soldiers who were already adequately clothed; and second, that if the German troops wore different uniforms to volunteers, they would be singled out at once and shot. Volunteers henceforth wore German uniforms and were distinguished only by their national cockade or unit mark.

The abolition of distinctions between volunteers and regular German soldiers extended to questions of rank as well. The Asiatic *Untermensch* of 1941 suddenly appeared with the epaulettes of a German officer on his shoulders. Lower-ranking German soldiers were required to salute first when meeting a volunteer of higher rank. At Köstring's instigation, a notorious SS brochure entitled *Untermensch* was withdrawn from circulation and corporal punishment of volunteer soldiers forbidden.

General Köstring swept aside those opposed to granting full equality to the volunteers with the statement that in case of refusal he could no longer guarantee the reliability of the three quarters of a million volunteers serving in the army, navy and air force. He accused everybody who resisted him of wrecking the fighting spirit of the volunteers and thus of the German army itself, for by 1943–44 every seventh soldier in the German army was a former Soviet. He would coolly remind his opponents that any mistake in the treatment of the volunteers would be paid for with the blood of German soldiers.

The second front in our campaign on behalf of the volunteers involved their material betterment. We knew well that such improvements were no substitute for full political equality but hoped that they would at least provide a strong impetus to the broader improvements that were so much needed. Needless to say, the Party vigorously opposed every practical measure we instituted, judging correctly that they flew in the face of Nazi doctrine.

Along with guaranteeing volunteers the same pay and food as German soldiers, one of our first actions was to establish special hospitals manned by doctors and nurses from the USSR, who could attend to the volunteers' needs in their own languages. By late 1944 we had founded

265

twenty such hospitals, ten of them to the rear of the fighting front. When the numbers of Soviet-trained doctors and nurses fell below the growing need, we created several medical schools in Germany and France where doctors, dentists and nurses could be trained in the volunteers' own languages. For those volunteers who had suffered debilitating wounds, special homes were established. Besides rehabilitation, volunteers wounded in action also received compensation. Furthermore, recreation centres for volunteers on leave were set up in Germany and Italy.

Much was also done to give volunteers access to education and culture. Special schools and programmes were set up to train volunteer officers, who could then replace the Germans assigned to their units. Libraries with books in the languages of the USSR were also built up, German films were dubbed into several Slavic, Turkic and Caucasian languages, much money was spent on theatrical groups, the Koran was published in large quantities, and a school for Muslim mullahs was set up in Berlin. Various newspapers in the languages of the USSR were founded by the national committees, with writers drawn from among the volunteers themselves. Besides all this, we organized trips to Germany for volunteers and arranged for thousands of them to spend their leaves with German families. Finally, we set up athletic programmes and competitions in many sports.

It was impossible to better the mood among the volunteers in the army without also taking steps to improve the lives of Soviet labourers in Germany, for many of the volunteers had relatives in the labour system. Until Köstring addressed himself to this problem, no attempts at improving the lot of the foreign labourer had succeeded. Volunteers complained bitterly of the fact that, when they visited their wives and relatives, they sometimes found them in camps behind barbed wire and wearing the hated '*Ost*' badge. If he wished to take members of his family to German cinemas and restaurants, which the volunteers were free to enter, the wives or parents would be stopped at the door. All this was the more loathsome for Russians and Ukrainians because the Azerbaijanis, Georgians, Armenians and Cossacks had been freed from such discrimination, thanks to Rosenberg's views on the minority question.

Our campaign on behalf of the *Ostarbeiter* faced fierce opposition from the Nazi officials, but certain gains were made. First, we got permission to send officers to inspect the living and working conditions of the forced labourers; if they found these unsatisfactory, they were authorized to give orders to the local authorities to change them. Those responsible for the abuses, even if they were civilian factory directors, could be brought to trial and imprisoned. This measure was instituted only in 1944, and its implementation was hampered by lack of officers to carry out the inspections. Beyond this, the *'Ost'* badge gradually disappeared. To be sure, these measures came far too late, were woefully inadequate, and left much undone, but Köstring worked with dedication to help the lives of these unfortunate people until the end of the war, when they were returned to the Soviet Union and to Stalin's 'Gulag Archipelago'.

The measures by which General Köstring and his staff endeavoured to better the circumstances of the former Red Army volunteers in the German forces were not the only factors affecting their well-being or fighting capacity. No less important was the attitude of their German comrades and the latter's capacity to understand the mentality of the various national groups involved. For example, Prussian-style commands simply would not work with the former Soviet troops. To improve relations between such different peoples, we set up several schools where German personnel dealing with the volunteers could attend courses on the languages, history and culture of the major Soviet nationalities. Equally important, Köstring attempted to visit personally practically every senior German officer with volunteers units under his command, and to explain to him the measures he should take to meet the volunteers' distinctive needs. During the autumn of 1943 and all of 1944 this took up most of our time.

The geographical range of my travels with Köstring vastly expanded in this period because volunteers were by then serving in practically every division in the army. Hitler had long since declared that the formation of a volunteer army of former Red Army troops would deprive Germany of all the fruits of its coming victory, since such an army would inevitably ask for a share in the booty as compensation for its achievements and its sacrifices. But while Hitler did manage to prevent the formation of an entire army of volunteers, he failed to stop their being added to the regular German fighting forces. In October 1943, large numbers of German troops were shifted from the USSR to the West. Nearly all German units by now included at least ten to fifteen per cent volunteers, for whom German replacements were no longer readily available, even had the German officers wanted them. In fact they did not, and many refused flatly to leave behind their volunteers, knowing them to be excellent soldiers. It infuriated Hitler that any German officer could prefer *Untermenschen* to good German soldiers.

Nearly all the generals whom we met were sympathetic to Köstring's message regarding volunteer helpers, though few had any great understanding of foreign peoples. There were exceptions like General Kurt Zeitzler, Chief of the General Staff, who in 1943 proposed to leave all volunteers on the Soviet front or to send them to work as labourers. Köstring rightly objected to this degrading suggestion. But for all the debates over the usefulness of the volunteers that occurred among people at a distance from the front line, I doubt if there were more than a handful of generals who accepted Hitler's ideas about the so-called *Untermenschen*.

My travels with Köstring also provided unique opportunities for me as a member of the Resistance movement, since it enabled me to gather large quantities of information on who could be depended on at the moment Hitler was assassinated. There were several periods during which it was essential for me to be at my post at headquarters in order to await the coup against Hitler, but since I always had adequate warning of such alerts, I would arrange in advance for Köstring and me to have a convenient break in our travels. When necessary, I had little difficulty in getting Köstring to issue orders requiring me either to travel somewhere or to stay put, as the situation required.

From Klamroth and Stauffenberg I already knew the names of several senior officers on whom we could rely. As a by-product of our official work, I tried to sound out others. This could not be done directly, of course. I could not simply shake their hands and tell them, 'Look here, I am also visiting you as a representative of the conspiracy'; a more subtle approach was called for. Luckily Köstring was known and respected by nearly every commander in the Army, and his conversations were exceptionally frank. Because he nearly always included me in them, I could frequently learn everything I needed without asking a single question.

From time to time I returned to Berlin to report to Stauffenberg, whom I recall visiting at least twice on the Bendlerstrasse in the last months of 1943 and many times in the spring of 1944. I also remember a meeting in Düppel, after the Bendlerstrasse had been bombed. At such sessions I would enumerate my various impressions, listing precisely whom I thought we could depend upon and who might pose a potential threat to the project. In Düppel I presented him with a radio that had belonged to my parents in order to prevent others from eavesdropping on such conversations as ours.

A figure who was central to the work of the Resistance was Admiral Wilhelm Canaris. Over a period of years, this man quietly worked to protect the organization against the danger of counter-attack by Himmler.

Canaris was able more than once to cover up actions that might have exposed the conspiracy. I first met Canaris during my travels in the summer of 1943. We spent a long evening together in a country house in the Ukraine. Canaris, Köstring and I were joined by Lieutenant Colonel Hermann Baun, head of the Wally II (intelligence) section of the *Abwehr* and a great expert on the USSR. A former consular secretary in Kiev, Baun's particular area of expertise was in sending spies behind the Russian lines. It was fascinating to listen to the conversation between Canaris and Köstring, two wise old men whose discussion ranged across every aspect of the world as they had known it. I was surprised to see how little Canaris fitted the image of a great admiral. There was something sad in his face and eyes which was evident throughout the evening. He impressed me not as a man of action but as an observer and philosopher, perhaps the most reflective member of the German military that I had met.

It was not necessary to tell Canaris how to treat the civilian population or the volunteers in the German army. Oberländer's *Bergmann* unit had been organized under his command, and Canaris had followed its development closely. Köstring said that we needed more people like Oberländer, with which Canaris emphatically agreed. Canaris sympathized with the plight of the volunteers, not merely because he had studied the situation as an officer but as a cultivated man whose humanity would not permit him to inflict suffering on others. So strong were these feelings, in fact, that he did not advocate the assassination of Hitler, preferring instead that he be arrested. This came out only later, of course, though one could have guessed it by meeting him. But though he would have stopped short of assassination, he had figured actively in the efforts of Colonel General Franz Halder to bring about a coup in 1938.

Köstring also frequently met General Reinhard Gehlen, the head of *Fremde Heere Ost*, an information section of the *Generalstab des Heeres*. This post gave Gehlen responsibility for gathering intelligence on the entire Soviet theatre of war so as to enable the General Staff to reach well-informed strategic decisions. He was hard-working and highly respected, by us particularly, since the intelligence he was gathering was also directly pertinent to our own activities respecting the volunteers. Gehlen was at one with Köstring on the need to treat the civilian population in general and the volunteers in particular with decency and respect. Until the end of the war he was among the most ardent supporters of all initiatives designed to improve the lot of the volunteers, and he took an active part in the effort to make use of General Andrei Vlasov's abilities.

Beyond this, Gehlen was among those top staff officers who fully appreciated the role the volunteers could play in inspiring an anti-Stalinist movement within the USSR. Gehlen's views on this matter were shared by a number of very intelligent officers on his staff, several of them future professors, with whom I was in constant touch. I never doubted that Gehlen himself supported the conspiracy and would have been delighted had 20 July been a success.

In the late autumn of 1943 we travelled to Paris, where Köstring met his old friend, General Karl-Heinrich von Stülpnagel. As usual, Köstring told him of the needs of the volunteer units in his area. Köstring had learned to his astonishment that in Paris the volunteers were being deployed to guard depots, including a repository where furniture confiscated from French Jews was being stored. He remarked that it was not his business to pass judgment on why that furniture was there in the first place, but he adamantly refused to allow volunteers to be used to guard it. He reasoned that if they were put in charge of guarding looted property, they would follow the Germans' example and begin looting themselves.

Stülpnagel, who had participated in the abortive Beck coup of 1938, did not hide his attitude towards Hitler, nor did many of his other officers, who were all part of the conspiracy. On 20 July, Stülpnagel carried out precisely the orders that Stauffenberg had given him; he arrested the SS officers in Paris and in a short time was in full control of the city. With the arrest of Stauffenberg however, Stülpnagel was himself arrested and ordered to return to Germany to answer for his actions. He drove by car from Paris and stopped near Verdun, where, as a young lieutenant in World War I, he had taken part in a bloody battle and won a high decoration. Arriving at the Meuse battlefield, Stülpnagel left his car, walked to the scene of his earlier glory, and put a bullet through his head. Unfortunately, he managed only to blind himself. Hitler put him in a hospital and the doctors succeeded in curing him, after which he was tried and hanged.

While in Paris on our visit to Stülpnagel, I visited his secretary, Countess Friederike Podewils, who had grown up with my wife. 'Mady' had just learned that her brother, a young artillery lieutenant, had been killed at Salerno and she was understandably distressed. In my mood at that time, I could not help but point out to her that her brother Max might have been fortunate, in that he had died quickly and heroically. It seemed to me by then that all we younger officers were doomed. I realized that this was scant consolation to her, and so invited her to dine with

Köstring and me, in the hope that we might cheer her up. After dinner, I took her by bicycle back to the Plaza, and returned to the Ritz on foot. The deserted city made a particularly gloomy impression on me as I pondered over the metamorphosis that had occurred since I was last in Paris as a young foreign service officer. Three weeks later, I learned that Countess Podewils' brother had not been killed at all but had been taken prisoner. He survived the war and is now German Ambassador in Vienna.

After our meeting with General Stülpnagel, Köstring and I visited General Alexander, Baron von Falkenhausen, the military governor of Belgium and Northern France. Von Falkenhausen was an old friend of Köstring and had earlier served as a military adviser to Chiang Kai-shek. I knew that he had been sceptical about National Socialism from the beginning and that he had taken a hand in the schemes of Beck, Halder, and others in 1938. I was therefore the more eager to observe him. We met in the autumn of 1943 outside Brussels at the large country house, Senaffe, where von Falkenhausen was staying. The estate was really magnificent, with all the silver plate and porcelain still intact. The dinner was simple but included fresh game that von Falkenhausen himself had shot and which had been prepared by an excellent cook.

Köstring preferred after a large dinner party to retire with his host for a more frank and intimate conversation. On this occasion Falkenhausen was joined by his chief of staff, Colonel Bodo von Harbou. Both gave ample evidence that they understood Germany's situation without illusions. Falkenhausen had been somewhat reticent about involving himself deeply in organizational work in connection with the conspiracy but he showed admirable independence in making contact with Belgians representing all shades of opinion within the country, including members of the local Resistance. It is impossible to know just how far Falkenhausen would have been willing to go on 20 July in his official capacity as military governor of Belgium and Northern France, for he was to be relieved of his post one week before the attempted assassination. The cause of his dismissal was fully in character: he had refused to send Belgian eighteen-year-olds to Germany as forced labourers. Whatever von Falkenhausen might have accomplished had he remained in his command, his constant contact with many of the principal conspirators gave grounds for him to be arrested after 20 July, along with von Harbou.

Of all the generals who were sympathetic to the conspiracy, none was more charismatic nor more highly regarded as a field leader than Field Marshal Erwin Rommel. He had joined the conspiracy rather late, and even after joining was cool towards proposals that Hitler be killed rather than arrested, but he was a genuine supporter nonetheless. Wounded while visiting the collapsing front on 17 June, 1944, he was put out of action at the critical moment. His loss was immeasurable. He was by far the most popular field marshal among the troops and his authority was seemingly boundless. He was to have given the order to stop hostilities in the West, which would have lead to the surrender of a significant part of the German army. Even when Hitler was not killed on 20 July, Rommel was so resolute that he would have issued his orders anyway, and I am convinced they would have been obeyed by a substantial part of the army, thus severely reducing Hitler's fighting capacity. As it was, Hitler despatched two senior officers, Lieutenant Wilhelm Burgdorf and Major General Ernst Maisel, to visit Rommel. They informed the wounded man that Hitler knew he had participated in the conspiracy. He was offered the alternatives of committing suicide or being tried by court martial and hanged. He chose the former and, in a stroke typical of Hitler, was accorded full military honours at the funeral.

Such figures as Tresckow, Gehlen, Stülpnagel, Falkenhausen, Rommel, and certain others were the illustrious exceptions to a depressing rule. The majority of the field marshals and commanding generals loyally stood by Hitler. At best they were neutral towards the conspiracy. No one epitomized the position of neutrality better than Field Marshal Erich von Manstein. A talented officer, Manstein was incapable of relating his own work in the army to the broader issues raised by Hitler's rule, though he in fact had several active conspirators in his immediate entourage. In the autumn of 1943, Stauffenberg told me about a recent conversation with the Field Marshal. Manstein had understood the military situation well but still refused to take action. At the end of his grim narrative, Stauffenberg summed up the situation by saying: 'If we are successful, Manstein will be with us; but if we fail, Manstein will not say a word.' Nor did he.

There were a number of commanders who were sympathetic to our work with the volunteers, even when it flatly contradicted Hitler's intentions, but remained aloof from the conspiracy. Such a man was Colonel General Heinz Guderian, the commander of the famous offensive against Abbeville in France and a prominent figure in the Russian campaign until Hitler withdrew him. Our meeting with Guderian occurred at his headquarters in the Mauerwald, after he had been appointed Chief of the General Staff of the army. We dined with Guderian, his aide, Major Bernd von Freytag-Loringhoven and Captain

272

Gerhard Boldt, later the author of *Last Days with Hitler*.

Guderian was a thoroughly amiable man and laughingly addressed me as *Herr Legationsrat*. Since his conversation with Köstring was a confidential one between two old friends, Freytag-Loringhoven, Boldt, and I were cast in the role of attentive listeners. Much was said about the importance of treating the volunteers well, and the generally disastrous situation on the two fronts was carefully reviewed. I was struck by the fact that Guderian seemed to agree with everything Köstring said about the Russian volunteers and about the Soviet army in general. Guderian had good reason to respect the Red Army by now. He was obviously a decent person, knew full well that the war was lost, and was immensely popular with his soldiers. He was held to be a kind of saint among the armoured troops, and could have been immensely effective in rallying them to the cause of the Resistance. Instead, he chose to do his duty to the bitter end, even assuming a new assignment after having first been briefly demoted. One can only wonder why he accepted this from Hitler, of whom he was so openly critical.

A striking case of wavering in the hour of decision was that of Field Marshal Günther von Kluge. Kluge succeeded Rundsted as Supreme Commander of the whole Western Front, and, like Stülpnagel, was stationed in Paris. After observing him during his conversations with Köstring, I was left with the feeling that he would mobilize and support the Resistance movement if others were first to remove Hitler. Besides my own impression of the man, there were other good grounds for thinking this. It was known to us that he had been in contact with Goerdeler and other members of the Resistance as far back as 1942 and that he had on more than one occasion given indications that he would be among the supporters of a coup. He was considered by the conspirators to be an appropriate person to assume a high position in the army following the fall of Hitler. When General von Stülpnagel seized control in Paris on 20 July, Kluge mobilized in support of the coup, but no sooner had the first news that Hitler might still be alive reached Paris than he began to waver. Even before word of Stauffenberg's capture reached him he had denounced Stülpnagel's decision to act unilaterally. Eventually he disavowed the conspiracy entirely. His tragedy was that he had done enough to warrant being summoned back to Berlin to explain his behaviour yet had done too little to change the direction of events. As he was returning to the capital, Kluge committed suicide. We will never know what it was that made him unwilling to take the risk of moving decisively to immobilize the Western Front.

It was not the neutrality or indecisiveness of the field marshals that most galled Stauffenberg and the rest of us, but the outright opposition of many of them to what we were seeking to do. Towards the end of the war, when the invasion of Italy was already under way and on the eve of the German retreat from Rome, General Köstring went down to Italy to visit Field Marshal Kesselring at his headquarters in the caves at Monte Soracte near Rome. Here the Italians had constructed a formidable building, like a battleship, where military enterprises could be conducted in full security. It was like a science-fiction film. We were joined by our former Permanent Under Secretary of State, von Weiszäcker, who was then Ambassador to the Vatican. The situation ouside the caves was in chaos; within, everything proceeded as if nothing were amiss. At both this meeting and during a second visit to Kesselring that I made when he was in the north of Italy near Vicenza, I understood fully that he would remain loyal to Hitler to the bitter end. Like Field Marshal Ferdinand Schörner and others, he did not lack the courage to act against Hitler but refrained from doing so on principle, and also with the hope that something might still be done to reverse the seemingly inevitable collapse.

Similar feelings seemed also to figure in Field Marshal Gerd von Rundstedt's adamant refusal to take part in the Conspiracy. Rundstedt had his headquarters at St Germain near Paris, where we visited him in late 1943. After dinner in his house, Köstring, Rundstedt's aide de camp, Major Hans-Victor von Salviati, and I sat down with him. It was a memorable occasion. We reviewed the military situation and Köstring argued that the war on the Eastern Front could not be won. Rundstedt entirely agreed. At this point Salviati boldly stepped into the conversation. He was a contemporary of mine and we knew of one another, but we had not met before. He was convinced of the desperation of Germany's position and of the need for senior officers to take a stand against Hitler. Allowing for the difference of age, he was on close terms with Rundstedt, in the same way as I was with Köstring. In the privacy of our conversation, he pressed Rundstedt hard, arguing that the field marshals had to take action; it was their duty as human beings and Christians to do so and others depended upon them. Had his remarks been overheard he could certainly have been shot and the rest of us demoted. But he persisted.

Rundstedt listened attentively but in the end shrugged his shoulders and said that he could not influence the Führer. Again and again Salviati argued that von Rundstedt was duty-bound to take action against Hitler

274

and that the entire country depended upon his doing so. To our disappointment, the tired old field marshal did not respond. Salviati was rewarded for his beliefs by being hanged after 20 July.

Rundstedt epitomized the failure of the field marshals as a group. He was relieved of command of his army group soon after our conversation, but was called back to active duty by Hitler after 20 July, 1944, in order to preside over the military court that was convened to expel the conspirators from the army. This step was necessary in order that they could be turned over to the civil courts for trial. Had the officers been court-martialled, they would have been shot, but if they were thrown out of the army and given a civil trial they could be hanged, which was Hitler's declared wish. What must have been Rundstedt's feelings as he presided over this court which condemned some of his closest comrades – Field Marshal von Witzleben, and the others?

I later accompanied General Köstring on a visit to Field Marshal von Rundstedt in December, 1944. He was now back at his old post as Supreme Commander in the West and had just launched the famous offensive on the 'Bulge'. His Chief of Staff was General Siegfried Westphal, who had served earlier as Rommel's chief of staff in Africa. Notwithstanding all that had happened, Rundstedt and his staff were gripped by enthusiasm as news of our advance poured in. It was grimly fascinating to watch the growth of a flickering hope that a reverse in the West was still possible. They had convinced themselves that the German effort at the 'Bulge' was a decisive counter-move and received every fresh report as justifying their faith. Neither Köstring nor I shared Rundstedt's optimism in the slightest. We were convinced that it was worse than futile to make a stand in the West and that we should instead have concentrated our few remaining forces against the Russians. Rundstedt was now working like a drowning man who drags down everyone else in a futile attempt to save his life.

Over and over I discussed the attitude of the leading generals with Klamroth, Stauffenberg, and Etzdorf. Had they been prepared to take resolute action, the fate of the Resistance might have been different from what it was, but all my 'research' with Köstring confirmed that they were not. Perhaps their failure to take action was due in part to the manner in which Hitler treated them. The field marshals all received excellent pocket money, and in many cases Hitler gave them property as well. Hitler perverted the old Prussian tradition, whereby the generals received titles as well sometimes as estates, but only when the wars were won. In addition, Hitler vastly inflated the number of field marshals, thus creating a large group of men whose authority was utterly dependent upon his own. It was a form of bribery.

Various other factors may have discouraged the field marshals and other top commanders from backing the conspiracy. No doubt their oath of loyalty to Hitler played an important part. For a long while they had no idea of the likely position of the Allies in the event of a successful coup against Hitler. Could a non-Nazi Germany expect any better peace terms than a Germany ruled by Hitler? If the Allies had issued a statement that the overthrow of Hitler would affect the settlement, however minimally, it would have had a profound impact and made the conspiracy far more attractive to wavering officers. Lacking such a statement, they were placed in the position of advocating measures that would lead to their country's surrender, with no sure compensatory benefits.

This is not to deny that contacts between the Resistance and various foreign governments took place. They did, thanks to the efforts of Adam Trott zu Solz and others. These contacts were significant but limited and led to nothing that provided the slightest support for the conspiracy.

I discussed this issue with Stauffenberg. We were deeply depressed by the Allies' silence. We never concluded that we should give up, since the fight against Hitler was at bottom a fight by Germans against their criminal government, irrespective of the position of outsiders. At the same time, we believed that if the Allied governments were confronted with the outcome of our work, they would be more willing to negotiate with the representatives of a freely elected government.

However reasonable this assumption, though, it carried little weight with the many officers who wavered on the edge of action. In this context, the Allies' doctrine of unconditional surrender dealt a deadly blow to the Resistance movement because it convinced many people that the overthrow of Hitler would not affect the terms of peace. There is no doubt in my mind that numerous generals and junior officers would have joined the Resistance had it not been for this well-publicized doctrine. Whenever it came up in discussions, I pointed out that it had been adopted by the Allies as a means of inducing some solidarity among their diverse interests, and also as a means of satisfying the Soviets, who continued to fear a Western defection. But while this reasoning may have been correct, it did not allay the deep fears caused by the spectre of unconditional surrender. Goebbels understood this well, and did everything possible to bring the Allies' announcement to the attention of every German.

However understandable the reluctance of the field marshals and senior commanders may seem in retrospect, our frustration knew no bounds at the time. When I reported to Stauffenberg my impressions of Köstring's conversations with senior members of the officer corps, I watched his disenchantment deepen. It confirmed his conviction that the Resistance movement had to depend not on the leading generals but on the young officers, with only a handful of senior officers playing supporting roles. Nor did he consider that the fine men involved with the civilian side of the Resistance could be the ones to eliminate Hitler. The civilians – Goerdeler, Count Moltke, Hassel, and the others – were well suited to hammer out programmes to be implemented after the elimination of Hitler, but not actually to do the deed. In one sense, he had arrived at this conclusion back in mid-1943, but not until the spring of 1944 did he finally abandon hope in the majority of the senior commanders.

19

THE JULY PLOT
AND ITS AFTERMATH

As if sensing the mounting danger, Hitler became warier, to the point that by early 1944 he was hesitant to visit the front or to leave the safety of his various headquarters. An attempt on his life that seemed almost certain to succeed involved a young and high-minded Captain, Baron Axel von dem Bussche-Streithorst. Appalled by having witnessed the mass murder of several thousand Jews in the Ukraine in 1942, Bussche had placed himself at Stauffenberg's disposal. Eventually they conceived a plan to mount a demonstration of new uniforms, during which Bussche was to conceal a small grenade or bomb in his clothing, fall on Hitler and pin him down until the explosives went off. Bussche was resolute but success in such matters often hangs on petty details. In this case the train carrying the new uniforms was hit by Allied bombs at the end of November, 1943, and the fashion show had to be postponed. By the time it could be rescheduled, Bussche had been gravely wounded on the Eastern Front and was in no condition to carry out the mission for which he would gladly have sacrificed himself.

I met Stauffenberg at least three times during the spring of 1944 as I paused on my travels back and forth across the continent. I remember particularly an argument that we had in the presence of Captain Count Schwerin von Schwanenfeld, who, some months later, was fated to be among the first to be tried by Hitler's People's Court. The argument was heated, but took place under the cover of the radio that I had given Stauffenberg precisely for such purposes. After so many thwarted attempts on Hitler's life, Stauffenberg was in despair. He reviewed every possible means of getting at the Führer and for each one found an obvious source of possible failure. I argued that the army would only follow the orders of the conspirators if Hitler were dead. Stauffenberg insisted that we had to proceed under any circumstances, convinced as we were that an attempt had again to be made.

In the late spring of 1944, Stauffenberg decided that he himself must place the bomb that would destroy Hitler. He had hoped that it would be possible to find someone more appropriate for the mission than himself. The decision to take matters into his own hands was taken as a last resort. As chief of the military conspiracy, he should not have had to move from his headquarters, let alone carry out such a mission as this. Moreover, his own battle injuries had left him unable to shoot a revolver, thus forcing him to turn to a bomb as the sole possible weapon in his arsenal.

To accomplish the mission he had assigned himself, Stauffenberg had first to fly to East Prussia to place the bomb and then return from Mauerwald to Berlin, thus absenting himself from the nerve centre at the most crucial moment. His decision meant that precious hours were to be lost, hours in which the already small possibility of a general revolt in the army was vitiated.

My personal assignment in the conspiracy had nothing to do with the actual assassination, which was to be co-ordinated and carried out by others, but rather was concerned with those many steps that would be necessary immediately afterwards in order to consolidate the attack on the regime. I was well aware that in July a major attempt on Hitler's life was to be made in Berchtesgaden. For several weeks I stood ready to take action. I made sure that Köstring and I were at Berchtesgaden. Our stay there did not arouse suspicion since the *Wehrmacht Führungsstab*, which was responsible for the Russian volunteers on the Western and the South-Eastern fronts, was at Berchtesgaden at that moment.

Köstring and I stayed at the Berchtesgadener Hof which was used by several people close to the conspiracy, among them General Wagner, Major General Stieff and General Lindemann. I saw Stauffenberg on 3 July, and again on the 6th, when he was summoned to brief Hitler in connection with his work with the so-called 'Reserve Army'. He seemed in full command of his powers, somewhat tired perhaps, but concentrated and outwardly calm.

Stauffenberg had a bomb with him when he came to Berchtesgaden on 6–7 July and again on the 11th. He did not detonate it, however, since Himmler and Goering were not present, and the possibility of the coup being suppressed following Hitler's assassination remained great if Himmler survived. On 14 July Köstring had to leave, as his staff was moving from East Prussia to Potsdam. He had not been brought in on the details of the conspiracy, but he was far from ignorant of my own involvement. I accompanied him to the airport in Salzburg. My nerves were strained to such a degree that I foolishly lost control of myself and blurted out: 'This time we'll blow up the devil.' I immediately regretted my outburst. Köstring looked at me without surprise and commented sadly on this Bastille Day: 'We Germans don't know how to make revolutions.' Without saying more he boarded the plane. Fortunately, the engines were already running and drowned our conversation.

The next attempt was set for 15 July in Wolfschanse in East Prussia. I was nervous, for I was convinced that with Stauffenberg himself set to act against Hitler, the chance of success was far greater than it had been in any previous attempt, and yet precisely because the assassination was to be done by him, the leader of the organization, the risk of failure in the crucial follow-up was greater than before. I expected to hear directly from Stauffenberg's aide, Haeften, when the deed was done and then to get my precise assignment from him. I waited all day, but no word came. I was puzzled and fearful that some disaster had occurred. Next morning I realized that the attempt had again been postponed.

Since the beginning of July I had put off a trip to the Army Group, Italy. Kesselring's Chief of Staff, Lieutenant General Röttiger, wanted urgently to discuss with me serious problems they were having with the 162nd Turkic Infantry Division. There had been cases of desertion. It was impossible to postpone this mission without arousing suspicion. The mood was extremely tense at the time, and we tried to be all the more alert against small lapses that could trigger a move against Hitler's enemies, real or imagined.

The trip to Italy was uneventful. The meeting with Röttiger took place at Montecatini between Florence and Pisa.

The return trip should have been swift and easy but turned out to be extremely difficult, since the Americans now controlled the air. Our own planes were grounded, so I had to take the train. American planes strafed the train at several points, causing the passengers each time to flee into the fields beside the tracks. The worst delays occurred at the Po, where the bridges and ferries were under attack. It was agonizing to see once more how rapidly our position was deteriorating, but since I did not know that the assassination attempt had been rescheduled for the 20th, I was not unduly bothered by the delay.

I arrived at my home in Kitzbühl in the late afternoon of 19 July, 1944. I went immediately to bed and fell sound asleep. Scarcely had I lain down before the telephone rang. Pussi answered. It was General Stieff, who wanted me to go to Salzburg at once. Knowing how exhausted I was Pussi could not bring herself to wake me up. She pretended that I had not yet returned from Italy and told him to try again next morning. As I was still asleep on the morning of the 20th, Pussi denied me once more. By midday it became apparent how closely I had escaped doom. Unwittingly Pussi had probably saved my life. The same evening she heard on the radio that Stauffenberg had made an attempt on Hitler's life and had failed. I nearly collapsed at the news. Pussi knew of my contacts with Claus and guessed correctly that I, too, was mixed up in the affair. We faced the situation together and tried to work out the best course of action.

Three possibilities were open to me. First, I could attempt to disappear into the Austrian mountains. This would have been quite possible, since I knew the mountains well and by this time there existed the beginnings of an Austrian Resistance movement with which I could readily have made contact. Second, I could make my way as fast as possible to Yugoslavia in order to cross the German lines and, with luck, make contact with Fitzroy Maclean, whom I knew to be there. Third, I could march into the lion's den and return to headquarters, which had just been moved from Mauerwald to Potsdam.

After long discussions with Pussi, I decided on the third course. To have taken either of the others would have been to admit to my own guilt and thereby invite the Nazis to execute my wife and parents. I had no choice but to pray to God and return to Potsdam.

Before leaving, I thought it best to register my presence in Kitzbühl with the local commandant, as was required by our regulations. In every large town there was a commandant assigned to wounded soldiers and soldiers on leave. In Kitzbühl, this responsibility was filled by Major Herter, whom I had already known for some time. I went to his office on the morning of the 21st. Just as I was signing my name, in walked an army colonel, who began at once to comment on the events of the day before. He announced that Stauffenberg and the other officers were not worthy of the bullets that had been used to carry out the sentences against them, and that it would have been far better to have broken every bone in their bodies instead. I felt degraded at not stopping him insulting one of my closest friends and a relative of my wife but, fearful of risking my own life, I said nothing. I felt miserable. Herter apparently found himself in a similar position. When I saw him after the war, he declared that this experience had been the most terrible of his life.

I left Kitzbühl on the morning of the 25th. After a terror-filled journey by train, I arrived at our new offices in Potsdam on the morning of the 26th. I went at once to the room that was assigned to me, intending to settle down to work as if nothing had happened. I sat down and surveyed the clean desk top. To my horror, I noticed a telephone message lying face up on the blotter. Dated 19 July and sent by Lieutenant Werner von Haeften, ADC to Stauffenberg, the message requested me to telephone Stauffenberg immediately. Clearly my delay had caused anxiety, and Stauffenberg and Haeften had been doing their best to reach me on the eve of the attempted assassination.

My knees went weak. This message had been lying there for six days, exposed to the world. Who had taken the call? Who had seen the note? Just as I was about to go to the lavatory to burn the slip of paper, my colleague from Crimean days, First Lieutenant Wilhelm Reissmüller, entered the room. Reissmüller had been in full sympathy with the conspiracy without actually taking an active part in it, and he understood well that I was intimately involved. He immediately poured me a glass of brandy to calm my nerves. By no means fully composed, I then went to report to General Köstring at his new office near mine. Upon seeing me, he exclaimed, 'What, *you're* still alive?'

Köstring advised me to disappear at once, since people were still being rounded up throughout the country. I agreed to do so, but added: 'General, may I suggest that you join me? Many of our friends have already been arrested, and I am not sure what would happen to either of us if we were to stay.' I did not have to remind him of his own collaboration with Stauffenberg and Schulenburg. We therefore resolved to get out of Potsdam at once.

We departed forthwith for Belgrade, flying first to Vienna and continuing by train via Budapest. As we left Budapest, three or four very handsome ladies, obviously members of the Hungarian or Austrian gentry, were standing on the platform about to board the overcrowded train. General Köstring invited them to join us. It was a wonderful distraction to hear them chatting about their children, riding, and life in the countryside, yet it was mournful to think that these ladies were even then about to be overwhelmed by forces that would completely tear up their lives.

Listening to them, I could not help but think of my own situation. Before leaving Potsdam, I had learned that Stauffenberg and Haeften had been executed. I also knew by then that my old schoolmate from Potsdam, Colonel Albrecht Mertz von Quirnheim, had been shot, and that nearly everyone else in the conspiracy with whom I had worked most closely was already under arrest. Etzdorf was still free at the time of my departure as I knew because I had met him by chance at the Potsdam barracks. We had neither shaken hands nor acknowledged each other, lest we reveal the link between us and thereby tip off the Gestapo. As he passed me, he said only, '*Davon später.*' – 'We'll talk later.' Had Etzdorf been rounded up, too?

I arrived in Budapest exhausted from such thoughts and grateful for the chance to rest briefly at the Gellert Hotel. After passing the night there, we proceeded to the airport to catch our plane for Belgrade. Disembarking from the plane in Belgrade, I caught sight of Lieutenant Colonel Karl Rathgens, who was being led in chains to a plane that would take him back to Berlin for interrogation.

Arriving in Belgrade, Köstring and I paid a visit to Field Marshal Baron Maximilian von Weichs, who was living at the former residence of Prince Paul, later the home of Tito. Given all that had happened, Weichs was none too pleased to see us. He was far too smart not to have had suspicions about me, and, as a relative of my wife, he knew, too, that another cousin of Pussi's, Colonel Count Rudolf von Marogna-Redwitz, had been active in the conspiracy while posted with the *Abwehr* counter-intelligence in Vienna, and had already been arrested.

In spite of his obvious anxiety, Weichs received us politely. Just as I was beginning to recover from my state of shock, General Köstring received a telegram ordering him back to the capital. Having learned that Schulenburg had been interrogated, and mindful of the intimate connection between Köstring and Schulenburg, we guessed that they now wanted to interrogate Köstring. I immediately said to him, 'General, I am going with you.' Just as quickly, he snapped back, 'No, you are not.' I insisted that I return with him, at which point Köstring drew himself up and barked: 'Herr Rittmeister von Herwarth! I have given you a military order and have the impression that you do not understand it. I am not prepared to discuss it with you, since I am the general and you the captain. You will stay here, damn it! If you come, I will give orders to have you thrown out of the aircraft.'

Köstring left at once for Potsdam. Convinced that there was nothing to be gained from sitting idly in Belgrade, I eagerly agreed to accompany Captain Prince Carl Wrede on an expedition to visit the Mihajloviçi commanders at Topola, a former summer residence of the Serbian kings, now in a 'no man's land' beyond the control of German forces, where I could feel safe. In our talks the Mihajloviçi proposed that the German army turn over equipment to them as it withdrew from Yugoslavia. In return, they were prepared to suspend action during the German retreat. We had to tell them that Hitler would certainly oppose their plan. The Mihajloviçi's dream of simultaneously resisting the Russians, Tito, and the Germans was quixotic, and their lack of equipment did not help matters. Their officers were a tenacious and rugged lot, bearded from their months in the mountains, but in excellent spirits. They failed to get any support from the withdrawing Germans. In May 1944 they had been abandoned in favour of Tito by the Allies as well.

Within a fortnight, my fears about Köstring's fate were dispelled by his unexpected return. He brought the welcome news that he had been recalled to Berlin for military consultations only and had not been interrogated at all. In fact, while in Potsdam, he had issued a particularly strong statement on the treatment of our volunteers. Unless relatives of the volunteers serving among the *Ostarbeiter* were exempted from such idiotic rules as the ban on visiting cinemas, and unless similar restrictions on the volunteers themselves were removed, Köstring refused to take responsibility for the loyalty of Russians serving in the German army.

During Köstring's absence I could not help but ask myself whether my friends who had been arrested after 20 July might not bring up my name under interrogation. Köstring brought back news that numerous of my close friends and collaborators had been tried by Dr Roland Freisler, president of the People's Court, and summarily executed. Among them were Lieutenant Colonel Klamroth and First Lieutenant von Hagen, my closest collaborators at Mauerwald. Like many others, Klamroth and Hagen had been tortured before being executed. Yet not even under torture did they, or any of the other officers who knew me well, reveal my connection with the conspiracy. I owe my life to the heroism of these loyal men, who submitted to torture rather than hand over their comrades. My friends went to their deaths without breaking the resolution they had shown throughout their involvement in the Resistance.

After Köstring's return to Belgrade, we decided to put yet more distance between us and Berlin and continued our expedition by visiting Athens, near which were deployed two battalions of Georgians and North Caucasians. Also posted near Athens was a special corps that had been formed for use in a proposed campaign in Syria. Arriving in Athens, we were received by General Felmy and his staff. Several officers of his suite were remarkable for their outspoken criticism on the course of the war. After a few days with them and a few more days with Colonel General Löhr near Salonika, we returned via Bulgaria (which was to withdraw from the war two days later) to Budapest, where we again spent several days. Enough time had now elapsed for us to feel it safe to return to Potsdam, where we arrived at the end of September. By now the arrests and executions connected with the plot against Hitler had run their course, and their place in the government's attention had been claimed by the disastrous situation on both fronts.

We remained in Potsdam until the beginning of 1945. It was a grim period for me, since I realized that everything we were doing in this place I knew so well was a waste of time. After 20 July certain changes were introduced into the army's procedures. First, we could no longer use the old familiar military salute (right hand to the cap), but had to stretch out the arm full length and shout 'Heil Hitler!' Second, every unit was assigned a so-called 'National Socialist Supervising Officer', whose functions were analogous to those of a political commissar in the Red Army. Technically, they were not empowered to interfere in military affairs, and had to confine their activity to raising the political morale of the troops. Their acronym – NSFO – was quickly transformed to 'NSF-Zero' indicating the contempt in which they were held by some of us. Those units whose officers were indifferent or hostile to National Socialism made every effort to get as NSFOs men who went through the forms of loyalty but would not interfere in any way in the officers' work. To our staff Köstring appointed Captain Karl Michel, a Party member who was clever enough to do nothing at all.

On 15 February, 1945, we were transferred to Bad Reichenhall. A few weeks later, Köstring and I went back to Berlin, this time returning to Reichenhall by car. On this brief trip all the signs of disarray were evident. It was astonishing to see the extent to which chaos had set in. In Czechoslovakia, it was impossible to determine whether a particular district was under German control or not. Many towns were surrounded by tank traps, but we had no idea against whom they were directed, whether Russians or Germans. We drove on via Passau to Salzburg and then to Bad Reichenhall. By then, the chaos that I had observed in Czechoslovakia was spreading throughout Germany.

I knew that my old Moscow colleague, Gustav Hilger, was with Ribbentrop's staff and living in Fuschl near Salzburg. While in Reichenhall I decided to pay him a visit. Bicycling to Fuschl, I found him thoroughly depressed and reproaching himself bitterly for having worked with Ribbentrop and thereby promoted Hitler's policies. His son had been killed on the Eastern Front near Orel. That he should have been killed in a war between Russia and Germany came as a terrible blow to both Hilger and his wife, since their love and loyalty was equally divided between the two countries.

Hilger was in such despair that he could think only of suicide. I therefore spoke to him as bluntly as I could, addressing him, as I usually did, as Papsi or Gustav Antonovich. I reminded him that as aide to Schulenburg he had always given good advice to Ribbentrop on all Soviet problems. I told him that he must not take his own life, since he had a wife and family to look after. As firmly as I could, I ordered him to be reasonable. I argued that he was so inept at all practical matters that if he tried to drown himself in the nearby lake he would probably fail, and if he used a pistol he would miss. This thoroughly angered Hilger, who resented the way I seemed to be ridiculing him. I assured him that I was not mocking him but trying to show him that he must survive, that we needed him, and that his family needed him. In the end, I got the impression that he was listening to me.

*   *   *

After the failure of the plot on 20 July, 1944, history lost all meaning for me. I knew that our further efforts could lead to no positive results. I asked myself why the failure had occurred and, more important, what might have happened had the attempt on Hitler's life succeeded. I came to two rather different conclusions. I knew that after the American-British landing in Normandy it was already far too late for any plot against Hitler to have significant consequences in the military or political realm. The war in the West was already lost, and there was no possibility of changing the situation in the East, where the Soviet forces were already hard by the German border. Given this, the only positive effect that the action against Hitler could have produced was to demonstrate to the rest of the world that there still existed people in Germany who were driven by their consciences to put an end to the dreadful system. No one had the slightest illusion that any great results were to be expected from their actions. The only frail hope was that the conditions of surrender would have been somewhat better if a non-Nazi government had been in power.

My second conclusion was more grim: I suspected that had Hitler been assassinated, there would have been many people in Germany who would have asked us by what right we had acted against their leader. Such people would have argued, or so it seemed to me, that even in 1944 Hitler might still have succeeded in winning the war. Given the persistence of this hope, the public mood might well have turned out to be much as it was after World War I, when extremists claimed that Germany had been 'stabbed in the back' and had had its deserved victory stolen from it. The Resistance, by seeming to have denied Germany that victory, could well have ended up as the scapegoat for Hitler's policies rather than their liquidator.

Even without going as far as this, I came gradually to appreciate the public's likely difficulty in accepting the basic premises upon which the conspiracy rested. Tens of thousands of families had sacrificed their husbands or sons. No human being could be expected to accept such losses easily. To admit that Hitler's regime was criminal meant accepting that the sacrifice of their beloved relatives had been in vain. Almost to the last moment they hoped for a miracle. In the end, of course, they were forced to acknowledge that all the sacrifices had been in vain, but they were brought to this conclusion through military defeat, rather than by the overthrow of Hitler by their fellow Germans.

20

VLASOV AND THE END OF THE VOLUNTEERS

In 1942 the army came to the conclusion that, along with a complete change in the administration of the occupied territories, political concessions could no longer be postponed. Lost in the vast plains of Russia the army had the feeling that the region could only be ruled with Russian help.

General Max von Schenckendorf, commander of the region under the administration of Army Group Centre, and his Chief of Staff, Lieutenant Colonel Kurt von Kraewel tried to institute a measure of self-government in the occupied territories around Smolensk, with the full approval of Stauffenberg and Altenstadt.

A capable Russian leader was found in the person of the well-known General Andrei Vlasov who had been in command of the Soviet army successfully defending Moscow in the winters of 1941 and 42. In the famous Smolensk manifesto, General Vlasov, as head of a committee for the liberation of Russia, proclaimed the establishment of a new democratic Russia on the basis of equality with her German ally, after the Soviet system had been overthrown by a mutual German–Russian effort. The manifesto met with great enthusiasm. When General Vlasov delivered speeches at mass meetings, the audience was under his spell and the volunteers were strongly impressed by his personality.

As there was no room in Hitler's conceptions for political and economic collaboration with the Russian people, he put an end to this promising experiment. He called the generals who believed in it 'foolish political generals'. So Vlasov was taken to Germany and restricted to making propaganda for the volunteers.

Köstring and I knew of Vlasov and his activities from the beginning. Köstring was not optimistic about the possibility of using Vlasov effectively until after Hitler had been eliminated. He saw Vlasov, correctly, in my view, as a convinced Russian nationalist to whom Hitler would be unwilling to make any concessions. Indeed, when Köstring was finally appointed General in charge of all the volunteer units in January 1944, he had been ordered quite bluntly by Field Marshal Keitel to 'keep your fingers out of the Vlasov affair', as Hitler was much opposed to it. To give Vlasov any encouragement would have contradicted Hitler's belief that Germans themselves had to make a sacrifice in blood to conquer Russia and that the Russians themselves should pay in sweat. Given this, Köstring considered it futile to push for the creation of anything like a Committee for the Liberation of the Peoples of Russia until after Hitler's assassination. For the same reason, we concentrated all our efforts on integrating former Soviet soldiers into the German army and seeing that they were well cared for.

Unfortunately, these were points which Vlasov's friend and German liaison officer, Captain Wilfried Strik-Strikfeldt, never understood. He realized correctly that in the long run the decisive step could only be the formation of a Russian army. What he did not appreciate was that this was impossible until after Hitler was removed, and that in the meantime there was valuable work to be done in the formation of small units of Russians, Ukrainians, Turkestani, Armenians, Georgians, and North Caucasians. Strik-Strikfeldt never quite forgave Köstring for his seeming lack of sympathy with Vlasov's cause and for his unwillingness to meet Vlasov before 1944. The fact is, our reticence was due only to our feeling that such a meeting would be disappointing to Vlasov, whose integrity and devotion to Russia we both respected highly.

Strik-Strikfeldt was one of the many Germans born and raised in tsarist Russia. He had even served as an officer in the imperial Russian army during World War I. He was a great idealist and a loyal German who, like Hilger, felt deeply for Russia. During the great famine that followed the Russian Civil War, Strik-Strikfeldt had organized a relief programme even before Hoover's programme was in operation. In this respect he was a most impressive personality. Between 1942 and 1944 he did everything in his power to build up an army for Vlasov and to create the necessary political basis for its existence. Doubtless, Strik-Strikfeldt took our coolness towards his various efforts as stubbornness, blindness, or worse. Unfortunately, it was impossible to tell him that we first wanted to assassinate Hitler and only then to initiate a new policy towards Russia!

In autumn 1944 Himmler, in view of the worsening military situation, decided to make use of General Vlasov. In contrast to his former negative attitude towards the Russians, he allowed Vlasov to create the Committee for the Liberation of the Peoples of Russia (KOHR). By this time the

Allies were poised on Germany's borders to the West and the Red Army was pushing ahead from the East. On 14 November, 1944, Köstring attended the founding ceremony in Prague, but he knew that no manifesto issued so late in the war could have the slightest effect, even if it was proclaimed from Prague, the scene of more than one Pan-Slavic Congress in the nineteenth century. Convinced that this last-ditch effort in collaboration with the SS could lead to nothing, Köstring avoided entering into any discussions with Vlasov at Prague and maintained the stance of an observer and well-wisher. Had he been frank, he would have told Vlasov that it would be best for him to go back to a prisoner-of-war camp.

Against the setting of the beautiful city of Prague, the ceremonies were dominated by an oppressive mood of failure. An unexpected problem generated by the Vlasov movement was the difficulty of co-ordinating it with the national committees of the various other peoples of the USSR that had been formed earlier under our direction, and in some cases, under the direction of Rosenberg. By 1942 there existed national committees for most of the larger ethnic groups in the USSR. A few of these saw no hope of liberating themselves from Stalin's control without co-operating with the Great Russians' committee under Vlasov. Many more strongly resisted the idea of any co-operation with Vlasov, precisely on the grounds that he *was* a Great Russian nationalist.

That Vlasov would have serious problems in gaining the support of the non-Russian volunteers was obvious from the outset, but it became particularly clear to me while attending a congress of the Turkestani Committee organized by Mende in Vienna in June 1944. Schulenburg and I were struck by the unwillingness of the group assembled there to co-operate in any way with the Russian volunteers or with Vlasov. At most, they would acknowledge him as head of the Great Russian nation and as *primus inter pares* among the leaders of the other nationalities. Vlasov had named his group the 'Committee for the Liberation of the Peoples of Russia'. In spite of this, the non-Russians denounced the name of Vlasov's committee as a renewal of the Great Russian policy of the tsars and of Stalin and declared that they had fought with Germany not only to overthrow the Soviet system but also to liberate their people from the Russian yoke.

Though neither Köstring nor I could help but be pessimistic about the Vlasov project, we did our best to help him. I recall a statement about the volunteers' attitude to the Jewish question that the editor of the Russian-language paper at Dabendorf submitted to Köstring for approval. Since it was entirely free of anti-Semitism, Köstring approved it at once and prepared to return it to Strik-Strikfeldt. As I was seeing to this, a senior officer and passionate National Socialist sarcastically commented that I apparently approved of the pro-Jewish views of the 'former Bolsheviks'. I allowed that I did, and, further, that I was not prepared to let the temporary idiocy of anti-Semitism ruin my own chances for advancement. The remark was calculated to appeal to the cynicism that lay just beneath the surface of many Nazis. It hit home, and the statement went out at once, in the form which Köstring had approved.

After the Prague meetings, permission was granted for Vlasov to organize two divisions of Russians, the 600th and the 650th. Himmler had promoted this project with a reluctant Hitler, who had consented to the formation of only two divisions and those only on the condition that the main stress should be placed on the propaganda value of the undertaking. Ribbentrop, meanwhile, had also jumped in to support the Vlasov project, hoping that it might help to restore his dwindling prestige. He also saw in Vlasov's army a means of weakening the influence of his old foe, Rosenberg, and of regaining a measure of influence in political affairs relating to the Soviet Union.

Colonel Heinz Herre, Köstring's former chief of staff, was seconded to help organize the two Vlasovite divisions. When the first of these had been put into shape, Köstring was invited to the Münsingen manoeuvre grounds in Württemberg to review it with Vlasov. The railway lines were under bombardment and we had great difficulty in getting under way. The officer who organized the trip had foolishly assigned Köstring a private compartment while booking Vlasov in a compartment with his ADC. Vlasov proudly objected and in the end I shared a compartment with Köstring while Vlasov was alone. By the time we arrived in Münsingen I was confirmed in my view that the entire enterprise was ill-fated. The troops passed grandly in review before Vlasov and Köstring, but I felt miserable and kept speculating about the ultimate fate of these brave Russians.

The 600th Division was soon sent off to the front near the Oder River, where it fought doggedly alongside a German infantry division against the advancing Red Army; in fact, it was reported that even at this late date a number of soldiers from the Red Army crossed the lines to join this unit. Shortly afterwards it was moved to Prague where it attempted to make an independent stand helping the Czech insurgents to fight the Germans. Contrary to the Soviet official legend, they and not the

291

Russians liberated Prague It was too late, however, and most of the troops were taken prisoner and eventually repatriated to the USSR, where Vlasov and his officers were executed. Such was the tragic ending of a noble Russian general.

As Himmler had decided to form Russian divisions, Köstring and his staff had to work with the SS military authorities. Köstring appointed my friend Reissmüller to do this liaison work. He had a fine Bavarian sense of humour and considerable patience, so he was the right person to cope with this difficult task. Reissmüller was infuriated at the assignment but carried out the mission. After one of the meetings he returned to us in a high rage. Apparently he had had a tremendous shouting match with his SS contacts, in the course of which he had called them idiots and blockheads for not realizing that the war was lost. The SS officers had greeted this with laughter, convinced that no one could have said such things seriously. Later, during the last days of February 1945, Reissmüller came back from another meeting with a yet more appalling tale. By this time even the SS officers thought it was time to get rid of Hitler and had approached Reissmüller to see if he was interested in joining their conspiracy. He turned them down, explaining that in his opinion it was far too late, hinting also that others had had that fine idea much earlier but had failed.

The SS scheme to eliminate Hitler that was revealed to Reissmüller originated with the SS Propaganda Unit 'Kurt Eggers'. The commanding officer of this unit was Günther d'Alquin, editor of the *Schwarze Korps*, the widely-read mouthpiece of the SS. Until 1944, at least, d'Alquin had been the unflagging propagandist for Germany's coming victory over her enemies, but he was not a fool and by the end of the year he had to admit that there was no hope left.

The SS's new attitude towards the volunteers had certain results. A typical example of the co-operation that resulted was the Yugoslavia-based Cossack division under the command of General Helmuth von Pannwitz. Pannwitz was a genuine *condottiere* who had managed to take over the Cossack units that had been formed earlier by Colonel Wessel von Freytag-Loringhoven. Pannwitz was dissatisfied with the way in which his two Cossack divisions were treated. He complained bitterly about the lack of uniforms and weapons. In the end, he agreed to allow his units to be provisioned by the SS since, as he put it, 'We'd take money from the devil if it would help.' As it happened, though, the units were commanded by regular army officers, mostly from the cavalry, including many Austrians, who flatly refused to adopt the SS uniforms. Thus you had one of those peculiar combinations that were only possible under Hitler: part-army, part-Cossack, part-SS.

General Köstring and I visited the XV-Cossack Cavalry Corps near Zagreb. We arrived from Berchtesgaden. The car trip from Zagreb to General von Pannwitz's headquarters was a colourful one, since mounted Cossacks had been assigned to accompany us. Every five hundred yards or so, two fresh Cossacks would appear and gallop wildly along with us until they were replaced by the next pair. The headquarters were impressive. In the evening we listened to a Cossack choir and an excellent Cossack band. We were left with the impression that this was an able fighting force, an impression that was shared by Tito and the Yugoslav forces against whom they fought. Unfortunately, they were a rough lot, and at times treated the population brutally.

This Cossack Corps was eventually to find itself behind the lines of the Red Army. It fought its way out bravely and with heavy loss of life, and finally reached the British lines. After the armistice, however, the group of survivors was extradited to the Soviets in accordance with the agreement among the Allies, but in violation of humanity and international law. Pannwitz was among those turned over to the Russians and was executed on Red Square. Most of the German officers managed to escape. Pannwitz stayed with his Cossacks, declaring that he had been with them in good times and would not desert them in bad.

I once encountered a smartly-dressed SS-sponsored Indian Unit when it was patrolling the Dutch coast in 1944. Their commanders had apparently considerable difficulty convincing them of the value of this exercise. They resorted to telling the Indians that one day the British would be thrown out of India and would certainly use their army and navy to try to force a return; hence, the German officers argued, the experience against the British on the Dutch coast would doubtless benefit the Indians one day. In the end, the Indians were transferred to the coast near Biarritz because they could not tolerate the Dutch climate. When the Indians did see action they immediately went over to the Allies, just as we had predicted. Throughout the entire period of their 'service' they had been receiving from England Red Cross packages filled with chocolate and cigarettes and had even shared them with German personnel.

In February 1945, Köstring had a meeting with Himmler, thinking that it would provide an opportunity to better the conditions of the various volunteer units and of the Soviet captives who had been assigned to work in German factories. Himmler had just taken over the group

293

Ober-Rhein which was operating in Alsace by this time and had its headquarters in Hornberg, in the Black Forest. We travelled to Himmler's headquarters, which were in a railway wagon. The trip there from Reichenhall showed clearly how total was Germany's chaos. We could go by train only as far as Offenburg, the trunk line having been bombed from there on. With immense difficulty we got through to headquarters by telephone and ordered a car. Throughout the remaining part of the trip we had to stop every ten or fifteen minutes and run for cover at the sight of strafing planes.

Before being ushered into Himmler's presence, I had to give up my pistol, my belt, and my briefcase. Stauffenberg's work had apparently put briefcases in bad repute among Hitler's confidants. It was a curious meeting. Far from looking like the leader of the dread SS, Himmler impressed Köstring and me as a very ordinary German. There was nothing interesting about him except his total ordinariness. He listened as Köstring set forth the needs of the volunteers. Contrary to our expectation, Himmler did not once contradict him. He evidently realized that the situation had become so desperate that the ends could justify hitherto unthinkable means. It was hard to imagine that this was the same man who had awed the Germans with his ruthlessness.

Morale in the volunteer units deteriorated from day to day during the last months of fighting. Once the German army began to retreat, the former Soviet soldiers found themselves every evening further than they had been in the morning from the homes they wanted to liberate. The number of defections increased as the *fata morgana* of their return to their homelands vanished.

Given what was taking place, the instances of heroism and loyal dedication among the volunteers during the last months of the war are the more astonishing. A stunning example of such heroism took place in April 1945, during an American air attack on Reichenhall, where Köstring and his staff were billeted.

It being a beautiful spring day, my fellow officers and I saw no sense in staying in the village after the alert was sounded, so we went out on the ridge overlooking it. Shortly afterwards the American planes roared overhead. With deep *Schadenfreude* we hoped they were on their way to Hitler's quarters at nearby Berchtesgaden. Suddenly the famous 'Christmas trees' were dropped over the town, indicating the bombing targets for the planes that followed. Minutes later the bombardment began, with more than a few bombs falling outside the town near where we were hiding in ditches.

When the bombing was over, we made our way into the town. Well before we got there, however, a Russian battalion that was on its way to the Italian front bravely plunged into the destroyed buildings in order to help the local population. The reaction of these soldiers was selfless and humane, and made us feel humiliated by comparison. The fifty or so members of this battalion were led by the admirable Major Riess, a highly-decorated former Soviet officer who spoke only a few words of German, in spite of his German name.

The following morning General Köstring awarded Riess' men war medals. As we watched this ceremony, we could not keep back the tears from our eyes. We realized that, while these brave Russian soldiers richly deserved the honour that was being bestowed upon them, the fact that they had received it would only worsen their situation after the surrender.

The loyalty that many volunteers showed until the bitter end sometimes manifested itself in tragi-comic situations. One afternoon shortly after the bombardment of Reichenhall, Lieutenant Reissmüller and I were sitting in our office when a former Russian general serving in the volunteer army entered the room, wearing his German general's uniform. According to normal procedures we should have stood up immediately, saluted, and then reported to him. I did so. Reissmüller, convinced that the war was over, felt this to be ridiculous pedantry and therefore greeted the Russian quite informally. The general turned to him at once and asked why he had not saluted. Reissmüller, amazed, sprang to attention, saluted, and delivered the expected report in a most formal manner.

The collapse of the volunteer units at the end of the war was most pronounced on the Western Front, since in that region there was no discernible connection between the war and the issues that motivated them. At one point just after D-Day I found myself in an awkward position because of a conversation I had had with one of our officers, Lieutenant Blanke, who commanded a volunteer unit in France. He asked me whether he should push his troops to the bitter end, and I told him I thought it best simply to find an appropriate way to surrender, since it made no sense for him to continue to sacrifice his soldiers' lives. When he then chose to surrender to the Allies, he was court-martialled *in absentia*. After the trial, a rumour spread that I had prompted Blanke's action, which brought me into acute danger during the final weeks of the war.

As the war drew to a close, we redoubled our efforts to protect the volunteers from extradition to the Soviets. All those units still fighting in the East had to be given up as lost, but we did succeed in transferring quite a lot of our Turkish and Caucasian units to the Western Front. Without any concrete evidence, we had assumed that the British and Americans would not extradite these volunteers to the Soviet Union. To be sure as possible on this crucial point, we tried to elicit some kind of statement from the Allies. To this end, we worked through the Ministry of Foreign Affairs and especially through Hilger. Through them we managed to make contact with the International Red Cross and other agencies, but no firm assurances were forthcoming.

The first Soviet volunteers were taken prisoner in Italy during the summer of 1944. When word of this reached us, we contacted our Foreign Ministry again and urged them to use every means to persuade the Allies to treat them as German soldiers and not as Soviet subjects. Specifically, we urged them to make contact once more with the International Red Cross and with the Swiss government. We pointed out that during World War I and II Czechs, Poles and other foreigners had fought and were fighting on the Allied side and were treated by us as prisoners-of-war in accordance with the Geneva Convention.

All our arguments had no effect after Germany had been completely knocked out and tens of thousands of volunteers had fallen into Allied hands. Our efforts came to naught. As is well known, the Western Allies lived up precisely to the obligation they entered into at Yalta, handing over to the Soviets all former volunteers, whether or not they wished to be repatriated. We did succeed in providing a small number of our volunteers with new papers that gave no indication that they had once been prisoners-of-war. Thanks to this, a few did manage to avoid extradition, particularly those who were fortunate enough to have developed a command of the German language.

When certain officers of the SS learned that we were in a position to obtain papers that indicated their bearers were part of the regular Germany army, they tried to play the same card. At the end of the war, when General Köstring, Reissmüller, and I were in Berlin on a visit from Reichenhall, several of the SS officers who earlier had been in contact with Reissmüller came to us and asked if we could not furnish them with army identification papers.

The fate of the volunteers that were handed over to the Soviet authorities is by now well known and does not need to be recounted again. Their tragic history is recounted in chilling detail in Nicholas Tolstoy's well-documented *Victims of Yalta,* and, at a later stage, in Alexander Solzhenitsyn's grandly sombre *The Gulag Archipelago*. The enlisted men and those who had worked in Germany as forced labour for the most part received little more than a period of re-education; the non-commissioned officers were sent to concentration camps at Kolyma and elsewhere in Siberia, generally for periods of up to twenty-five years; and most of the officers were shot.

The most astonishing instance of Western refusal to extradite volunteers was due to the courageous attitude of Prince Franz Josef of Liechtenstein, his Prime Minister, Dr Alexander Frick, and the people of Liechtenstein. At the end of the fighting, the remnants of a Russian corps under General Smylovskii were interned in Liechtenstein and cared for by the small population. The Soviets approached Liechtenstein demanding their extradition but Prince Franz Josef flatly refused. He acted thus, partly because he was accurately informed about the volunteers in the German army, due to the fact that a cousin of his wife was married to Erwein Count Eltz, the chief intelligence officer for Pannwitz's Cossack corps; also because he and his small nation had the guts to act upon the dictates of their consciences. Neither conscience nor courage was in good supply in 1945.

The history of the 800,000 volunteers did not end when most of them were turned over to the Russians in 1945. Many presumably died in Stalin's camps, but some survived. Some even reappeared in my own life, often in the most unexpected manner. Much later, in the summer of 1959, I was invited by a Greek friend to join him for a Mediterranean cruise. Arriving at Athens airport at night I was all but overcome by the heat. Making my way off the plane, I was addressed in broken German by a man who identified himself by declaring: 'Non-commissioned Officer Panayotou of the Kuban Cossacks, at your service, sir!' For a moment I was completely puzzled, and thought that I had encountered a ghost. Then I recognized him as one of our volunteers, a man of Greek origin who at the end of the war had fallen into the hands of the British. He explained that the British had turned him over to the Russians, who sent him to Siberia for a twenty-five-year sentence. He believed it was the visit of Chancellor Adenauer to Moscow in 1955 that led to his release. In a way he was right. Adenauer had negotiated for the release only of German soldiers in Russian concentration camps, but the Soviets mistakenly released many of the former Soviet volunteers in the German army as well.

Upon his release, my acquaintance made such a storm with the local Soviets on the grounds of his Greek nationality that they finally let him go and he arrived in Athens with no relatives or friends to whom to turn.

Eventually he made his way to the German Embassy where my old friend Theo Kordt was serving as Ambassador. Kordt listened to his story, discovered the connection between this former groom in our cavalry and me, and immediately offered him a job as a driver in the German Embassy. When finally he retired he was awarded the Order of Merit of the new Federal Republic of Germany.

21

THE END OF THE WAR

Shortly after General Köstring's marriage in January 1943, I had made the preposterous promise to his wife that I would return him safely to her at the end of the war. Recalling this promise at the end of April 1945, I told Köstring that Reissmüller and I would now take him home. While this was to be far from simple, we were lucky to be starting our trip in Reith near Reichenhall rather than from a point more remote from Unterwössen. We were not at all sure that we would succeed, since his home at Unterwössen was already occupied by the Americans. We were optimistic, however, since I had broken through the lines many times while on reconnaisance patrols during the war. I had to insist on one point: that our command structure be turned upside down. I would be in charge, Reissmüller would be second, with Köstring at the bottom. If both Reissmüller and I were put out of action, Köstring had orders simply to sit down and wait until he was picked up either by the Germans or the Americans.

Köstring consented, and we first drove by car to the headquarters of the First Panzer Army, the same army that Kleist had commanded in the Caucasus. It was quartered at St Johann, some ten kilometres from Kitzbühl. I went to see Major General Hauser, Chief of the General Staff, from whom I had to get a signed document discharging General Köstring from the German army with honour. Upon learning of our scheme to deliver Köstring, Hauser objected that Unterwössen was already occupied by the Americans. I retorted that, as a cavalryman like himself, I had had ample experience in crossing enemy lines. He then hesitated to make up the document without full authorization from Schleswig, or from wherever the 'capital' had moved to by then. I pointed out to him that the war would be over in three of four days. If he was not prepared to sign, however, I asked that he give me the documents so that I could complete them myself and sign them 'Herwarth von Bittenfeld, General of the Cavalry'. He laughed and told me to do whatever I liked, asking if there was anything else that he could do for me. I assured him that there was, namely, to give us his car, since our own alcohol-burning car could not make any progress in higher altitudes except in reverse gear. Besides being inconvenient, such a method lacked the heroic tone that the occasion demanded. With Hauser's car we could take General Köstring directly to Kössen, whence we would proceed by foot. Knowing that the front was only a few miles away, Hauser was concerned that he might never see his car again, but I gave him my word of honour as a cavalryman that he would, and he released it for our use.

Before leaving, I met a cousin of my wife and of Stauffenberg, Colonel Rudolf von Lerchenfeld. He was among those many who decided to stay put until he was made a prisoner-of-war. He considered my project crazy, but I avowed that I would far rather stay active right down to the end. Lerchenfeld ended up as a prisoner-of-war and I did not.

After reaching Kössen in Hauser's car, the three of us set out along the high road to Schleching. Köstring was gravely concerned that we would encounter American troops. I explained to him that I had deliberately chosen a route on which the bridge was destroyed; since the Americans had already won the war, I reasoned, there was no reason for them to get their feet wet. No sooner was he pacified on this point than we turned a corner and encountered a group of SS soldiers and their commanding officer. Had they been less numerous, we might have forced our way, but as it was there was no choice but to meet their leader, whom I greeted with a hearty 'Heil Hitler, *Sturmbannführer!*' I quickly introduced General Köstring and explained that this renowned expert on the Soviet Union was travelling under orders from Schleswig to make contact with the Americans and explore means of combining forces with them against the Soviet Union. The SS officer swelled with enthusiasm for the plan, and sent us forward with his best wishes. After a further exchange of 'Heil Hitler' we departed. Köstring was astonished, calling me a shameless liar.

Soon, we felt it necessary to detour into the hills so as to avoid other such encounters. Scarcely had we done so than we walked into a shepherd's dwelling occupied by a unit of the *Reichsarbeitsdienst*. This hut was in the hills directly above Unterwössen, where Köstring lived. In fact, it turned out to have been owned by Köstring's wife! We decided to wait there until evening so that we would not have to enter the village by day. The rest of the afternoon we spent talking with these people about everything except what we were engaged in.

Towards nightfall I went alone to reconnoitre the river bank,

Köstring's farmhouse being on a small hillock on the other side of this small stream and across the highway beyond. At length I located a foot bridge that was unguarded and at about 10:00 p.m. we crossed the river. No sooner were we on the other side than we saw American jeeps driving to and fro on the highway, fortunately with their headlights on. After waiting for some while in the ditch beside the road, we finally rushed to the other side and headed for the farm. Leaving Köstring and Reissmüller in a copse, I went ahead to the house. Seeing no jeeps there, I concluded that no Americans were about, and knocked on the door. A maid answered and was about to shout out when I silenced her. After reporting to Frau Köstring that the General was returning, I returned to the copse to fetch Köstring and Reissmüller. Reaching the house, Reissmüller and I withdrew and sent Köstring ahead for the reunion with his wife. After a few minutes Reissmüller and I came out and I asked Köstring whether he would go down to the wine-cellar for a bottle with which to celebrate our noble achievement, or if I would have to take the keys myself. He went for the wine at once, and we celebrated with an excellent meal, which we ate sitting in full uniform in a village occupied by the Americans. Köstring remained somewhat ill-at-ease, however, fearful lest we be captured while celebrating. I reminded him that the Americans were Christian soldiers, and that Christian soldiers do not make war after 10:00 p.m. I was right.

After a long sleep, we held a mustering-out ceremony which was at once formal and poignant. After this, we put away our uniforms and Frau Köstring fitted out Reissmüller and me in suits that had belonged to her first husband, Ambassador Köster.

With no plan in mind other that to get home as soon as possible, I paid a visit to the American commandant at Unterwössen. With some slight deception, I introduced myself as an Austrian eager to get back to my home in Kitzbühl. I asked if he could provide me with travelling papers, which he refused to do. He did give me one useful piece of advice, though. He recommended that I keep off the roads and avoid encounters with both American *and* German troops. The Americans had placed a former SS unit in charge of rounding up the many German soldiers still roaming the district, so his advice was well given. I congratulated him, and assured him that he would one day understand just what he had done. For myself, I was eternally grateful to this captain, since he possibly saved me from falling into the hands of a *Sturmbannführer* for a second time.

Shortly after our departure, I took the road to the left towards

Kitzbühl and Reissmüller took the right fork towards Ingolstadt. Only much later did I learn what happened to him after our parting. Apparently, when Reissmüller came out into the plain near Lake Chiemsee, he avoided the roads and travelled instead through the fields and meadows. In spite of his caution, however, he was arrested by a patrol of Americans who noticed that his forehead was only partially sunburned, the rest having been covered by his officer's cap. Reissmüller quickly realized that the camp at Grassau in which he had been interned was not for him and therefore escaped through the barbed wire, and, moving only by night, returned to his home in Ingolstadt, where he eventually found work as an ambulance driver for the Americans.

I continued along the same route as I had travelled with Köstring, this time making my way along the hillside. At Kössen I had to cross the valley and make my way up another valley towards St Johann. Along the way, I encountered a professor from Munich serenely chasing butterflies with a net. I smiled and realized that peace had truly arrived. He was able to give me advice as to where best to cross the stream. Following his advice, I arrived safely on the other side. Happily sauntering up the valley near the creek, my idyll was suddenly broken by outbursts of rifle fire and the explosion of hand grenades. I plunged to the earth and lay there, my heart pounding, as bullets whined overhead. I feared that some detachment of fanatical SS troops was putting up resistance to the Americans and that I would be caught in their desperate stand, after passing safely through the whole war. When the firing finally ended, I stood up. Some American soldiers approached me, as surprised at my presence as I was by theirs. Agitated, I asked the Americans what had been going on. They smiled and told me to calm down; they had been shooting squirrels and fishing for trout with hand grenades. After giving me a packet of cigarettes to help me settle down a bit, they sent me on my way. By now my feet were sore, and I covered the last kilometres barefoot, with a large pack of canned goods for my family on my back.

Arriving home, I discovered that our house was occupied by Americans but that Pussi and the family had been allowed to keep one room on the attic floor. There they lived with our cook, Pata Pelz, who had been with us in Russia, and Valia, a young Russian from Sevastopol. My daughter Alexandra was four years old now, and Pussi, Alexandra, Pata, and Valia were all crowded together in this room. I was immeasurably happy to join them.

Although the arrangement can hardly be considered convenient, when the Americans finally departed they left everything in perfect order, even to the untouched wine and spirits that lay under the bed. They were also kind to our children, to whom they gave packets of chocolate and the like.

My return to Kitzbühl gave me a brief respite, during which I devoted myself to trying to get a bit of bread and *Blutwurst* with which to feed the family, and to doing some gardening. While I was pottering away at these modest tasks, one day my wife was unexpectedly arrested and jailed. Thinking that this had occurred on my account, I went at once to the OSS and informed them that I had never been a Nazi, and that two of my last three chiefs – Counts Schulenburg and Stauffenberg – had been executed on account of their connection with the Resistance movement. But it was not my history that bothered them so much as Pussi's. They had learned that she had been in contact at various points with officials in charge of the forced-labour workers. That much was true. What they had not understood until Valia, our Russian maid, and I explained it to them was the fact that, since Pussi spoke Russian, French and Italian, she had been called in to work as an interpreter and advisor on foreign labour. Through this she had been able to do much to defend the forced labourers, who called her their 'Guardian Angel'. On Sundays many of them came to Pussi's home to ask for help and every kind of advice. Her experience confirmed the general opinion that the Russians and Ukrainians were the best foreign labourers, often more efficient than the German workers. More than once she had warned the responsible officials that she understood from the German High Command that anyone who harmed this labour force would diminish the spirit of the Soviet volunteers and therefore weaken the fighting power of the German army.

The foreign labourers remembered gratefully that she had acted on their behalf with understanding and devotion. Valia undertook to rally them in Pussi's defence. A band of workers demonstrated in front of the Military Government offices and demanded her immediate release, threatening to break open the jail if this was not done at once. After three days Pussi was free.

Her arrest had been caused by a confusion of two lists: one of people whom the SS considered reliable and a second of people whom they suspected. Inadvertently the Americans had arrested people from both lists.

Shortly after this, an order came through requiring all former German officers and soldiers who had not been dismissed before 1 February, 1945, to report to a camp at Woergl. Reluctantly, I decided to obey it. Before going to Woergl, however, I happened to pay a visit to a cousin of my wife's whose husband had not yet returned from the army.

While I was visiting her, an enormous American officer entered the room, his field helmet still on his head. He explained that he had orders to examine the house for requisitioning. As he looked around, he asked if the children present were mine. When I answered him in English, he responded by noting that we were drinking tea and asked if he could join us. No sooner did we invite him than he sent away his orderly to bring cookies for the children. I assured him that we had no intention of making his work difficult, and he assured us in return that he would do everything in his power not to inconvenience my cousin.

With these pleasantries behind us, he asked my name. Upon hearing it, he burst out laughing and asked if I was the husband of that funny woman for whom the foreign workers had mounted the demonstration. This was obviously the best possible recommendation, and he asked me immediately what I intended to do next.

I explained to him that I was on my way to Woergl and he told me that that would be a complete waste of time. He would hire me on the spot as his interpreter. Since he had to go to Innsbruck next day anyway, he promised to drop me at the prisoner-of-war camp. If I had not been discharged by the time he returned two hours later, he would speak to the commanding officer himself. We departed together for Woergl the following morning. The camp left a decidedly unpleasant impression. Of course, Germany had lost the war and the soldiers in this camp had served in her armies, but it was depressing nonetheless to hear the tone of the interrogations and to see a captured soldier tied to a stake by way of punishment. When I was being interrogated I mentioned this fact, acknowledging, of course, that it was none of my business.

As the interrogation continued, Bob Kennefax, the American whom I had met at the home of my wife's cousin, reappeared and took me back to Kitzbühl. After spending a few weeks working for Kennefax, he told me, his unit, the 42nd Infantry Division, was being transferred to Salzburg to be replaced by the French in our area. On the grounds that the Americans and not the French had won the war, Kennefax objected to this decision and warned me that many German soldiers had been taken to France already to work on reconstruction projects. In the end he proposed that I come with him to Salzburg, which I did.

Taking leave of Pussi and the family once more, I headed for Salzburg, where I found room with an old friend from the cavalry, Lieutenant Colonel von Jena. No sooner had I arrived than Kennefax's division was transferred to Vienna and I was left with no useful work, no food rations, and with pains in my back growing more severe every day. As I wandered around Salzburg, I came across the office of the Department of State and dropped in, on the off-chance of learning the whereabouts of some of my old friends. The people there were polite but of no help, so I prepared to return to Kitzbühl. A day later I received an invitation to dinner from Kennefax, who was in town again briefly. He told me to wait on the bench in front of Jena's house at 6:00 p.m. I arrived on time and waited fifteen minutes and then an hour. Finally, I got up and was hobbling back towards our garden gate when a car screeched to a stop and an American officer sprang towards me. As I cried out in pain he embraced me, kissed me on both cheeks, and shouted: 'Johnnie, you don't recognize me? It's Charlie!'

'Good Lord, Charlie, what are you doing here?' I exclaimed. He told me I had damn well better stand at attention since he was a lieutenant colonel and I only a captain. As I did so, he explained that he was the officer in charge of the Office of Strategic Services (OSS) for Austria. He told me that the officer whom I had met had casually mentioned to him that some English-speaking German by the name of Johnnie had dropped his name. Thayer immediately guessed that it was me and launched a man-hunt, which I had escaped by staying in Jena's house with my lumbago. Having finally caught me, he began bombarding me with questions. I interrupted him to say that he could order me to do whatever he pleased, but meanwhile, I had three requests to make: some medical treatment for my back, some food, and a good drink. At his usual pace, Thayer took me to a doctor and then dragged me at once to the officers' mess. As we entered, he ordered everyone to stand to attention while he introduced me as a 'gallant captain in the German army'. I spent nine weeks with Charlie and worked with him for the OSS.

Every day I went down to the offices that had been established in the old monastery of St Peter's and helped in whatever way I could. During that time, Charlie asked me to set down what I recalled of my wartime experiences in Russia. I have drawn on that memorandum at several points in these pages.

While working for Charlie, I brought the OSS into contact with Prince Albrecht of Bavaria, the eldest son of Crown Prince Ruprecht. He had just been released from a concentration camp and the Americans were keenly interested in talking to him. I recall also participating in discussions with Karl Seitz, the very straightforward former Lord Mayor of Vienna from the years before 1938. Seitz, as I recall, tried to give the

305

Americans some sense of the tangled nature of the Austria situation by reminding them of the positive attitude of Austrian Socialists towards reunion with Germany after World War I. The Americans in the officers' mess listened with puzzled faces as he urged them to look at the Austrian cemeteries, where they could find the gravestones of many Austrians who had sacrificed their lives fighting in Hitler's armed forces. Since the photographs of the soldiers in German uniforms could easily have been removed from the stones, it would have been easy for the families to erase evidence of this tie to Germany. They had not done so. He assured them of Austria's gratitude to the Americans for liberating them from Hitler and establishing Austria's independence, but urged them to grasp the complexity of the situation, lest they act hastily.

It was in Salzburg that I learned the fate of our Russian volunteers. Charlie Thayer explained to me that, according to the convention with the Soviets, all volunteers were to be handed over to the Russian side. I urged him for God's sake to be magnanimous and to accept the word of any soldier who said that he was part of the German army. But by this time the Americans and British had already started to carry out their side of the agreement with chilling punctiliousness.

We tried as best we could to work out a way of getting in touch with Pussi in Kitzbühl. Charlie finally came up with a plan for issuing me with papers so that he could take me to the French Zone for interrogation. This was accomplished quickly and we reached Pussi in Kitzbühl that same day. Pussi was delighted to see Charlie and he was equally pleased to see her and my daughter, whom he had not met. We explained to Pussi that I had to report at once to the French commander, but she assured us that this was unnecessary since she had already established contact with him. Indeed, she delivered an invitation for us all to dine that evening with the head of the French counter-espionage authority.

The French soon issued me papers to enable me to move about freely in Austria and Germany. I think this was due to the fact that one of my French friends, de Juniac, had given information about me to the French occupation forces in Austria. Charlie, meanwhile, arranged to have me attached to the historical investigating team that the Americans had established at Wiesbaden under the direction of Colonel Pope.

After my arrival I set to work and wrote a memorandum on the Ukrainian question and several other papers about my wartime experience. To my astonishment I met there my former ambassador, Herbert von Dirksen, and the Under Secretary of State, Andor Hencke, who had served for many years in the Soviet Union. Both were still under arrest. They were no less astonished to meet me working as a free man for the investigating team.

During my stay in Wiesbaden, I became close friends with Captain Peter Harnden, an architect by profession and a member of the team. Peter had studied German before the war in Munich, staying as paying guest in the family of Professor Anton Pfeiffer, a brother of my Moscow colleague Peter Pfeiffer. Peter Harnden got engaged to Princess Missie Wassiltschikoff who was living near Wiesbaden at Johannesberg, the estate of her brother-in-law, Prince Paul Metternich, a descendant of the famous Austrian chancellor. One evening, sitting in the officers' mess, we fell into a lively discussion about whether I should emigrate to America. I had long considered this possibility because I was afraid that the division of Germany into four zones might be permanent. I could not imagine the rebirth of a German state with a Foreign Office which I could join again. In the course of our conversation my friend Reissmüller appeared with a letter from Anton Pfeiffer, who by now was Minister of State and head of the Bavarian State Chancellery. On behalf of the Bavarian Minister President, Wilhelm Hoegner, he asked me whether I was prepared to work in the Bavarian State Chancellery. While we were discussing this new turn of events, a telegram arrived for Peter, informing him of his transfer to the American Consulate General in Munich. Peter exclaimed: 'This is surely the voice of destiny. Let us both go to Munich and reconstruct Bavaria.'

In the autumn of 1945 we both left for Munich and the following winter Peter and Missie got married in Kitzbühl. As Missie was Orthodox the wedding was celebrated in a Catholic gothic chapel by a Russian priest who had fled from the Soviet Union. One sunny day we walked in procession to the chapel. Following the Russian tradition my daughter Alexandra marched in front, carrying an icon. Next came Missie and Peter in American uniform, followed by the three best men, Captain Count La Brosse from the French Military Government in Kitzbühl in French uniform, and Paul Metternich and myself who had both served as German officers. The three of us had alternately to hold a heavy crown over the heads of the young couple. We were all aware of the significance of this ceremony which united people from four nations that, a short time before, had fought a grim war against each other.

Arriving at this point in my life, I had to admit that I had been very lucky. I had been able to stay safely in the Moscow Embassy during Hitler's rise to power; I was never wounded in the war; I had escaped being executed after 20 July, 1944; by pure coincidence I had run into

Charlie Thayer; and now a challenging job in the reconstruction of Bavaria was awaiting me – all this was enough to make me extremely grateful to the Lord Almighty and to remind me that what really counts in life is the companionship of faithful friends.

INDEX

Herwarth, Johnnie von—*cont.*

on, 20; his love for mother, 20; background of family, 20–21; sympathies expressed on outbreak of World War I, 21; becomes soldier, 24; returns to school, 24; employed in locomotive factory, 24; joins *Deutsche Erdöl A.G.*, 25; studying at Breslau, 26; examination for Foreign Service, 26–7; enters Foreign Service, 27; appointed secretary to Otto von Simson, 29; desire to go to Soviet Union, 33; avid studying of Russian affairs, 33–4; ordered to Moscow, 34; arrival in Moscow, 35; impressions of Moscow, 37; makes cultural visits in Russia, 44ff; contact with Russians, 49ff; social life in Soviet Union, 53; impressions of Josef Stalin, 54; seconded to Swedish legation, 61; sporting diversions in Moscow enjoyed, 68–9; life at American *dacha*, 69–70, 73–4; promotion of, 72; assesses Hitler's intentions, 73; special relationship with American and British ambassadors, 74; decides to enlist in Army, 74; opines Stalin liquidator of Communism, 79; serves under Herbert von Dirksen, 82; his indebtedness to von Schulenburg, 95; as Ambassador to England, 95; a non-Aryan, 99; his promotion to Secretary of Legation, 101; completes service in reserve, 102; promoted sergeant, 103; becomes engaged, 103; marriage to Elisabeth von Redwitz, 104; attends Olympic Games, 1936, 106; to Nuremberg, 107; his opinion of Hitler's oratory, 107; addresses *Wehrmachtsakedemie*, 117ff; informed must leave Foreign Office, 120; nominated as Third Secretary, 120–21; resolve to stay in Foreign Service, 121; plans and departs on trip to Odessa, 122–3; to Berlin, 123; discusses European situation with Brigadier Fitzroy Maclean, 125; warns Berlin of likely French and British resistance to German coup in Czechoslovakia, 134ff; appointed to Consulate General in Memel, 136; posted to Moscow, 140; avers Hitler

would sign agreement with Stalin, 145; meets Guido Relli, 146; efforts focused on American Embassy, 153; meets Charles Bohlen, 154; information leaked to Bohlen, 154ff; conviction Hitler's intentions to attack Poland, 161; wish to join Army, 162, 166; accompanies von Ribbentrop to Moscow, 165; in Army, 168; opines Britain and France would enter war, 169; action with First Cavalry Regiment, 170ff; involvement in invasion of France, 179ff; promoted to Second Lieutenant, 181; returns to Poland, 181; in Moscow, 183; returns to regiment, 185; detached from Army, 185; returns to regiment, 187; attached to Dietrich Schwencke, 187; to Moscow, 188; meets wife in Moscow, 190; returns to regiment, 192; seconded to Corps command in Radom Llll, 193; lectures on Soviet Union, 193; transferred back to regiment, 194; involvement in invasion of Soviet Union, 197ff; cordial reception for Russian civilians, 201ff; attitude of prisoners-of-war, 204; sent to Ohrdruf, 208–9; seconded as officer of Dept. 13 of Ministry of Foreign Affairs, 211; objection by von Ribbentrop to protocol compiled by, 214; leaves Ministry of Foreign Affairs, 214; transferred to Army, 214; to 'Spala', 214; assigned to staff of *Wehrmachtsbefehlhaber im Generalgouvernement*, 214; his special task, 215; assigned to Army's General Staff, 215; offers to assign responsibilities for volunteers declined, 221; appointed to inspection commission, 229; asked opinion regarding von Ribbentrop, 236; in Simveropol, 237; asked opinion of Gustav von Steengracht's appointment, 237–8; urged by Field Marshal von Kleist to inform Hitler of parlous situation, 238; attends conference in Berlin, 242; arrives in East Prussia 243; leaves Crimea, 245; assigned to Organizational Division of General Staff HQ Mauerwald, 245; conversa-

316